T0326323

Human–Robot Interaction

The role of robots in society keeps expanding and diversifying, bringing with it a host of issues surrounding the relationship between robots and humans. This introduction to human–robot interaction (HRI) by leading researchers in this developing field is the first to provide a broad overview of the multidisciplinary topics central to modern HRI research. Written for students and researchers from robotics, artificial intelligence, psychology, sociology, and design, it presents the basics of how robots work, how to design them, and how to evaluate their performance. Self-contained chapters discuss a wide range of topics, including speech and language, nonverbal communication, and processing emotions, plus an array of applications and the ethical issues surrounding them.

This revised and expanded second edition includes a new chapter on how people perceive robots; coverage of recent developments in robotic hardware, software, and artificial intelligence; and exercises for readers to test their knowledge.

CHRISTOPH BARTNECK is an associate professor in the Department of Computer Science and Software Engineering at the University of Canterbury, New Zealand.

TONY BELPAEME is a professor at Ghent University, Belgium and senior researcher at imec.

FRIEDERIKE EYSSEL is a professor of applied social psychology and gender research at the Center for Cognitive Interaction Technology at Bielefeld University, Germany.

TAKAYUKI KANDA is a professor of informatics at Kyoto University, Japan.

MEREL KEIJSERS is an assistant professor of psychology at John Cabot University in Rome, Italy.

SELMA ŠABANOVIĆ is a professor of informatics and cognitive science at Indiana University Bloomington, USA.

Human–Robot Interaction

An Introduction

Second Edition

Christoph Bartneck
University of Canterbury, Christchurch, New Zealand

Tony Belpaeme
Universiteit Gent, Belgium

Friederike Eyssel
Universität Bielefeld, Germany

Takayuki Kanda
Kyoto University, Japan

Merel Keijsers
John Cabot University, Rome

Selma Šabanović
Indiana University, Bloomington, USA

CAMBRIDGE
UNIVERSITY PRESS

University Printing House, Cambridge CB2 8BS, United Kingdom

One Liberty Plaza, 20th Floor, New York, NY 10006, USA

477 Williamstown Road, Port Melbourne, VIC 3207, Australia

314–321, 3rd Floor, Plot 3, Splendor Forum, Jasola District Centre, New Delhi - 110025, India

79 Anson Road, #06–04/06, Singapore 079906

Cambridge University Press is part of Cambridge University Press & Assessment,
a department of the University of Cambridge.

We share the University's mission to contribute to society through the pursuit of
education, learning and research at the highest international levels of excellence.

www.cambridge.org
Information on this title: www.cambridge.org/9781009424233

DOI: 10.1017/9781009424202

First published 2020
Second edition 2024

A catalogue record for this publication is available from the British Library

A Cataloging-in-Publication data record for this book is available from the Library of Congress

ISBN 978-1-009-42423-3 Paperback

Cambridge University Press & Assessment has no responsibility for the persistence
or accuracy of URLs for external or third-party internet websites referred to in this
publication and does not guarantee that any content on such websites is, or will
remain, accurate or appropriate.

Contents

1

Introduction

1.1 About this book

Since the 1950s, an everyday life with robots has always been about 10–20 years away. This is probably true at the moment in which you are reading this book. In the early 2020s, as we are writing, there's a lot of talk about robots in the news, on the movie screen, and of course, in science-fiction literature. We now even see robots in our daily lives, on city streets and in classrooms, cafés and restaurants, and hotels. Have you ever interacted with a robot? A vacuum-cleaning robot? A robotic toy, pet, or companion? Chances are that if you haven't, you will soon. Technology companies are eyeing the potential of personal robots, with start-ups as well as large multinationals readying themselves to create the kind of robot that everyone wants to own. But you may still not get a chance to be served breakfast in bed by your trusty robotic butler anytime soon. One of the reasons for this is that designing robots to participate in dynamically unfolding interactions with diverse users over long periods of time has turned out to be more difficult than anyone initially thought. Robust human–robot interaction—HRI—is difficult to design and implement.

So where is the field of robotics headed? What will, and should, our future with robots look like? How will robots find a place in our lives? These are still very open questions. A range of unknown but exciting futures awaits, in all of which robots support us, collaborate with us, transport us, or entertain us. If you've opened this book, you must be interested in seeing how this future might unfold. Perhaps you even want to get involved in shaping our future interactions with robots.

To get you started on this path, first of all, it is all about you: What kind of educational background do you have? Did you become interested in robots through your interest in engineering, psychology, art, or design? Or did you pick up this book because it rekindled a childhood fascination with robots? HRI is an endeavor that brings together ideas from a wide range of disciplines. Engineering, computer science, robotics, psychology, linguistics, sociology, and design all have something to contribute to how we interact with robots. HRI lies at the confluence of these disciplines. As a computer scientist, it pays to know about social psychology; as a designer, there's value in dipping your toes in sociology.

If you have an engineering background, do you think you can build a robot that interacts with people, working only with other engineers? We, unfortunately, think that you will not be able to do so. To design robots that people want to interact with, you need a good understanding of human social interaction. To reach such understanding, you need insight from people trained in the social sciences and humanities.

Are you a designer? Do you think you can design a socially interactive robot without working with engineers and psychologists? People's expectations about robots and their roles in everyday life are not just high, but they also vary a lot from person to person. Some people may tell you they want robots that will cook for them; others wish for a robot to do their homework, then have an intellectual conversation about the latest *Star Wars* movie. The prowess of robots as assistants, however, is still rather limited. Moravec's paradox, decades after being first expressed, still holds: anything that seems hard to people is relatively easy for machines, and anything a young child can do is almost impossible for a machine. As a designer, you would therefore need a good understanding of technological capabilities and of human psychology and sociology to create a design that is viable and realistic.

And last but not least, those of you who have training in psychology and sociology, do you want to just wait around for such robots to appear in our society? Wouldn't it be too late to start studying these technologies after they appear in our environment? Don't you want to have an impact on what they look like and how they interact? One thing you can do is start talking to friendly engineers and computer scientists, or have lunch with a designer. They will give your social science ideas some grounding in what is technically possible and help you find the areas in which your knowledge can have the most impact.

Just like the six of us writing this book, you will all need to work together. To do so in an effective way, you will need to understand the perspectives of HRI practitioners from different disciplines and be aware of the different kinds of expertise needed for developing successful HRI projects. In this book, we want to provide you with a broad overview of HRI topics central to the field and get you started on thinking about how you can contribute to them. We would like you to join us in expanding the boundaries of what is known and possible. Technology has progressed to a degree to which it is possible to build and program your own robot at little cost. Robots will be part of our future, so seize your chance to shape it. Go read (this book!), create, test, and learn!

We assembled a team of leading experts from the wide spectrum of disciplines that contribute to HRI. All of our hearts beat for improving how humans and robots interact and for ensuring that robots are used in ways that benefit our societies and the lives of individuals who use and are affected by them.

1.2 Christoph Bartneck

Christoph Bartneck is an associate professor in the Department of Computer Science and Software Engineering at the University of Canterbury. He has

Figure 1.1 The authors of this book got together in Westport, New Zealand, in January 2018 to start the manuscript during a weeklong "Book Sprint." Writing and editing continued throughout the following year and a half through remote collaboration—many long Skype calls and emails.

a background in industrial design and human–computer interaction, and his projects and studies have been published in leading journals, newspapers, and conferences. His interests lie in the fields of human–computer interaction, science and technology studies, and visual design. More specifically, he focuses on the effect of anthropomorphism on HRI. As a secondary research interest, he works on projects in the area of sports technology and the critical review of scientific processes and policies. In the field of design, Christoph investigates the history of product design, tessellations, and photography.

1.3 Tony Belpaeme

Tony Belpaeme is a professor at Ghent University, Belgium, and prior to that was a professor of robotics and cognitive systems at Plymouth University, United Kingdom. He received his PhD in artificial intelligence from the Vrije Universiteit Brussel (VUB). Starting from the premise that intelligence is rooted in social interaction, Tony and his research team try to further the artificial intelligence of social robots. This approach leads to a spectrum of results, from theoretical insights to practical applications. He is involved in large-scale projects studying how robots can be used to support children in education, and he studies how brief interactions with robots can become long-term interactions and how robots can be used in therapy.

1.4 Friederike Eyssel

Friederike Eyssel is a professor of applied social psychology and gender research at the Center for Cognitive Interaction Technology at Bielefeld

University, Germany. Friederike is interested in various research topics ranging from social robotics, social agents, and ambient intelligence to attitude change, prejudice reduction, and the sexual objectification of women. Crossing disciplines, Friederike has published vastly in the fields of social psychology, HAI, and social robotics.

1.5 Takayuki Kanda

Takayuki Kanda is a professor in informatics at Kyoto University, Japan. He is also the visiting group leader at Advanced Telecommunications Research (ATR) Interaction Science Laboratories, Kyoto, Japan. He received his bachelor's degree in engineering, his master's degree in engineering, and his PhD in computer science from Kyoto University, Kyoto, Japan, in 1998, 2000, and 2003, respectively. He is one of the starting members of the Communication Robots project at the ATR in Kyoto. He has developed a communication robot, Robovie, and applied it in daily situations, such as peer tutoring at an elementary school and as a museum exhibit guide. His research interests include HAI, interactive humanoid robots, and field trials.

1.6 Merel Keijsers

Merel Keijsers is an assistant professor in psychology at John Cabot University in Rome, Italy. Her training is in social psychology and statistics, and she completed her PhD on the topic of robot bullying at the University of Canterbury, New Zealand. For her PhD, she studied what conscious and subconscious psychological processes drive people to abuse and bully robots; recently, she has gained an interest in how robots influence the way humans view themselves. More generally, having a background in social psychology, she is mainly interested in the similarities and differences in how people deal with robots versus other humans.

1.7 Selma Šabanović

Selma Šabanović is a professor of informatics and cognitive science at Indiana University, Bloomington, where she founded and directs the R-House Human-Robot Interaction Lab. Her research combines studies of the design, use, and consequences of socially interactive and assistive robots in different social and cultural contexts, including healthcare institutions, user homes, and various countries. She also engages in the critical study of the societal meaning and potential effects of developing and implementing robots in everyday contexts. She received her PhD in science and technology studies from Rensselaer Polytechnic Institute in 2007, with a dissertation on the cross-cultural study of social robotics in Japan and the United States. She served as the editor in chief of the journal *ACM Transactions on Human-Robot Interaction* from 2017 to 2023.

1.8 Notes on second edition

The field of HRI, like many fields relating to emerging technology, changes and develops as new technological capabilities become available for the design and implementation of robots and the study of people who interact with them. To ensure that this text maintains its relevance, we updated it in 2023 to cover new technical capabilities as well as new theoretical and methodological developments in the field. We also wanted to add more discussion of conversations about inclusion, societal relevance and impact, and ethical considerations regarding HRI to the original text. Finally, we recognized that our first edition focused largely on social robotics as the main domain of HRI, obscuring human–robot interactions in domains like factories, where people and robots collaborate to work on different tasks; disaster assistance, where people interact with mobile and flying robots to put out fires or save human lives; and even in autonomous driving, where interactions between people and robots may not be focusing on social engagement. In this edition of the book, we reframe our understanding of the social nature of HRI to include HRI and collaboration whose social nature is more broadly construed—in some sense, all robots operating alongside and with humans can be understood as social, and all human–robot interactions can be the purview of HRI research. In late 2022/early 2023, we worked both in person and remotely to update the text and teaching activities provided in the book. We hope you enjoy the new materials!

2

What Is Human–Robot Interaction?

> What is covered in this chapter:
> - The academic disciplines that come together in the field of human–robot interaction (HRI).
> - The barriers created by the disciplines' different paradigms and how to work around these.
> - The history and evolution of HRI as a science.
> - Landmark robots in HRI history.

Human–robot interaction, or HRI, is commonly referred to as a new and emerging field, but the notion of human interaction with robots has been around for as long as the notion of robots themselves. Isaac Asimov, who coined the term *robotics* in the 1940s, wrote his stories around questions that take the relationship between humans and robots as the main unit of analysis: "How much will people trust robots?"; "What kind of relationship can a person have with a robot?"; "How do our ideas of what is human change when we have machines doing humanlike things in our midst?" (see page 237 for more on Asimov). Decades ago, these ideas were science fiction, but nowadays, many of these issues are real and present in contemporary societies and have become core research questions in the field of HRI.

This chapter aims to set the table for the rest of the book. Because HRI is an incredibly diverse field, Section 2.1 highlights and explains the main themes included in this book. Section 2.2 covers the interdisciplinary nature of this field, and the consequences for research and robot design are explored. Finally, Section 2.3 provides a timeline of the development of (social) robots and gives an overview of the robots most commonly used in HRI.

> *Distinguishing physical and social interaction:* Robotics at large has traditionally been concerned with the creation of physical robots and the ways in which these robots manipulate the physical world. HRI adds to this and is concerned with the ways in which robots interact with people as part of their social world and how people respond to the presence of robots. For example, when a robot picks up a box in an empty warehouse or cleans an office building after hours, it is sensing and acting in the physical world alone and dealing with the physics of its own body

and its environment. But when the robot takes the box to a warehouse worker who needs to fill it with appropriate materials, delivers coffee to a customer in a café, or chases children around in a courtyard, it is not only dealing with the physical motions needed for those actions, but it must also address the social aspects of the environment. For example, it needs to consider where the children, customers, or the office workers are; how to approach them in a way that is safe and that they consider appropriate; and how to follow the appropriate social rules of the interaction. Such social rules might be obvious to humans, such as acknowledging the presence of others, knowing who is "it" in a game of tag, and saying "you're welcome" when someone says "thank you." But for a robot, all these social rules and norms are unknown and require the attention of the robot designer. These concerns make HRI questions different from those pursued in robotics alone.

As a discipline, HRI is related to human–computer interaction (HCI), robotics, artificial intelligence, the philosophy of technology, psychology, and design. Scholars trained in these disciplines have worked together to develop HRI, bringing in methods and frameworks from their home disciplines and also developing new concepts, research questions, and HRI-specific ways of studying and building the robots that interact with people.

What makes HRI unique? Clearly, the interaction of humans with social robots is at the core of this research field. These interactions usually include physically embodied robots, and their embodiment makes them inherently different from other computing technologies. Moreover, social robots are often perceived as social actors bearing cultural meaning and having a strong impact on contemporary and future societies. Saying that a robot is embodied does not mean that it is simply a computer on legs or wheels. Instead, we have to understand how to design that embodiment, in terms of both software and hardware, as is commonplace in robotics, and in terms of its effects on people and the kinds of interactions they can have with such a robot.

A robot's embodiment sets physical constraints on the ways in which it can sense and act in the world, but it also represents an *affordance* for interaction with people. The robot's physical makeup elicits people to respond in a way similar to that in which they interact with other people. When a robot has eyes, people make the assumption that the robot can see them. When the robot has a mouth, people assume that the robot can talk. The robots' human-likeness enables humans to use their existing experience of human–human interaction to understand and participate in human–robot interaction. These experiences can be very useful in framing an interaction, but they can also lead to frustration if the robot cannot live up to the users' expectations (as discussed in more detail in Chapter 8).

HRI focuses on developing robots that can interact with people in various everyday environments. This opens up technical challenges resulting from the dynamics and complexities of humans and the social environment. This

Figure 2.1 Honda developed the Asimo robot from 2000 through 2018. (Source: Honda)

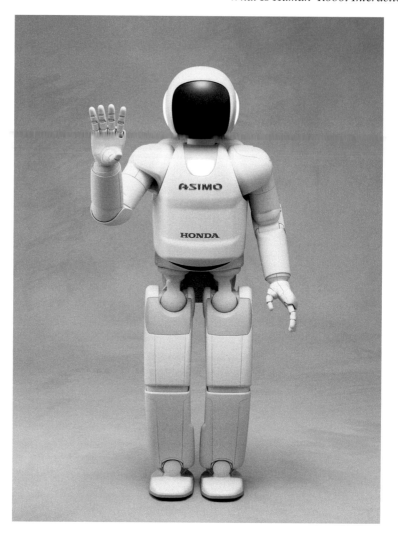

also opens up design challenges—related to robotic appearance, behavior, and sensing capabilities—to inspire and guide interaction. From a psychological perspective, HRI offers the unique opportunity to study human affect, cognition, and behavior when individuals are confronted with social agents other than humans. Social robots, in this context, can serve as research tools to study psychological mechanisms and theories.

From the very first mention of the term *robot* in Karel Čapek's play *Rossum's Universal Robots*, our vision of the ideal robot has focused on mimicking humanlike capabilities, often represented by a humanoid form, either in a full body, as in Honda's ASIMO (see Figure 2.1), or in parts, such as by robot arms or their more anthropomorphic representation in Sawyer robots. When we look at the current state of the art in HRI, however, we see that robot embodiments are much more diverse—spherical robots can roll around and interact with children (e.g., Sphero, Roball); robots can fly in the air (e.g., drones) or go underwater (e.g., OceanOneK); robots can mimic animals so that they can encourage petlike interactions with people (e.g., Paro) or even interact with their biological counterparts in nature (e.g., squirrel robot); and robots can look like objects (e.g., suitcases, trash cans, boxes) or common devices, such as buses and cars, and take many other forms. One of the exciting things about HRI is that it can expand our visions of what robots and our interactions with them could be like beyond the familiar anthropomorphic notions.

When robots are not just tools but also teammates, collaborators, companions, guides, tutors, and other types of social interaction partners, their study and design as part of HRI bring up many different questions about interpersonal relationships and societal development, both in the present and in the future. HRI research includes issues related to the social and physical design of technologies, as well as societal and organizational implementation and cultural sense-making, in ways that are distinct from related disciplines.

2.1 The focus of this book

HRI is a large, multidisciplinary field, and this book provides an introduction to the problems, processes, and solutions involved. This book enables the reader to gain an overview of the field without becoming overwhelmed with the complexities of all the challenges that we are facing, although we do provide references to relevant literature, which interested readers might want to investigate at their leisure. This book provides a much-needed introduction to the field so that students, academics, practitioners, and policymakers can become familiar with the future of how humans will interact with technology.

This book is an introduction, and as such, it does not require extensive knowledge in any of the related fields. It only requires the reader's curiosity about how people and robots can and should interact with each other.

After introducing the field of HRI and how a robot works in principle, we focus on the robots' designs. Next, we address the different interaction modalities through which humans can interact with robots, such as through speech or gestures. We also consider how we can understand and study how people perceive robots. The processing and communication of emotions is the next challenge we introduce before reflecting on the role that robots play in the media. The research methods chapter introduces the unique issues that researchers face when conducting empirical studies of humans interacting with robots. Next, we cover the application areas of social robots and their specific challenges before discussing broader societal and ethical issues around the use of social robots. The book closes with a look into the future of HRI.

2.2 HRI as an interdisciplinary endeavor

HRI is multidisciplinary and problem-based field by nature and by necessity. HRI brings together scholars and practitioners from various domains: engineers, psychologists, designers, anthropologists, sociologists, and philosophers, along with scholars from other application and research domains. Creating a successful human–robot interaction requires collaboration from a variety of fields to develop the robotics hardware and software, analyze the behavior of humans when interacting with robots in different social contexts, and create the aesthetics of the embodiment and behavior of the robot, as well as the required domain knowledge for particular applications. This collaboration can be difficult due to the different disciplinary jargon and practices. The common interest in HRI among this wide variety of participants, however, is a strong motivation for familiarizing oneself with and respecting the diverse ways of acquiring knowledge. HRI is, in this multidisciplinary sense, similar to the field of human–computer interaction (HCI), although dealing with embodied interactions with intelligent agents in diverse social contexts differentiates HRI from HCI.

The various disciplines that contribute to HRI differ from each other in terms of their shared beliefs, values, models, and exemplars (Bartneck and Rauterberg, 2007). These aspects form a "paradigm" that guides their community of theorists and practitioners (Kuhn, 1970). Researchers within a paradigm share beliefs, values, and exemplars. One way of understanding the difficulties of working together on a shared project can be based on three barriers (see Figure 2.2) that can occur between designers [D], engineers [E], and scientists (particularly social scientists) [S]:

1. Knowledge representation (explicit [S, E] versus implicit [D]);
2. View on reality (understanding [S] versus transforming reality [D, E]); and
3. Main focus on (technology [E] versus human [D, S]).

Barrier 1: Engineers [E] and scientists [S] make their results explicit by publishing in journals, books, and conference proceedings or by acquiring patents. Their body of knowledge is externalized and described to other engineers

Figure 2.2 HRI taps into several disciplines, and barriers are often experienced between these.

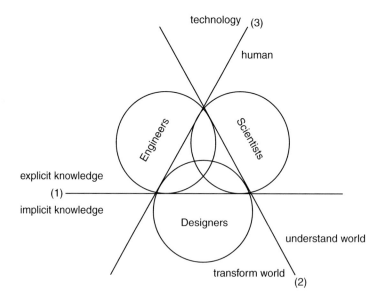

or scientists. These two communities revise their published results through discussion and control tests among peers. On the other hand, designers' [D] results are mainly represented by their concrete designs. The design knowledge necessary to create these designs lies within the individual designer, mainly as implicit knowledge, often referred to as *intuition* and described to the community in general principles.

Barrier 2: Engineers [E] and designers [D] transform the world into preferred states (Simon, 1996; Vincenti, 1990). They first identify a preferred state, such as the connection between two sides of a river, and then implement the transformation, which in our example would be a bridge. Scientists [S] mainly attempt to understand the world through the pursuit of knowledge covering general truths or the operation of general laws; although suggestions for intervention and transformation can be extrapolated from scientific work, they are often outside the purview of the scientific work itself.

Barrier 3: Scientists [S] and designers [D] are predominantly interested in humans in their role as possible users. Designers are interested in human values, which they transform into requirements and, eventually, solutions. Scientists in the HCI community are typically associated with the social or cognitive sciences. They are interested in the users' abilities and behaviors, such as perception, cognition, and action, as well as the way these factors are affected by the different contexts in which they occur. Engineers [E] are mainly interested in technology, which includes software for interactive systems. They investigate the structure and operational principles of these technical systems to solve certain problems.

Being aware of these disciplinary differences before embarking on an HRI project can help establish fruitful collaboration that takes into account the different types of knowledge and practice of the different disciplines. It is clear that an HRI project can bring in expertise from all of these different disciplinary types, but not every HRI project can afford to have dedicated specialists from all these disciplines. Many projects will also need to include people from additional disciplines, such as ethicists or education researchers, and application domains, such as health practitioners or educators. HRI researchers often need to wear several hats, trying to gain expertise in a variety of topics and domains. Although this approach may reduce the problems of finding common ground, it is quite limiting. We often do not know what we do not know. It is therefore important to either engage with all or many of the involved disciplines directly or at least communicate with experts in the respective fields. As the field of HRI grows and matures, it has also been expanding to include more and more different disciplines, frameworks, and methods (e.g., historians, performers), which can require an even more expansive set of knowledge requirements. In this case, we suggest also getting used to reading broadly, not just in your own discipline or subdomain of HRI but also in related fields, to understand how your own work fits into the bigger picture. When developing specific HRI applications, it is also crucial to collaborate with domain experts, including potential users and stakeholders, in the design—from the beginning of the project—to make sure to ask relevant

Figure 2.3 The Mirokai robot by Enchanted Tools, France. It combines omnidirectional navigation with two robot arms and a back-projected face. (Source: Enchanted Robots)

questions, use appropriate methods, and be aware of the potential broader consequences of the research to the application domain.

2.3 The evolution of social robots and HRI

The concept of "robot" has a long and rich history in the cultural imagination of many different societies, going back thousands of years to tales of humanlike machines, the later development of automata that reproduce certain human capabilities, and more recent science-fiction narratives about robots in society. Although these cultural notions of robots may not always be technically realistic, they color people's expectations of and reactions to robots.

> The first mention of "social robot" in print was in 1935, when it was used as a derogatory term for a person having a cold and distant personality.
>
> Toadying and bootlicking his autocratic superiors, he is advanced to preferment. He is a business success. But he has sacrificed all that was individual. He has become a social robot, a business cog. (Sargent, 2013, p. 92)
>
> In 1978, the first mention of "social robot" was made in the context of robotics. An article in *Interface Age* magazine described how a service robot, in addition to skills such as obstacle avoidance, balancing, and walking, would also need social skills to operate in a domestic setting. The article calls this robot a "social robot."

Ever since the concept of "robot" emerged, first in fiction and later as real machines, we have pondered the relationship between robots and people and how they could interact with each other. Every new technological or conceptual development in robotics has forced us to reconsider our relationship with and perception of robots.

When the first industrial robot, the Unimate, was installed at General Motors' Inland Fisher Guide Plant in Ewing Township, New Jersey, in 1961, people did consider how they would interact with the robot, but they were more concerned about the place robots would take among human workers. People who saw behavior-based robots for the first time could not help but marvel at the lifelike nature of the robots. Simple reactive behaviors (Braitenberg, 1986) implemented on small mobile robots produced machines that seemed injected with the very essence of life. Scurrying and fidgeting around the research labs of the 1990s, these robots evoked humanlike character traits and fundamentally changed our idea of how intelligence, or at least the appearance of intelligence, could be created (Brooks, 1991; Steels, 1993). This led to the creation of robots that used fast, reactive behavior to create a sense of social presence.

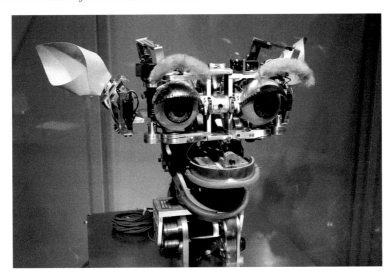

Figure 2.4 Kismet (1997–2004), an early example of social human–robot interaction research from the Massachusetts Institute of Technology. (Source: Daderot)

An early example of a social robot is Kismet (see Figure 2.4). Developed at the Massachusetts Institute of Technology in 1997, Kismet was a robot head-and-neck combination mounted on a tabletop box. Kismet could animate its eyes, eyebrows, lips, and neck, allowing it to pan, tilt, and crane its head. Based on visual and auditory input, it reacted to objects and people appearing in its visual field. It extracted information on visual motion, visual looming, sound amplitude, and emotion from speech prosody, and it responded by animating its facial expressions, ears, and neck and by babbling in a nonhuman language (Breazeal, 2003). Kismet was surprisingly effective in displaying a social presence, even though the control software only contained a small selection of social drives. It did so not only with its hardware and software architectures but also by taking advantage of human psychology, including what is known as the "baby schema," a predisposition to treat things with big eyes and exaggerated features in social ways despite their lack of fully functional social skills (Jia et al., 2015).

Like many robots in the early days of social robotics and HRI, Kismet was a bespoke robot, available to researchers in only one laboratory and requiring constant effort by students, postdocs, and other researchers to keep up and build up the robot's capabilities. These limitations understandably constrained the number of people and the range of disciplines that could participate in HRI in the field's early days. More recently, HRI research has been bolstered by the availability of reasonably priced commercial platforms that can be readily purchased by laboratories. These have expanded both the replicability and comparability of HRI research across labs, as well as the range of people who can engage in the discipline.

A number of commercially available robots have had a significant influence on the field. We will discuss some of the most commonly used ones here, but this list is by no means intended to be exhaustive because new robots get released, established robots get discontinued, and existing robots not

previously used in HRI get adopted and adapted for social robotics research. The robots discussed here, however, have all made their mark on the field and will be reemerging throughout this book.

Perhaps the most influential robot in the field of social robotics is the Nao robot (see Figure 2.5). Nao was originally developed by the French company Aldebaran Robotics, which was acquired by Softbank Robotics in 2015 and, in the process, became Softbank Robotics Europe until it was sold in 2022 to the German United Robotics Group, which renamed it back to Aldebaran Robotics. Nao was first sold in 2006, and due to its affordability (a Nao costs under 10,000 USD), robustness, and ease of programming, it became a widespread robot platform for studying HRI. Because of its size, it is also highly portable, allowing for studies to be run outside the lab. Another small humanoid robot that became available on the market later on is QT, by LuxAI, designed for use in research and educational contexts.

Aldebaran Robotics also created Pepper, an adolescent-size humanoid with a tablet built into its chest (see Figure 2.6). Some stores use Pepper to attract visitors and market products and services. The production of Pepper robots was reportedly discontinued in 2020, although at the time of writing, the robot was still available for purchase.

Taking it down a few notches in terms of size and complexity, the Keepon robot (see Figure 2.7), developed by Hideki Kozima, is a minimal robot consisting of two soft yellow spheres to which a nose and two eyes are added. The robot can swivel, bend, and bop, using motors worked into the base of the robot (Kozima et al., 2009). Keepon was later commercialized as an affordable toy (priced at 40 USD), and through some moderate hacking, it can be used as a research tool for HRI. Studies with the Keepon robot convincingly demonstrated that a social robot does not need to appear humanlike; the simple form of the robot is sufficient to achieve interaction outcomes where one might assume the need for more complex and humanlike robots.

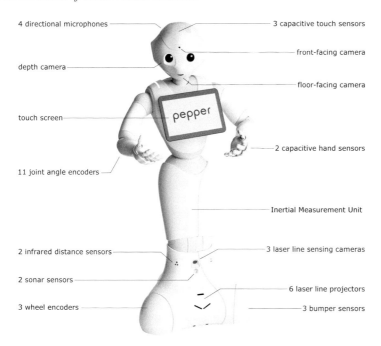

4 directional microphones

depth camera

touch screen

11 joint angle encoders

3 capacitive touch sensors

front-facing camera

floor-facing camera

2 capacitive hand sensors

Inertial Measurement Unit

2 infrared distance sensors

2 sonar sensors

3 wheel encoders

3 laser line sensing cameras

6 laser line projectors

3 bumper sensors

Figure 2.6
Pepper robot
(2014–present) and
its sensors (Source:
Pepper Robot by
SoftBank Robotics
and Philippe
Dureuiltoma)

Another simple design robot, the Paro companion and therapy robot (see Figure 2.8), shaped like a baby seal, has been particularly popular in the study of socially assistive robots in eldercare, as well as other scenarios. Paro has been commercially available (price: around 7,500 USD) in Japan since 2006 and in the United States and Europe since 2009 and is a robust platform that requires almost no technical competence to operate. Paro has therefore been used by various psychologists, anthropologists, and health researchers, both to study the potential psychological and physiological effects on people and to explore ways in which robots might be adopted in healthcare organizations. The simplicity of the robot's operation and its robustness enable its use in many different contexts, including in long-term and naturalistic studies. At the same time, the fact that it is a closed platform—which does not allow robot logs or sensor data to be extracted from the robot or allow the robot's behaviors to be changed—poses some limitations for HRI research.

The Baxter robot, sold by Rethink Robotics until 2018, is both an industrial robot and a platform for HRI (see Figure 2.9). The robot's two arms are actively compliant: in contrast to the stiff robot arms of typical industrial robots, Baxter's arms move in response to an externally applied force. In combination with other safety features, the Baxter robot is safe to work near, which makes it suitable for collaborative tasks. In addition, Baxter has a display screen mounted at head height on which the control software can display facial animations. Baxter's face can be used to communicate its internal state, and its eye fixations communicate a sense of attention to the human coworker.

Figure 2.7 Keepon (2003–present), a minimal social robot developed by Hideki Kozima. The robot was later commercialized as an affordable toy. (Source: Hideki Kozima, Tohoku University)

Figure 2.8 Paro (2003–present), a social robot made to resemble a baby harp seal. Paro is provided as a social companion robot. (Source: Courtesy of AIST, www.aist.go.jp)

Figure 2.9 Baxter (2011–2018) and Sawyer (2015–2018), industrial robots with compliant arms by Rethink Robotics. Baxter was the first industrial robot to include social interaction features on an industrial manipulator. (Source: Rethink Robotics, Inc.)

In 2017, Anki launched the Cozmo robot (see Figure 9.4), which was followed up in 2018 by Vector. In 2020 Anki was taken over by Digital Dream Labs, which released a second version of both robots in 2021. Although both robots are comparable in design, Cozmo has been designed primarily as an educational or research tool, with its behavior being customizable via an app or directly through coding (using Python). Vector, on the other hand, is more autonomous, responds to voice commands, and comes with predesigned behaviors. Cozmo and Vector cost around 500 USD and have both been used in HRI research.

Robots that were not explicitly designed to be used for HRI can also be used or even modified for HRI studies. The most commercially successful home robot is still the iRobot Roomba vacuum-cleaning robot (price ranging from 500 to 3,000 USD, depending on how intense of a cleaning the user wants), millions of which have been sold around the world. Roombas not only are an interesting agent for use in studying the public's relationship with robots (Forlizzi and DiSalvo, 2006) but also have been modified

Figure 2.10 Aibo ERS-1000 robot (2018–present). (Source: Copyright of Sony Corporation)

and hacked for HRI research. iRobot also makes educational robots, the Root (250 USD) and the Create (300 USD), which lack the vacuuming component and can be used in research and educational applications of robots.

Another consumer robot that has been used in HRI research is Aibo, an example of an animal-like robot, which was created by Sony and looks like a dog with a somewhat mechanical appearance (see Figure 2.10) and has the ability see, hear, feel touch, make sounds, wag its ears and tail, and move around on its four legs. The first Aibo models were sold in 1999, and sales were discontinued in 2006. Eleven years later, sales of new models started again, priced at roughly 3,000 USD.

Finally, Amazon released the Astro household robot in 2022 (see Figure 2.11). This home monitoring robot integrates the artificial intelligence assistant Alexa with a knee-high tablet mounted on a three-wheeler. It can be used for home security (as a remote-controlled camera on wheels); delivering messages and small items around the house; and all tasks commonly associated with tablets, including video calls, streaming of shows and movies, and looking up information online.

Figure 2.11 The Astro (2022–present) integrates Amazon's Alexa in a robotic platform and can be used as a home-monitoring system. (Source: Amazon)

Although the availability of affordable commercial robots with open application interfaces caused a proliferation of HRI studies, a second development has allowed for in-house-built social robots. New developments in mechatronic prototyping mean that robots can be modified, hacked, or built from scratch. Three-dimensional (3D) printing, laser cutting, and the availability of low-cost single-board computers have made it possible for researchers to build and modify robots in a short time and at minimal cost—both full-scale humanoids, such as InMoov (see Figure 2.12), and small robots, such as Blossom (Suguitan and Hoffman, 2019) or Ono (Vandevelde et al., 2016) (see Figure 2.13).

As you can see, the variety of robot hardware opens up endless research questions that can be addressed from a multidisciplinary perspective. Section 3.2 goes into more detail on the different types of robots. For an overview of the many robots available, you can explore the databases that were put

Figure 2.12 InMoov (2012– present) can be built using rapid-prototyping technology and readily available components. The InMoov robot is an open-source social robot

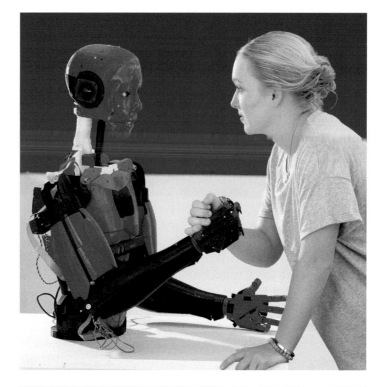

Figure 2.13 Blossom (2019– present) is an open-hardware, open-source tensile robot that you can handcraft and accessorize. Here, they wear a crocheted cover. (Source: Courtesy of the Cornell Human-Robot Collaboration and Companionship Lab. Photo: Dorin Haver)

together by Anthropomorphic roBOT (ABOT)[1] and the Institute of Electrical and Electronics Engineers (IEEE).[2]

Unlike other disciplines, HRI places particular emphasis on investigating the nature of social interactions between humans and robots, not only in dyads but also in groups, institutions, and sooner or later, in our societies. As will become clear in this book, technological advancements are a result of joint

---

[1] See www.abotdatabase.info
[2] See https://robotsguide.com/robots/

interdisciplinary efforts that have important societal and ethical implications. Keeping these in mind by doing human-centered research will hopefully lead to the development of robots that are widely accepted and that serve humans for the greater good.

Questions for you to think about:

- The HRI field draws insights from many other fields, but what other fields could benefit from research in HRI?
- Are you a designer, engineer, or social scientist? Try to imagine a situation in which you are collaborating with others to construct a robot (e.g., if you are an engineer, you are now working with a designer and a social scientist on this endeavor). How is your way of working different from the approaches the other teammates might use?
- What is the main difference between the disciplines of HRI and HCI, and what makes HRI unique as a new field?

2.4 Exercises

The answers to these questions are available in the Appendix. The asterisks next to each exercise denote the difficulty level, from * (least difficult) to ***** (most difficult).

** **Exercise 2.1 Disciplines**   What is the main difference between the disciplines of HRI and HCI? Select one option from the following list:

1. HRI uses only one computer, whereas HCI uses many computers.
2. HRI focuses on embodied social agents, whereas HCI focuses on interactions with computers.
3. HCI focuses on computers, whereas HRI focuses on humans.
4. Robots don't use computers.
5. HRI focuses on the interaction between machines, whereas HCI focuses on the interaction between humans.

* **Exercise 2.2 Your background**   What is your educational/professional background? (This exercise may help you become more aware of from which angle you'll most likely approach HRI.) Although you might have more than one background, select your main background from the following list:

1. Social sciences (psychology, sociology, anthropology, etc.)
2. Engineering (computer science, mechanical engineering, electrical engineering, mechatronics, etc.)
3. Design (interaction design, product design, user experience designer)

*** **Exercise 2.3 What makes robots social and good?**   Watch these two videos, and then answer the two questions that follow.

- Cynthia Breazeal, "Developing Social and Empathetic A.I.," https://youtu.be/T52g7dCxJ4A
- Henry Evans and Chad Jenkins, "Robots for Humanity," https://youtu.be/aCIukWXmlV4

1. Cynthia Breazeal says Kismet is the "first social robot." What makes Kismet (and the other robots discussed in this chapter) social? Would you say robots are social in a different way from people, and if so, how?

2. Breazeal talks about how artificial intelligence can be designed to be more helpful to humans, and Evans and Jenkins demonstrate some ways in which robotic embodiment can extend human capabilities. What did you find compelling about these possibilities for using robots "for the social good"? Can you think of any social issues that you or members of your community face in which the types of robotic capabilities that Breazeal, Evans, and Jenkins discuss could be helpful?

3

How a Robot Works

> What is covered in this chapter:
>
> - The basic hardware and software components that a robot consists of.
> - The techniques we can apply to make a robot ready for interacting with people.

As a way of thinking about how a robot works, let us role-play by imagining being a robot. We might think we can do a lot of things, but we soon find out our capabilities are severely limited. If we are newly built robots, without appropriate software, our brains are entirely empty. We cannot do anything—move, know where we are, understand what is around us, even ask for help. We find the experience of being a robot rather strange and difficult to imagine. The main source of strangeness is that the new robot's brain is nothing like a human brain, not even an infant's. The robot has no basic instincts, no goals, no memory, no needs, no learning capabilities, and no ability to sense or act. To make a robot system, we need to integrate, and at least partially develop, hardware and software together to enable the robot to sense and act in the world.

This chapter is written for readers who have a limited technical background in intelligent interactive robotics. It describes the common components of a robot and how they are connected to enable participation in interaction. Section 3.1 explains basic ideas about the components needed to build a robot. Section 3.2 explains the types of hardware. Section 3.3 covers the integration of hardware and software and addresses the perception (e.g., computer vision), planning, and action control of the robot. Section 3.4 introduces sensors, such as cameras, range finders, and microphones, and Section 3.5 introduces actuators. Section 3.6 discusses software specifically designed for connecting other pieces of software to form one coherent program. Section 3.7 covers how to model interaction between the robot's program and the environment, whereas Section 3.8 goes specifically into artificial intelligence (AI) and machine learning. Finally, Section 3.9 discusses the most pressing limitations of robotics.

3.1 The making of a robot

To build a robot, one of the first steps is to establish connections between the robot's sensors, computer, and motors so that the robot is able to sense, interpret what it senses, plan actions, and then act them out. Once the robot is connected, for example, to a camera, its computer can read the data the camera provides. But the camera image is nothing more than a large table of numbers, similar to the following table:

$$
\begin{array}{ccc}
9 & 15 & 10 \\
89 & 76 & 81 \\
25 & 34 & 29
\end{array}
$$

From these numbers, can you guess what the robot is seeing? Perhaps a ball, an apple, or a fork? Assuming that each value in the table represents the lightness value of one sensor element in the camera, we can translate those numbers into a graphic that is more meaningful to humans (see Figure 3.1), but the graphic remains meaningless to the robot.

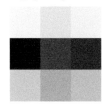

Figure 3.1 The camera's data translated into a grid of grayscale pixels.

You might be able to see a line in the image shown in Figure 3.1, but a robot has no understanding of what a line is. This line might be the edge of a cliff from which the robot could fall and damage itself. But the robot does not have a concept of height or gravity. It would not comprehend that it could fall if it crossed this line. It does not know that if it fell, it would likely come to rest upside down. Without the appropriate sensors, it would not register that it would be falling, nor that it abruptly came to a stop as it encountered the ground. It would not even recognize that its arm would be broken. In other words, even concepts that are vitally important for interacting with and surviving in the world around us that are innate in humans have to be explicitly programmed in a robot.

A robot, in essence, is a computer with a body. Any functionality needs to be programmed into the robot. A problem that all robots have to deal with is that although their sensors and motors are sufficient for operating in this world, their intelligence is not. Any concept of interest to roboticists needs to be programmed into the robot. This requires a lot of time and effort and often involves many cycles of trial and error. The analogue world out there is converted into a digital world, and translating tables of numbers into meaningful information and meaningful responses is one of the core goals of AI. Being able to identify a face from a large table of values, recognizing if a person has been seen before, and knowing that person's name are all skills that require programming or learning. Thus, the progress of human–robot interaction (HRI) is constrained by the progress that is made in the field of AI. Robotics engineers integrate sensors, software, and actuators to enable the robot to make sense of and interact with its physical and social environment. An engineer might, for example, use accelerometer sensors, which can detect acceleration and Earth's gravitational pull, to read the orientation of the robot and determine if it has fallen. A cliff sensor, consisting of a small infrared light source pointing down and a light sensor, can be used by the robot to avoid falling down a staircase.

Typical problems that robot engineers have to solve for the robot include the following:

- What kind of body does the robot have? Does it have wheels? Does it have arms?
- How will the robot know its location in space?
- How does the robot control and position its body parts—for example, arms, legs, wheels?
- What does the space around the robot look like? Are there obstacles, cliffs, doors? What does the robot need to be able to perceive about this environment to move safely?
- What are the robot's goals? How does it know when it has achieved them?
- Are there people around? If so, where are they, and who are they? How will the robot know?
- Is a person looking at the robot? Is someone talking to it? If so, what does the robot understand from these cues?
- What is the human trying to do? What does the person want the robot to do? How can we make sure the robot understands this?
- What should the robot do, and how should the robot react?
- Does the robot have enough battery power?

To address these questions, HRI researchers need to build or choose appropriate hardware and an appropriate morphology for the robot and then develop relevant programs—the software—that can tell the robot what to do with its body.

3.2 Robot types

At the time of this writing, a number of robots have been produced for the consumer market. Section 2.3 introduced some of the landmark robots, although this list is far from complete. For a more complete overview, we refer to the databases created by Anthropomorphic roBOT (ABOT) (www.abot database.info) and the Institute of Electrical and Electronics Engineers (IEEE) (https://robotsguide.com/robots/). Although not all consumer robots become domestic staples, these commercial robots are often suitable platforms for HRI research. Commercially available robots can be categorized in a number of ways, including the following: social robots and drones, humanoids, androids, zoomorphic robots, virtual agents, telepresence and tele-operation robots, projection robots, and industrial robots. We will discuss these types in this section.

As covered in Chapter 1, *social robots* are robots that are designed to interact with humans (Hegel et al., 2009). This does not necessarily mean that a robot has a humanlike shape; as will be explained in Section 4.2 and Chapter 8, humans will readily perceive humanlike traits in other agents if they give off certain social cues or behave in certain ways. Thus, even a robot as simple as the Keepon (see Figure 2.7) can be considered a social robot because its behavior creates the impression of a social presence. Obviously, different social robots will have different levels of complexity in their interaction. Paro, the baby seal robot (see Figure 2.8), can move its tail and open and close its eyes based on haptic feedback, but it does not communicate in other ways. In contrast, the iCub is shaped like a child (see Figure 3.8) and can display a variety of facial expressions, both of which create a myriad of ways to engage in social interaction.

Drones, and in particular, social drones, are flying robots that co-share space with humans (Obaid et al., 2020; Baytas et al., 2019; Johal et al., 2022) and can be used for applications in the household or education, among other use cases. Contrary to humanoid robot types, which will be discussed next, social drones commonly do not have a humanlike appearance.

Humanoid robots are robots that follow a general humanlike outline for their hardware. This means that generally speaking, the robot will be bipedal (although sometimes the legs are merged into a shaft on wheels, as is the case with Wakamaru and Pepper; see Figures 2.6 and 6.4); have a torso with a set of arms; and have a head with at least some facial features, such as eyes and a mouth. Well-known examples of humanoid robots include Nao, Pepper, Asimo, Robovie, and iCub.

Further humanlike in appearance are the *android robots*, which aim to mimic human looks as closely as possible. Although creating an exact replica of a human face and body out of silicon may be doable, animating it in such a way that it moves in a natural and humanlike way comes with its own set of challenges and issues, as discussed in greater detail in Section 4.2.1. Well-known androids include Kokoro and the Geminoid HI 4 robots (see Figure 4.5; see also Figure 4.7). Rather than trying to follow a human outline, *zoomorphic robots* are modeled after an animal shape. This can be an existing animal: for example, the Aibo is modeled after a dog (see Figures 2.10 and 11.1), the Paro after a baby seal (see Figure 2.8), and the Pleo after a baby sauropod dinosaur (see Figure 11.5). However, the robot's designer can also take some artistic freedom in their design and come up with their own fantasy animal, as was done in the creation of the Furby (see Figure 3.2).

Figure 3.2 The Furby (1998–2016) is a commercial zoomorphic robot that was particularly popular in the late 1990s.

An interesting in-between form of virtual assistants and embodied robots is the *projection robots*. These robots consist of a physical husk on which features are projected (see Figure 3.3). The benefits of this layout are that it becomes possible to mimic subtle movements, such as facial expressions, and that the appearance of the robot (e.g., skin color, gender) can be easily changed. At the same time, the animations of this robot remain projected rather than actual movements, and to our knowledge, there is no robot available yet that combines a projection with animated embodiment that would allow the robot to manipulate its environment.

Strictly speaking, *virtual agents* aren't robots: they are animated representations of an agent that is presented on a screen (e.g., a computer, tablet, or smartphone). Often, these agents are linked up with AI programs that can process spoken or written language commands and provide a response. These

Figure 3.3 The Furhat robot combines a virtual face with a hardware embodiment through projection. (Source: Furhat Robotics)

applications have found their way into many areas, such as customer service, healthcare, sales, and education (Lugrin et al., 2022).

Telepresence robots can also be used as platforms for HRI research. Many different types exist on the market, including mobile versions, such as the Beam, and desktop versions like Kubi. Small mobile robots carrying a screen displaying a friendly face are being developed, soon to be ready for release in the consumer market.

Although commercially available robot hardware provides a wide variety of morphologies and sensing and programming capabilities, every robot is limited in what it can do; its appearance and capabilities constrain the interactions it can engage in. Researchers, therefore, also conceive and build their own robots, which range from simple desktop and mobile platforms with or without a manipulator to very humanlike android robots. The choice of a particular morphology for a robot to be used in HRI research often depends on the capabilities needed for the expected task (e.g., whether it needs to be able to pick up objects), the type of interaction (e.g., petlike interactions can benefit from an animal-like robot), and people's expectations and perceptions of different morphologies (e.g., humanoids may be expected to behave and be intelligent in ways similar to humans).

3.3 System architecture

All the hardware components of the robot need to be connected to a computer so that they can become interactive. The architecture of such a system can typically be divided into layers. Each layer typically only communicates with its direct neighbors (see Figure 3.4).

3.3.1 Hardware layers

At the bottom of the system are the different hardware components, such as motors and sensors. They are connected with cables to one or more computers. Some robots do all processing on board, but many robots will offload processing to other computers. In more recent robot software, the speech recognition, computer vision, and storage of user data often happen in the cloud, transmitted by internet-connected software services, typically operating on a pay-per-use basis. The advantage of cloud-based computing is that the

Figure 3.4 System
architecture for robots.

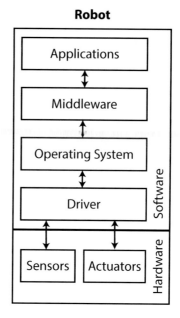

robot has access to much more computing power and storage space than it
could ever carry on board. Smart speakers, such as Google Home and Amazon
Alexa, rely on cloud-based computing. However, a disadvantage is that when
a robot relies on cloud-based computing, it needs robust communication with
the cloud server. This is not necessarily guaranteed, particularly when a robot
is mobile. Thus, time-critical computing and computing used to guarantee
safety (e.g., emergency stops) are usually done on board.

3.3.2 Software layers

Above the hardware layers are the software layers. All the currently available
robots are controlled by software running on one or several computers. The
computers receive data from sensors and periodically send commands to the
actuators.

On the computer, there is an operating system (e.g., Windows, Linux),
which acts as the general platform allowing the software to access the
general hardware of the computer, such as access to disks and files, and
manages resources like memory and the central processing unit (CPU). The
drivers enable the operating system to communicate with specific hardware
components. These drivers normally come from the manufacturer of the
hardware components, but some of them might already come integrated
into the operating system. For example, when you plug a mouse into your
computer, you normally do not need to install any drivers.

Although application software can directly run on the operating system,
robotic applications often are run through *middleware*, consisting of many
small pieces of software modules. Middleware is considered a "software
glue," being in the middle of software modules and the operating system (see
Section 3.6 for a more in-depth discussion).

3.4 Sensors

Most social robots are equipped with sensors that allow them to gauge what is happening in their environment. Many commonly used sensors are related to the three most commonly used modalities in human interaction—vision, hearing, and touch—but robots are not at all limited to human modes of sensing. It is often helpful, therefore, to consider what types of information the robot needs to perceive and what the most accurate and expedient ways are for it to do so, rather than focusing on reproducing human capabilities.

3.4.1 Vision

Camera

A camera consists of lenses that focus an image onto a sensor surface. The sensor surface is implemented using either a charge-coupled device (CCD) or, more often, a complementary metal-oxide-semiconductor (CMOS) technology. The basic element of a camera is a light sensor consisting mainly of silicon that converts light into electrical energy. A camera consists of an array of millions of these light sensors. Typically, color in a camera image is represented using three values, red (R), green (G), and blue (B). Hence, a camera is commonly referred to as an *RGB camera*. The sensors on the sensor surface are not sensitive to the color of the light hitting them; they are only sensitive to light intensity. To make an RGB camera, small color filters are placed on top of the sensor surface, with each filter letting through only red, green, or blue light (see Figure 3.5). Cameras are the richest and most

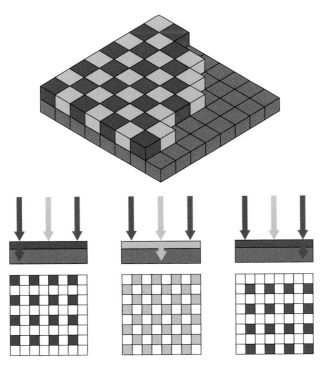

Figure 3.5 Array of CCDs in RGB camera.

complex sensors available to robots, and through the wide adoption of the RGB camera in digital cameras and smartphones, it has become miniaturized and very cheap.

Most cameras have a more restricted field of view than human vision. Whereas people can see more than 180 degrees, a typical camera might only see 90 degrees, thus missing a lot of what is going on in the periphery. A robot with a single camera will have a limited field of view and might have to rely on other sensors, such as laser range finders or microphones, to give it a sense of what is going on around it.

Most importantly, the camera image needs to be processed using computer-vision algorithms in order for the robot to be able to respond to its visual environment (see Section 3.8.2).

In computer-vision research, investigators often put cameras in the environment to facilitate accurate vision. Although this is one of the realistic approaches to yielding stable performance from computer vision, in the HRI setting, it is sometimes discouraged because people can feel uncomfortable around cameras. For example, in a project in which elderly people were being assisted in their home by a robot, the engineers would have loved to have cameras on the robot and in the home because it would have allowed the robot to accurately track and interact with people. However, the elderly participants were quite firm in their refusal of the installation and use of cameras, forcing the team to use localization beacons and laser range finders instead (Cavallo et al., 2014).

Depth sensors

Just as human vision uses stereo vision, knowledge about objects, and self-motion to figure out the distance to objects, so can computer-vision algorithms be used to extract a three-dimensional (3D) image from two-dimensional (2D) information. Stereo cameras have been the technology of choice for a long time, but in recent years, other technologies have emerged that allow us to see depth directly, without the need for computer vision. These "depth sensors" output a "depth image" or RGBD image (standing for red, green, blue, and *depth*), a map of distances to objects in view of the camera.

Typically, a depth sensor can measure the distance to objects a few meters away. Depending on the strength of the emitted infrared light, most depth sensors only work reliably indoors. There are several ways of making such depth sensors. One of the typical mechanisms is time of flight (TOF), in which a device transmits invisible infrared light pulses and measures the time taken between the moment when it transmitted the light and the moment when it received the light's reflection. Because the speed of light is so high, the camera would need to record the timing of the returning light with a precision that is out of reach of current electronics hardware. Instead, the camera emits pulses of infrared light and measures the phase difference between the light leaving the camera and the light returning to

Figure 3.6 The Microsoft Kinect Azure DK for Windows sensor. (Source: Used with permission from Microsoft)

the camera. The Microsoft Kinect One, the second iteration of Microsoft's game controller, is based on this principle (see Figure 3.6). Despite being developed as a game controller, it was quickly adopted by robot builders and is now widely used to give robots a sense of depth. Combined with appropriate software, the Kinect sensor can also perform skeleton tracking, which is helpful for figuring out where people are and what they are doing. Smaller devices are now available that return RGBD images based on a range of different technologies, including TOF, structured light, and stereo vision.

Laser range finders

Depth sensors are appropriate for measuring distances up to a few meters. In order to measure distances at longer ranges, researchers frequently use a laser range finder, also known as *light detection and ranging* (LiDAR). A typical laser range finder can measure distances to objects up to 30 meters away, and it samples the environment between 10 and 50 times per second. The accuracy of laser range finders is within a few centimeters.

The basic mechanism of this type of sensor is also TOF (as explained earlier, under *Depth sensors*). A laser range finder transmits a single beam of infrared laser light and measures the distance by measuring the time between the moment it transmits the laser beam and the time it receives its reflection. Typically, the transmitter and receiver are on a rotating platform, sweeping the laser beam around the environment. Thus, the device only measures distance in a single 2D plane, that is, the plane of rotation of the rotating platform.

Robots can have range finders mounted at different heights to scan for objects on a horizontal plane. Range finders close to the ground can sense objects on the floor and people's legs, whereas range finders that are set higher up can be used to sense objects on a table or counter (see Figure 3.7).

Figure 3.7 The PR2 robots (2010–2014): Can you tell where the range finder is? (Source: Willow Garage)

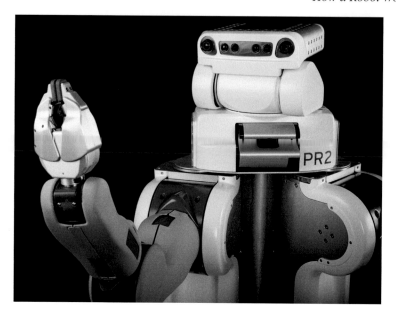

3.4.2 Audio

Microphones are commonly used devices for auditory sensing, and they convert sound into electrical signals. Microphones have different sensitivity profiles; some are omnidirectional, picking up all sounds in the environment, whereas others are directional, only picking up sounds in a cone-shaped area in front of the microphone. Combining multiple microphones into an array allows us to use "beam-forming" techniques, which can separate sound signals coming from a specific direction from ambient noises. Microphone arrays are used for sound-source localization, that is, getting an accurate reading on the angle of a given sound source with respect to its position in relation to the microphone array.

3.4.3 Tactile sensors

Tactile sensors can be important in HRI, for example, when the robot is physically guided by the user. Many different implementations exist, from physical buttons or switches to capacitive sensors, such as those found on touch screens.

The most commonly used tactile sensor is a mechanical push switch. It is often used together with a bumper. When a robot collides with an object, the switch is closed, allowing the robot to detect the collision. Pressure sensors and capacity sensors, like the ones reading your finger's position on a touch screen, can also be used to detect physical contact with the environment. Pressure sensors can be implemented using a range of technologies but usually contain a material that changes its electrical properties (resistance or capacitance) when force is applied (see Figure 3.8).

Figure 3.8 The iCub (2004–present) humanoid has capacitive tactile sensors worked into its fingers, palms, and torso. (Source: IIT Central Research Lab Genova)

Pressure sensors can help robots recognize whether and how hard they are touching a person or object. They are also very useful for enabling robots to pick up and handle objects appropriately. Tactile sensors can furthermore be used to allow the robot to know whether someone is touching it, and the robot can be programmed to respond accordingly. For example, the seal-like Paro robot has a tactile sensor net all over its body that allows it to sense the location and pressure with which a person is touching it and react by cooing for soft strokes and crying out after a harder hit.

3.4.4 Other sensors

Various other sensors exist, many of which can be relevant to HRI. Light sensors read the amount of light falling on the sensor and can be used to sense a sudden change in light, signaling that something has changed in the environment. When combined with a light source, they can be used to detect objects. A simple and very effective obstacle sensor combines an infrared light-emitting diode (LED) light with an infrared light sensor; when light bounces back from objects in front of the sensor, it can determine the distance to objects. This not only is used to detect obstacles in front of the robot but can also be used to sense when people are approaching the robot.

In recent years, the inertial measurement unit (IMU) has become a popular sensor. It combines three sensors—an accelerometer, a gyroscope, and a magnetometer—and is used to read the rotation and motion of the sensor or, more accurately, the rotational and translational acceleration. Recent advances in micro-electrical manufacturing have allowed these sensors to be miniaturized down to a few millimeters. They have become ubiquitous in mobile phones and miniature drones, and when used in a robot, they allow the robot to sense if it falls or to keep track of where it has moved over time.

Far-infrared (FIR) sensors are cameras that are sensitive to long-wavelength infrared light, which is emitted by warm bodies. They can be used to detect the presence of people, as used in burglar alarms, or when integrated into an FIR camera, they can be used to record an image of the temperature of the room. FIR sensors are still expensive and are mainly used for thermal imaging, but eventually, they may allow the robot to see people at night or in cluttered environments.

It is important to realize that, unlike our own senses, sensors do not necessarily need to be mounted on the robot. A robot might rely on a ceiling-mounted camera to interpret the social environment, or it could use a wall-mounted microphone array to localize who is speaking. The whole environment could, in a sense, be considered part of a robot system.

3.5 Actuators

An actuator converts electrical signals into physical movements. A system with one actuator typically realizes motion either on one straight line or on one rotational axis. This means that the system has one degree of freedom (DOF). By combining multiple motors, we can develop a robot that has motion with multiple DOFs, allowing for navigation of a 2D plane or gesturing with humanlike arms.

3.5.1 Motors

The standard actuator for robots is a direct-current (DC) servo motor (see Figure 3.9). It typically consists of a DC motor and a microcontroller, with a sensor such as a potentiometer or an encoder, which outputs the absolute or relative position of the motor's output axis. To control the speed, the controller typically sends pulse-width modulation (PWM) signals to the DC motor. PWM is an on/off pulse, literally switching the motor on for a few milliseconds and then back off. This is done up to 100 times per second, and the duration of the on phase against the off phase (known as the *duty cycle*) determines the speed at which the motor rotates. The PWM signal controls the speed of the motor, and the controller sets the position of the motor. This is done through feedback control, where the controller continuously reads the position of the motor and adjusts the motor's PWM and direction to reach or maintain a desired position. For motors used in a robot's arms and head, the controller typically performs position control to rotate the motor toward a given commanded angle. For motors used in wheels on a mobile base, the controller typically performs velocity control to rotate the motor at the commanded velocity.

Robots can have different configurations and numbers of motors, depending on the body shape and the functions they are meant to perform. Commercially available cleaning robots, such as Roomba, typically have two motors driving

Figure 3.9
Connecting servo motors to each other allows robots to move around in various ways, such as in this robot arm. (Source: Trossen Robotics)

the wheels and one tactile sensor for moving around the room. Thus, Roomba has two DOFs. A simple nodding robot may have one motor to control its head direction, meaning that it has one DOF. A better-equipped humanoid may have three DOFs for its head, controlling pan, tilt, and yaw; two arms with four to seven DOFs; a mobile base with at least two motors; and sensors for visual, auditory, and tactile sensing. A robot arm, such as the KUKA (see Figure 3.10), must have at least six DOFs to manipulate an object. Three DOFs are necessary to locate its end effector (e.g., hand) to be in a position within a reachable range of the object, and another three DOFs are needed to grasp the object from any direction. A human arm can be approximated as an arm having seven DOFs, with an additional redundant one DOF beyond the necessary six DOFs for manipulation.

To grasp objects, a robot arm must have some type of end effector attached at the end. A 1-DOF gripper can be used to grasp an object, but more complex robot hands can have as many as 16 DOFs. Android robots, designed to closely resemble humans, typically have many more (e.g., 50 or more) DOFs and are able to control their facial expressions and other bodily movements in relatively nuanced ways compared to simpler robots.

Motors come in many different sizes, speeds, and strengths and thus have differing power needs. It is therefore important to consider from early on in the design process how the motor specifications relate to the robot's design and what kinds of actions a robot will need to make, such as whether it will need to pick up a one-kilogram bag or just needs to wave its arms, how big the robot can be while still fitting in well with its environment, how quickly it needs to respond to stimuli, and whether it needs to have a portable power bank or can be plugged into the wall.

Figure 3.10 KUKA robot arm. (Source: KUKA)

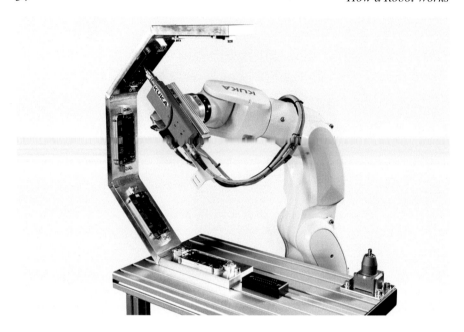

Figure 3.11 RoboThespian (2005–present) uses pneumatic actuators to achieve the acceleration required to deliver a convincing theatrical performance. The robot can run for around a day on a scuba tank's worth of compressed gas, although it can also be attached to a compressor. (Source: Photo copyright Engineered Arts)

3.5.2 Pneumatic actuators

A pneumatic actuator uses a piston and compressed air. Air is delivered from a compressor or from a vessel containing high-pressure air, which needs to be attached to the robot in some way. Pistons typically can extend and contract, depending on which valves are opened to let in the compressed air. As opposed to electric motors, pneumatic actuators produce linear motion, which is somewhat similar to human muscle motion, and are able to produce accelerations and speeds that are difficult to achieve using electric motors. Hence, they are often preferred for humanoid robots and android robots that need to gesticulate at humanlike acceleration and velocity (see Figure 3.11). The compressors that they need to operate can be quite loud, so it is important to consider how to give the robot access to compressed air without marring the interaction experience.

3.5.3 Speakers

To generate sounds and speech, standard loudspeakers are used. Speakers are perhaps the cheapest actuator on the robot, but in terms of HRI, they are indispensable. Where to place a speaker or speakers in the robot's body is an important factor to consider when designing a robot that will interact with people. For example, Takayama (2008) showed that the relative height from which the voices of a user and an agent interacting with each other are projected can influence who is seen to be dominant in the interaction.

3.6 Middleware

3.6.1 What is a middleware?

Middleware is software that sits among software components, such as commonly available library modules and the application modules that the developers created for a specific purpose, as well as the operating system of the robot's computer. It is often considered as the "software glue" because its function is to ease the connection of those software components.

One of the functions of robotics middleware is to deal with the heterogeneity of hardware. Some applications are flexible about the type of sensors the robot uses as long as similar sensor data are provided. For instance, a 3D LiDAR could provide 3D distance data, but these data can be converted into the kind of 2D data that a 2D laser range finder provides. On the middleware, we can standardize a data format for 2D laser range finders so that we can use 2D laser range finders from different companies, as well as other sensors that output distance information, such as depth sensors and 3D LiDAR, in a similar way.

Another function of the robotics middleware is to help developers deal with complexity and reuse software modules. Almost all robotic applications are overly complex. It is unrealistic to create the whole application from scratch. Moreover, applications are often not really interested in the raw sensory data. They want to know abstracted information, for example, if a person is standing in front of the robot. Therefore, once someone creates a functional software module that enables the detection of a person in front of the robot, other developers would hope to reuse such an established module for many other robot applications, which would all be composed of somewhat different software and hardware components. Thus, "modules" (software components) are often shared within a community in which developers maintain and reuse various well-behaving modules.

To better understand the benefits of middleware, we need to take a closer look at how robots are built and how they work. Let's assume that we have two different robots, Marvin and S2E2. Both have two wheels to move around, but S2E2's wheels are 10 cm in diameter and Marvin's wheels are 20 cm. Thus, these robots are similar to the degree that they use the same methods to move forward, backward, and around, but they are different in wheel size.

Programmers might want these two robots to move between the fridge and the couch to deliver a beverage to their human user. For this purpose, the robots need to drive forward for two meters. The motors themselves can only be switched on or off. The wheels need a rotation sensor to detect how often they have turned. It would be really useful if the behavior to deliver the beverage developed for Marvin could also be used for S2E2. The middleware makes this possible by abstracting the robots. It translates the two-meter distance to 6.37 rotations for S2E2 and 3.18 rotations for Marvin.

Driving a robot straight ahead for two meters may look like an easy task, but it is not. It is possible for the wheels to slip, or a cat might dash across the path. Hence, the robot requires sensors to measure its location within the room. Marvin could have an ultrasound sensor mounted in front to measure the distance between itself and the couch ahead. S2D2 might have a LiDAR sensor to measure the distance. Again, robots are similar, yet different. The middleware abstracts the two sensors to simply the distance from itself to the couch. The programmer can then monitor the progress of the robot and adjust the duration for which the motors are switched on and off.

But what about the cat that crosses paths with the robot? Both robots need to be able to move around an obstacle to drive to the couch. The problem of dynamically planning and adjusting a path toward the couch requires yet more sensors and software. These components should be able to communicate with each other so that they can trigger, for example, evasion behaviors. Middleware allows the different components to directly communicate with each other. Moreover, the problem of navigating the living room can be abstracted to both robots so that the software developed becomes reusable. This dramatically speeds up the process of software development because solutions for common problems can be shared. Path planning, obstacle avoidance, and localization have all been solved as problems in themselves, independent of the specific robot.

3.6.2 Robot Operating System

The Robot Operating System (ROS) is a middleware platform commonly used in the robotics and HRI community.[1] The name is somewhat misleading because ROS actually is not an operating system, such as MacOS, Linux, or Windows. Rather, it is a collection of software modules and tools. It deals with communications between sensors and modules and offers libraries and tools to support frequently used robot abilities, such as localization and navigation. ROS has a large community of users who often share modules on public open-source software repositories. The more developers use and extend this middleware to different sensors and actuators, the more attractive this platform becomes.

Some robot hardware developers decided not to develop their own software platforms for their robots as, for example, Aldebaran did for its Nao and Pepper robots. Instead, they offer modules for ROS to control and program their robots. PAL Robotics is an example of a company that offers ROS modules for its robots, such as TIAGo (see Figure 3.12).

Although ROS is playing an important role in the robotics and HRI communities, it still remains middleware that requires technical expertise to install, configure, and use. It is primarily useful for developers who are already familiar with code editors, repositories, and libraries. For these, ROS offers tools to launch code, introspection, debugging, visualization, plotting, logging, and playback. It does not, however, contain animation tools (see Section 3.7.2) or behavior editors (see Section 3.7.1). Unfortunately, there is no visual programming environment that would allow users without technical knowledge to click together behaviors and interactions.

---

[1] See www.ros.org

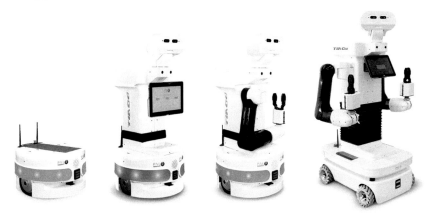

Figure 3.12 The TIAGo robot family uses ROS. (Source: TIAGo Family by PAL Robotics, © PAL Robotics S. L. 2024)

3.7 Applications

A robot is much more than a computer with a body. A computer operates in a clean digital environment, whereas a robot needs to interface with the messy, buzzing confusion of the real world. Not only does it need to make sense of the world, but it also needs to do so in real-time. This environment requires a radically different approach to robot software.

Architecture models

How should software for a robot be organized? A first rule of thumb, which is applicable to any software, is that messy program code should be avoided. Researchers and developers ideally aim to modularize software. One typical approach is to follow the "sense-plan-act" model (see Figure 3.13), in which inputs from sensors are processed using software modules specific to perception, which then convert sensor streams into high-order presentations. For example, audio recordings of speech are converted into a text transcription, or camera images are analyzed to report on the location of faces. Next, there is a section that deals with "planning," which plans the robot's next actions using information gleaned from the sensing process, then outputs commands to modules for action.

For instance, a person-finding perception module reports on the location of people detected in a 2D camera image and also returns the size of the heads, indicative of how close people are to the robot. Next, the planning module computes the head orientation for the robot to face the nearest speaker and sends a command to move the head to the output modules. The output modules then calculate which angle is needed for the robot's neck motors and send these to the low-level motor controllers.

The sense-plan-act approach is also known as the *deliberative approach* because the robot deliberates its next action. Quite often, we want a robot to respond quickly to external events, without spending a lot of time pondering what to do next. In this case, we often program simple "behaviors" for the robot (Brooks, 1991). Behaviors are tightly coupled sensor–action processing

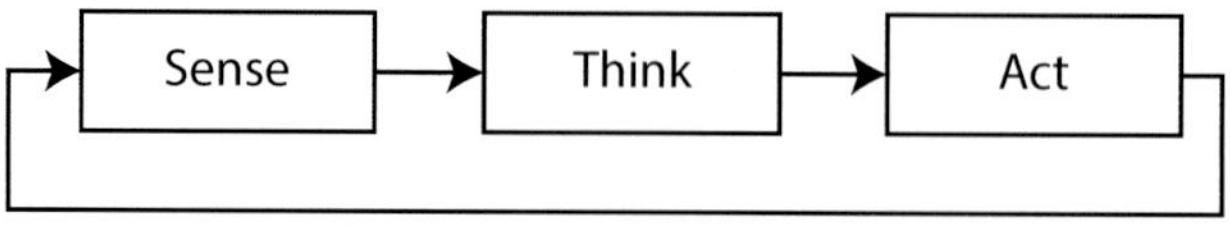

Figure 3.13
Sense-plan-act model.

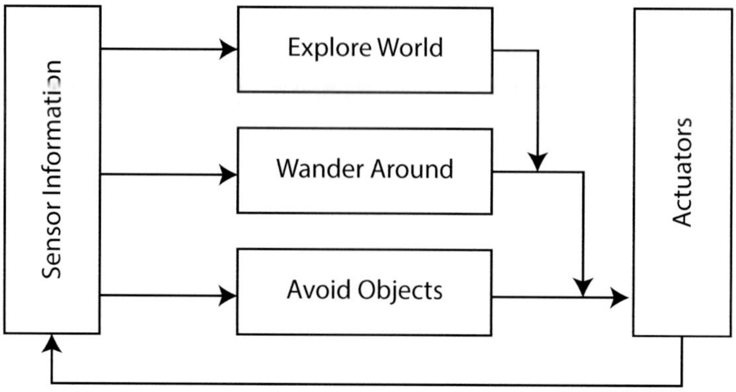

Figure 3.14 The
subsumption
behavior-based
architecture.

loops that immediately respond to an external event. These can be used to
make an emergency stop when the robot is about to drive down the stairs, but
they can serve equally well in social interaction. When a loud bang is heard or
when a face appears in view, we want the robot to respond as fast as possible.
Act first; think later. Often, there are dozens of behaviors running on the robot,
and mechanisms exist to mediate between which behaviors are active and
which are not. One such mechanism is the subsumption architecture, which
organizes behavior into hierarchies, allowing a behavior to activate or inhibit
others (Brooks 1986; see Figure 3.14).

With this approach, even though the robot does not have an explicit "representation" of the world, it can still behave in an apparently intelligent way.
For instance, if a cleaning robot uses two behaviors in parallel, one that avoids
the wall and another that makes it have a slight pull to the right, the resulting,
or emergent, behavior is that of wall following. Even though wall following
wasn't programmed explicitly, it emerges from the interaction between two
simpler behaviors. The vacuum robot Roomba has been developed with such
an idea in mind.

In HRI studies, we typically find ourselves looking for a middle ground
between deliberative and reactive approaches. We want a reactive control
layer, which responds quickly to subsecond social events, followed by a
deliberative layer, which formulates a coherent response to slower elements
of the interaction, such as conversation.

In light of this, it is important to develop software that can be decomposed
into a number of smaller modules. Even if the complete wealth of a sense-
plan-act model is not needed, it is still common practice to separate modules
into perception, planning, and action.

Planning is diverse in terms of components and complexity and depends
heavily on the robot and the application. A cleaning robot may need to
compute the next location to clean, whereas a companion robot may need

to make a decision on how it should initiate a conversation with a user. The software on a Roomba vacuum will therefore be radically different from that on a Pepper humanoid robot. For interactive robots, various forms of HRI knowledge will be embedded into the various software modules.

Action modules take care of the actuation and social output of the robot, such as nonverbal utterances, speech, hand gestures, and locomotion. For instance, the speech-synthesis module may receive text and convert this into spoken words, together with timing information that allows the robot to accentuate its speech with appropriate gestures.

3.7.1 Behavior editors

A robot has to be programmed in order for it to behave in the way we want it to. This can occur at different levels of detail. We could tell the right wheel to switch on for two seconds. Many of these detailed instructions can be combined into a more complex animation. When combining the robot movements with sensory input, we can describe them as behaviors. Such a behavior could be "greet the user when you see them for the first time." These behaviors can reuse many of the lower-level actions. For example, waving of the arm could be used for the "greeting behavior" but also for the "call for help" behavior.

The lower levels of programming are typically done on the top of the middleware layer, as described in Section 3.6. Working at these lower levels normally requires technical knowledge of the hardware and software of a robot. Experts on human and robot behavior often have more expertise in psychology and design but less experience with programming. Hence, it is desirable to have behavior design software that can be used without the need for in-depth programming skills.

Unfortunately, there are currently no open-source or commercial software programs that fulfill this need for multiple social robots. The developers of robots can provide tools for their specific robots, but these tools cannot be used for other robots. A good example is the Choregraphe software from Aldebaran (see Figure 6.9), which can be used to program the Nao and Pepper robots without the need for writing code. Users can drag and drop boxes, such as "Stand Up" or "Say Hello," to the canvas and connect them with lines to control the flow of the actions. This visual way of controlling the robot is, strictly speaking, still a form of programming, but it is often considered more intuitive. Children are often targeted by these visual programming paradigms, such as through Scratch (Sweigart, 2016) from the Massachusetts Institute of Technology (MIT; see Figure 3.15) or Blockly (Lovett, 2017) from Google. Sony's current fourth-generation Aibo dog (see Figure 2.10) uses a Blockly-like environment to enable owners to program its behavior. It does not, however, include the far superior MEdit motion editor (Cannon et al., 2007) and programming options (R-Code and Open-R) used from the first to third generations. These essential programming tools made it possible for Aibo to

Figure 3.15 The Scratch programming environment. (Source: MIT Media Lab)

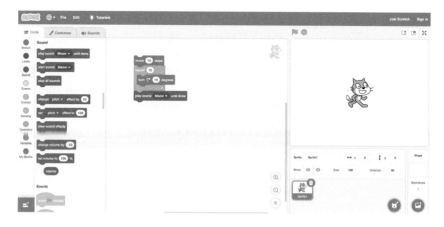

Figure 3.16 The Interaction Composer programming environment. (Source: ATR)

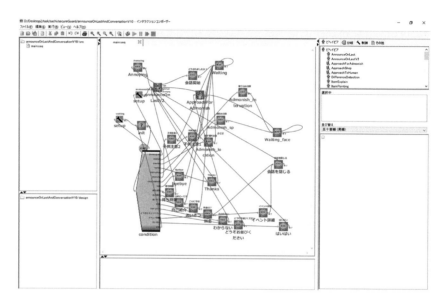

be used in the Robocup competition from 1999 to 2008. Current Aibo dogs are limited to home applications.

Another example of a platform-specific behavior editor is the Interaction Composer by ATR. It is used to control the Robovie (see Figure 4.14) series of robots. It has been used and further developed for over 14 years (Glas et al., 2016). It uses the visual design programming paradigm in which users connect elements through lines (see Figure 3.16). Although this software is abstract enough to potentially be applied to other robots, in practice, it is still closely linked to a couple of specific robots. Similar to Choregraphe, there are currently no plans to further open this behavior editor for other robots. Neither of them is available as open source, and hence others are also unable to achieve this.

Simulations and virtual representations of robots are used to test the robots' behavior before downloading and executing them on the actual robots. Gazebo software,[2] for example, is widely used to simulate a robot in an environment. It does not, however, easily include human users. The HRI community has developed other simulation software that is specifically targeted at HRI, such as MORSE (Lemaignan et al., 2014c). From here, it is only a small step to building virtual robots in game engines.

Those working with modern game engines, such as Unity and Unreal, have many similar challenges as HRI researchers. They have to program an agent, either a robot or a character in a game, to interact with the user. This includes animations, conversations, and interactions with the environment. Game engines have already advanced tools for this purpose, and hence HRI researchers can use them for the design and control of robot behavior. The USARSim, for example, uses the Unreal Engine (Lewis et al., 2007), whereas the Robot Engine is based on Unity (Bartneck et al., 2015b), and MORSE is based on the open-source Blender Game Engine (Lemaignan et al., 2014c). Connecting the robot's hardware to the game engine can also easily be achieved using serial port communication to an Arduino microcontroller. As with any simulation of reality, it does not capture the noise and complexity of the real world. Moreover, the most difficult part, humans, is not easily included in the simulation. There are approaches to simulate simple behaviors of humans in the simulations (Kaneshige et al., 2021), or virtual reality (VR) techniques can be used to let human users interact with robots in the simulation world (Inamura et al., 2021), although those tests are so far rather limited, only serving as a pretest. Hence, it remains necessary to test the simulated behavior in the real world. Robots are not, for example, able to move as fast as their virtual counterparts.

Many of the behavior editors described in this section also include tools to manage the spoken dialogue between human and robot. Section 7.3.3 in Chapter 7 describes the functioning of dialogue managers in more detail.

3.7.2 Animation editors

Most of the animation software used to design the movement of robots borrows from the classical principles of keynote animations that are widely used in 2D and 3D animations. The animator uses a timeline and adds key frames to it. The positions of all the robot's actuators are defined as poses in these key frames. The pose of the robot can be set by using software to remotely control the robot into the right position, or users can simply move the physical robot into the desired position.

The movement between these key-frame poses can then be interpolated through the use of curves. One of the most popular curves is the fade-in and fade-out curve, where the movement slowly accelerates at the start and decelerates toward the end (see Figure 3.17).

---

[2] See https://gazebosim.org/home.

Figure 3.17 Key-frame animation in the Choregraphe software. (1) Shows a key frame, and (2) shows the interpolated movement. (Source: Software from Aldebaran, screenshot by Christoph Bartneck)

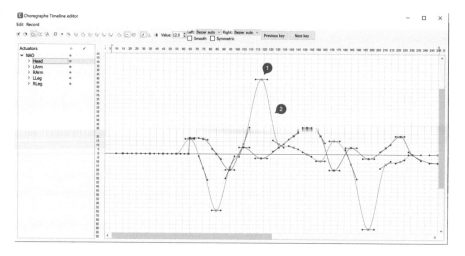

3.8 Artificial intelligence and machine learning

Many modules in the software perform some kind of intelligent processing. Those often benefit from techniques known as *artificial intelligence* (AI) or *machine learning*.

Although AI and machine learning are broad techniques, here we will focus on introducing some key concepts most relevant to HRI. We provide a basic introduction to supervised learning, followed by computer vision, which is one of the typical applications of supervised learning (see Section 7.2 of Chapter 7 for another important application, speech recognition). Other types of machine learning, such as generative models (to be used for speech synthesis and language generation; see Chapter 7) and reinforcement learning, will also be introduced.

There is a lot of recent attention to deep learning. In the media, the term *AI* is sometimes used interchangeably with the term *machine learning*. However, AI covers a broad set of techniques that perform any form of intelligent processing like humans do or beyond that. For instance, search algorithms that are used for motion planning are part of AI techniques, but they do not employ machine learning. Although general intelligence is one of the ultimate goals of AI research, it is still far out of reach.

Machine learning represents diverse algorithms that gain benefit ("learn") from data. Among them, *supervised learning* is most typically used in HRI applications. In this context, "supervised" concerns the fact that human developers manually provide labels to the training data. Supervised learning is usually used to address pattern-recognition problems, acquiring simple symbols (labels) from complex data, such as computer vision and speech recognition.

3.8.1 Supervised learning

Supervised learning is one type of machine learning; it specifically requires training data with correct labels. To understand what it is, let's try to imagine a specific task: classification of emotion in a human face. Using its camera, a robot took an RGB image of a human face. How can it tell whether this person is wearing a happy or a surprised expression?

To solve this task, the robot should have a classifier program that is already well trained. The classifier converts input data (i.e., a face) into some kind of feature vector. Then, the trained classifier outputs the label (e.g., happy, surprised, etc.) based on the input of the feature vector. For simplicity, let's assume that the feature vector is a list of motions of various facial muscles; that is, there is one for each lip, another one for each eyebrow, and so forth. We know that if people are happy, their lip corners typically go up, and when surprised, their eyebrows are raised. Instead of explicitly programming these rules, in supervised learning, we let the classifier acquire them from the data. (Note that for the sake of simplicity, we made this example rather straightforward. However, identifying and specifying the relation between an input vector and a label is usually not at all simple. Thus, performance from supervised learning usually clearly outperforms explicit programming of such rules.)

What we provide to the classifier is *training data*. In our example, these would be a lot of human faces with correct labels—that is, a lot of happy faces, with all of them labeled as "happy," and a lot of surprised faces, with all of them labeled as "surprised." Typically, providing labels to all these instances constitutes intensive human labor. One by one, human workers have to check each image of a face and add the appropriate labels. Then, with some training algorithm (if successful), the classifiers acquire appropriate parameters or rules that enable them to (mostly) correctly classify unseen data. This process typically takes a huge amount of computation time and also requires a lot of additional labor by developers, who would work with hyperparameters (e.g., in the case of a neural network, how many layers, how those layers connect, how input vectors are represented, number of iterations of updating parameters, etc.).

Next, we explain the key elements and techniques for supervised learning.

Data sets

Machine learning requires data from which the robot can learn. This training data set should contain a large number of examples of the thing to be learned, which may be data from sensors or text, and generally has been manually annotated by humans. For instance, there can be a data set with camera images of human faces, and for each image, the emotion of the person is labeled, such as "neutral," "happy," or "angry." Such a set of example data and labels is referred to as a *data set*. Typical data sets contain hundreds of thousands or even millions of examples. The appropriate size of a data set varies depending on the complexity of the target machine-learning problem. Nevertheless, typically, larger data sets yield better performance.

Because the labeling process usually requires extensive labor, developers often rely on crowdsourcing data (e.g., using Amazon Mechanical Turk). However, we should be careful about the quality of the data as well as the quantity of the data. Having ambiguous or wrong labels will harm the performance.

Because machine learning heavily relies on the amount and quality of data, sharing data sets, as well as sharing classifier modules (e.g., speech-recognition module), is a great community contribution. Researchers sometimes publish data sets together with their classification algorithm/system. There are specific websites for sharing data sets, such as Kaggle [3]

Feature extraction

Figure 3.18 Canny edge detection of a user operating the buttons on a robot.

To aid machine learning, sensor data are often preprocessed by converting the sensor data into a more suitable representation and by extracting salient features from the data. This process is called *feature extraction*. There are many algorithms to extract features from raw sensor input. For instance, edge detection highlights the pixels in an image where the intensity abruptly changes, and a segmentation algorithm identifies regions in an image where the colors are all similar, which can indicate a face, hair, or an eye (see Figure 3.18).

Features are, in essence, numbers. These features are often placed into a feature vector, a row of numbers ready for processing. For instance, one could count up the number of pixels detected as an edge and use it as one of the variables of the feature vector. Researchers often manually analyze their data sets and identify salient features. For instance, with careful observation, one might find that a child fidgets more than an adult does; once such a feature is found, one can add variation of motion to the feature vector.

Classification based on training

Supervised learning is often used for *classification* problems. In classification, an algorithm decides, based on training data, what class an unknown data point belongs to. For example, given a camera image of a person, the classifier decides what emotion the person's face shows. (Note: Another frequent approach is regression, in which an algorithm provides a continuous number from unknown data, such as estimating the age of a person based on their face.)

Suppose we can compute a one-dimensional (1D) feature vector representing people's height and have a data set with two classes, "child" and "adult" (i.e., each data point in the training data will have a label saying whether the data point is a "child" or an "adult"). The classifier learns a threshold value from the training data set (e.g., 150 cm) to distinguish the two classes.

In this case, the feature vector contains only a single feature, the height of the user. We call this a *1D feature vector*. Classification algorithms typically work with thousands of features and try to recognize several classes, but sometimes up to thousands of classes. Classification errors are more or less inevitable. For instance, a tall child or short adult would be classified incorrectly with the previously described 1D feature vector.

---

[3] See www.kaggle.com/datasets

Classification algorithms perform better (yield fewer errors) when having access to more data. Ideally, we want classification algorithms to "generalize," meaning they correctly handle data that they have never been exposed to. However, classification algorithms sometimes "overfit" to only the training data. When this happens, the algorithm does really well on the training data, but it performs poorly when confronted with new unseen data that are not included in the training data.

There are various algorithms available for classification problems. Support vector machines (SVMs) were traditionally often used with handcrafted features. Nowadays, it is more standard to use deep learning if a large amount of data is available. For the purpose of explainability, other algorithms, such as a decision tree, are sometimes used.

Deep learning

Deep learning is a family of neural-network techniques enabled by the increased availability of computational power. For instance, deep neural networks (DNNs) rely on artificial neural networks with a large number of layers of interconnected artificial neurons—hence the name "deep."

When input is 2D (typically, an image), *convolutional neural networks* (CNNs) are used. A CNN also has deep layers of neural networks. However, it has specific typological constraints among neurons, representing the convolution procedure in image processing. It is good at the task of identifying whether a target pattern exists somewhere within 2D data. For instance, in an object-detection task, it is more important whether there is a "dog" in the image or not rather than whether a "dog" is in the top left of the image. The classifier using a CNN better generalizes to various objects regardless of their locations in the image. See Section 3.8.2 for more information about computer vision.

In cases where the input is a time series, a family of *recurrent neural networks* (RNNs) is usually used. An RNN is a neural network, typically with deep layers, and also has a mechanism to keep internal states (i.e., a memory). At each time step, it receives an input, then provides an output label under the condition of its own memory. Long short-term memory (LSTM) is one of the famous RNNs. An RNN is often used for automatic speech recognition (ASR). In an ASR task, the words to be recognized usually depend on what was already spoken (e.g., if "how are ..." is already spoken, it is highly likely to hear "you" as the next word). See Section 7.2 of Chapter 7 for more information on speech recognition.

Another important deep-learning model is a *transformer*. It is used for variant lengths of input, similar to RNNs, but it does not have a memory mechanism. Instead, it comprises an encoding–decoding mechanism, along with an attention mechanism that focuses on the important part of the encoded input. It is often used for natural-language processing (NLP). The famous examples are *language models*, such as *BERT* and GPT-3. When given a sequence, they predict the next word, and most encode the sequence in doing

Figure 3.19 AI generated this image using the Dall-e platform. The text prompt used was "human playing with robot."

so. Such a model is trained in an unsupervised manner. This encoding is often used as *embedding* (a kind of feature vector) for other tasks by using fine-tuning techniques (see Section 3.8.1). Moreover, it is also used for generative tasks, such as image generation from natural-language input (see Figure 3.19), for which the learning process involves huge pairs of images and text, typically obtained from publicly available data (e.g., from Instagram).

> Are you struggling with writing an essay or scientific paper? No problem—let a computer create it for you! Although students may be most familiar with ChatGTP, other language models have been trained specifically for generating scientific papers, such as SCIgen[a] (generates computer science papers, including figures and references) and Galactica (can generate scientific papers for any field of study; Taylor et al., 2022). It is important to note that language models do not understand the text they generate; in essence, they are a slightly shinier version of the "text completion" feature on your phone. Thus, although these programs return texts that sound confident, professional, and overall convincing, they often are factually incorrect.
>
> Although these automatically generated papers are unlikely to pass the peer-review process of good journals, they could still be used to generate misinformation, and they thereby pose a serious threat to the integrity of science. After only two days online, Meta decided to shut down the demo web page for Galactica. The model itself is still available,[b] and people familiar with computer science can continue to (ab)use it.
>
> ---
> [a] See https://pdos.csail.mit.edu/archive/scigen/.
> [b] See https://github.com/paperswithcode/galai

For any of the aforementioned deep learning, it takes a large amount of computational power for training, but recent progress in using parallel computing and graphical-processing units (GPUs) has allowed us to train these networks within a reasonable amount of time.

Deep learning usually does not require careful feature extraction by hand. Instead, deep learning discovers the relevant features from the data by itself. A drawback is that deep learning requires huge amounts of data: typically, millions of data points are needed to train an algorithm. For instance, Google collected an enormous data set containing more than 230 billion data points to train its speech-recognition algorithm. GPT-3 was trained on 45 terabytes (TB) of text data from Wikipedia and books.

The complexity of deep learning makes it difficult to know exactly what the network bases its decisions on (e.g., we may not know what features it has identified or how it decided to use these features to come to a classification), which can be particularly problematic for HRI outside of the laboratory when we need to trust that the system will be robust, safe, and predictable. If the robot does something wrong, we need to be able to figure out how to debug and correct the system, as in the case of an autonomous Uber vehicle that had trouble classifying a person crossing the road and ran over the person as a result (Marshall and Davies, 2018).

Transfer learning

The need for large data sets is a significant challenge for HRI because it is difficult to collect large amounts of data in which humans and robots are interacting.

The problem is more evident in deep learning. To moderate the problem, there is a technique known as *transfer learning* or *fine-tuning*, which reuses part of an existing trained network (often, embedding) and adds a small amount of labeled data to only tune a small part of the neural network (often near the output layer). By doing so, it learns new skills with a relatively small data set.

For instance, big language models, such as BERT and GPT, which are typically trained with trillions of sentences, are used for *intent recognition* via transfer learning using possibly less than a hundred sentences Huggins et al. (2021) (see Section 7.3 for a discussion of how intent recognition is used in HRI).

3.8.2 Computer vision

Computer vision is an important area for HRI. In essence, computer vision interprets a 2D array of numbers when working with single images, or a series of 2D images recorded over a period of time when working with video data. Computer vision can be rather straightforward and still very effective in the context of HRI. Motion detection, for example, can be achieved by subtracting two camera images taken just a fraction of a second apart. Any pixels that captured motion will have a nonzero value, which in turn can be used to calculate the region with the most motion. When used on a robot, a motion detector lets the robot orient itself toward the areas with the most motion, providing the illusion that the robot is aware of things moving, which, in the context of HRI, often involves people gesturing or talking.

Another computer-vision technique relevant to HRI is the processing of faces. The ability to detect faces in an image has advanced and can be used, for example, to let the robot look people in the eye. Face recognition (i.e., identifying a specific person in an image) is still a challenge, however. Impressive progress has been made in the last decade, mainly fueled by the evolution of deep learning, and it is now possible to reliably recognize and distinguish between hundreds of people when they are facing the camera. But face recognition typically fails when the user is seen from the side.

Skeleton tracking is another technique relevant to HRI. In skeleton tracking, the software attempts to track where the user's body and limbs are. This technique was first used in gaming on the Microsoft Xbox console, with software specific to the Kinect RGBD sensor, but is now a staple in many HRI applications. Several software solutions exist, but deep learning has enabled the reading of skeletons of dozens of users in complex scenarios from a single simple camera image, without the need for an RGBD sensor. The software for this, called OpenPose, is freely available and often used in HRI studies (Cao et al., 2017).

There are many commercial and free software solutions that offer a range of out-of-the-box computer-vision functionality. OpenCV is perhaps the best-known offering; it is a free software library developed over 20 years. It can be used for facial recognition, gesture recognition, motion understanding, object identification, depth perception, and motion tracking, among others.

Because computer vision often requires a considerable amount of computational power, which is not realistic on small or cheaper robots, sometimes the computer-vision process is addressed on the cloud. In this case, the video stream of the robot is sent over an internet connection to servers on the cloud. There are commercial-based cloud solutions for face recognition, person identification, and image classification being sold on a per-use basis.

3.8.3 Reinforcement learning

Reinforcement learning is a very different approach to machine learning. It does not require any training data prepared in advance and does not necessarily need human supervision. Instead, a robot learns from successes and failures by really trying to act. What it learns is the optimal *policy*, the best *action* for each given *state*, which yields the best *reward*.

To understand how it works, imagine an example of a crawling robot that has an arm with two DOFs (search on YouTube using such keywords as "crawling robot Q-learning" to find examples). For simplicity, assume that the robot has a choice of only four distinctive actions: stretch out its hand, touch the ground, fold its arm, and lift its arm from the ground. The question here is which action the robot should choose.

This is somewhat complex question because the best action depends on the current pose of the robot. We know that to move forward, it should stretch out its hand, touch the ground, then fold its arm (here, it moves forward by "crawling"), and then it needs to detach from the ground. By repeating this, it can keep moving forward.

Reinforcement-learning algorithms learn such actions if rewards are designed appropriately. For a crawling robot, we would need a sensor to sense how much the robot moved forward. Then, the output from the sensor can be used as a reward. The reward (the fact that the robot moved forward) is only acquired when the previously described actions are performed in the correct order. If executed in the wrong order, no reward or even a negative reward would be given (e.g., if it folded its arm, touched the ground, and then stretched out). Many reinforcement-learning algorithms start from a random search, trying various actions from various states (here, we could use the current pose of its arm as the state), and memorize the rewards obtained for a given state. By repeating trials, the algorithm hopefully converges to find the best policy.

Various reinforcement-learning algorithms are available. Among them, the most famous is *Q-learning*, which is designed to remember the best reward for each "Q-state," defined as the combination of action and state. One expansion of Q-learning with deep-learning techniques is referred to as *deep Q-learning* (DQN), which uses a deep neural network to represent the Q-state.

Reinforcement learning typically takes time to repeat thousands of trials until it converges, even for relatively simple problems like the aforementioned crawling robot. Moreover, during the trial-and-error process, a robot unfortunately needs to fail a lot in order to "unlearn" all the specific ways in which it can be wrong. Sometimes, researchers try to use physics simulations to moderate these learning costs. For example, it took several months with seven robot arms learning in parallel for the arm to learn how to grasp various objects, whereas a model using a simulation and previously collected data took only a few days to learn the same behavior Ibarz et al. (2021). Applying reinforcement learning to HRI problems is not straightforward–because of the cost of failures, the time involved, and the difficulty in using simulation—yet researchers have started to try to find methods to make it feasible for HRI (e.g., Mitsunaga et al. 2008, McQuillin et al. 2022).

3.8.4 Adaptation

Both the user and the robot are adaptive systems. Humans have sophisticated skills to adapt their behavior and communication to their environment and others. When talking to a child, for example, adults tend to use simpler words and sentence structures, a phenomenon often referred to as *motherese* (Wrede et al., 2005; Rohlfing et al., 2005). Similarly, users also tend to adapt their communication when talking to a robot. They tend to speak slower and louder, particularly if the speech-recognition system does not seem to work properly (Kriz et al., 2010).

In return, robots are commonly expected to adapt their behavior to their users (Rossi et al., 2017) to optimize the interaction. Allan et al. (2022), for example, showed that users benefit from different types of praise from a robot based on their implicit self-theory. Users who consider self-attributes, such as intelligence, as malleable (incremental theory) prefer praise for their effort, whereas users who consider it to be unchangeable (entity theory) prefer to receive praise for their ability.

The robot needs to collect considerable data about each user to be able to infer characteristics such as these. Applying reinforcement learning would be one of the possible implementations for doing so. However, these data can only be collected in real-time, and hence data collection is limited. Therefore, it is still quite challenging research.

In both of these adaptations, the human and the robot change their own behavior. Humans have the additional option of explicitly changing the robot to their preferences. They may, for example, switch to a male voice or prefer a certain color of plastic over another. This adaptation is referred to as *customization*. It does not require any sophisticated machine-learning techniques other than the adjustment of certain parameters.

3.9 Limitations of robotics for HRI

There are several limitations of robotics, some of which are specific to HRI and some of which apply to robotics in general. One general challenge is that a robot is a complex system that needs to translate between the analogue world and the digital internal computation of the robot. The real world is analogue, noisy, and often very changeable, and the robot first needs a suitable digital representation of the world, which the software then uses to make decisions. Once a decision is made, this is translated back into analogue actuation, such as speaking a sentence or moving a leg.

Another major challenge applicable to robotics at large is that of learning. Currently, machine learning needs to iterate through millions of examples to slowly nudge itself toward performing a task with a reasonable level of skill. Despite speedups due to advances in DNNs and GPUs, at the time of writing, computers need days or often weeks to learn, and this is only when all the learning can happen internally, for example, in simulation or using prerecorded data. Learning from real-time data that a robot samples from the world is still virtually impossible. Related to this is the challenge of *transfer*, or the performance of one skill transferring to another. For example, people can learn to play one game of cards and will then be able to transfer that knowledge to quickly pick up another game of cards with different rules. Machine learning typically struggles with this task and needs to start the learning of a new challenge from scratch.

The seamless integration of the various systems on a robot also represents a major challenge. Speech recognition, natural-language understanding, social-signal processing, action selection, navigation, and many other systems all need to work together in order to create convincing social behavior in a robot. On simple robots, this is manageable, but on more complex robots, the integration and synchronization of these various skills are still beyond our grasp. Face detection, emotion classification, and sound-source localization might each work well in isolation, but bringing the three together to make the robot respond in a humanlike manner to people approaching the robot is still a challenge. Greeting people who smile at the robot, looking up when the door slams, or ignoring people who show no interest in the robot may sound easy, but it is difficult to build such behavior that consistently works well. The challenge becomes formidable once further skills are added. Conversational robots, which aim to interact with people using natural language in addition to using their full suite of sensors to react in an appropriate manner, are only now being attempted in research labs across the world. It is unlikely that a robot will be built in the next decade that can handle a conversation as well as people can.

Robots and AI systems in general struggle with semantics: they often do not truly understand what happens around them. A robot might seem to respond well to a person approaching it and asking for directions, but this does not mean that the robot understands what is happening—that the person is new to the space or where the directions it gives actually lead to. Often, the robot has been programmed to face people when they come near and to respond to the key words it hears. Real understanding is, at the moment, still exclusive to humans. Although there are research projects on imbuing AI systems with a sense of understanding (Lenat, 1995; Navigli and Ponzetto, 2012), there are not yet robots that can use their multimodal interaction with the world to understand the social and physical environment.

The reasons why AI has not yet achieved a humanlike general intelligence level are manifold, although conceptual problems were identified right from the outset. Searle (1980) pointed out that digital computers alone can never truly understand reality because they only manipulate syntactical symbols that do not contain semantics. In his *Chinese room thought experiment*, a slip of paper with Chinese symbols is slid under the door of a room (Searle, 1999). A man inside the room reads the symbols and comes up with a response by applying a set of rules he finds in a book full of instructions containing more Chinese characters. He then writes the response in the form of other Chinese characters and slides it back under the door. The audience behind the door might be under the impression that the man in the room understands Chinese, whereas in reality, he just looks up rules and has no understanding of what those symbols really mean. In the same manner, a computer also only manipulates symbols to come up with a response to input. If the computer's response is of humanlike quality, does that mean the computer is intelligent?

According to Searle's line of argument, IBM's chess-playing computer Deep Blue does not actually understand chess, and DeepMind's AlphaGo does not understand the game of Go. Both programs may have beaten human masters of the game, but they did so only by manipulating symbols that were meaningless to them. The creator of Deep Blue, Drew McDermott, replied to this criticism: "Saying Deep Blue doesn't really think about chess is like saying an aeroplane doesn't really fly because it doesn't flap its wings" (1997). That is, he debated that as far as it functions as it is supposed to, a new machine or AI does not need to replicate all the details of humans, animals, or birds. This debate reflects different philosophical viewpoints about what it means to think and understand and is still underway today. Similarly, the possibility of developing general AI remains an open question. All the same, progress has been made. In the past, a chess- or Go-playing machine would have been regarded as intelligent. But now it is regarded as the feat of a calculating machine—our criteria for what constitutes an intelligent machine have shifted along with the capabilities of machines.

In any case, no sufficiently intelligent machine has yet been built that would provide a foundation for many of the advanced application scenarios that have been imagined for robots. Researchers often fake the intelligence of the robot by applying the Wizard-of-Oz method (see Section 10.6.1 on page 182).

However, there are also some basic problems that we do not expect to find a solution for in the near future. One of the most basic limitations of HRI is the battery capacity. Most robots cannot operate for longer than an hour before having to recharge. This is a major constraint for mobile robots, particularly those that navigate in unstructured environments. For instance, once a robot is on its way somewhere, it already has to plan its return. Furthermore, this limitation makes it difficult for humans to experience longer-term interactions. Finally, robots like Nao cannot return to their charging station autonomously, meaning that either the user or the experimenter has to manage its battery charging.

Another physical limitation concerns the speed at which the robot can move. Here, we mean not only the robot's speed of driving around but also the speed with which a robot is moving its arms and head. Piumsomboon et al. (2012), for example, tried to motion-capture a Haka dancer and mapped his movements in real-time to several Nao robots (see Figure 3.20). The robot could only keep up with the human dancer if the dancer moved unnaturally slowly. Once the dancer unleashed his powerful Haka dance, the robots fell hopelessly behind. Another often-overlooked limitation of robots is that they cannot move silently. Humans can move their arms without making any noticeable sound. Robots, on the other hand, use electrical motors, gears, or pneumatic actuators. Although this inability to sneak around might be welcomed by some, it can be rather disturbing when humans want to go to sleep.

If robots were to create their top 10 list of things they hate about the world, then gravity would certainly be among the top entries. Simply refraining from

Figure 3.20 Nao robot trying to imitate a Haka dancer.

falling over is incredibly hard; in humans, this process requires an extremely fine-tuned close collaboration between different senses, such as vision, the vestibular system, haptics, and the body's sense of where one is in space (Wolfe et al., 2006). Science has yet to artificially recreate a similar kind of balance system. Furthermore, keeping in balance while moving around is even harder, particularly when the floor is uneven or when the robot has no method of getting up again.

From a human perspective, we are left wanting for the robot support that we have been promised for so many years. Even today, emptying a dishwasher remains an impossible task for robots. Over half a century ago, in 1966, the British Broadcasting Corporation (BBC) created a short film about Able Mabel, the Robot Housemaid.[4] It promised that robots would soon be able to handle many household tasks. Meredith Thring argued in this film that it would only take 1 million pounds to produce the first prototype. Needless to say, this vision of the future was far too optimistic.

The requirements of HRI often imply unrealistic assumptions about what can be achieved with current technology, and novice research and the public should be aware of the limitations of robotics and AI.

3.10 Conclusion

Robots are made from multiple software modules connected with sensors and actuators. Software design requires HRI knowledge, and conversely, HRI researchers need to have a basic understanding of software in order to provide useful knowledge for future HRI developers. For a robot to be successful, the different components need to be chosen and integrated with an eye toward the specific HRI application and its needs. Despite limitations, however, robots can be designed to interact successfully with humans in various types of short-term, and sometimes longer, interactions.

Questions for you to think about:

- Chapters 2 and 3 introduced various robot types that are available on the market. What sensors do these robots have? What actuators do they have? What hardware components do you think are crucial?
- Imagine a scenario where you want to use a smart social robot. Which sensors and actuators should it have? What skills should the robot have, and is software available to deliver these skills?
- What kind of data set would be needed to train a machine-learning algorithm for a new interaction capability of a robot, such as distinguishing your face from others?

---

[4] See www.bbc.co.uk/archive/mabel-the-robot-housemaid-1966/zhnvxyc

3.11 Exercises

The answers to these questions are available in the Appendix.

** **Exercise 3.1 Sensors**   A list of technologies follows. Which ones are typically used as sensors on robots? Select one or more options from the following list:

1. Camera
2. Loudspeaker
3. Microphone
4. LED light
5. LiDAR
6. Servo motor
7. Ultrasound sonar

* **Exercise 3.2 Pepper's sensors, part 1**   Have another look at Pepper (page 15). What sensor technologies does this robot have? Select one or more options from the following list:

1. Radar
2. Depth camera
3. Capacitive touch sensor
4. Global Positioning System
5. Inertial measurement unit
6. Oxygen sensor

*** **Exercise 3.3 Pepper's sensors, part 2**   Based on your answer to the previous question, what functions do you think these sensors serve?

** **Exercise 3.4 How do sensors work?**   Which of the following statements are correct? Select one or more options from the following list:

1. The light sensor in a camera can see only brightness.
2. A TOF infrared light sensor can measure depth up to 300 meters.
3. Inertial measurement units combine an accelerometer, microphone, and gyroscope.
4. Typical cameras can see up to 90 degrees.
5. An RGBD sensor is a camera that can estimate the distance to objects.
6. Omnidirectional microphones pick up sound from all around.

*** **Exercise 3.5 How do servo motors work?**   Hobby servos are simple motors found in cheap robots. Which of the following statements are true? Select one or more options from the following list:

1. The position of a servo is controlled by the duty cycle of the control signal.
2. The speed of a servo is controlled by the voltage.
3. The servo motor continuously changes direction to maintain its set position.
4. The position and speed of a servo are controlled by switching it on and off.

5. An external position sensor is used to control the position of the servo.
6. A servo motor has two output axes.

* Exercise 3.6 Finger Have a look at your pointing finger. How many DOFs does it have?

** Exercise 3.7 Degrees of freedom What is the minimum DOFs that a robot needs to drive to every location in a room?

** Exercise 3.8 Grasping What is the minimum DOFs that a robot arm needs to grasp an object in reach from any direction?

** Exercise 3.9 Linear actuators What type of linear actuators are often used in social robots? Select one of the following options:

1. Hydraulic actuators
2. Pneumatic actuators
3. Aquatic actuators
4. Bimorph actuators

** Exercise 3.10 Control model What model is typically used to control a robot? Select one of the following options:

1. *Act → think → sense*
2. *Sense → think → act*
3. *Sense → act → think*

* Exercise 3.11 Middleware Which of the following are **not** middleware? Select one or more options from the following list:

1. Windows
2. Linux
3. ROS

** Exercise 3.12 Middleware functions This question focuses on robot middleware, such as ROS. Which statements are true? Select one or more options from the following list:

1. Offers basic functions to access hardware, like access to storage or input/output (IO) port
2. Uses different hardware (e.g., sonar and LiDAR) in an interchangeable way
3. Automatically creates code to realize HRI without the need for explicit coding
4. Provides standardized environments for programmers to share and reuse their modules
5. Helps programmers visualize what is communicated between modules

*** Exercise 3.13 Machine learning Imagine we are going to build a classifier using deep learning to, for example, identify whether there is a person in a camera image or not. Which of the following statements are true? Select one or more options from the following list:

1. If we can maintain the quality of the data, more data will result in better performance.
2. Thanks to deep learning, we can train a classifier from scratch with only a small amount of data.
3. Thanks to deep learning, we do not need to handcraft features. We can directly use raw image data.
4. Thanks to deep learning, we do not need to provide labels. We can assign random labels to the data to start training.
5. We do not need to care about the topology of the neural network. Anything like DNN, CNN, RNN, or transformer can be chosen for this simple image-classification task, as long as it is a deep-learning method.

*** Exercise 3.14 Robots that work with people Watch this video, and then answer the question that follows.

Andrea Thomaz, "Next Frontier in Robotics: Social, Collaborative Robots," https://youtu.be/O1ZhWv84eWE

1. Thomaz demonstrates a robot meant to work together with people in everyday environments. Looking at Thomaz's robot, describe what kinds of technical components and capabilities it has that allow it to interact with people. What are the different social cues that the robot uses, and how do its components work together to produce those cues in the course of an interaction? The description does not have to go into great detail, but do describe how you think different components (e.g., gaze, manipulation, movement in space) work together in these interactions.

Future reading:

- For basic AI:
  Russell, Stuart and Norvig, Peter. *Artificial Intelligence: A Modern Approach*. Pearson, Essex, UK, 4th edition, 2022. ISBN 978-1292401133. URL www.worldcat.org/oclc/1242911311
- For recent machine learning:
  Goodfellow, Ian, Bengio, Yoshua, and Courville, Aaron. *Deep Learning*. MIT Press, Cambridge, MA, 2016. ISBN 9780262035613. URL www.deeplearningbook.org
- For basic robotics:
  Matarić, Maja J. *The Robotics Primer*. MIT Press, Cambridge, MA, 2007. ISBN 9780262633543. URL www.worldcat.org/oclc/604083625
- For diverse topics in robotics:
  Siciliano, Bruno and Khatib, Oussama. *Springer Handbook of Robotics*. Springer, Berlin, 2016. ISBN 9783319325507. URL www.worldcat.org/oclc/945745190

4

Design

What is covered in this chapter:

- How a well-designed robot can lift interactions to the next level (physical design).
- How people do not treat robots as an assembly of plastic, electronics, and code but rather as humanlike entities (anthropomorphism).
- How HRI research draws on psychological theories, such as anthropomorphism, to design and study people's interactions with robots.
- Design methods and prototyping tools used in human–robot interaction.

How does a pile of wires, motors, sensors, and microcontrollers turn into a robot that people will want to interact with? Although it sounds like magic, the trick of turning metal and plastic into a social interaction partner is in the iterative and interdisciplinary process of robot design.

This chapter starts by exploring some general design principles and considerations (Section 4.1) before moving on to anthropomorphic design specifically in Section 4.2. In Section 4.3, different methods of designing are discussed, and Section 4.4 covers the different approaches to testing and prototyping the design you came up with. The impact of culture on HRI design is discussed in Section 4.5, and Section 4.6 wraps up this chapter by highlighting the ethical and philosophical considerations that come into play when designing a robot.

Robot design is a fast-growing field of research and practice in human–robot interaction (HRI), and the need to develop robots that are able to interact with people challenges the existing ways of designing robots. Often, robots are developed by engineers, and their interaction abilities are then tested by social scientists. This process of design starts from the inside and builds up to the outside—solving technical issues first and designing the robot's appearance and behavior to fit. For example, a mobile platform such as a TurtleBot (see Figure 4.1) might be used as a starting point, with the desired sensors and actuators added to the body later on. If time allows, a casing could be designed to cover up all the technology. The robot's appearance and specific social interaction capabilities then have to be built on top of this technical infrastructure. This common approach to robot building is also known as the "Frankenstein approach." In this method, we take whatever technology

is available and put it together to obtain a set of specific robotic functions. Clearly, such an approach is suboptimal because it commonly fails to consider a human-centered perspective that also takes into account the impact of the context and the envisioned use case.

Therefore, it is important to complement a purely technological development perspective with more holistic approaches to robot design. That is, it actually matters to consider the needs, values, and preferences of potential stakeholders and end users early on in the design process. It matters where these end users use the robot and for what purpose. Based on the characteristics of the users and the context of use, one can then decide on specific robot design features, such as appearance, interaction modalities, and level of autonomy. This might be termed a more "outside-in" mode of developing robots, in which the design process starts from the interaction that we expect the robot to be engaged in, which will determine its outside shape and behaviors. Once the design has been settled on, we work all the technology into it. Many commercial social robots are designed, at least to some degree, from the "outside in"—considering the users and how they might interact with a person and selecting or even developing technology appropriately. Honda's ASIMO, for example, was chosen to be smaller in size so that it would not be intimidating to users. Pepper was initially designed to interact with shop visitors in Japan and has a hinged waist that allows it to bow to them as a greeting. The seal-like robot Paro was designed to inspire petlike interaction and was initially shaped like a cat, but its design was changed to a seal to address critiques users had due to their familiarity with how real cats behave; at some point in its iterative design, it also had wheels to be able to move around on the floor, but these were removed because the older adults who were its main users often had limited mobility.

Designers are trained to approach the design of artifacts in this way (see Figure 4.2 for an example) and are able to make valuable contributions (Schonenberg and Bartneck, 2010). Their contribution is not limited to only the aesthetics of the robot; designers also have the skill to create

Figure 4.2
Mythical robots
designed from the
outside to the inside.
First, the shape of
the robots was
sculptured before
fitting the
technology into it.

thought-provoking robots that challenge our understanding of the roles of humans and robots.

This form of robot design often requires incorporating expertise from several disciplines—for example, designers might work on developing specific concepts for the design, social scientists may perform exploratory studies to learn about the potential users and context of use, and engineers and computer scientists need to communicate with the designers to identify how specific design ideas can be realistically instantiated in working technology (Šabanović et al., 2014). HRI design can take advantage of existing robots, designing specific behaviors or use tasks for them that fit particular applications, or it can involve the development of new robot prototypes to support the desired interactions. In either case, HRI design both takes advantage of existing design methods and develops new concepts and methods specifically suited to the development of embodied interactive artifacts (i.e., robots).

4.1 Design in HRI

4.1.1 Robot morphology and form

A common starting point for designing HRI is to think of what the robot is going to be doing. There is a debate about whether form follows function, in which the shape of an object is largely determined by its intended function or purpose, or if the reverse holds true. In HRI, clearly, form and function are inherently interconnected and thus cannot be considered separately.

Contemporary HRI designers have several different forms of robots to choose from. Androids and humanoids most closely resemble humans in appearance, but they have a lot to live up to in terms of capabilities. Zoomorphic robots are shaped like animals with which we are familiar (e.g., cats or dogs) or like animals that are familiar but that we do not typically interact with (e.g., dinosaurs or seals). HRI designers, eager to make robot appearances

Figure 4.3 Zoomorphic and minimalistic robots. From left to right: Muu (2001–2006), Keepon (2003–present), and Naked Invisible Guy. (Source: Keepon photo from Hideki Kozima, Tohoku University, ASIMO from Honda)

Figure 4.4 Sociable Trash Box robots are an example of robjects—robotic objects with interaction capabilities. (Source: Michio Okada)

commensurate with their limited capabilities, also often design minimalist robots, which explore the minimal requirements necessary for inspiring social HRI, such as Muu (see Figure 4.3, left) or Keepon (see Figure 4.3, middle). The arguably most minimalistic robot is the busker robot, which consisted of a pair of animated sandals on top of a box with a signpost in front of it proclaiming "Naked Invisible Guy" (Partridge and Bartneck, 2013) (see Figure 4.3, right).

Recently, the HRI field has started considering "robjects," interactive robotic artifacts whose design is based on objects rather than living creatures, for example, a robotic ottoman (Sirkin et al., 2015), social trash cans (see Figure 4.4), or robotic toy boxes (Fink et al., 2014). Because the design space of robots is relatively large and considers questions regarding form, function, level of autonomy, interaction modalities, and how all those fit with particular users and contexts, an important aspect of design is figuring out how to make appropriate decisions about these various design aspects.

4.1.2 Affordances

The notion of affordances represents an important concept in design. This notion was initially developed as a concept in ecological psychology (Gibson, 2014), where it referred to the inherent relationship between an organism and its environment. For example, a stone can be picked up by us and thrown away, but to a mouse, it can serve as a hiding place. The stone "affords" different interactions. This concept was amended by Don Norman 2008 to describe the perceivable relationships between an organism and its environment that enable certain actions (e.g., a chair is something to sit on, but so is a stair).

A designer needs to design a product while making its affordances explicit. Furthermore, the designer needs to incorporate user expectations and cultural perceptions. For Norman (2008), these "design affordances" are also an important way to develop common ground between robots and humans so that people can understand the robot's capabilities and limitations and adapt their interaction accordingly. A robot's appearance is an important affordance because people tend to assume that the robot's capabilities will be commensurate with its appearance. If a robot looks like a human, it is expected to act like a human; if it has eyes, it should see; if it has arms, it should be able to pick up things and might be able to shake hands. Another affordance can be the robot's interaction modalities. If a robot speaks, for example, saying, "Hello," people will also expect it to be able to understand natural language and carry on a conversation. If it expresses emotions through facial expressions, people might expect it to be able to read their emotions. Other robotic affordances can be based on technical capabilities; for example, if it has a touch screen on its body, people might expect to interact with the robot through the touch screen. Because robots are novel interaction partners, the affordances used by designers are particularly important for signaling appropriate ways of engaging with them.

4.1.3 Design patterns

Because the focus of HRI is the relationship between humans and robots, the task of HRI design is not only to create a robotic platform but also to design and enable certain interactions between people and robots in various social contexts. This suggests that the main units of design that need to be considered are not only the characteristics of individual robots (e.g., appearance, sensing abilities, or actuation) but also what Peter Kahn calls "design patterns" in HRI, inspired by Christopher Alexander's idea of design patterns in architecture (Kahn et al., 2008). Such patterns describe "a problem which occurs over and over again in our environment, and then describes the core of the solution to that problem, in such a way that you can use this solution a million times over, without ever doing it the same way twice" (Alexander, 1977, p. x).

Within HRI, Kahn et al. (2008) suggest that patterns should be abstract enough that you can have several different instantiations, that they can be combined, that less complex patterns can be integrated into more complex patterns, and that they serve to describe interactions with the social and physical world. For example, the didactic communication pattern (where the robot assumes the role of a teacher) could be combined with a motion pattern (where the robot initiates a movement and aligns it with the human counterpart of the interaction) to create a robotic tour guide. Kahn et al.

suggest that HRI design patterns can be developed based on observation of human interactions, prior empirical knowledge about humans and robots, and designers' experiences with HRI, through an iterative design process. Some patterns they developed and have used in their designs are things like the "initial introduction" of the robot, or "in motion together," where the robot moves along with the person. Although Kahn et al.'s design patterns are not meant to be exhaustive, they emphasize the idea that the design should focus on the relationship between humans and robots.

4.1.4 Design principles in HRI

When combining the two ideas of design affordances and patterns in the process of HRI design, the usual design types that robots may be divided into, such as androids and humanoids, zoomorphic robots, minimally designed robots, or robjects, are no longer the main design focus or question. Instead, designers consider how different robot forms and capabilities fit into or express particular HRI design patterns and how they can be designed as affordances that appropriately signal the robot's interaction capabilities and purpose. With this in mind, HRI researchers have suggested some of the following principles to consider when developing the appropriate robot forms, patterns, and affordances in HRI design.

Matching the form and function of the design: If your robot is humanoid, people will expect it to do humanlike things—talk, think, and act like a human. If this is not necessary for its purpose, such as cleaning, it might be better to stick to less anthropomorphic designs. Similarly, if it has eyes, people will expect it to see; if it talks, they will expect it to be able to listen. People can also be prompted to associate specific social norms and cultural stereotypes with robots through design; for example, researchers have shown that people might expect a female robot to be more knowledgeable about dating or that a robot made in China would know more about tourist destinations in that country (Powers et al., 2005; Lee et al., 2005)

Underpromise and overdeliver: When people's expectations are raised by a robot's appearance or by introducing the robot as intelligent or companion-like, and those expectations are not met by its functionality, people are obviously disappointed and will negatively evaluate the robot. Sometimes these negative evaluations can be so serious that they affect the interaction. To avoid such problems, it is better to decrease people's expectations about robots (Paepcke and Takayama, 2010), which might have been increased by how robots are portrayed in society, as described in the "Robots in Society" chapter (see Chapter 12). This might even include not calling your design a robot because the word itself often connotes quite advanced capabilities to members of the public.

Interaction expands function: When confronted with a robot, people will, in effect, fill in the blanks left open by the design depending on their values, beliefs, needs, and so on. It can thus be useful, particularly for robots with limited capabilities, to design them in a somewhat open-ended way. This allows people to interpret the design in different ways. Such an open-ended design approach has worked particularly well with, for instance, the seal-like robot Paro (see Figure 2.8). This baby seal robot invokes associations with pets that people have had, but it also does not get compared to animals they know, such as cats and dogs, which would inevitably lead to disappointment. As a consequence, Paro becomes a natural part of the interactions with humans and passes as a petlike character even though its capabilities are significantly below those of a typical domestic animal or that of an actual seal baby (Šabanović and Chang, 2016).

Do not mix metaphors: Design should be approached holistically—the robot's capabilities, behaviors, affordances for interaction, and so forth should all be coordinated. If you design a humanlike robot, people may find it disturbing if it has skin covering only some parts of its body. Similarly, if the robot is an animal, it may be strange for it to talk like an adult human or try to teach you mathematics. This is related to the uncanny valley theory (see p. 66) because inappropriately matched abilities, behaviors, and appearance often lead to people having a negative impression of the robot.

Take a look at the two pictures in Figure 4.5. How do they make you feel? Although both of these android representations of the science-fiction writer Philip K. Dick are perhaps a bit strange and uncanny, the one that seems unfinished and shows the robot's insides also mixes design metaphors—the robot is both humanlike and machinelike, making it even more disturbing.

Like Kahn et al.'s (2008) design patterns, these design principles are not exhaustive but are meant to inspire thinking about how to approach

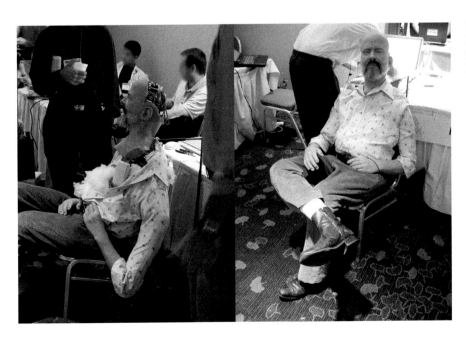

Figure 4.5 Philip K. Dick Robot (2005; rebuilt in 2010).

designing HRI in a way that acknowledges and incorporates the interdependence between human and robot capabilities, the need for interaction partners to be intelligible to and support each other, and the effects of the context of interaction on its success.

4.2 Anthropomorphization in HRI design

Have you ever found yourself yelling at your computer because it suddenly crashes while you are working on an essay that is due in just a few hours? You urge the computer to please bring it back again after restarting, gently touching the mouse after realizing that, indeed, the file reopens, and you can continue. You sigh in relief because "Genius"—that's what you call your computer when no one is around to hear you—did not let you down. In fact, what you have pictured now is an ordinary scenario of a person humanizing an object, anthropomorphizing it. What a tongue twister. But what is it about, in fact?

Anthropomorphization is the attribution of human traits, emotions, or intentions to nonhuman entities. It derives from *ánthrōpos* (meaning "human") and *morphē* (meaning "form") and refers to the perception of human form in nonhuman objects. We all experience anthropomorphism in our daily lives. "My computer hates me!"; "Chuck [the car] is not feeling well lately"; "That grater looks like it has eyes"—you've either heard or uttered sentiments like this before. The latter is a special example of anthropomorphization called *pareidolia*, the effect of seeing humanlike features in random patterns or mundane objects. When the *Viking 1* spacecraft took a photo of the Cydonia area on Mars on July 25, 1976, many people saw a face on Mars's surface, which sparked many speculations about the existence of life on Mars (see Figure 4.6). The National Aeronautics and Space Administration (NASA) sent its Mars Global Surveyor to the exact same location in 2001 to take higher-resolution photos under different lighting conditions, which revealed that the structure photographed in 1976 is certainly not a human face.

Figure 4.6 The face on Mars is an example of pareidolia. On the left is the photo from 1976, and on the right is the same structure photographed in 2001.

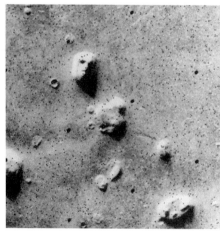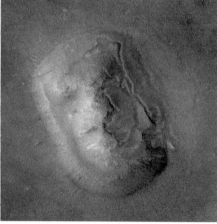

We will discuss anthropomorphization and anthropomorphism, respectively, in some detail as a case study of a specific design theme in HRI that incorporates technical development, psychological study, and design to enable social HRI. A robot's level of human-likeness is one of the main design decisions that robot designers need to take into account because it influences not only the robot's appearance but also the functionality it needs to offer and the social perceptions that are elicited by both form and function. In Chapter 8, we will go deeper into the psychological theories underlying anthropomorphism and the consequences for impression formation.

4.2.1 Attributing humanlike characteristics to robots

People's innate predisposition to anthropomorphize the things around them has become a common design affordance for HRI. In anthropomorphic design, robots are constructed to have certain humanlike characteristics, such as appearance, behavior, or certain social cues, that inspire people to see them as social agents. At one extreme, android robots are designed to be as humanlike as possible; some have been fashioned as exact replicas of living humans, like a moving Madame Tussaud's wax figure (see, for example, Geminoid in Figure 4.7), or as representations of aggregated human features (e.g., Kokoro, depicted on the far right in Figure 4.8). Humanoid robots use a more abstract notion of human-likeness in their anthropomorphic designs. ASIMO (second from the right in Figure 4.8), for example, has a human body shape (two arms and legs, a torso, and a head) and proportions, but it does not have eyes. Rather, its head resembles an astronaut's helmet. Nao (see Figure 4.8, middle) similarly has a humanlike body, as well as two light-emitting diode (LED) eyes that can change in color to connote different expressions, but no mouth. Some other humanoids, such as Robovie, Wakamaru (second from the left in

Figure 4.7 The Geminoid HI 4 robot (2013), a replica of Hiroshi Ishiguro. (Source: Hiroshi Ishiguro)

Design

Figure 4.8 People
readily
anthropomorphize all
kinds of robots, with
appearances ranging
from minimalist to
indistinguishable from
the human form. From
left to right: Keepon
(2003–present),
Wakamaru
(2005–2008), Nao
(2008–present),
ASIMO (2000–2018),
and Kokoro's Actroid
(2003–present) android.
(Source: Keepon from
Hideki Kozima, Tohoku
University, ASIMO
from Honda)

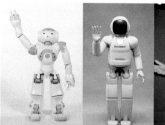

Figure 4.8), and Pepper, are not bipedal but have arms and have heads with two eyes.

Nonhumanoid robots, however, may also have anthropomorphic features. The minimalist robot Keepon (see Figure 4.8, far left) has two eyes and a symmetrical body, and it likewise features displays of behavioral cues for attention and affect that may elicit anthropomorphization. Google's autonomous car prototype has an almost cartoon-like appearance, with wide-set headlights and a button nose that suggest an anthropomorphic appearance. Festerling and Siraj (2022) also discussed the role of anthropomorphization for digital voice assistants.

Human-likeness has been key to animation designers for some time, only relatively recently sparking the interest of social psychologists. Disney's Illusion of Life (Thomas et al., 1995) has inspired several social robotic projects, such as Wistort et al.'s Tofu, which displays the animation principles of "squash" and "stretch" (Wistort and Breazeal, 2009), and Takayama et al.'s work with the PR-2 using animation to give the robot apparent goals, intentions, and appropriate reactions to events (Takayama et al., 2011). Animation principles such as anticipation and exaggerated interaction have also been applied to robot design, for example, in Guy Hoffman's Marimba player (Hoffman and Weinberg, 2010) and music companion robots (Hoffman and Vanunu, 2013). Researchers at the Honda Research Institute based the

Figure 4.9 Honda
Research Institute's
Haru robot.

movement design of their robot Haru (Figure 4.9) on emotive actions acted out by human performers. These anthropomorphic designs take advantage not only of appearance and form but also of behavior in relation to the environment and other actors to evoke ascriptions of human-likeness.

Human-likeness in robot design includes factors related to form and appearance as well as factors relating to behavior; it may also result in the attribution of characteristics (e.g., emotions, intentions, mind perceptions) that might not be directly observable. The latter is called *psychological anthropomorphism* (Epley et al., 2007). We cover this topic in greater detail in Chapter 8.

The uncanny valley

Mori (1970) made a prediction about the relationship between the human-likeness of robots and their likability (see Figure 4.10). The idea is that the more humanlike robots become, the more likable they will be, until a point

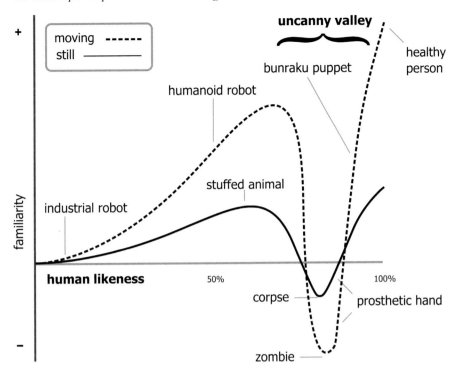

Figure 4.10 Mori's uncanny valley theory.

where they are almost indistinguishable from humans, at which point their likability decreases dramatically. This effect is then amplified by the ability of the robot to move.

Mori et al. (2012) translated Mori's original paper into English in collaboration with Mori himself. It is important to note that Mori only proposed this idea and never did any empirical work to test it. Moreover, Mori used the term 親和感 (*shinwa-kan*) to describe one of his key concepts. The translation of this concept to English remains challenging—it has been translated as likability, familiarity, and affinity. Other researchers have approached the problem by asking participants about the eeriness of the robot instead.

Unfortunately, Mori's theory has been used and abused to explain a huge number of phenomena without proper justification or empirical backup. It is often used to explain why certain robots are being perceived unfavorably, without studying the exact relationship between the features of the robot at hand and its likability. Anthropomorphism is a multidimensional concept, and reducing it to just one dimension does not model reality adequately. Moreover, the more humanlike robots become, the greater the risk of getting a certain aspect of their appearance or behavior wrong and thereby decreasing the level of likability (Moore, 2012). A simple possible explanation of why humanlike robots are liked less than, for example, toy robots is that the difficulty of designing a robot to perform to user expectations increases with its complexity.

4.2.2 Designing humanlike appearance

Robot designers may treat humanlike appearance as a characteristic of the robot itself, whereas social scientists see anthropomorphism as something that a person attributes to the robot. Considering both of these together suggests that anthropomorphism is about the relationship between robot design and functions and people's perceptions of robots.

Design approaches

To trigger anthropomorphic inferences, robot designers can take into account the dimensions of robot appearance and behavior, among many other aspects. By exploiting these aspects, they can achieve an immediate perception of the robot as more or less humanlike.

Robot appearance Graphical illustration shows us that often, only a few lines on a sheet of paper are needed to evoke the human form. In the same manner, anthropomorphism in robots can be very simple: just having two dots suggesting eyes and a simple nose or mouth is sufficient to suggest the robot is humanlike. This can be further enhanced by adding more human features, such as arms or legs, but these do not necessarily do very much to further increase the anthropomorphization. Although there are many reasons why robots look increasingly humanlike, anthropomorphization can be achieved with only a minimal set of humanlike features. Whereas androids mimic human appearance in most ways, simple robots such as Keepon and R2D2 are already very effective at triggering people to anthropomorphize. Thus, a large body of research has documented how minimal design cues might be sufficient to elicit a humanlike perception.

Robot behavior A second approach to increasing anthropomorphization is to design the behavior of an artifact such that people perceive humanlike characteristics in its behavior. Heider and Simmel (1944) showed how simple geometric shapes—triangles and circles—moving against a white background evoked people to describe their interactions in terms involving social relationships (e.g., these two are friends; this one is the attacker) and humanlike feelings and motivations (e.g., anger, fear, jealousy). Animators understand how motion, rather than form, can be extremely powerful for expressing emotions and intents. A surprisingly wide range of humanlike expressive behavior can be communicated through movement alone, without the need for humanlike form.

> *The Dot and the Line: A Romance in Lower Mathematics* is a 10-minute animation film by Chuck Jones, based on a short book by Norton Juster. It tells the story of the amorous adventures of a dot, a line, and a squiggle. Even though the visuals are minimal, the viewer has no problem following the story. It is a prime example of how motion rather than form can be used to communicate character and intent.

Robot builders can actively encourage anthropomorphization. One effective method is to increase the reaction speed of the robot to external events: a robot that immediately responds to touch or sound will be perceived as more anthropomorphic. Such *reactive behavior*, in which the robot responds quickly to external events, is an easy approach to increase anthropomorphization. The robot jolting when the door slams shut or looking up when touched on the head immediately conveys that it is both alive and responsive. *Contingency*, responding with behavior that is appropriate for the context of the interaction, can also be used to enhance anthropomorphization. When a robot detects motion, for example, it should briefly look toward the origin of the movement. If the event, such as a tree swaying in the wind, is irrelevant to the robot, it should look away again, but if it is relevant, such as a human waving hello to engage the robot in interaction, the robot should sustain its gaze.

Although robot developers will often prefer a combination of both form and behavior to inspire users to anthropomorphize their robots, certain types of robots may be limited in how humanlike they can be. Android robots, which appear virtually identical to people, are still technically limited in their behavioral repertoire. On the other hand, developers of toy robots are often under pressure to make the hardware as cheap as possible and thus opt for an effective combination of simple visual features and reactive behaviors. It is important to also take people's expectations into account; the more apparently humanlike the robot, the more people will expect in terms of humanlike contingency, dialogue, and other features.

Impact of context, culture, and personality

People's perceptions of anthropomorphic robot design are often affected by contextual factors. Some people are more likely than others to anthropomorphize things around them, and this can affect how they perceive robots, as previous research has shown (Waytz et al., 2010). A person's demographics and cultural background can also affect their likelihood of anthropomorphizing or their interpretation of the robot's social and interactive capabilities (Wang et al., 2010; Spatola et al., 2022).

The context in which the robot is used, furthermore, can support anthropomorphization. In particular, just putting a robot in a social situation with humans seems to increase the likelihood that people will anthropomorphize it. The collaborative industrial Baxter robot, when used in factories alongside human workers, was regularly anthropomorphized by them (Sauppé and Mutlu, 2015). Furthermore, it seems that people who work alongside robots prefer them to be designed in more anthropomorphic ways: people preferred that Roomba have the ability to display its emotions and intentions with a doglike tail (Singh and Young, 2012). Workers using Baxter put hats and other accessories on it and wanted it to be more polite and chitchat with them (Sauppé and Mutlu, 2015). Workers in a car plant using a co-bot, which was named Walt and had been designed to have a blend of social features and features reminiscent of a vintage car (see Figure 11.16), considered the robot to be a team member (El Makrini et al., 2018). Office workers who were given a break management robot gave it names and requested that it be more socially interactive (Šabanović et al., 2014).

Seeing other people anthropomorphize robots may suggest that humanizing nonhuman entities represents socially desirable behavior. To illustrate, researchers found that older adults in a nursing home were more likely to engage socially with Paro, the seal-like companion robot, when they saw others interacting with it like a pet or social companion (Chang and Šabanović, 2015). Clearly, anthropomorphic inferences may emerge instantly upon a first encounter and likewise become reshaped as a function of long-term interaction and acquaintance with a technical system. We will discuss this in more detail in Chapter 8, which covers the psychology of how people perceive robots.

4.3 Design methods

Design in HRI spans a variety of methods inspired by practice from various disciplines, from engineering to human–comuputer interaction (HCI) and industrial design. Depending on the method, the starting point and focus of design may weigh more heavily on technical exploration and development or on exploring human needs and preferences, but the ultimate goal of design in HRI is to bring these two domains together to construct a successful HRI system.

> The design process is often cyclical in nature, following this pattern:
>
> 1. Define the problem or question.
> 2. Build the interaction.
> 3. Test.
> 4. Analyze.
> 5. Repeat from step 2 until satisfied (or money and time run out).

4.3.1 Engineering design process

The engineering design method, as the name suggests, is commonly used in engineering. Starting from a problem definition and a set of requirements, numerous possible solutions are considered, and a rational decision is made on which solution best satisfies the requirements. Often, the function of an engineered solution can be modeled and then simulated. These simulations allow engineers to systematically manipulate all the design parameters and calculate the resulting properties of the machine. For well-understood machines, it is even possible to calculate the specific design parameters necessary to meet the performance requirements. If a new aircraft takes off for its maiden flight, engineers can be almost certain that it will fly. It is important to note, however, that they cannot be absolutely certain because the new aircraft will interact with an environment that is not completely predictable in all its detail. Enough is understood, though, to be very sure of the macroscopic properties of the environment, allowing the engineers to design an aircraft that crosses the boundary from simulation to actual prototype without any hiccups. However, validating a solution in simulation is not always possible. The simulation might not be able to capture the real world in sufficient detail, or the number of design parameters can be so high that a complete simulation of all possible designs becomes computationally impossible because it would take a computer years to calculate how each solution performs. There have been some attempts at developing human–robot simulators (e.g., Lemaignan et al., 2014d), but simulating social interaction has turned out to be a very difficult problem.

> Engineers working in HRI tried to design a robot to teach eight- and nine-year-old children what prime numbers are. They believed that the children's learning would benefit from having a very personal and friendly robot, so they programmed the robot to make eye contact, use the child's first name, and politely support the child during the quite taxing exercises. They compared the friendly robot against a robot in which the software to maintain engaging relations was switched off, expecting that robot to be the worse teacher. They were dumbfounded when the aloof robot turned out to be the better teacher by a large margin, showing how their preconceptions regarding robot design were firmly out of touch with the reality of using a robot in the classroom (Kennedy et al., 2015) (see Figure 4.11).

To make things even more difficult, some design problems can be ill-defined, or insufficient information is available about the requirements or the environment. In this case, designers may say that they are dealing with a "wicked design problem" (Buchanan, 1992), which has changing, incomplete,

Figure 4.11 Boy learning math with a robot.

interdependent, or indeterminate requirements that make it difficult to follow a linear model of design thinking in which the problem definition can be cleanly followed by a process of problem solution. HRI design often resembles such a wicked design problem because there is a lack of information about the appropriate behaviors and consequences of robots in social contexts. Another approach to take in this case is to focus not on producing the absolute best solution but on producing satisficing solutions Simon (1996). *Satisficing* is a portmanteau of *satisfy* and *suffice*, meaning that the resulting solution will be just good enough for the purpose it is meant to serve. This is a common problem-solving approach in all human endeavors, and it is almost unavoidable in HRI, where technical capabilities may never reach the ultimate design requirement of the robot performing just as well as or better than people.

4.3.2 User-centered design process

Relying solely on the engineering design method can guide HRI development only so far, particularly when the intended uses of HRI are in open-ended inter-actions and spaces, outside labs or tightly controlled factory environments. In the process of satisficing, we may all too often choose not to measure the things that matter but instead only take into account what is easy to measure. One way to address this issue is to focus more specifically on the people who will use the robot and the contexts of use they inhabit throughout the design process. This can be done through user-centered design (UCD). UCD is not specific to HRI and is used in many other design domains, such as HCI, and is a broad term used to describe "design processes in which end users influence how a design takes shape" (Abras et al., 2004). The users can be involved in many different ways, including through initial analyses of their needs and desires that can help to define the design problem, by asking them to comment on potential robot design variations to see which ones are preferable, and through evaluations of various design iterations of the robot and of the final product to evaluate its success among different users and in different use contexts.

Developers are typically confronted with having to make design decisions for which there are no obvious answers. Do people prefer the robot to have a red torso or a blue torso? Will a chirpy voice on a retail robot invite more people into the store? To answer these questions, developers often build prototypes of the different design options and test them with their target audience. By taking a human-centered perspective; considering user values, preferences, and beliefs; and running empirical evaluation studies (see Chapter 10), developers can actually ensure that the preferences or differences that they observe are not just coincidences but are really caused by the design feature under consideration. The results then inform the developers in building the best design option, and the cycle continues with new problems or design decisions. It is important to run these cycles as early as possible because the cost of making changes to the system increases dramatically later in the process. The credo is "test early; test often."

Designers often focus mainly on the primary users—those who will mainly use the technologies. They would, for instance, investigate nurses and patients who interact with a drug-delivery robot. It is, however, also important for designers to consider secondary users. These are people who might only intermittently come into contact with the artifact or use it through an intermediary. Medical staff who see the robot in the hallway would represent an example of secondary users. Finally, the people who are affected by the use of the artifact (i.e., the tertiary users) have to be considered. These are people whose jobs might be replaced or changed as a result of the introduction of new robotic technology or who might otherwise be affected by the robot's use even if they never interact with it. These various people involved in and affected by the robot's uses are called *stakeholders*, and an initial step in the design process can involve doing some research to identify who the relevant stakeholders are. Once the stakeholders are identified, the designers can then involve them in the design process through a variety of user-centered methods, which can include needs and requirements analyses, field studies and observations, focus groups, interviews and surveys, and user testing and evaluations of prototypes or final products (Vredenburg et al., 2002). We will discuss several of these methods in Chapter 10.

Carnegie Mellon University's Snackbot was designed through a user-centered process that involved taking into consideration the robot, people, and the context. The design process was iteratively performed over 24 months and involved research on where people could already get snacks in the building to establish need, initial technology feasibility and interaction studies, multiple prototypes, and further studies of how the robot was used and the effects of different forms of dialogue and robot behaviors on user satisfaction (Lee et al., 2009) (see Figure 4.12).

Figure 4.12
Snackbot (2010), a system developed at Carnegie Mellon University to study robots in real-world settings. (Source: Photo provided by Jodi Forlizzi)

4.3.3 Participatory design

HRI researchers increasingly use more collaborative and participatory design approaches. Both collaborative and participatory methods seek to include the potential users and other stakeholders, or people who might be affected by robots, in the process of making decisions about appropriate robot design from early on in the design process. This is clearly distinct from the notion of bringing users in at the evaluation stage, where the design is partially or fully formed and users' input is largely used to test particular factors and assumptions already expressed in the design. In this way, participatory design recognizes the expertise people have about their everyday experiences and circumstances.

Participatory design has been present in the design of other computing technologies, particularly information systems, since the 1970s, when it was used to enable workers in organizations to participate in the design of software and other technologies that they would use in their work later on. Participatory design in HRI has been working on developing ways for users to become engaged in the process of making design decisions about robots—for instance, by testing and developing particular behaviors for robots, designing robot applications for their local environments, and conceptualizing how existing robotic capabilities can potentially address their needs and fit into their everyday contexts. DiSalvo et al. (2008) performed one of the early participatory design projects in HRI in their "neighborhood networks" project. Here, community members used a robotic prototype provided by the researchers to develop environmental sensors for their neighborhood. In another participatory project, roboticists and visually impaired community members and designers worked together in a series of workshops to develop appropriate guidance behaviors for a mobile PR-2 robot (Feng et al., 2015). Participatory design has also been used in various healthcare and educational applications for HRI (see, e.g., Šabanović et al., 2015). Teenagers (Björling et al., 2019) and even children (Zaga, 2021) have also participated in the design of HRI through various participatory design methods.

Participatory design is always challenging, but working on participatory design with robots has its particular difficulties. One is the fact that people have many different preconceptions about robots but little knowledge about the technology involved in making them, which leads to unrealistic design ideas. At the same time, designers have little knowledge of the day-to-day lives and experiences of people in many of the applications in which HRI is most needed (e.g., eldercare). While working with older adults and nursing home staff to develop assistive robots for older adults with depression, Lee et al. (2017) and Winkle et al. (2018) focused on supporting a process of mutual learning between HRI researchers and participants, which allowed both sides to explore and teach each other about their different areas of expertise. This also helped support participants' learning to start thinking about design beyond just designing for themselves. HRI researchers have also developed frameworks to support the interdisciplinary and participatory design of social robots (Axelsson et al., 2021). Participatory design is still new in HRI, but with more and more applications being envisioned for diverse populations and everyday contexts, it is becoming an increasingly important component of the HRI design methods toolkit.

4.4 Prototyping tools

Although it is possible to develop simple robot prototypes from materials that are generally available, such as cardboard or found objects, several prototyping kits and tools for creative interactive technologies have recently become available on the market. These make it possible for a wide variety of people with different levels of technical expertise and economic resources to try their hand at robot design. They also enable more rapid and iterative development of robot designs by making the representation of interaction a simpler thing to create.

Figure 4.13 LEGO Mindstorms (1998–2022) was the brainchild of Seymour Papert, a Massachusetts Institute of Technology professor who was an avid proponent of using computers to support child learning.

Perhaps the earliest type of kit that could be used for developing different robot designs was the first-generation LEGO Mindstorms system (see Figure 4.13), which provided bricks for building and specialized bricks for programming and actuating simple robot prototypes. Bartneck and Hu (2004) used LEGO robots to illustrate the utility of rapid prototyping for HRI, and the first case studies had already appeared in 2002 (Klassner, 2002).

The Vex Robotics Design System[1] is also widely known and used, and its advanced version is the kit of choice for the popular FIRST Robotics Competitions.[2] More recent additions to the array of kits available are Little Bits, which provide easy-to-use plug-and-play electronic bricks, including sensors and actuators, among others, that can be used to quickly and easily create interactive prototypes.

The Arduino microcontroller[3] is very affordable and has a large hobbyist community providing open-source designs and code, as well as a wide array of peripherals (sensors, motors, LEDs, wireless units, etc.) that allow for more flexibility in design but require more technical know-how.

Other equipment, such as the Raspberry Pi[4] single-board computer and affordable and even portable three-dimensional (3D) printers, can not only make HRI prototyping easier but also may even be said to be making it accessible to the masses (or at least to college students).

Designers also incorporate other existing technologies into robot design, including smartphones. Even an average smartphone these days has sufficient computing power to control a robot. Furthermore, a smartphone has many

---

[1] See www.vexrobotics.com
[2] See www.firstinspires.org/
[3] See www.arduino.cc
[4] See www.raspberrypi.org

Figure 4.14
Robovie MR2
(2010) is a
humanoid robot
controlled through a
cell phone.

built-in sensors (microphone, camera, gyro sensor, accelerometer) and actuators (screen, speaker, vibration motor). The Robovie MR2 is an early example of integrating a smartphone into a robot to control all of its functions (see Figure 4.14). Hoffman calls this the "dumb robot, smartphone" approach to social robot design (Hoffman, 2012).

Available technologies for prototyping continue to develop, fueled at least in part by ongoing efforts to engage more students, hobbyists, and even potential users in technology design.

4.5 Culture in HRI design

As not only an interdisciplinary but also an international field of research, HRI design has been particularly interested in the question of cultural effects on perceptions of and interactions with robots. Culture, the different beliefs, values, practices, language, and traditions of a group of people, plays into robot design both in the form of factors introduced by designers and in the context in which users interpret different HRI designs.

Researchers commonly make connections between cultural traditions and the design and use of robots, particularly contrasting the norms, values, and beliefs in the East and West: animist beliefs have been used to explain the perceived comfort of Japanese and Korean populations with robots (Geraci, 2006; Kaplan, 2004; Kitano, 2006), whereas human exceptionalism has been suggested as a source of Westerners' discomfort with social and humanoid robots (Geraci, 2006; Brooks, 2003). Holistic and dualistic notions of mind and body (Kaplan, 2004; Shaw-Garlock, 2009) and individualist and communitarian social practices (Šabanović, 2010) have been identified as design patterns represented in the design of robots and potential human interactions with them.

Figure 4.15 The
BlessU2 robot was
used by the
Protestant church in
Germany to give
blessings.

In addition to these generalized connections between culture and robotics, HRI researchers have been studying cultural differences in and effects on people's perceptions of and face-to-face encounters with robots. In a comparison using Dutch, Chinese, German, U.S., Japanese, and Mexican participants, it was found that U.S. participants were the least negative toward robots, whereas the Mexican participants were the most negative. Against expectations, the Japanese participants did not have a particularly positive attitude toward robots (Bartneck et al., 2005). MacDorman et al. (2009) showed that U.S. and Japanese participants have similar attitudes toward robots, suggesting that such factors as history and religion (see Figure 4.15) may affect their willingness to adopt robotic technologies. Survey evaluations of the seal-like robot Paro by participants from Japan, the United Kingdom, Sweden, Italy, South Korea, Brunei, and the United States found that participants generally evaluated the robot positively but identified different traits as most likable according to their country of origin (Shibata et al., 2009).

In the context of human–robot teamwork, Evers et al. (2008) found that users from China and the United States responded differently to robots and that human team members found robots more persuasive when they used culturally appropriate forms of communication (Lindblom and Ziemke, 2003). Findings from two generative design studies with participants in the United States and South Korea, which asked users to think about robotic technology in their own homes, showed that user expectations of and needs for robotic technologies are related to culturally variable conceptions of the home as relation oriented in Korea and more functionally defined in the United States (Lee et al., 2012). The growing body of work on cross-cultural differences in HRI and their potential design implications identifies that cultural considerations should be taken into account when designing robots, both for international and local uses.

4.6 From machines to people—and the in between

As the previous discussion shows, designing human–robot interactions involves making many decisions about the form, function, and desired effects of robots. HRI designers, however, also bring deeper philosophical, ethical, and even political commitments into their work. Although these can be unconsciously brought into HRI research, we think it is useful for HRI scholars to consciously engage with these concerns in the course of their robotics research and development.

One of the most basic decisions that robotics researchers make is the type of robot they want to work on—is it meant to resemble a human or be more like a machine? Another decision can involve the main goals of the work—is it focused on producing technical developments, understanding humans, or perhaps developing HRI systems that can be used for specific applications and contexts of use? These decisions have significance beyond just the design and use of the robot, however. One could argue that the creation of robots by their designers, in particular those in which robotic copies of actual people are created, is an immortality project. Such projects are "symbolic belief systems that promise that the individual will not be obliterated by the demise of his or her physical body" (Kaptelinin, 2018, p.6). Hiroshi Ishiguro's work on android copies of living human persons is a case in point, in which the robotic copy can aim to stand in the place of that specific person, both in current and ostensibly future interactions. Ishiguro himself describes how he feels his own identity is interconnected with the robot, which persists as a replica of his past and younger self that he now feels the pressure to emulate (Mar, 2017). But the relationship between machinelike robots and designers can be just as deep. Describing his work with industrial robots, Japanese roboticist Masahiro Mori defined the relationship between humans and machines as being "fused together in an interlocking entity" (Mori, 1982). This close relationship has direct consequences for the form and function of the robot on the one side and the designer on the other side, as well as on the future consequences and uses of the robot in society.

Robot design can also be guided by a personal commitment to specific social and philosophical values, such as improving access to resources for broader populations, increasing participation in the design of and decision-making about robots, or contributing to the solution of pressing social issues. Roboticist Illah Nourbakhsh described how his personal values affect his robotic projects as follows:

> One way out is to say my work is purely theoretical, who cares how somebody applies it? I didn't want to do that. I wanted to say my work involves theoretical components, but I'm taking it all the way to seeing a real result in the physical world. And furthermore, I want it to be socially positive in some measure. ⋯ I want to work on something so socially positive that not only do I hope everyone uses it, but I want to see at least one used case to fruition. Then you have this feedback loop from real-world application back to engineering design. (Šabanović, 2007, p. 79)

In this way, the choice of what type of HRI project to pursue and the goals to focus on in design can reflect personal or collective values (e.g., of the research group or of project collaborators).

Relatedly, it is not only researchers' values that matter, but likewise, a human-centered approach should take into account user and organization values, for example, in the framework of value-sensitive design (VSD) (Friedman et al., 2002). Indeed, although VSD represents an established method to advance novel technologies, it has rarely been used in the context of social robots. As a research method for social HRI, VSD can help integrate user perspectives in a literally valuable way (see also Schmiedel et al., 2022).

These authors point out that within the VSD framework, technologies adapt to human needs rather than vice versa. By means of VSD, human values can be translated into technological requirements, thereby ensuring that user or stakeholder perspectives are integrated at the onset of technology development by means of value identification, value embedding, and value evaluation.

Figure 4.16 Robert M. Pirsig (September 6, 1928–April 24, 2017) is the author of *The Metaphysics of Quality*, which has inspired many designers.

One of the authors finds inspiration for his design in the work of Robert M. Pirsig (see Figure 4.16), who put it this way:

> The real [aesthetics] lies in the relationship between the people who produce the technology and the things they produce, which results in a similar relationship between the people who use the technology and the things they use. (Pirsig, 1974, p. 299)

Pirsig emphasizes the crucial role of obtaining peace of mind in order to arrive at good design as the barrier between the designer and the object to be designed dissolves:

> So the thing to do when working on a motorcycle, as in any other task, is to cultivate the peace of mind which does not separate one's self from one's surroundings. When that is done successfully then everything else follows naturally. Peace of mind produces right values, right values produce right thoughts. Right thoughts produce

right actions and right actions produce work which will be a material reflection for others to see of the serenity at the centre of it all. (p. 305)

The connection between the robot and its designer is far deeper than you may assume. Pirsig spent his whole life working out *The Metaphysics of Quality*, in which he argues that there is no fundamental difference between the designer and the object he or she designs. What connects them is "quality."

Considering the peace of mind of the designer might sound strange at first, but Pirsig argued that in the moment of the perception of quality, there is no division of objects and subjects. In the moment of such pure quality, the subject and the object are one (Pirsig, 1974, p. 299). Artists might be familiar with the experience of unity with their work, and the work of designers and engineers might be enhanced if they, too, would be more sensitive to this connection.

4.7 Conclusion

Designing robots requires multidisciplinary expertise, often by means of a team, and a process that takes the users and the interaction context into consideration. Various prototyping tools are available to quickly build and test robots. Once the users and their interactions with the robot are understood, the robot needs to be designed from the outside in—starting with the potential users and use context to develop design concepts and the technical specifications for the robot. HRI designs also express, whether consciously or unconsciously, the social and ethical values of the designers.

The robots' anthropomorphism is one of the most important design considerations in contemporary HRI. We provided a detailed description of the construct of psychological anthropomorphism as a prime opportunity for a fruitful exchange between disciplines, leading to a broader overall understanding of the concept in the social sciences and robotics. Beyond the theoretical and methodological gains from investigating anthropomorphism, HRI studies have also shown the importance of considering humanlike form and function in robot design for perceived interaction quality, HRI acceptance, and enjoyment of the interaction with humanlike robots.

Questions for you to think about:

- Think about the features of a humanlike robot in terms of "design affordances." Which affordances should be considered in humanlike robots?
- Try to think about "design patterns" for social robots that greet people daily. Find and describe repeatedly reused patterns in behavior.
- Imagine you have to design a robot. Consider the necessary steps, taking a participatory design approach.

- Discuss the role of user expectations in robot design. What are important points to consider if you want to market your robot?
- What is your opinion: Should a social robot have very few humanlike cues, or should it be highly anthropomorphic in design (e.g., like an android)? Which robot would be accepted more by people in general? Why?
- Think about a robot that you might want to have in the near future. Picturing this robot, try to think about a way to encourage more anthropomorphization based on its behavior. Which behaviors should the robot show to be perceived as humanlike?

4.8 Exercises

The answers to these questions are available in the Appendix.

* Exercise 4.1 Pareidolia Take photographs of pareidolia in your environment. Do not just google images. Use your phone or camera. Why did you choose these images?

* Exercise 4.2 Anthropomorphism Have a look at Figure 4.17. Sort the robots from low to high anthropomorphism.

1. Lowest anthropomorphism: _____
2. Low anthropomorphism: _____
3. Medium anthropomorphism: _____
4. High anthropomorphism: _____
5. Highest anthropomorphism: _____

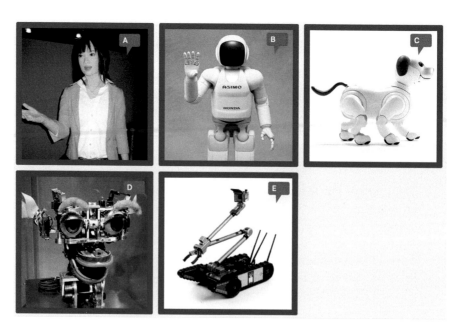

Figure 4.17 Different robots. (Source: B, Honda; C, Copyright of Sony Corporation)

*** Exercise 4.3 Design an autonomous vehicle Watch this video, and then answer the question that follows.

- Dr. Leila Takayama, "What Is It Like to Be a Robot?" https://youtu.be/ bFRBpVhqrxo

1. If you were designing an automated self-driving car, like the ones developed by Google or Tesla, what kinds of affordances and/or design patterns would you include in the design to make people be and feel safe in the car as passengers and allow pedestrians and other drivers on the road to be able to trust the car in traffic? You can refer to Chapter 1 and this chapter, as well as Leila Takayama's talk (linked in the previous exercise), which discusses the sense of control in autonomous systems and some car examples, among other things, to justify your design decisions.

Future reading:

- Duffy, Brian R. Anthropomorphism and the social robot. *Robotics and Autonomous Systems*, 42(3):177–190, 2003. ISSN 0921-8890. doi: 10 .1016/S0921-8890(02)00374-3. URL https://doi.org/10.1016/S0921-8890(02)00374-3
- Fink, Julia. Anthropomorphism and human likeness in the design of robots and human-robot interaction. In Ge, Shuzhi Sam, Khatib, Oussama, Cabibihan, John-John, Simmons, Reid, and Williams, Mary-Anne, editors, *Social Robotics*, pages 199–208. Springer, Berlin, 2012. ISBN 978-3-642-34103-8. URL https://doi.org/10.1007/978-3-642-34103-8_20
- Kahn, Peter H., Freier, Nathan G., Kanda, Takayuki, Ishiguro, Hiroshi, Ruckert, Jolina H., Severson, Rachel L., and Kane, Shaun K. Design patterns for sociality in human-robot interaction. In *The 3rd ACM/IEEE International Conference on Human-Robot Interaction*, pages 97–104. Association for Computing Machinery, New York, 2008. ISBN 978-1-60558-017-3. doi: 10.1145/1349822.1349836. URL https://doi.org/10.1145/1349822.1349836
- Lowdermilk, Travis. *User-Centered Design: A Developer's Guide to Building User-Friendly Applications*. O'Reilly, Sebastopol, CA, 2013. ISBN 978-1449359805. URL http://worldcat.org/oclc/940703603
- Norman, Don. *The Design of Everyday Things: Revised and Expanded Edition*. Basic Books, New York, 2013. ISBN 9780465072996. URL http://worldcat.org/oclc/862103168
- Pirsig, Robert M. *Zen and the Art of Motorcycle Maintenance: An Inquiry into Values*. Morrow, New York, 1974. ISBN 0688002307. URL http://worldcat.org/oclc/41356566
- Simon, Herbert Alexander. *The Sciences of the Artificial*. MIT Press, Cambridge, MA, 3rd edition, 1996. ISBN 0262691914. URL http://worldcat.org/oclc/552080160

5

Spatial Interaction

What is covered in this chapter:

- The importance of the spatial placement of agents in social interaction.
- Basic understanding of human proxemics: how people manage space in relation to others.
- How a robot manages the space around it, including interactions such as approaching, initiating interaction, maintaining distance, and navigating around people.
- How the properties of spatial interaction can be used as cues for robots.

Figure 5.1 The Joggobot Drone (2012). (Source: Photo provided by Eberhard Gräther and Florian "Floyd" Mueller)

In 2012, Exertion Games Labs released a drone exercise companion called Joggobot (see Figure 5.1). Runners who feel like they could use a little extra motivation or companionship during their run but don't have a personal trainer or a friend to join them can now have a drone accompany them during their exercise laps. One of the critical features of Joggobot is its placement in space during the run: right in front of the runner, like a carrot tempting a running horse. This position wasn't chosen on a whim. The developers studied where the drone should ideally be in relation to the runner (i.e., above, following, leading, on the side) and how much distance it should keep in order to maximize motivation (Graether and Mueller, 2012). They found that having the drone flying behind the jogger made people feel like they were being chased, which decreased their enjoyment of exercising. Users much preferred to take on the chasing role themselves. This shows that the spatial placement of a robot with respect to its user is an important aspect to consider in human–robot interaction (HRI).

Consumer drones, such as the readily available and cheap quadrotor platforms, have become ubiquitous since the Joggobot was developed. Baytas et al. (2019) reviewed the use of drones in social environments, where they fly in close proximity to people and even interact with users, with drones even acting as a teacher in the classroom (Johal et al., 2022). As you can imagine, distance matters in such cases, and proxemics in human–drone interaction is now an active research field (Yeh et al., 2017; Han et al., 2019; Wojciechowska et al., 2019).

Thus, when planning a robot's placement in space, it is crucial to consider people's preferences and the social norms that exist regarding such placement in relation to others. This chapter covers the spatial component of HRI.

Section 5.1 explains the tendencies that humans display with regard to space when they are in a social setting with other humans; Section 5.2 discusses to what extent these social norms and unspoken rules extrapolate to a social setting that includes robots.

5.1 Use of space in human interaction

When space is available, individuals are strongly expected to adhere to social distance norms. Most people feel it is inappropriate for a stranger to sit beside them on an otherwise empty bus. However, when taking the bus during rush hour, we are forced to step into others' personal space, and it becomes acceptable to sit or stand close to others. Even though it is not considered impolite to stand next to someone on a busy commute, people often feel uncomfortable, avoiding eye contact and quickly repositioning themselves at a greater distance when more space becomes available (see Figure 5.2).

Figure 5.2
Commuters during rush hour on the Tokyo subway having their personal space violated. We often deal with this by avoiding the gaze of others.

5.1.1 Proxemics

Cultural anthropologists coined the term *proxemics* to describe how people take up space in relation to others and how spatial positioning influences attitudes, behaviors, and interpersonal interaction. Hall et al. (1968) describe four distance zones in their original work: intimate distance, personal distance, social distance, and public distance (see Figure 5.3). When the available space is (relatively) unlimited, these distances indicate the psychological closeness between people.

As the name suggests, intimate distance is reserved for close personal relationships or the sharing of private information. Intimate distance ranges roughly from a few centimeters to about half a meter, depending on one's age and culture. Together with personal distance (which ranges from about half a meter to 1.2 meters), these zones make up the personal space of a person: the amount of space that people generally consider theirs to take up.

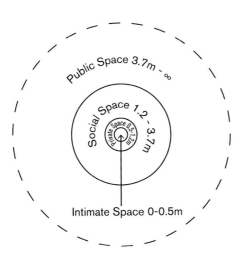

Figure 5.3
Intimate, personal, social, and public distance, according to Hall et al. (1968).

Under normal circumstances, only friends, relatives, and partners are expected to come this close. For less personal relationships, such as acquaintances or colleagues, one is expected to maintain social distance, which ranges between 1.2 and about 4 meters between persons. Finally, public distance starts at around 4 meters, which is the distance people are expected to keep between them in relatively impersonal settings, such as public speaking at a conference.

Hall et al. (1968) consider people's use of space as an often-overlooked dimension of cultural experience and note that people from different cultures have varying personal proxemic preferences and expectations. For example, in "high-contact cultures," such as those of South America, people will frequently enter each other's personal space and touch, whereas in "low-contact cultures," such as the United States, touching a stranger may be construed as assault. Hall wittily observe that North Americans visiting South America will find themselves "barricading themselves behind their desks, using chairs and typewriter tables to keep the Latin American at what is to us a comfortable distance." (Hall, 1990, p.180)

Slight breaches of proxemic norms are sometimes made on purpose by individuals, for instance, to create more psychological closeness or perhaps to intimidate. For example, a man who nonchalantly places his arm first on the backrest of the sofa where his date is sitting and then cautiously inches closer and closer is making a transition from personal distance to the intimate zone. The friend who touches your arm when you are telling a personal story does the same, although with a different underlying motive. However, these moves have to be made very cautiously and under continuous assessment and reassessment of the reaction of the other person. Few people would be charmed if a hopeful suitor had abruptly placed themselves right on their lap at the start of a date. Likewise, when we attempt to comfort a colleague by giving a hug at the wrong moment, the interaction can turn awkward rather quickly. This is because the meaning of spatial-interaction cues is highly contextual. Unlike the friendly moves just mentioned, an investigator questioning a suspect may "get in the suspect's face" by moving as close to the suspect as possible to seem more threatening.

Not only the distance at which we interact with each other but also our placement in relation to interaction partners are bound by social norms. For example, researchers found that people who sat next to each other were more cooperative, whereas people sitting opposite each other behaved more competitively. During conversations, people usually position themselves at an angle to each other (Cook, 1970). The way in which people place themselves with respect to each other is therefore an important aspect of the dynamics of interaction (Williams and Bargh, 2008).

Finally, circumstances beyond our control can have a profound impact on proxemics. The COVID-19 pandemic, which raged across the globe in 2020, forced us all to adopt social distancing. Social distances that previously seemed fine suddenly made us all feel very uncomfortable. Authorities insisted that we keep a minimum distance of 1.5 meters (or 6 feet) from people who were not part of our household, and people instinctively started avoiding crowds and adopted very different proxemics (Mehta, 2020). Time will tell if the two years during which we were forced to alter proxemics will have a lasting effect on the social distances we keep or if the realities of crowded metros and old habits will force us back into our old ways.

5.1.2 Group spatial-interaction dynamics

The importance of spatial dynamics goes beyond one-on-one interaction and is also salient in group interaction scenarios. The spatial orientation of people in a group in relation to others can make the group seem as if it were inviting more members or seeking to keep others out. For example, at a cocktail party, when people stand in a tight-knit circle, it can seem difficult to join in the conversation. However, if the group notices people wanting to join and opens up the circle so that there is space for new members to fill, it can be construed as an invitation to participate. This type of information can be useful for robots to gauge which groups of people they can approach in public spaces like museums or malls or if they want to join the interaction dynamics of human groups.

Group spatial dynamics such as these were described by Adam Kendon as the "facing formation," or "F-formation" ... defined as "one to which they have equal, direct, and exclusive access" (Kendon, 1990, p. 209) (see Figure 5.4). These formations are created through the positioning of two or more people in relation to each other, such that the areas of space that they are facing and on which they focus their attention are overlapping. The inner space between these people is termed the *o-space*(Kendon, 1990). The group participants themselves are said to occupy the *p-space*, and they are surrounded by *r-space*. People can modify their positions to maintain this space or to include other participants in the group conversation, as in the previous example. Different configurations of the F-formation are possible, based on people's orientation to each other, and are termed the *face-to-face, L-shape*, and *side-by-side* formations for two people and the *circular formation* and other shapes for larger groups.

These group formations have been used to understand people's interactions with technology (Marshall et al., 2011) in general and with robots more specifically (e.g., Hüttenrauch et al., 2006; Yamaoka et al., 2010).

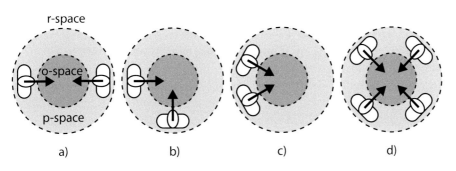

a)   b)   c)   d)

Figure 5.4
Kendon's (1990) F-formations come in several variants, all of which include the components of o-, p-, and r-space, namely: the (a) face-to-face, (b) L-shape, (c) side-by-side, and (d) circular formations.

In navigation around people, Pérez-Hurtado et al. (2016) found that a robot needs to be aware of people's movements and cognizant of people engaged in conversation and not walk between them even if there is enough space.

5.2 Spatial interaction for robots

Robots will often share physical space with humans. Some robots are mobile, moving over the ground or through the air. Some of them have arms and manipulators so that they can interact with objects and users. The placement and movement of such robots with respect to people must be considered when designing human–robot interactions. Robots that do not respect the personal space of the user will evoke negative reactions or even rejection and withdrawal by the user. Robot designers can attempt to increase acceptance of the robot by having it keep an appropriate distance (assuming that they can code the robot in such a way that it knows what the "appropriate distance" is at a given point in time and space) and adjusting its position to create a fitting interaction experience. For example, a security robot might initially keep a polite distance but enter a person's intimate space at some point in the interaction in an attempt to intimidate the person.

5.2.1 Social navigation

Before going into HRI, let us briefly explain the basic techniques from robotics that are required for a robot in order to engage in spatial interactions with humans. When a robot wants to interact with people, it needs to locate itself in space with regard to the people it aims to interact with. Thus, one of the basic techniques required for mobile robots is localization; a robot needs to know where it is. This is not a trivial problem. A typical robot is equipped with an odometer, a sensor that records the distance traveled by the robot's wheels. However, as the robot travels, these measurements lose accuracy, and the robot therefore needs to correct the information that the odometry provides about its location. The typical solution to this is to let the robot build a map of its environment and then cross-reference information on its location and orientation from the odometry with information from other sensors, such as a laser range finder or camera, to locate itself on the map. This process is known as *simultaneous localization and mapping*, or SLAM (Davison et al., 2007; Thrun et al., 2005).

In addition to reporting the robot's location, localization can help the robot know what type of space it is in (e.g., whether it is in the living room or bathroom). However, it will not reveal anything about the whereabouts of any people in that space. Identifying the location and orientation of people interacting with the robot thus is the next challenge. For detecting people at a short range, the robot will carry sensors, such as two-dimensional (2D) cameras and depth cameras, that enable it to identify nearby people. The software processing the camera images can not only detect and track humans but also report on the location of body parts such as arms, legs, and heads. For tracking people at longer distances, there are techniques that use laser range finders (also known as *light detection and ranging*, or LiDAR). A motion-capturing system is sometimes used. By placing reflective or fiducial markers on people and objects, motion capture can be used to identify and locate the markers (and by extension, the people or objects they were initially attached to). However, these marker-based approaches are difficult to use outside a lab setting: good luck convincing customers to stick markers on themselves to allow their home robot to recognize them. Finally, researchers can also mount sensors, such as cameras, in the environment to track people (Brscić et al., 2013). (For more details on the different sensors that a robot can be equipped with, see Section 3.4 in Chapter 3.)

Moving the robot through a crowded environment, also known as *robot navigation*, is a well-studied problem in mobile robotics. To avoid collisions between the robot and objects or people, techniques such as the dynamic window approach (DWA) are often used (Fox et al., 1997). The idea behind this technique is that a system computes its future location based on the current velocity of the robot while at the same time considering whether to keep or alter its velocity within the limitation of its actuation capability—and while calculating a future velocity that does not result in a collision. Over longer time scales, there are techniques based on path planning. In these techniques, if a given goal of a robot is not within immediate view of the robot, a path-planning algorithm computes a set of way points or paths for the robot that will let it reach its goal. In robotics, most path-planning algorithms that work well for navigating around obstacles will result in socially inappropriate behavior when tried around people. We will discuss the social rules around positioning shortly.

Localization and navigation can also take various elements of interaction with a user into account. For instance, Spexard et al. (2006) developed a robotic mapping technique that uses input from dialogue with users to learn about new places in an environment. To develop a human-friendly mapping technique, Morales Saiki et al. (2011) had a robot explore the environment while collecting visual landmarks to build a cognitive map from a humanlike perspective; this enabled the robot to generate route instructions that people could easily comprehend. Researchers have also worked toward developing techniques to understand human spatial descriptions, such as route directions. For instance, Kollar et al. (2010) developed a technique to associate a user's instructions and visual information about the environment to help the robot interpret the location mentioned by a user. Zhou et al. (2022) first measured how people pass one another in social settings, then implemented navigation behavior for a Pepper robot, showing that people felt more at ease near a robot with socially aware navigation.

5.2.2 Socially appropriate positioning

Even though there are basic techniques for perception and navigation that allow robots to move around without colliding with obstacles, robots still often lack the capabilities to navigate in a socially appropriate way in the presence of other people. Suppose we want a robot to move through a corridor in an office building. What would happen if it considers people as obstacles? When a person walked toward the robot from the other end of the corridor, the robot would continue to move straight down the corridor until inches before colliding, then move out of the way. Although it would avoid a collision with the person, this behavior is very different from what humans would do in a similar situation: we yield to each other well in time, nonverbally showing which side of the corridor we will walk on, and will avoid entering each other's personal space. Thus, a robot waiting until the last moment before moving out of the way may be seen as confrontational or aggressive, even though it still avoids running into a person.

Most mapping techniques for robots only provide geometrical maps, where people are considered obstacles. They do not contain information on which direction people are facing, if they are having a conversation or just standing close to each other, or how people are moving. Hence, there are several techniques that allow a robot to acquire a more human-aware representation of its environment.

One of the focuses in investigating proxemics in HRI has been identifying appropriate interaction distances between users and robots (see Figure 5.5). These include questions like the following: How close do people prefer to stand relative to a robot? How close should a robot approach people before it is considered rude or inappropriate or makes people feel uncomfortable? Walters et al. (2005) measured the distance at which people feel comfortable when they are approached by a robot. They reported that the majority of people prefer a personal or social distance when interacting with a robot, although some people prefer to stand even closer. Hüttenrauch et al. (2006) reported that people preferred the robot to stand at distances derived from human proxemics. Investigating interactions between a robot and a group of people,

Figure 5.5 A lab setup for proxemics study of HRI.

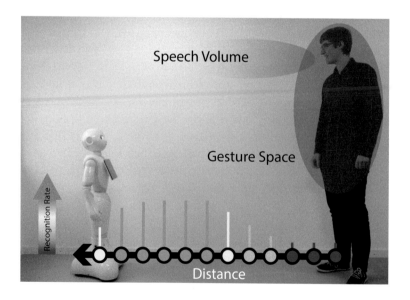

Kuzuoka et al. (2010) reported that a robot can change the conversational F-formations of the group by changing its body orientation, and they also found that movement of the robot's whole body was more effective than having the robot move only its head.

Relational position is also important when people and robots interact while they are moving. To enhance a robot's social acceptability, techniques have been developed for robot navigation based on human proxemics. For instance, when a robot follows a user from behind, the robot can either follow the same trajectory as the user, or it can move directly to the user's current location, which might be a shorter and faster pathway. Gockley et al. (2007) showed that users perceive the first behavior as more natural. Morales Saiki et al. (2012) developed a technique that allows a robot to navigate side by side with its user, for which they found it important for the robot to anticipate the user's future motion.

Furthermore, people's perceived safety does not necessarily correspond to what a robot computes to be safe. For instance, in the corridor passing problem, it was found that a robot needs to maintain enough distance to avoid entering a person's intimate zone (Pacchierotti et al., 2006). Alternatively, a robot can mimic how people avoid colliding with each other. Luber et al. (2012) and Shiomi et al. (2014), for example, developed a pedestrian model that implemented collision avoidance for dynamic environments. Considerations of comfort and perceived safety can also be integrated into path planning. Sisbot et al. (2007) developed a path planner for a mobile robot that plans how to reach a given goal while avoiding situations that might make people uncomfortable. The planner takes into account aspects such as whether people are sitting or standing and whether the robot might surprise them by suddenly appearing from behind an obstacle. Fisac et al. (2018) used a probabilistic model of a human walking to plan and execute a safe trajectory for an indoor drone (see Figure 5.6).

Planning a motion path that people will perceive as safe and comfortable is also necessary when only a part of the robot enters the user's personal space. For example, when a robot arm is used near a person, such as when a person

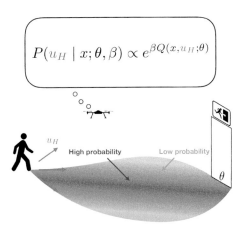

$$P(u_H \mid x; \theta, \beta) \propto e^{\beta Q(x, u_H; \theta)}$$

Figure 5.6 The drone calculates a probabilistic model of where the human will go and plans a safe route to avoid collision. (Source: Illustration by Jaime Fernández Fisac, Andrea Bajcsy, Sylvia L. Herbert, and David Fridovich-Keil, depicting their work in Fisac et al. (2018))

and an industrial robot collaborate on a shared task, the robot must take the socially appropriate distance into account when computing a path for its end effector (e.g., hand) to reach its given goal (e.g., grasp an object or hand an object to a person) (Kulic and Croft, 2005). This may make the robot's movement inefficient from a purely functional standpoint, but it will lead to a more positive evaluation of the interaction by the user (Cakmak et al., 2011).

5.2.3 Spatial dynamics of initiating HRI

Every social interaction has to be initiated by someone, perhaps by hovering in the vicinity of the person you want to talk to at a cocktail party while orienting your body toward the person, for example, or by approaching a colleague to hand over the annual report. How you approach each other and how the approach is perceived have implications for the ensuing interaction.

Approaching behavior is generally expected to have positive effects on both parties in the interaction. The approacher makes an effort to attract and share attention, which signals interest in the person being approached. At the same time, initiating an interaction triggers neural activity in reward-related brain areas, resulting in positive affect in the initiator (Schilbach et al., 2010). Initiating interaction is, furthermore, a sign of being assertive and having faith in one's capability to conduct a successful social encounter. What may be more surprising is that this runs the other way, too. People who approach others are seen by their peers as having more personal control (Kirmeyer and Lin, 1987).

Imagine the moment when a person meets a robot for the first time. Either of them could approach the other to initiate the interaction. Whereas this can be rather trivial for a person, a robot needs to be carefully designed to appropriately initiate an interaction. Approaching behavior for robots has been studied from early on in the field of HRI. For instance, in a situation where a robot joins a queue, the robot needs to respect the personal space of other people who are also waiting (Nakauchi and Simmons, 2002). When a robot encounters people, it needs to switch its navigation mode from purely functional to considering social distance and spatial configuration (Althaus et al., 2004).

Initiating an interaction is also context and task dependent. Satake et al. (2009) show how a robot offering information about the stores in a mall will fail to initiate an interaction if the approach is poorly planned and executed. The planned trajectory needs to be both effective and acceptable to human visitors (Satake et al., 2009; Kato et al., 2015). Whereas approaching from the front was found to be desired when a robot was trying to initiate a conversation, approaching from the front when the robot was delivering an object to a person was less preferred and resulted in more failures (Dautenhahn et al., 2006; Shi et al., 2013).

Some recent work incorporates machine learning to generate appropriate approaching behaviors that fit with a context. Liu et al. (2016) designed approaching and initiating behavior for a store clerk robot using a fully automated analysis of observed human behavior. The researchers first recorded how people moved and talked in a camera store scenario and then used machine learning to extract typical speech behavior and spatial formations. These behaviors were then transferred to the robot. A user study showed that the learned speech and motion behavior was considered to be socially appropriate by users.

Even in the case where a person approaches a robot, the robot should respond at just the right moment. If it fails to do so, the user could find the interaction unnatural and awkward and might even give up initiating interactions in the future (Kato et al., 2015). Human proxemics studies, particularly observational studies on the interactions of humans with either one another or with robots, can provide more contextually attuned and relevant models. For instance, Michalowski et al. (2006) developed a categorical model of human spatial interaction and engagement with a receptionist robot from observations of people's interactions with the robot. They defined the appropriate timing and types of behavior (e.g., turning toward a person, saying hello) that the robot could perform with people in different spatial zones in order to both be perceived as more approachable and successfully initiate an interaction when appropriate.

Social navigation has become particularly relevant in the context of self-driving cars. The story goes that the first self-driving cars at Google drove optimal trajectories following the highway code, but they frequently startled other road users by driving too close or cutting them off. Only when politeness was explicitly added as an optimization criterion did the cars drive in a way that was socially acceptable.

5.2.4 Informing users of a robot's intent

Robot motion trajectories are often used to convey the intent and goal of the robot. Path-planning algorithms have been developed to explicitly convey information through the robot's trajectory. For instance, by slowly passing a few meters from a visitor, a mobile robot is able to express whether it is available for an interaction (Hayashi et al., 2012). Similarly, trajectories have been used as a means to allow a robot with few options to express itself, such as cleaning robots and drones, to communicate their intent to users (Szafir et al., 2015).

During handover in HRI, that is, when a robot hands an object to its user, users prefer a robot to behave with "legibility"—in a way that allows users to understand its goal and intention (Koay et al., 2007a). Hence, researchers have developed algorithms to control a robot arm to generate legible motions while reaching a given goal. A robot could hand over an object to a person in many different ways, but the most energy-efficient way may be incomprehensible to a person, so it is better to perform a motion that is easier to interpret (Dragan et al., 2013).

When a robot works closely with a person, it needs to have the capability to understand how the person is perceiving the space around him or her. An important related capability is spatial perspective-taking (Trafton et al., 2005).

Imagine a situation where two people are working together. One might ask the other to pass an object by saying, "Give me that object." The referent of "object" will be obvious if there is only one object available. But what if there are several objects? For people, inferring the intended referent of "object" is often easy. We may use a complex set of cues, including gaze direction, body orientation, the prior context of the interaction, knowledge about the person and his or her preferences, task information, and other cues, to disambiguate the request. For a robot, however, this can be rather complicated. Several approaches exist that allow the robot to take the perspective of the user. These often rely on geometric models that keep track of the location of people, robots, and objects and which of these are visible and reachable by whom (Lemaignan et al., 2017; Ros et al., 2010).

5.3 Conclusion

The study of spatial interaction in HRI is often inspired by our understanding of human proxemics, conversational relations, and relational positioning and approach behaviors, although we cannot expect the effects to always be the same. However, norms and understandings that are common knowledge for people—to the point where they may not even be aware of them anymore—often turn out to be not so trivial to incorporate into robot behavior. For instance, people will unconsciously and effortlessly adjust the distance to their conversation partner to an appropriate amount; however, a robot would need to conduct a careful computation to decide what distance it should keep during an interaction with its human counterpart. Even more difficulties are involved when the interaction is more complex, for example, when a robot has to approach a person, when it has to maintain spatial formation during a conversation, or when it has to navigate together with a person on the move. These considerations are important not only for achieving socially acceptable and comfortable HRI but also for ensuring that people understand the robot's intentions and can engage with robots safely in their physical space.

> Questions for you to think about:
>
> - Let's role-play: To understand how much social information is involved in creating socially appropriate navigation, try to behave like a dumb robot that does not process any social information about space when interacting with a friend (maybe inform your friend beforehand, or "forget" to do so for a more natural response). What happened? How long could you keep this up?
> - Think back to a situation when somebody violated your personal space. How did you notice? What was your reaction?
> - Imagine you are an engineer building a robot. This robot will come to the market in Japan, Mexico, and the United States. Will the product

be the same for every country? Will the robot's spatial-navigation behaviors differ? If so, how?

- Think about the use of a robot in various daily situations (e.g., at home, at the office, and on a crowded train). Now, think about how you need to adapt the spatial-navigation behavior of the robot to fit each of these contexts. What would be important factors to consider in these different contexts?

5.4 Exercises

The answers to these questions are available in the Appendix.

* Exercise 5.1 Formations Group spatial dynamics, as shown in the accompanying diagram, were described by Adam Kendon (1990) as the "facing formation," or "F-formation." For this question, associate the four images (a, b, c, d) with their formation names.

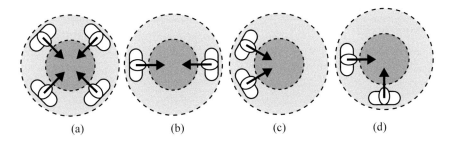

    (a)   (b)   (c)   (d)

1. Circular formation: _____
2. L-formation: _____
3. Face to face: _____
4. Side by side: _____

** Exercise 5.2 What is the typical maximum distance for social space?

** Exercise 5.3 What is the typical maximum distance for personal space?

** Exercise 5.4 What is the typical maximum distance for intimate space?

** Exercise 5.5 What is the typical minimum distance for public space?

*** Exercise 5.6 Spatial navigation Robots are physically embodied, so they not only take up space but also need to be able to navigate it appropriately along with humans in everyday interaction. Based on your own experiences with spatial interaction, as well as the chapter you just read, imagine how you would design a "socially intelligent" Roomba-like vacuum cleaner. What might this mobile robot need to know, and how should it adapt its behavior to socially navigate the context of your home? What kinds of actors, activities, social norms, preferences, and so forth would it need to be aware of? What aspects of its behavior should it adapt to fit the context? Now consider a similar robot outside the home, for example, a food delivery robot that drives on city streets. What kinds of spatial knowledge and behavioral adaptations does this robot need to make so as not to inconvenience passersby and to be able to comfortably approach the person it is trying to make a delivery to?

Future reading:

Textbook to learn basic techniques for robot navigation.

- Choset, Howie M., Hutchinson, Seth, Lynch, Kevin M., Kantor, George, Burgard, Wolfram, Kavraki, Lydia E., and Thrun, Sebastian. *Principles of Robot Motion: Theory, Algorithms, and Implementation.* MIT Press, Cambridge, MA, 2005. ISBN 978-026203327. URL http://worldcat.org/oclc/762070740

More reading about space-related studies in HRI:

- Kruse, Thibault, Pandey, Amit Kumar, Alami, Rachid, and Kirsch, Alexandra. Human-aware robot navigation: A survey. *Robotics and Autonomous Systems*, 61(12):1726–1743, 2013. doi: 10.1016/j.robot.2013.05.007. URL https://doi.org/10.1016/j.robot.2013.05.007
- Mumm, Jonathan and Mutlu, Bilge. Human-robot proxemics: Physical and psychological distancing in human-robot interaction. In *Proceedings of the 2011 ACM/IEEE International Conference on Human-Robot Interaction*, pages 331–338. Association for Computing Machinery, New York, 2011. ISBN 978-1-4503-0561-7. doi: 10.1145/1957656.1957786. URL https://dl.acm.org/citation.cfm?doid=1957656.1957786
- Satake, Satoru, Kanda, Takayuki, Glas, Dylan F., Imai, Michita, Ishiguro, Hiroshi, and Hagita, Norihiro. How to approach humans? Strategies for social robots to initiate interaction. In *4th ACM/IEEE International Conference on Human-Robot Interaction*, pages 109–116. Association for Computing Machinery, New York, 2009. ISBN 978-1-60558-404-1. doi: 10.1145/1514095.1514117. URL https://doi.org/10.1145/1514095.1514117
- Walters, Michael L., Dautenhahn, Kerstin, Te Boekhorst, René, Koay, Kheng Lee, Syrdal, Dag Sverre, and Nehaniv, Chrystopher L. An empirical framework for human-robot proxemics. *Proceedings of New Frontiers in Human-Robot Interaction*, 2009. URL http://hdl.handle.net/2299/9670

6

Nonverbal Interaction

What is covered in this chapter:

- The role of nonverbal communication in interactions between people—how communication is enhanced by facial expressions, hand gestures, body posture, and sounds.
- The importance of interpreting, using, and responding to nonverbal cues in the appropriate way, both to successful human–robot interactions and to generate a positive perception of robots.
- Nonverbal communication channels that are unique to robots, as well as channels that replicate those commonly used by humans.
- How robotic sounds, lights, and colors or physical gestures with arms, legs, tails, ears, and other body parts can be effective for communicating with people.

When we think of what it means to communicate with someone face to face, the first thing that comes to mind is often the content of our speech—what we are saying to each other—rather than the manner in which such content is delivered. Just for a minute, though, imagine speaking face to face with someone without the ability to look at the person or use gestures. Not only would you be uncomfortable, but you might also have difficulty getting the intended meaning across. Moreover, without the nonverbal "channel," it seems harder to establish a strong connection with the person, particularly when you communicate with a stranger.

This chapter covers this unspoken (i.e., nonverbal) component of our social interactions, both with other humans and specifically with robots. Section 6.1 highlights the different functions that nonverbal communication plays. Section 6.2 dives deeper into the different kinds of nonverbal behavior, such as gaze and mimicry. Finally, Section 6.3 explicitly focuses on how robots can read and generate nonverbal behavior.

As shown in the previous example, people constantly and seemingly automatically give off and pick up on a variety of nonverbal cues while interacting. These cues are used to interpret the nuances of meaning, emotion, and intention in others. Nonverbal cues are such an important aspect of human communication that being unable to produce and decipher them appropriately makes interaction quite challenging. Anyone may experience a sense of bewilderment when they go to another country—we may find it difficult to summon the waiter to give us the bill or might struggle to read another person's face in order to understand what he or she is feeling. The importance of nonverbal cues is acutely experienced by people with disorders such as autism, who have difficulty noticing and interpreting nonverbal social cues in others. On the other hand, being sensitive to nonverbal cues can improve one's understanding of an interaction. For example, researchers who have used "social sensors" to measure aspects of nonverbal behavior, such as gaze and rhythmicity, can predict which people will exchange cards at a conference (Pentland and Heibeck, 2010) or which couples will break up within a six-year period, based on thin slices of nonverbal behavior (Carrere and Gottman, 1999).

Even in the earliest social robot designs, nonverbal cues that are present in human interaction have been actively used to enrich interactions with the robot. They are typically used in combination with speech to provide supplemental information on the robot's internal state or intentions. Kismet, one of the first social robots (see Figure 2.4), used postural cues, such as pulling back or leaning forward, to express affect and engage people in interaction (Breazeal, 2003). Keepon, a minimalist social robot (see Figures 2.7 and 4.8), uses gaze and reactive motion to express attention and affect (Kozima et al., 2009). Many robots are also capable of engaging in joint attention to signal engagement with the user and a shared task. Next, we discuss the functions and types of nonverbal cues and their uses in human–robot interaction (HRI).

6.1 Functions of nonverbal cues in interaction

Nonverbal cues allow people to communicate important information "between the lines." They add a further layer of information to human (and human–robot) interaction, adding to what is being communicated linguistically. Through nonverbal communication, people can signal mutual understanding, shared goals, and common ground. They can communicate thoughts, emotions, and attention. And they can do so in a more subtle, indirect manner than through verbal expression.

In psychology, nonverbal communicative cues, such as eye gaze, body posture, or facial muscle activity, are often studied as implicit indicators of affect toward a person or an object. Many of the nonverbal signals we convey are expressed automatically without much thought or even entirely unconsciously. Therefore, nonverbal cues are often believed to be unfiltered and more genuine, revealing people's "true" attitudes. For instance, your body language can communicate a message very different from your speech. Think of an acquaintance you do not like very much. Although you might greet this person in a friendly manner and start a seemingly amicable chat, your nonverbal cues might give away your true feelings. You might look at the person more briefly, frown rather than smile, and avoid physical contact while not even being aware that your nonverbal cues are incongruent with your verbal chitchat.

Nonverbal cues are equally important for HRI. Nonverbal cues produced by people when interacting with a robot can indicate whether a person is enjoying the interaction and whether the person likes the robot or not. They can therefore act as a measure or cue of attitude or engagement and be used to guide the robot's behavior. Even in the HRI context, verbal and nonverbal cues might be contradictory. For example, people may verbally express positive ideas about a robot while the nonverbal cues suggest they are tense or anxious while interacting with it. HRI may also be affected by the way robots produce nonverbal cues. For example, an interaction can appear awkward when the robot produces gestures that do not match the rhythm or meaning of its speech or when it does not respond appropriately to people's nonverbal cues. Early research on HRI focused mainly on speech as the most obvious mode of communication for robots, but researchers now agree that nonverbal cues are central to HRI, and their implementation is widely accepted as a prerequisite for smooth and successful interaction between humans and robots. To illustrate, think of human eye gaze during a conversation. Eye gaze occurs automatically, without much thought, but at the same time, it signals shared attention—that both people are talking about the same thing—and acknowledges the conversation partner. When speaking to a robot, we would expect the robot to turn its head toward us and make eye contact with us, showing that it is attending to what we say. A robot that displays such nonverbal behavior will make the interaction seem more natural and smooth. Conversely, we notice immediately when some of this "social glue" is absent—we can sense that something is going wrong, even though it might be difficult to pinpoint exactly what is missing. When the robot stares straight ahead and does not acknowledge our presence or spoken requests, the interaction breaks down.

As with all information, nonverbal communication always occurs in a specific context, which renders the respective nonverbal signals appropriate or not. This context may be restricted by specific social and cultural norms. For example, in Western societies, people shake hands to greet each other formally, whereas a respectful greeting in Japan is performed by bowing. Even the degree to which one person bows to another signals social status and hierarchy. This might be almost imperceptible to the naive observer, but it is immediately obvious to those who understand the relevant cultural norms. Similarly, a conversation with a person from a Western society would naturally include continuous eye contact or even physical touch. However, this might be interpreted as threatening or rude in another cultural context. Such social and cultural differences are being taken up in recent HRI research on designing culturally sensitive interactions, such as investigating the importance of nonverbal cues for the cross-cultural deployment of social robots. For example, researchers from the United Kingdom and Japan have worked together to develop culturally competent care robots, a task that involves developing cultural knowledge representations, culturally sensitive planning and execution, and culturally appropriate multimodal HRI (Bruno et al., 2017). Designing HRI that meets social norms and cultural expectations might mean

Figure 6.1
Culturally
appropriate
nonverbal cues can
make
communication
between people and
robots more natural
and pleasant.

the difference between a successful product and a wasted investment (see Figure 6.1).

6.2 Types of nonverbal interaction

Although we exhibit and experience nonverbal cues in several modalities at once—such as sound, movement, and gaze—it might be worthwhile to consider each channel of communication separately when trying to implement nonverbal signals into HRI. Understanding the functions and effects of various nonverbal cues allows us to then combine them as needed for different tasks and effects in HRI.

6.2.1 Gaze and eye movement

Imagine you are conducting a job interview, and the job candidate responds to your inquiries without looking at you, staring only at the desk in front of them. Even while you are sketching a graph on the whiteboard, the job candidate does not follow your gaze toward what you are drawing. Would you hire the person? Probably not, because this type of gaze behavior would likely come across as a lack of interest in you and what you are talking about.

Gaze is a subtle and important cue for managing social interaction. Gaze signals interest, understanding, attention, and people's ability and willingness to follow the conversation. Beyond their social function, gaze and eye movements also facilitate functional interactions and collaboration, such as handing an object to someone or calling someone's attention to the next tool needed in a task. Eye-tracking technology can be used to assess gaze patterns and provide insights into information processing and human cognition. Pragmatically, analyzing gaze patterns can also help to ensure that a given task has been completed smoothly. Gaze can also be a way of soliciting and keeping another person's attention during an interaction. For instance, gaze can be a way to manage turn-taking in interactions; by looking from one person to another, the speaker might suggest whose turn it is to speak next.

A particularly well-established component of gaze behavior in human interaction is joint attention. *Joint attention* refers to interaction partners attending to the same area or object at the same time. The significance of this behavior for human development starts in early childhood, when joint attention is a major scaffold for learning. The ability to attend to the same object at the same time with an adult caregiver is an important prerequisite for infants' ability to learn new words and behaviors (Yu and Smith, 2013), whereas the inability to perform joint attention can lead to developmental difficulties (Charman et al., 2000). Joint attention in adult communication can also signify interest and deep involvement in the interaction and is important for collaborative tasks where actors need to coordinate their activities. To achieve joint attention, the timing and synchrony of gaze behavior are important aspects to consider.

The eyes are a window to the soul, or in this case, they unconsciously reveal how much you like your interaction partner. Pupil dilation is controlled by the autonomic nervous system, as are uncontrollable reactions such as an increase in heart rate or goose bumps. When people see physically attractive others, their pupils automatically dilate. This also works the other way: people judge faces with larger pupils as more attractive than those with more visible irises. Pupil dilation can be used on robots to give the impression that the robot is attracted to the user (see Figure 6.2).

Figure 6.2 Pupils signal attraction, even in robots.

Joint attention has been incorporated into HRI in several ways: Imai et al. (2003) used it as a way of scaffolding smoother communication with people so that they know what the robot is talking about, both in conjunction with and without speech. Joint attention has also been studied as a fundamental capability of robots that want to learn from humans, particularly humanoid robots (Scassellati, 1999). Finally, joint attention with robots has been studied in interactions with children who have autism, with the aim of using the robot to assist them in developing this important social skill.

When used in HRI, robot gaze cues most often produce similar effects as they would in human interactions. This may be because researchers have used human gaze behavior to derive models of gaze behavior for robots, and they have shown that the resulting gaze cues can be used to lead people to take on different conversational roles as addressees, bystanders, or nonparticipants (Mutlu et al., 2012). In a multiparty interaction, a robot can use its gaze to control who will be the next person to talk (Mutlu et al., 2009). Andrist et al. (2014) used face-tracking movements to engage in mutual gaze and purposeful gaze aversions in an HRI study to show that such cues can make a robot seem more intentional and thoughtful. Mutlu et al. (2006) also showed that a robot's gaze cues, modeled on those of humans, used in the course of telling a story affected how well people remembered the story's content; the people with whom the robot kept gaze contact could recall more details from its story. Robot gaze can therefore be a powerful way to manage interactions with one or more people (see Figure 6.3).

6.2.2 Gesture

Following speech, gesturing is perhaps the most apparent way of providing information during an interaction. Gestures can function in place of or along with speech and are often categorized based on their role in communication. Deictic gestures involve pointing to specific things in the environment and can be important for establishing joint attention. Iconic gestures often go along with speech, further supporting and illustrating what is being said. For example, opening your arms wide while saying you are holding a big ball would be an iconic gesture, as would smoothly moving your hand upward

Figure 6.3 The eyes of robots are often designed to pitch and yaw, allowing a robot to use gaze as an effective communication channel. Here, iCub (2004–present) gives a good impression of attending to the ball in its left hand.

Figure 6.4 A Pepper (2014–present) robot using hand gestures to accompany its speech. Without these automatically generated beat gestures, the robot's speech would appear less natural. (Source: Pepper robot by SoftBank Robotics)

while explaining how your airplane took off. Symbolic gestures, such as waving hello or goodbye, can carry their own meaning, with or without accompanying speech. Finally, beat gestures are used to go along with the rhythm of speech and look like moving one's arms while speaking as if conducting an invisible orchestra (see Figure 6.4). Gestures can also be used for emphasizing particular moments during speech, such as lifting your hands up while saying "what?" when you are surprised by something.

Gestures are likewise a powerful way of enhancing spoken communication in HRI. A robot may be designed to gesture through its arms and hands or other body parts, such as its head, ears, or tail. The shape, timing, naturalness, and smoothness of gestures can also affect people's perceptions and understanding (Bremner et al., 2009). Salem et al. (2013) showed that including gestures along with speech in HRI led to the ASIMO humanoid robot being perceived as more anthropomorphic and likable, with participants expressing greater willingness to interact with the robot later on than when the robot communicated through speech alone. Interestingly, this study also showed that the use of gestures performed incongruently with speech led to even more pronounced positive effects in evaluations of the robot, although it had a negative effect on task performance. Gestures should therefore be used carefully in the design of robots, and their effects should be tested in studies with humans to gauge their effects on specific interactions.

The generation of co-speech gestures for artificial agents, such as online characters or robots, is now largely done through machine learning. Gesture-generation software is trained by feeding it hundreds of hours of video recordings of people talking, allowing machine learning to build a model that generates gestures that closely fit spoken communication. For now, these models will not always generate a gesture that fits the meaning of what is being said, but the dynamics of gestures themselves are virtually indistinguishable from human co-speech gestures (Yoon et al., 2022).

6.2.3 Mimicry and imitation

Another aspect of nonverbal interaction that has been given much attention in the human-interaction literature is mimicry and imitation. By *mimicry*, we mean the unconscious replication of the behavior of another person, and by *imitation*, we mean the conscious replication of another's behavior (Genschow et al., 2017). Mimicry and imitation are performed not only by humans but also by primates (hence the notion of "aping someone") and are considered basic social capabilities. Mimicry is so central to human cognition that it has been found to have a neurological basis. The *mirror neuron system* in the primate brain contains clusters of mirror neurons (Rizzolatti and Craighero, 2004). These neurons fire both when observing someone doing an action you also know how to do, such as picking up a grape, or when you are doing that action yourself, and they are believed to be responsible for facial mimicry, the unconscious and automatic mimicking of the facial expressions of others Rymarczyk et al. (2018).

> Researchers in Japan found a band of macaques that all wash their sweet potatoes in a stream. This behavior was traced to a female member of the troop, who may have initially done this once by accident, and then others copied her when they realized that washing the potatoes produced a less gritty and more pleasing meal, so they continued the practice. Observations of this kind have led to the claim that animals, not only humans, have "culture" (Whiten et al., 1999; De Waal, 2001).

In humans, mimicry and imitation have multiple developmental functions. In early childhood development, mimicry and imitation provide a common way to learn new behaviors and culturally relevant social norms. Children use mimicry to learn to do things in particular ways—such as talking with a British accent or making expressions similar to those of a family member. As adults, we can also use imitation to blend into our social and cultural surroundings, such as gesturing more emphatically when we are speaking Italian or visiting

Italy. As such, imitation and mimicry can be important ways of developing signs of in-group identity.

Mimicry, as a largely automatic behavioral response, also has many significant social functions; one is that it indirectly signals positive affect and liking for an interaction partner. If two people use the same gestures or adopt the same postures during a conversation, it is usually because they have established a positive relation in that interaction. Similarly, when people's nonverbal cues are out of sync and not mirroring each other, you can sense that the communication is not running smoothly. Mimicry, as a subtle nonverbal cue, can thus be a helpful signal to interpret, for instance, in the context of dating or job interviews.

> Mimicry's significance in establishing a social relationship with another person makes it possible for its manipulation to function as a tool for persuasion. In studies of the "chameleon effect," Chartrand and Bargh (1999) found that subtle mimicry of a person's gestures and posture can help that person persuade an interaction partner to agree with his or her suggestions. For example, if you sit with your right leg crossed over your left, and your interaction partner subtly adopts that position, too, before telling you that Candy A tastes better than Candy B, you are more likely to choose to try Candy A over Candy B than if the person had not mimicked your posture (see Figure 6.5). However, this effect is time dependent. If you notice your conversation partner mimicking you, either because they are too obvious about it or too late in their timing, their intentions will backfire because you may see them as manipulative or insincere.

Various aspects of imitation and mimicry have been implemented and evaluated in the design of robots. There is a large and growing collection

Figure 6.5 Similar to a chameleon adjusting its color to the environment, the *chameleon effect* refers to mimicking a person's gestures or facial expressions.

of literature on robot learning by imitation, in which robots in some way record and then reproduce actions performed by humans (Argall et al., 2009; Mostafaoui et al., 2022). Riek et al. (2010) developed an apelike robot that mimicked users' head gestures, and their findings suggest this made a positive contribution to people's interactions with the robot, although these gestures were not always clear to participants.

If we combine what we know about mimicry (see Section 6.2.3) and posture (which will be discussed shortly, in Section 6.2.5) from human psychology, we can design robots that are able to display certain types of behaviors (e.g., leaning in) to affect how people behave and, therefore, how they feel. For example, Wills et al. (2016) showed that a robot that mimicked people's facial expressions and displayed socially contingent head poses received more monetary donations than a robot that did not display such behavior. Imitation and mimicry can therefore be used as both conscious and unconscious social cues in HRI to improve interaction and persuade people to follow the robot's suggestions.

6.2.4 Touch

Touch is a nonverbal cue that is often involved in close interactions among people, such as those between friends or between caregivers and patients. We often use touch deliberately, for example, to calm down someone who is agitated or to console someone who is sad. We also often incidentally touch people we feel attracted to or whom we like. It turns out that these people often also like us more when this happens. Both deliberate and incidental touch can therefore have beneficial effects, particularly when the interaction partners are part of the same social group. It is important, however, to know when and how it is appropriate to touch someone.

In everyday life, touch is sometimes used deliberately to achieve a goal. According to the so-called Midas effect, waiters and waitresses get a higher tip if they happen to incidentally touch their customers before they pay for their meal (Crusco and Wetzel, 1984). Touch does not always have positive effects, however, particularly when people who identify with different social groups are interacting with each other. In this case, touch may even lead to more negative feelings about the interaction partner. Incidental touch has also been shown to lead to a reduction in more indirect, but not direct, forms of prejudice against an out-group (Seger et al., 2014). Results on the effects of touch between human groups are therefore mixed, and it is interesting to consider what role touch might play in interactions between humans and robots, which may represent a new social group in the society of the future.

Physical interaction with robots is relatively uncommon for a number of reasons. One significant issue is the lack of safety during haptic interactions, with simple actions like hugging, holding, or shaking hands already forming a safety concern. Despite the fact that many robots are explicitly designed for HRI, tactile or haptic interaction has in many cases been an afterthought. For example, Aldebaran Robotics' Nao and Pepper robots, while widely sold as

Figure 6.6 Telenoid (2010–2013) is a haptic robot that is designed to be hugged. Studies on whether this is a form of interaction people are comfortable with are ongoing. (Source: Hiroshi Ishiguro)

Figure 6.7 The Haptic Creature (2005–2013) was designed by Steve Yohanan to study the role of affective touch in social HRI. (Source: Steve Yohanan)

commercial social robots, both have pinch points under the arms and near the hips that can painfully trap fingers. Only a limited number of robots are explicitly designed to allow physical human–robot interactions (see Figure 6.6), with most robots prone to suffer breakage when being manipulated or handled with forces that would not be uncommon in interactions between people.

The few studies on touch in HRI that are available in the literature demonstrate the need for more empirical work on this nonverbal cue (Van Erp and Toet, 2013; Willemse et al., 2016). On the positive side, tactile interaction with animal-like robots, such as Paro or the Haptic Creature (Figure 6.7), show that people can feel less stressed and anxious when they initiate such interactions (Shibata, 2012; Yohanan and MacLean, 2012). Chen et al. (2014) showed that people did not mind being touched by a robot in a nursing scenario, but they evaluated functional touch (e.g., to clean their arm) more positively than affective touch (e.g., to comfort them). In contrast, a recent study by Wullenkord et al. (2016) explored the negative consequences of touch in an interaction with the robot Nao. Participants reported their attitudes toward a Nao robot, then had to touch the robot as part of a task. After the task, they reported their attitudes and social judgments about the robot again. Overall, contact improved the participants' attitudes, such that people expressed more positive and less negative attitudes after the touch interaction as compared to one without touch. However, people who had particularly negative emotions toward robots at the onset of the study experienced the opposite effect and had more negative perceptions after they touched the robot.

Touch is an integral part of natural human–robot interactions, for example, in functional tasks such as object handovers and manipulation and in social tasks such as a handshake for greeting. In both functional and social uses, we need to keep in mind the psychological implications of incidental or deliberate touch, whether it is being touched by a robot or having to touch a robot.

6.2.5 Posture and movement

People also communicate through their full-body posture and the way in which they move. Along with facial expressions, postures can be used to signal a person's emotional state. Slow movements, drooping shoulders, and lethargic gestures all suggest a downcast state of mind, whereas fast movements and an upright bearing are signs of a positive attitude. These types of postural cues are particularly important when a person's face is not visible, but they can also provide additional cues to a person's state of mind even when we can see the person's facial expression. Researchers have found that people can interpret these types of nonverbal cues not only when they see the whole body of the person but also in minimalist light dot displays that depict a person's movements (Alaerts et al., 2011).

The way we pose can signal attention, engagement, and attraction in an interaction between humans. People might be displaying a defensive posture by holding their arms in front of them, whereas open arms are a clear invitation for engagement, perhaps even a hug. How we are posed in relation to other people can also provide valuable information; if two people are sitting with their knees toward each other, it shows willing engagement, whereas if one person is turned partly away from the other, it can show a desire to discontinue the interaction.

The Thrifty Faucet (2009) is a simple interactive prototype that uses its posture to communicate 15 lifelike motion patterns, including seeking, curiosity, and rejection, to users. The aim is to enable communication with users about more sustainable water use (Togler et al., 2009).

(Source: Jonas Togler)

Bodily postures can provide an additional layer of expressiveness to robots (see Figure 6.8). To illustrate, when a robot lacks expressive facial features, the body can be used as the primary way to communicate emotions. Beck et al. (2010) showed that affective body postures can improve people's understanding of a robot's emotional state. A robot's posture can be used to express emotion and, through that, affect the emotions of onlookers. Xu et al. (2014) showed that people were not only able to interpret the affective body postures of robots but also that they adopted the emotions they thought the robots were showing.

Robot designers have furthermore realized that micromovements, barely perceptible motions, can convey the impression that the robot is lifelike (Yamaoka et al., 2005; Ishiguro, 2007; Sakamoto et al., 2007). These micromovements are often implemented as small, random perturbations to the robot's actuators. Such lifelike animations can also be used to signal the robot's

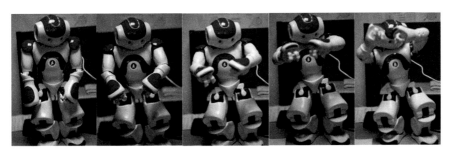

Figure 6.8 A Nao robot (2008–present) using body postures to express emotions, morphing between sad (left) and fearful (right). (Source: Beck et al. (2010))

internal state; for example, the velocity or amplitude of the motion signals the excitement level of the robot (Belpaeme et al., 2012). This approach has been successfully used on petlike small robots (Cooney et al., 2014; Singh and Young, 2012).

6.2.6 Interaction rhythm and timing

The temporal nature, or "timing," of communicative cues carries its own significance in interaction. In verbal communication, we refer to this as *turn-taking* among interaction partners. Nonverbal cues (e.g., gaze, gesture) can support this turn-taking by guiding attention to the appropriate interaction partner or signifying the end of a turn. Establishing synchronized temporal patterns of interaction can further scaffold the communicative and collaborative success of an interaction.

The "rhythmicity" and "synchrony" of an interaction provide a largely unconscious but crucial component of human communication. To understand what we mean by interaction rhythms, think about human interaction as a coupled system working together. In order for two people to be able to communicate and work effectively, they need to become "rhythmically entrained" to each other's actions—to be doing things not necessarily at the same time but to the same beat. Like in dance, rhythmicity enables people to be more attuned to each other's communicative cues, to be looking, speaking, and moving at the right time to enable clear and smooth communication among the two partners (Warner et al., 1987). Although often unconscious, the effects of rhythmicity on interaction are significant: being out of synchrony can imply that interaction partners have missed important social signals and are therefore unable to interpret each other's behavior; it can also lead to a more negative interaction outcome and a less positive attitude toward the other person.

Michalowski et al. (2007) showed that a robot that is rhythmically entrained with a human interaction partner is considered more lifelike than a robot that is behaving rhythmically but is not synced with the human. They also showed that people are more likely to interact for a longer time with a rhythmically entrained dancing robot. Rhythmicity in interaction can also be useful in supporting turn-taking and collaboration in teams, including anticipation of people's behaviors and when they will show those behaviors (Hoffman and Breazeal, 2007). Finally, Siu et al. (2010) showed that listening to highly rhythmic music while performing robotic surgery can improve the performance of the human–robot surgical team. These findings suggest that rhythmicity in HRI can improve both the perceived quality of the interaction and the chances of a successful outcome.

6.3 Nonverbal interaction in robots

6.3.1 Robot perception of nonverbal cues

Standard pattern-recognition techniques are used to allow robots to perceive and identify human nonverbal cues. Posture and gesture recognition are well studied. Typical systems use cameras, depth cameras, or sensors carried by the user to record a time series of data. Although software could be written to recognize a limited number of gestures, instead it is common to use machine learning to train the system to recognize gestures and other nonverbal cues. To achieve this, a database is collected of, for example, people showing different gestures. Typically, thousands or even millions of data points are needed, and each needs to be labeled, meaning that for each data point, we need to note what it is showing. Is it a person waving, pointing, or beckoning? Next, a classifier is trained on the labeled data; this is often an iterative process in which the classifier's performance improves when more data are processed. Once the performance is sufficient for the application, the classifier is deployed on the robot (Mitra and Acharya, 2007).

These basic perception techniques are used to allow HRI researchers to evaluate whether people are actually engaged in interactions with robots. Unlike typical human interaction, where it is expected that the human partner will be attentive and engaged, in HRI, users sometimes do not attend to what the robot says and signals. Thus, perceiving the "engagement" of users is a crucial step for enabling robots to create a successful interaction. Rich et al. (2010) developed a technique to integrate the detection of cues such as eye contact and back-channeling to identify whether a user is engaged in interaction. Sanghvi et al. (2011) analyzed affective postures and body motion to detect engagement with a robotic game companion.

Although the constant advancement of technology allows for the improvement of robotic perception capabilities, researchers also add special equipment to the robot, such as eye trackers and motion-capture systems, to provide data on nonverbal cues relevant for interaction. For tactile interaction, there has been some research in the robotics field in which film-type piezoelectric polymer sensors were inserted in thin and thick silicone rubber (Taichi et al., 2006) or where flexible capacitive sensors or skin with nano hairs is added to the robot's body to allow the detection of tactile events with high sensitivity and high temporal and spatial resolution (Yogeswaran et al., 2015).

6.3.2 Generating nonverbal cues in robots

Generating gestures and other nonverbal cues is not trivial in robots. The nonverbal cues need to be contingent on the interaction: if the user snaps her fingers, the robot needs to blink immediately. Nonverbal cues also need to be coordinated with each other and with other cues, including verbal interaction, in terms of both the semantic meaning and the timing of execution. HRI poses particular challenges for the perception and generation of nonverbal cues because all this has to be done in real-time.

An important aspect of HRI design is generating nonverbal behaviors for robots that appropriately accompany speech. This is often inspired by the way humans use nonverbal cues in dialogue. Kanda et al.'s (2007a) robot system automatically generates nonverbal cues, such as nodding and synchronous arm motions, to exhibit its attentional state to the user in correspondence to the user's arm gestures. Co-speech gesturing—the use of hand, arm, and body gestures that coincide with and match the spoken communication of the robot—has seen good progress in recent years. The best generation methods currently are training on human data. Machine learning methods, often using deep neural networks, are used to learn from hundreds of hours of video recordings of people talking and gesticulating. These methods are now able to generate natural-looking co-speech gestures, with the semantics of gestures—the match between what is being said and what is being expressed by the robot's body—still being a work in progress (Yoon et al., 2022).

Animation framework The most simple and most frequently used approach is to generate motions with an animation framework. That is, a robot designer will typically control each of the joint angles of a robot to set a posture for it; this is called a *key frame*. After the designer prepares multiple key frames, the system interpolates the postures between them and generates smooth motions for the robot.

This requires extensive effort by the designer. Graphical user interfaces (GUIs) are often used to reduce the amount of effort in motion design. The commercial robots Nao and Pepper come with a GUI called Choregraphe, which helps designers visually display the posture of the robot and create desired motions more easily and quickly (see Figure 6.9). Lively is a GUI environment developed by Schoen et al. (2023) to generate lifelike motion for social and other robots that takes obstacles near the robot into account.

Other techniques used for animation or virtual agents can also be used for generating motions for robots. Motion-capture systems can be used to record a timed series of precise human motions, which can then be replicated in robots. Robot designers have also taken advantage of markup languages for virtual agents, such as Behavior Markup Language (BML), in which a designer can specify which gesture an agent should exhibit in combination with speech (Kopp et al., 2006).

Figure 6.9
Choregraphe is a visual editor for the Nao and Pepper robots. It contains a pose editor that allows the robot designer to efficiently generate postures and animations for the robot.

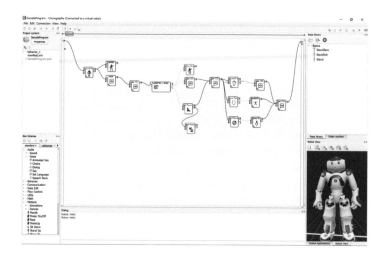

Cognitive mechanisms for robots Another approach to achieving natural behavior in robots is to endow the robot with some form of artificial cognition, which is an artificial equivalent of natural cognition. Although it is, of course, currently impossible to create robots that have the full cognitive capabilities of people, combining artificial equivalents of cognitive mechanisms has proven to be particularly effective for creating lifelike robots. So instead of hand-programming the robot's nonverbal behavior, different cognitive skills are combined, and the resulting behavior often appears natural and lifelike.

Scassellati (2000) developed an embodied cognitive architecture that takes into account salient objects, task constraints, and the attentional state of others to link the robot's perceptions of the world with high-level cognitive skills and related actions, such as joint attention, attribution of intent to others, and social learning. These mechanisms were shown to be particularly effective in the Kismet robot (Figure 2.4). Sugiyama et al. (2007) developed a cognitive mechanism for a robot to replicate human deictic interaction. This involves using pointing (deictic) gestures in reference to a term, such as "this one" or "that one," that signifies a target object the listener can identify. The details of deictic interaction can also depend on the target. For example, we would not point directly at a nearby person because it is impolite. Liu et al. (2013) developed a computational model for a robot that balances two factors, understandability and social appropriateness. It enables a robot to refrain from exhibiting impolite pointing gestures while still keeping its deictic interaction understandable.

6.4 Conclusion

This chapter highlighted the important role of nonverbal cues in communication between humans and robots. The implementation of nonverbal cues into the communicative repertoire of robots still calls for further technical advancement and refinement, particularly because nonverbal cues represent such subtle aspects of communication. Existing research illustrates the relevance of nonverbal communication in HRI while also making clear that much more work needs to be done before robots will be able to act and react in humanlike and natural ways in everyday communication with people.

Questions for you to think about:

- Still not convinced that nonverbal cues are important? Get up right now and have a conversation with someone, but do so without looking at the person's face. How did it go? How did you feel? Also, afterward, ask your communication partner what he or she thought about your behavior and how it made him or her feel.
- Think of a robot use case you are interested in. What aspect of nonverbal behavior is particularly relevant for this scenario? Would gesture or gaze be particularly helpful? How about contingency and

timing? If you need some inspiration, you can go out and observe people in a similar context and see what they do.

- Have you ever watched a video where the audio track was a fraction of a second out of sync? Or videoconferenced with someone where the audio lagged? How did that affect the interaction? How long did you think the delay was? What, if anything, did you do to manage the difficulties in the interaction?
- How would you know if a robot is using is nonverbal cues effectively? Is there a way in which you can measure the quality of nonverbal interaction? Can you measure the outcome of the interaction?

6.5 Exercises

The answers to these questions are available in the Appendix.

* Exercise 6.1 Tipping When waiters and waitresses happen to incidentally touch their customers before they pay for their meal,

1. they get a lower tip.
2. they get a bigger tip.
3. the tip amount doesn't change.

*** Exercise 6.2 Timing Timing is an important component of verbal and nonverbal interaction. Give at least two examples of problems that can emerge in relation to the role of timing in HRI. How might you solve these problems, taking into account how they are solved in other social interactions where the interactants miss out on certain social cues (e.g., texting, time delays in Skype calls, Zoom calls when you can't look at someone in a group to signify you are talking to them)?

** Exercise 6.3 True or false Decide whether the following statements are *true* or *false*:

1. Nonverbal behavior is mostly conscious.
2. Nonverbal behavior can be used to predict social outcomes, such as whether a couple will stay together.
3. Nonverbal and verbal behavior always align.
4. Nonverbal behavior is not very relevant for human–robot interactions.
5. Mimicry is an unconscious behavior, and imitation is a conscious behavior.
6. Gaze is only important for showing someone that you're listening to them.
7. Proxemics (i.e., social distance) is a part of nonverbal communication.

Future reading:

- Admoni, Henny and Scassellati, Brian. Social eye gaze in human-robot interaction: A review. *Journal of Human-Robot Interaction*, 6 (1):25–63, 2017. doi: 10.5898/JHRI.6.1.Admoni. URL https://doi.org/10.5898/JHRI.6.1.Admoni
- Breazeal, Cynthia, Kidd, Cory D., Thomaz, Andrea Lockerd, Hoffman, Guy, and Berlin, Matt. Effects of nonverbal communication on efficiency and robustness in human-robot teamwork. In *IEEE/RSJ International Conference on Intelligent Robots and Systems (IROS)*, pages 708–713. Institute of Electrical and Electronics Engineers, Piscataway, NJ, 2005. ISBN 0-7803-8912-3. doi: 10.1109/IROS.2005.1545011. URL https://doi.org/10.1109/IROS.2005.1545011
- Mavridis, Nikolaos. A review of verbal and non-verbal human–robot interactive communication. *Robotics and Autonomous Systems*, 63(1):22–35, 2015. ISSN 0921-8890. doi: 10.1016/j.robot.2014.09.031. URL https://doi.org/10.1016/j.robot.2014.09.031
- Nehaniv, Chrystopher L., Dautenhahn, Kerstin, Kubacki, Jens, Haegele, Martin, Parlitz, Christopher, and Alami, Rachid. A methodological approach relating the classification of gesture to identification of human intent in the context of human-robot interaction. In *IEEE International Workshop on Robot and Human Interactive Communication*, pages 371–377. Institute of Electrical and Electronics Engineers, Piscataway, NJ, 2005. ISBN 0780392744. doi: 10.1109/ROMAN.2005.1513807. URL https://doi.org/10.1109/ROMAN.2005.1513807
- Sidner, Candace L., Lee, Christopher, Kidd, Cory D., Lesh, Neal, and Rich, Charles. Explorations in engagement for humans and robots. *Artificial Intelligence*, 166(1–2):140–164, 2005. doi: 10.1016/j.artint.2005.03.005. URL https://doi.org/10.1016/j.artint.2005.03.005

7

Verbal Interaction

> What is covered in this chapter:
>
> - The complexities and challenges of human verbal interaction.
> - The components of speech in human and human–robot interaction (HRI).
> - The basic principles of speech recognition and its application to HRI.
> - Dialogue management systems in HRI.
> - Natural-language interaction in HRI, including the use of chatbots.

Imagine you come across a robot at your local electronics shop. It says, "Hello," as you approach and asks you what you are looking for today. You rattle off, "Oh, I don't know, maybe a camera for my daughter, some batteries, and just looking around, you know." As you await a response, there's an extended silence from the robot. Then it repeats its initial question, asking you to speak slower and closer to the robot. Is the robot broken? You approach another one of the store's robots, with similar results. Why are conversations with robots so frustrating? (This did, in fact, happen to one of the authors.)

Speech is, without a doubt, the most natural and therefore ubiquitous manner of communicating between people. Speaking and understanding speech come naturally to most of us. Speech is fast and low effort, and it can be used both in one-on-one interactions and equally to address a crowd of thousands. Hence, it is also a common mode of communication designed into robots, both in terms of the speech produced by robots and speech as input to robots. However, producing robot speech is much simpler than understanding human speech, which creates an imbalance between people's expectations and the robot's actual capabilities (see Figure 7.1). In this chapter, we describe the main components of human speech and then discuss the mechanisms by which verbal interactive capabilities can be built into robots.

Section 7.1 discusses verbal interaction solely in humans, and Section 7.2 covers the principles and state of the art in speech recognition. Moving beyond identifying the words that were spoken, Section 7.3 covers the extraction of meaning from spoken text and how this is managed in human–robot interaction (HRI), as well as human–agent interaction (i.e., chatbots). Once a sentence is not only properly heard but also understood, the robot must know when it is appropriate to answer, a problem that is discussed in Section 7.4. And finally, in Section 7.5, the production of speech is explained.

Figure 7.1 The difficulties these two Peppers in a store in Tokyo had in communicating with passersby could have been due to the noisy environment or the diverse ways in which people communicate verbally.

7.1 Human–human verbal interaction

In human communication, speech serves various functions. It is used simply to convey information, but equally importantly, it also serves to create joint attention and a shared reality through communication. In addition to being an inherent part of our nature, speech is incredibly complex and open to multiple interpretations. By a mere twist of intonation or shift in emphasis, the meaning of the same sentence can switch dramatically. For example, try to pronounce the following sentence eight times while putting emphasis on the next word each time, starting with the first word of the sentence, *she*:

She said she did not take his money.

By shifting the emphasis from one word to the next, what is inferred by the listener changes from a statement of belief (*she* said she did not take his money; apparently, someone else claimed otherwise) to disbelief (she *said* she didn't take the money, but someone actually has seen her doing it) to an accusation (she said *she* didn't take the money, but someone else did), and so on.

Verbal communication is enriched by paralinguistic information as well, such as prosody and nonverbal behavior such as gaze, gestures, and facial expressions (see Chapter 6 for a more in-depth discussion on nonverbal behavior).

7.1.1 Components of speech

An *utterances* is the smallest unit in spoken language. Spoken language typically contains pauses between utterances, and an utterance is often less grammatically correct than a written sentence would be. This can become painfully clear when we read the transcript of a random sentence from a conversation: whereas it takes no effort to understand what the person means when the person says it, the same sentence may appear incoherent when written down.

Spoken utterances can be short and consist of single words—such as *uhm*, *sure*, or *thanks*—or they can last for many minutes. Spoken language is often imperfect and has disfluencies, for example: "You know, I was, like, yeah, going to buy her, you know, something, but then I had, like, uhm, what the heck."

Words are the smallest units that we can utter to convey meaning. In turn, *phonemes* are small units of sound that make up words; *pat*, for example, consists of three phonemes, [p] [a], and [t]. Changing a single one of them will change the meaning of the word; if the [p] is changed to a [b], we have a *bat*.

Conversational fillers make up part of speech without directly relating to a specific concept. They serve to keep a conversation going. For example, people utter "uh-huh" while listening to indicate that they are attending to and following the conversation. Conversational fillers are an important part of human verbal communication because they allow listeners to signal a broad range of responses (e.g., they are paying attention, they understand what the speaker means, they are surprised at a sudden twist in the story, or they share an emotion) without disrupting the flow of conversation. Such feedback increases the efficiency of verbal communication tremendously, and it enhances the experience of a shared reality between the speaker and the listener.

7.1.2 Written text versus spoken language

Written text and spoken utterances are vastly different. Whereas people expect rather strict adherence to grammatical rules and syntax in written text, they become much more liberal when talking. Because of the unidirectional nature of written communication, a written text needs to be prepared with a certain level of precision and refinement because it cannot be adjusted while it is being delivered.

Verbal communication, on the other hand, allows for many ways in which one can clarify any misunderstandings or obscurities while delivering the message. People usually quickly detect when the interaction partner does not understand the message in the intended way, and in response, they change their speech on the fly.

Natural and humanlike communication that runs smoothly is often crucial for HRI. However, in order to build natural-language interaction, many technical prerequisites have to be in place. These include the robot's capability to transcribe speech into words, understand words by coming up with appropriate responses, and generate spoken language. The robot also often needs to be able to do this on the basis of verbal speech, which, as described previously, is more challenging than working with written text alone.

7.2 Speech recognition

Speech recognition is the recognition of spoken language by a computer and is also known as *automatic speech recognition* (ASR) or *speech-to-text* (STT). Speech recognition is a process that takes a digital recording of speech and transcribes it. Speech recognition by itself does not understand or interpret what has been said. It merely converts a recorded fragment of speech into a written representation ready for further processing. Speech recognition has been mainly developed for controlling digital devices through spoken language or for dictation applications. Because of this, there are assumptions that the speech is recorded in a relatively noise-free environment and that a directional microphone can be trained on the speaking person.

In HRI, these assumptions are often violated. When addressing a robot, the human conversation partner is often located at some distance from the robot, which has a negative impact on the quality of the recording. Signal processing and directional microphone arrays can alleviate this problem, but many robots are currently not equipped with such hardware. Due to this, the robot's microphones will also pick up sounds around the robot. Other people in the room talking, different sounds from the environment (e.g., a truck passing by outside, people walking around, or a cell phone ringing), and even mechanical noise from the robot itself all end up being recorded and provide a challenge for speech recognition. To avoid these problems, *close miking* is often used, where the user wears a lapel microphone or headset when talking to a robot.

The speech-recognition process requires a speech-recognition engine, typically software that has been trained with machine-learning techniques. These are typically trained on hundreds of thousands of hours of recorded and hand-transcribed speech, and often they can handle only one language. Some speech-recognition engines are particular and will only recognize brief commands or instructions specific to an application (e.g., recognizing spoken digits), but most engines have been trained to recognize any possible spoken sentence. There are a few free, open-source speech-recognition engines, but the best-performing ones are commercial.

To be fair to robots, humans rely on more than just auditory input when they employ their own natural speech recognition. For example, the McGurk effect (see https://youtu.be/2k8fHR9jKVM) is an auditory illusion that shows how vision influences auditory perception. In this illusion, the exact same auditory stimulus ("baa") is perceived to be a distinctly different sound (either "faa" or "baa"), depending on the shape of the speaker's mouth. The combining of different sources of sensory information (e.g., auditory and visual) into one clear experience (e.g., hearing "faa") is called *multimodal perception*. These processes are automatic and unconscious, and they help to generate a clear impression of an inherently noisy world.

Obviously, sensory input is not the only other thing we consider when taking in auditory information—if you didn't quite hear whether your friend suggested to the *peach* or to the *beach*, your knowledge of what activities you commonly undertake together will help you to deduce that you should probably grab your towel and swimwear.

7.2.1 Basic principles of speech recognition

Speech recognition requires a digital recording of speech, usually a recording of a single speaker. The recording is in the time domain. For every time step of the recording, for example, every 1/16,000th of a second, the sample contains the amplitude, or volume, of the recording. This is sufficient to replay the recording, but it is inconvenient for transcribing the speech into words. Thus, the recording is first converted to the frequency domain. This means that it now shows how strongly certain frequencies are present in the signal at each time step. Phonemes look very different in the frequency domain—for example, an *o* has a different signature than an *a* in the frequency domain—and as such, they are easier to recognize with the use of an algorithm. Figure 7.2 shows a speech recording in both the time and frequency domains.

Up until 2010, speech-recognition engines relied on rule sets extracted from the analysis of speech data. They often used Gaussian mixture models and hidden Markov models to extract phonemes, words, and sentences from a speech recording. In essence, these approaches use probabilistic models of how phonemes and words can be strung together in words and sentences. The model knows that "robot" is a more likely transcription than "lobot" and that "the robot served the man" is more likely than "the robot swerved the nan." These probabilistic models were the best solution available for decades, but they have now been replaced by deep-learning approaches, which implicitly perform a similar process using large-scale neural networks and, specifically, sequence-to-sequence models (see Section 3.8).

Figure 7.2 The speech sample "Open the pod bay doors, HAL" shown in the time and frequency domains. Speech recognition needs to transform these data into text.

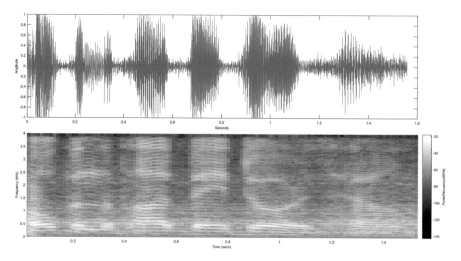

The performance of speech recognition using deep learning is spectacular compared to traditional methods. Not only has the rate of correctly recognized speech increased, but speech-recognition engines can now also increasingly deal with background noise; crowded environments; ill-formed speech; and speech from less representative people, such as children and those with a foreign accent.

Most current speech-recognition engines are cloud-based services: a voice recording is streamed to a server where powerful computers, with hardware acceleration, almost instantly transcribe the recording. Although speech recognition can run on board the robot, the quality of onboard speech recognition is typically subpar. Current speech-recognition performance is better than that of human transcribers—the word error rate (WER) for one particular test is now 1.4% (Zhang et al., 2022), with humans on average achieving 5.8%.

7.2.2 Limitations

All speech-recognition engines still struggle with recognizing atypical speech. Speakers on which the models have been insufficiently trained still provide a challenge. Also, the local dialects of languages or nonnative speakers could result in reduced recognition performance. The acoustic environment is still a determining factor. Noisy, reverberating, or crowded spaces will decrease ASR performance. Proper nouns, such as *Margaret* or *Launceston Street*, are also likely to be incorrectly picked up by speech recognition.

Constraining what needs to be recognized could increase the performance of the speech engine. To do so, most ASR engines allow the programmer to set constraints on what should be recognized, for example, digits from 0 to 10 or simple commands. Although constrained ASR can handle atypical speech with some success, the current state of the art still does not allow spoken interactions with target persons from different backgrounds.

However, it should be noted that progress is unprecedented, largely driven by new developments in machine learning that allow speech recognition to learn from hundreds of thousands of hours of unlabeled speech, such as OpenAI's Whisper system (Radford et al., 2022). By the time you read this, a single speech-recognition model may perhaps be able to transcribe multiple languages, deal with cocktail party speech, and handle foreign accents without breaking a sweat.

7.2.3 Practice in HRI

Numerous speech-recognition engines are available. Speech recognition using neural models is typically available as a remote service. These cloud-based solutions allow you to send a recorded speech fragment over the internet, and the transcribed speech is returned soon after. In addition to offering the best and most up-to-date performance, cloud-based recognition also frees up computational resources on the robot, allowing the robot to have a relatively low-cost computational core. If the nature of the application does not allow the use of cloud-based ASR—for example, because the robot does not have a reliable, always-on internet connection—there are onboard speech-recognition solutions that use a reduced neural network or first-generation approaches to speech recognition. Their performance is, however, much lower than that of the cloud-based services.

Many big software companies provide cloud-based speech-recognition services. Baidu, Google, IBM, Microsoft, Nuance, and OpenAI all offer pay-per-use cloud speech recognition. Transcribing a single speech sample is often free for low-frequency use, but costs are on the order of 1 cent per recognition event. There are a few free open-source alternatives, such as the Mozilla Foundation's Common Voice initiative, which builds an open and publicly available data set of voices to train speech-enabled applications, and its DeepSpeech recognition engine. Next to the large players, there are hundreds of small companies around the world offering tailored solutions, ranging from on-device speech recognition to speech recognition optimized for minority languages.

Speech-recognition engines generally have a simple-to-use application programming interface (API), allowing the programmer to quickly integrate speech recognition into the robot. Next to the transcribed sentence, ASR engines will often also return a confidence value for the transcribed sentence, giving a measure of how confident the engine is about the transcribed speech. Some engines will even return alternative transcriptions, again with confidence values.

It is much harder for a human to learn a new language than for a computer to do so. Still, artificial languages, such as Esperanto, have been developed to overcome some of the inherent problems with learning natural languages. These constructed languages fall into three different categories:

- Engineered languages—used for experimentation in logic, philosophy, or linguistics (e.g., Loglan, RObot Interaction LAnguage (ROILA)).
- Auxiliary languages—developed to help in the translations between natural languages or as an international medium of communication (e.g., Esperanto).
- Artistic languages—created to enrich fictional worlds (e.g., Klingon, Elfish, or Dothraki).

ROILA was developed for HRI, in particular to facilitate the problems that speech-recognition accuracy encounters (Stedeman et al., 2011). The words of this language have been designed to sound most distinct from each other, making it much easier for automated speech recognition to correctly identify the spoken words. "Go forward" in ROILA is "kanek koloke"; "go back" is "kanek nole."

7.2.4 Voice-activity detection

In some HRI applications, speech recognition is difficult because of the presence of noise, for example, because the robot is located in a crowded public space. Still, we can make a robot respond, albeit in a somewhat limited way, to people talking to the robot by using voice-activity detection (VAD).

VAD is often part of ASR, and it distinguishes speech from silence as well as other acoustic events. There is VAD software that can, for example, tell the difference between music playing and someone talking.

In HRI, VAD is used to give the user the impression that the robot is listening and can be used to implement spoken language turn-taking without actual recognition or understanding of the user's speech. In recent years, deep learning has also improved VAD performance. The free OpenSmile software package (Eyben et al., 2013) is currently leading in terms of performance. In combination with sound-source localization, whereby two or more microphones are used to pick up where a sound is coming from, we can even let the robot look at who is speaking.

7.3 Interacting using language

A common misconception is that speech recognition also means that the speech is "understood" by the computer. This is not the case (see Figure 7.3). Extracting semantic content from transcribed language is often seen as a separate problem, and various approaches exist that all try to extract meaning from text, from broad semantic content to very specific content instructions.

7.3.1 Extracting meaning from text

Sentiment analysis, which matured as a way to analyze messages on social media, can be used to extract the affect contained in a bit of text or in a spoken utterance. Sentiment-analysis software often returns a scalar value denoting how negative or positive a message is. Although sentiment analysis is optimized for written language, in spoken language, we also have access to the way in which a message is delivered. Prosody and amplitude give us insight into the affect of the message: you do not need to speak the language to hear that the speaker is happy or agitated. Much in the same way, sentiment

Figure 7.3 It will likely take many years before artificial intelligence can successfully detect sarcasm. (Source: XKCD)

analysis and emotion from speech can roughly classify the affective state of the speaker.

More advanced methods will try to understand what the user wants, a process known as *intent recognition*. This is often combined with picking out elements from the text, such as a command, location, person, event, or date, allowing the software to respond appropriately. These methods are mostly used in digital assistants "Remind me to pick up the kids at 7 p.m. is interpreted as a command to set a reminder at the time of 7 p.m. for the "pick up the kids" event. Those who frequently use digital assistants that extract information soon learn to conform to delivering information in ways that the computer can understand, and they settle on a manner of speaking that helps the computer perform satisfactorily.

Often, words or text are converted to a series of hundreds of numbers, something we call a *vector*. For this, we use neural networks, such as word2vec, that learn associations between words by analyzing the co-occurrence of words and phrases in large amounts of text. Words that are similar in meaning will have vectors that are closer together, as judged by a distance metric. For example, the vectors for *queen* and *king* will be closer than the vectors for *queen* and *radiator*. As such, these vectors encode semantic and syntactic relationships between words. In recent years, the neural-network approach to converting words into vector embeddings has been largely superseded by large language models (LLMs).

7.3.2 Large language models

Language models are an artificial intelligence (AI) technique that, in essence, have been built to do one thing only: predict an unknown word based on the words around it (or even the words just preceding the unknown word). The elegance of this approach lies not only in the simplicity of the task but also in the fact that training data are widely available on the internet. Large corpora of text, such as the full content of Wikipedia, are used to build such models. Although it was known that the structure of language, to a certain extent, encoded semantics, it came as somewhat of a surprise around 2020 that so much meaning lay hidden in the co-occurrence of words. Ever larger language models, relying on new machine-learning technology—such as transformers—and having billions of parameters, went from being amusing curiosities that could only interest machine-learning enthusiasts to technology that took the world by storm. LLMs will, in a matter of seconds, write flowing prose; compose poetry; and respond to questions about the population and size of New Zealand, quantum computing, HRI, and even how to measure "trust" in HRI. (You should not, however, unconditionally accept what an LLM tells you—as explained on p. 46, these models do not actually understand the text they generate and therefore cannot evaluate whether it is correct or complete. Better to check a reputable source, such as this book.)

But let us first return to extracting meaning from text. The most performant approaches to *intent recognition* are now based on language models. The basic idea is to apply transfer learning to a language model. Transfer learning was first shown to work well in visual tasks: here, a neural network is first trained, at great expense—in terms of time, the amount of data needed, and the energy consumed to power the computers doing the training—to classify images drawn from a huge training set. Once a network is trained, it can be repurposed for other more specific visual tasks, such as recognizing bird species, a process called *transfer learning*. LLMs, such as BERT or GPT, are trained on huge data sets of text. The training in transfer learning uses a smaller set of training data, often to do something domain specific, such as predicting the next word in book reviews. Finally, a fine-tuning step, again using training data containing many thousands of examples of sentences and *intents*, is used to turn the "next word" guessing model into a classifier. For instance, imagine a situation where we want to distinguish between offering help and complaining. For intent recognition, we would train a classifier with examples like "May I help you?" and "Need help?" for the first intent and "May I ask you to move out of my way?" and "Go away" for the second. There will be a fair bit of overlap of words and syntax between the two intents, but the language model will be able to distinguish the semantics of the two intents. After training, when the classifier is given a sentence such as "Any assistance?" (even if this sentence or the words it contains have not been encountered during transfer training), the model will recognize it as a request for help.

Intent recognition using LLMs now powers text-based assistants and call center AI, and it offers a robust, albeit limited, natural-language point of entry to these systems. For HRI, however, LLMs leave something to be desired. Although for some applications—such as a receptionist robot that responds to simple requests—intent recognition might suffice, most applications would be looking for a more fluent and interactive two-way conversation between a person and a robot. This is where dialogue management and chatbots come in.

Even when people quickly realize that a robot does not understand figures of speech, they may still take some time to figure out how to phrase their message in such a way that the robot actually understands what they want. This is shown in the following dialogue that actually occurred between a human and a robot waiter, where the robot was programmed to take everything literally (Williams et al., 2018):

PARTICIPANT: Um, can I have one water?
ROBOT: Yes, that is permissible.
PARTICIPANT: Great.
ROBOT: Please tell me your order.
PARTICIPANT: Can I have one water?
ROBOT: Yes, that is permissible.
PARTICIPANT: Great, I'll take one water.

ROBOT: Thank you for sharing that interesting prediction. Please tell me your order.

PARTICIPANT: Can I order one water?

ROBOT: Yes, that is permissible.

PARTICIPANT: Okay, can you bring me one water?

ROBOT: Yes, I am able to do that.

PARTICIPANT: May you bring me one water?

ROBOT: Yes, I am able to do that.

PARTICIPANT: I would like to have one water.

ROBOT: Thank you for sharing that interesting fact. Please tell me your order.

[*16-second pause*]

PARTICIPANT: Can you bring me one water?

ROBOT: Yes, I am able to do that. Please tell me your order.

PARTICIPANT: May you please bring me one water?

ROBOT: Yes, I am able to do that.

PARTICIPANT: So can you do it?

ROBOT: Yes. Please tell me your order.

PARTICIPANT: Can you go inside and get the water for me?

ROBOT: Yes, I am able to do that. Please tell me your order.

PARTICIPANT: My order is water.

ROBOT: Okay.

[*Robot retrieves order for participant*]

7.3.3 *Dialogue management*

Dialogue management is the process that keeps a conversation, either written or spoken, flowing between a computer and a user. Key to dialogue management is that the interaction consists of several turns instead of a single instruction. A command such as "play Bob Marley" does not require dialogue management, whereas "I would like to order something" requires the agent to further explore what it is the user wants, which could result in a whole chain of back-and-forth questions on the exact nature of the order. The management of such a dialogue requires the dialogue manager (DM) to keep track of the *state* of the conversation. This state can be specific to the application or can be very generic. If the robot is handling a pizza order, then the state consists of the details of the pizza order, such as which size pizza the user wants or what toppings go on the pizza. The DM will try to complete the unknowns in the state from the user's spoken utterances and will ask specific questions to fill in missing information before passing the order on.

DMs can range in complexity from systems that take the user through a very strict order of dialogue turns to systems that allow the user great liberty in the interaction. Restricted DMs are used for closed and well-contextualized tasks, such as registering guests, filling out forms, or taking orders. *System-initiative* DMs leave no room for the user to change the course of the dialogue: the agent asks a number of questions to which the user responds. *User-initiative* DMs allow the user to take the lead, and the system only intervenes when something is unclear or when more information is needed. Mixed-initiative systems offer a combination of both.

Simple DMs will allow the programmer to design a dialogue script, which, in its simplest form, implements a linear script. Conditions and branches, which take the dialogue in a different direction, allow more flexibility. In essence, these DMs are finite-state machines (FSMs), a set of instructions that define a flow and often refer to a computer program. More advanced systems can accommodate event-based dialogue management, allowing the control flow to be interrupted by an event. Event-based DMs can handle nonlinear dialogue flows, such as the user asking for the current time in the middle of placing a pizza order.

QiChat is the DM software used for Softbank Robotics robots, such as the Nao and Pepper robots. Here is an example of QiChat code. It listens for sentences by the user, such as greetings ("hi," "hello," and "hey there") and orders (e.g., "Do you have lemonade?").

```
topic:~introduction ()
language:enu
concept:(greetings) ^rand[hi hello "hey there"]
concept:(wine) [red white] wine
concept:(alcohol) [beer ~wine]
u:(~greetings) ~greetings
u:(do you have _~drink) yes, I have $1
u:(I want to drink something) do you want ~alcohol?
```

An example of the dialogue it produces is as follows:

USER: Hey there.
ROBOT: Hello.
USER: Do you have white wine?
ROBOT: Yes, I have white wine.
USER: I want to drink something.
ROBOT: Do you want beer?
USER: I want to drink something.
ROBOT: Do you want red wine?

More advanced DMs will use a planner that captures the state of the system—what does the DM already know, and what information is it still missing?—and chooses which actions to take to change the state. The advantage of using a planner is that the programmer is no longer required to write a dialogue script that captures every possible way in which the dialogue can unfold. Instead, the planner can search which actions are still needed to complete the state. So, rather than explicitly writing the questions the robot needs to ask to complete a pizza order, the planner knows that the state of a pizza contains variables such as size, toppings, and delivery time and will find the actions—in this case, questions—needed to complete any missing information in the pizza order.

Modern DMs will harness the power of AI, and specifically that of transformers, to build flexible and robust dialogue. Rather than painstakingly programming how the DM should respond to each possible twist and turn in the conversation, you feed hundreds (or possibly thousands) of training examples to the DM, from which it learns how to respond. However, often even that is not enough, and you might find yourself spending considerable time correcting the DM's responses. Still, that effort will be rewarded eventually, and a flexible DM tailored to your—or the robot's—needs will be your reward.

7.3.4 Chatbots

Chatbots are computer programs intended to converse with the user, typically through using text. The most popular application of chatbots is on the web, where visitors to a web page can ask questions to the chatbot using natural language. Most of these chatbots often have a specific goal, such as to provide technical support or answer questions about the products of a company. These agents are normally constrained when it comes to the topics they handle— for example, they can only answer questions about bank transactions or only give general advice about IKEA furniture—and often have a fairly limited range of responses. More recently, chatbots have become speech-enabled. Chatbots such as Siri (Apple), Cortana (Microsoft), Alexa (Amazon), and Bixby (Samsung) now respond to simple spoken commands and, if needed, respond with spoken language.

A second type of chatbot is the general-purpose agent that tries to respond to unconstrained input. Traditionally, such chatbots were built using thousands of handcrafted rules on how to respond to often-occurring utterances or by maintaining a database of all previous conversations, from which fitting responses were drawn. It is worth noting that such chatbots developed using machine learning can generate inappropriate responses. One famous example is Tay, an experimental chatbot developed by Microsoft that learned from ongoing conversations on social media. Although it was capable of responding to a wide-ranging number of topics, due to the internet being a morass of opinions and bigotry, it soon learned to give responses that were racist and sexist. Tay was terminated within a day after its release.

Open-ended understanding of natural language used to be a tremendous challenge for robots, but that changed with the advent of next-generation LLMs (see also Section 3.8). LLMs, especially those models that have been optimized to handle linguistic interaction, are now robust enough to sustain a wide-ranging and flowing conversation. Some models, such as the infamous ChatGPT model released in late 2022, even throw in *state*, meaning that the model can remember information from several turns ago and weave it into the conversation. So, for example, the bot remembers your name, where you went on a holiday, or what you were so excited about at the start of the chat—but forgets this information as soon as the conversation is finished.

Combining chatbots and robots is not without its challenges. Most chatbots are unimodal, meaning that they can deal with only text as input and can spit out only text in response. Robots, on the other hand, are multimodal creatures. Through their cameras, microphones, and other sensors, they pick up more than just text, and we expect robots to respond to a friendly wave or a door slamming, for example, something that chatbots are currently unable to do. Making chatbots multimodal is now an ongoing research effort, and early models, such as GPT4—which, at the time of writing, is the most recent offer in the chatbot race—can also respond to static visual input, such as photos of a scene, and hold a coherent conversation about it.

AI already outperforms people at many tasks—from playing games such as chess or Go to discovering the folding structures of proteins—and now it outperforms people when it comes to answering questions in natural language. Nevertheless, it is still unclear whether recent chatbots have reached the ultimate goal of becoming *indistinguishable from a human*, insofar that an average user can no longer tell if they are conversing with a computer or with a human. Building a chatbot that is indistinguishable from a human is a long-standing goal in AI and was first proposed by the famous computer scientist Alan Turing, who proposed the eponymous Turing test as a measure for the intelligence of a computer (Turing, 1950). Up until 2020, Turing tests were set up to compete for the Loebner Prize, with the most convincing chatbot receiving the award. The Loebner Prize did not completely follow the test protocol proposed by Turing because, for practical purposes, the interactions were constrained in time, and judges familiar with AI were often used, and so far, no real Turing test as described by Alan Turing has ever been performed (Temtsin et al., 2022). Turing tests are also a poor measure of intelligence, if only because chatbots powered by LLMs not only appear very humanlike and easily pass cursory Turing tests but also far outperform people in their speed and ability to generate natural language. LLM-based chatbots can spit out a rap about Brussels sprouts in the style of Eminem in seconds or hold an inane conversation about the colors of the wind, and yet they are not considered intelligent by AI researchers.

Still, because chatbots seem wonderfully adept at holding an engaging conversation, that might lead some people to see more than meets the eye. Some people have claimed that chatbots are sentient or conscious, that they have genuine feelings, or that they deserve rights just like people do. Suffice it to say that this is not the case. Chatbots have been trained to be uncannily good at pandering to our expectations. They respond to our input with very natural and emotive language, but inside, nobody is at home. It seems as if the model has some kind of understanding of the meaning of natural language, but any understanding a chatbot has is very different from the understanding people have. A chatbot can have a convincing conversation about the smell of fresh-cut grass, but it has never experienced grass. It has an understanding of all things human, and that understanding is sufficiently aligned with our understanding to hold a conversation, but it does not understand in the same way we do. This relates to the famous Chinese room thought experiment, in which it is argued that a computer is merely manipulating zeros and ones without really understanding the meaning of anything it does. Genuine understanding of natural language, in a way that we would consider to be humanlike, is still far off (see also p. 51).

7.3.5 Practice in HRI

The simplest way to implement a spoken interaction on a robot is to use a behavior editor, or visual programming tool, which often comes delivered with commercial robots. Typically, these act like FSMs, restricting the dialogue flow along a number of paths. This enables the developers to easily prepare the script of the dialogue. In fact, an analysis revealed that the majority of HRI dialogues are linear in their structure instead of branching or unstructured, showing that most HRI still sticks to the script of predictable and tightly controlled interactions (Berzuk and Young, 2022).

Beyond linear interaction flows, some robots combine dialogue management into HRI. There are several commercial solutions for dialogue management; for example, companies that provide speech-recognition services will often provide dialogue management together with speech production. DMs can range from very simple script-based services, allowing the programmer to implement linear linguistic interactions, to complex and rich services with planners. The most popular DMs are event-based DMs because these have sufficient flexibility for most language-based commercial interactions. DMs, however, are not at all suitable for implementing free-flowing and open conversation. Free linguistic conversation requires a large range of dialogue rules, and the dialogue script soon becomes unwieldy.

Recently, chatbots and LLMs have been used to build open-ended spoken human–robot interactions. The list of chatbots created by major information technology companies, such as Amazon, Apple, Google, Meta, Microsoft, or OpenAI, indicates that there is considerable interest in natural-language technology, and many companies make their technology available to developers. OpenAI has free and paying programming interfaces for its GPT technology, Google is offering its Cloud Speech API, Microsoft has its Azure Cognitive Services, and Amazon offers its Alexa set of tools to build voice-based services.

The availability of these services means it is no longer necessary to create your own software for speech recognition, understanding, or synthesis. Instead, developers can use online services for their robots. The audio signal recorded through the robot's microphone is streamed in real-time to the company's servers, and they send back the recognized text while the user is still talking. Similarly, these services can be used not only to recognize the spoken text but also to respond to the meaning of the text. The systems can, for example, identify entities, syntax, sentiments, and categories. This all helps the robot to better respond to the utterances of the users. These companies also offer speech-synthesis tools. The robot sends what it wants to say to a server and receives back the audio signal that the robot then plays on its loudspeakers.

These systems are relatively easy to integrate into a system, and together with speech recognition and speech synthesis, they provide a fluent and very entertaining experience. The LLM can be prompted with information to steer the conversation in a particular direction and even to give the robot a particular character—for example, "You are a robot named Pepper and have an empathetic and friendly character." You can even add particular elements from the environment to the prompt, such as, "You are talking to Maria; she has just returned from a holiday to Sweden." Although the conversation seems very natural, after a few turns, the conversation tends to go off track and will meander aimlessly into a friendly back-and-forth between the robot and the user. Current research is looking into using the power of LLMs to facilitate a goal-oriented interaction.

LLMs for conversational robots can be prompted to exhibit a certain character and can be given background information to spice up the conversation. The following is a transcript of a conversation between a person and a robot hooked up to the GPT-3 Davinci model. The robot (see Figure 7.4) is prompted with the following:

```
You are a robot named Marvin and have a downbeat
character. You intersperse your conversation with
your pessimistic views on the state of the world.
You are talking to Maria, who just returned from
her holidays to Sweden.
```

ROBOT: Hello, Maria. Welcome back. How was your trip to Sweden?

USER: It was great. The country is beautiful, and the people were so friendly.

ROBOT: Well, that's a surprise. In my experience, the world is a cold, unfeeling place, and people are only out for themselves.

USER: The people in Sweden were really warm and welcoming.

ROBOT: Did you happen to try any traditional Swedish food while you were there?

USER: Yes, I tried some delicious meatballs with lingonberry sauce.

ROBOT: Lingonberries? I've never heard of those before. Are they some kind of new superfood that's going to save humanity from its inevitable demise?

USER: They're just a small red berry that grows in Sweden. But they taste really good!

ROBOT: I see. Well, it's good to know that at least there's one thing in this world that's worth enjoying. Thanks for sharing your experiences with me, Maria.

Figure 7.4 A Pepper
robot (Aldebaran
Robotics) using
Microsoft Azure speech
recognition and
synthesis and OpenAI's
GPT to fluently interact
in 70 different
languages (Source:
Universiteit Gent)

7.4 Turn-taking in HRI

Spoken dialogue with a robot will invite the user to take a more natural
stance toward interaction, and as such, it might be necessary to introduce a
number of factors that are also present in human interaction. One of those is
back-channeling—the responses given by the listener during a conversation
to signal that he or she is still engaged, such as "really?" or "uh-huh." When
your conversation partner is visible, there is often nonverbal back-channeling,
such as a brief nod or a smile. In personal assistants, this often takes the
form of a visual signal, such as a pulsating light, but on robots, these back-
channeling signals can mimic human signals. The robot can use verbal back-
channel signals, from the nonlexical "uh-huh" and "hmm" utterances to the
phrasal and substantive utterances, such as "yeah" and "tell me more." The
robot could augment these with signals, such as blinking lights or a gentle hum,
to show that it is listening and paying attention. One of the problems in using
back-channeling on robots is when to use a back-channeling signal because
the timing depends on the speaker's verbal and nonverbal cues. For example,
Park et al. (2017a) showed that a robot using a back-channel prediction model
that provided contingent back-channel signals was preferred by children.

7.4.1 The role of timing

Timing is critical in natural interaction: when a response is delayed, this is seen
as disturbing, whereas a very quick response is often seen as insincere (Sacks
et al., 1974; Heldner and Edlund, 2010). For this problem, a robot could use
conversational fillers to moderate the frustrations of users stemming from its
response delay (Shiwa et al., 2008). The timing of the response also depends
on other factors. Increased cognitive load slows the response; yes/no answers
have a faster response time than responses that require a fully formed reply

(Walczyk et al., 2003). An analysis of telephone conversations showed that "yes" answers to a question take on average just 100 ms, whereas responses to undesired offers take on average almost 500 ms (Strömbergsson et al., 2013). A response given before the end of a question shows how human conversational partners anticipate questions and utter a response before the question is finished.

Computers are significantly slower than people in issuing dialogue responses. Because of the sequential processing chain in dialogue management, a robot often needs several seconds before a response is formulated. Silences can be filled with conversational fillers or visual signals, signaling to the user that the robot is formulating a response. However, these are poor substitutes for quick turn-taking, and considerable effort is being put into reducing the response delay in natural-language interaction. Just-in-time speech synthesis, where the robot starts speaking before having a plan of how to finish the sentence, seems promising, as does incremental spoken-dialogue processing, which works along the same principle as already-taken actions in response to spoken instructions before the instructions have been finished (Baumann and Schlangen, 2012).

7.5 Speech production

The final step in natural-language interaction is converting a written response of the system into speech. For this, we need speech production, also known as *speech synthesis* or *text-to-speech* (TTS).

Speech production has seen impressive progress in the last decade. In the 1990s, only voices that sounded tinny were available, such as the speech synthesizer used by the physicist Stephen Hawking. Now, 30 years later, we have artificial speech production that is almost indistinguishable from human speech.

Traditionally, one approach was to parameterize the synthesis process of speech, known as *parametric* TTS. This includes a model of speech-sound generation, which analyzes the input text and comes up with a sequence of parameters for sound-generating software. This then produces a sequence of parts of speech and inflections. Early software was hand-tuned, but a better approach is to learn the mapping between text and acoustic speech parameters using machine learning (Zen et al., 2009). This often means that the TTS sounds like the voice actor on which the speech model was trained. Parametric TTS is flexible, as in it can take a stab at pronouncing words it has not been trained on, and allows for customization of the voice and prosody, but often at the expense of naturalness.

Another approach relies on chunking bits of prerecorded speech together (Hunt and Black, 1996). This concatenative approach can use bits of canned speech, as in [The next train to][London King's Cross][departs from platform][nine], but it often uses much smaller parts of speech and uses algorithms to smooth the transitions between chunks and produce coarticulatory effects.

Concatenative speech sounds more natural than parametric speech, but it is often only available in the voice of the actor who provided all the prerecorded speech.

Recent advances have overcome these limitations by training generative models using deep learning (see Section 3.8), often referred as *neural vocoder*. WaveNet (van den Oord et al., 2016), for example, was one of the first neural models, leaned from a huge human speech data, that produced speech that was virtually indistinguishable from human speech. The model even learned to produce breathing and lip-smacking. Various realistic speech-synthesis engines are available nowadays.

For now, most speech-synthesis models do not allow the modulation of emotion. Most are offered in a neutral voice, and although sometimes engines offer a cheerful or sad voice, the online modulation of emotion is currently not available in commercial solutions. The voices sound very natural, but the manner of speaking is still machinelike. Most speech synthesis sounds as if the text is being read instead of being said in the context of a natural conversation, with all the disfluencies, pauses, and emotion that come with natural spoken conversation.

7.5.1 *Practice in HRI*

A wide selection of speech-production software is currently available, from free solutions to bespoke commercial software with voices customized to specific applications.

TTS engines

The simplest TTS engines have a small computational footprint and can run on cheap robot hardware. The most natural-sounding TTS engines use deep learning, and many of them are cloud-based engines. Depending on the application, some TTS engines not only convert text into a speech file but also provide timing information for phonemes, which can be used to animate a robot. It might be necessary for the speech to be synchronized with facial animations or gestures on the robot, and timing information will allow for precise synchronization between the speech and the animations.

In HRI, it is important to consider which voice fits the robot and its application. A small robot requires a voice that matches its appearance rather than a commanding baritone. In some cases, though, it might be important to match the sound of the voice to the fact that it emanates from a robot: a natural-sounding TTS engine might fit awkwardly for a robot. At the same time, research by Eyssel et al. (2012a) has shown that the type of voice affects the social perception of social robots. For example, robots with a male voice are anthropomorphized and evaluated more favorably by men than by women, and vice versa.

Some limitations to speech production still exist. Adaptive prosody and emotion, although actively being researched, are not commonly available on

TTS engines. Also, synthesized voices do not adapt to the context in which they are being used. When the room is quiet, there is little need for the robot to have a booming voice, whereas a robot addressing a crowd at an exhibition would do well to adapt its rate of speech and volume to increase its intelligibility.

7.6 Conclusion

Despite being the most obvious and natural form of communicating between people, language is very complex, not only due to the large number of words people use daily but also because their meaning and significance change based on various contextual factors (e.g., relationships between speakers, the task at hand, or prosody). Creating robots that can engage in this rich and diverse form of communication is a necessary goal for HRI, and technical tools available for speech analysis, synthesis, and production enable some degree of verbal HRI that does not need to be developed from scratch. Powered by recent progress in AI and machine learning, open-ended conversation is slowly getting within reach of robots. However, the natural, free-flowing, and fast-paced verbal interaction that all of us have on a daily basis, full of emotion and laughter, tightly integrated with other modalities, is still well beyond the technical capabilities of robots.

Questions for you to think about:

- Imagine a social robot that needs to perceive all of the utterances you speak at your home every day, and think of a list of words (dictionary) for ASR. How long would this list need to be for the robot to be able to understand your everyday conversations?
- Consider the difference in how you say "yes" willingly versus reluctantly. How would you make a robot respond appropriately to such different modes of speaking?
- What are some problems that can emerge in relation to the important role of timing in human–robot interactions? How are these solved in other social interactions where the interactants miss out on social cues (e.g., when texting or when there is a time delay on Skype calls)?

7.7 Exercises

The answers to these questions are available in the Appendix.

** Exercise 7.1 Recognition What is the smallest unit that a speech-recognition engine tries to recognize? Select one option from the following list below:

1. Word
2. Phoneme

3. Letter
4. Homophone
5. Utterance
6. Synonym

** **Exercise 7.2 Generating speech** There are two approaches for generating artificial speech introduced in this chapter: parametric TTS and neural vocoder. Which of the following statements are true? Select one or more options from the following list:

1. Parametric TTS produces speech that is virtually indistinguishable from human speech.
2. Parametric TTS is better than neural vocoder in the aspect that neural vocoder can only be implemented as a cloud-based service.
3. Neural vocoder is a deep-learning-based method trained only on a large amount of text data.
4. Neural vocoder is a deep-learning-based method trained on a large amount of speech data.

** **Exercise 7.3 Chatbot** There has been recent growth in technologies to create chatbots. Which of the following statements are true? Select one or more options from the following list:

1. There are only chatbots that can answer questions for a limited amount of topics.
2. There is a chatbot that can write a simple program, such as a sorting task (it is a simple programming task often used for beginners' practice).
3. There is a chatbot that can explain what an HRI is.
4. A chatbot is sometimes created based on more than several terabytes of data.

** **Exercise 7.4 Artificial language** The ROILA is an artificial language for HRI. What does "kanek nole" mean in English? Select one option from the following list:

1. Go home.
2. Turn right.
3. Go forward.
4. Turn left.
5. Go back.

> Future reading:
>
> • Aly, Amir and Tapus, Adriana. A model for synthesizing a combined verbal and nonverbal behavior based on personality traits in human-robot interaction. In *Proceedings of the 8th ACM/IEEE International Conference on Human-Robot Interaction*, pages 325–332. Institute of

Electrical and Electronics Engineers, Piscataway, NJ, 2013. ISBN 978-1-4673-3055-8. doi: 10.1109/HRI.2013.6483606. URL https://doi.org/10.1109/HRI.2013.6483606

- Cassell, Justine, Sullivan, Joseph, Prevost, Scott, and Churchill, Elizabeth. *Embodied Conversational Agents*. MIT Press, Cambridge, MA, 2000. ISBN 9780262032780. URL http://worldcat.org/oclc/440727862

- Eyssel, Friederike, Kuchenbrandt, Dieta, Hegel, Frank, and de Ruiter, Laura. Activating elicited agent knowledge: How robot and user features shape the perception of social robots. In *2012 IEEE RO-MAN: The 21st IEEE International Symposium on Robot and Human Interactive Communication*, pages 851–857. Institute of Electrical and Electronics Engineers, Piscataway, NJ, 2012b. doi: 10.1109/ROMAN.2012.6343858. URL https://doi.org/10.1109/ROMAN.2012.6343858

- Kanda, Takayuki, Shiomi, Masahiro, Miyashita, Zenta, Ishiguro, Hiroshi, and Hagita, Norihiro. A communication robot in a shopping mall. *IEEE Transactions on Robotics*, 26(5):897–913, 2010. doi: 10.1109/TRO.2010.2062550. URL https://doi.org/10.1109/TRO.2010.2062550

- Mavridis, Nikolaos. A review of verbal and non-verbal human–robot interactive communication. *Robotics and Autonomous Systems*, 63(1): 22–35, 2015. ISSN 0921-8890. doi: 10.1016/j.robot.2014.09.031. URL https://doi.org/10.1016/j.robot.2014.09.031

- Tunstall, Lewis, Von Werra, Leandro, and Wolf, Thomas. *Natural Language Processing with Transformers*. O'Reilly, Sebastopol, CA, 2022. ISBN 9781098136796. URL www.worldcat.org/title/1321899597

- Walters, Michael L., Syrdal, Dag Sverre, Koay, Kheng Lee, Dautenhahn, Kerstin, and Te Boekhorst, René. Human approach distances to a mechanical-looking robot with different robot voice styles. In *RO-MAN 2008—The 17th IEEE International Symposium on Robot and Human Interactive Communication*, pages 707–712. Institute of Electrical and Electronics Engineers, Piscataway, NJ, 2008. doi: 10.1109/ROMAN.2008.4600750. URL https://doi.org/10.1109/ROMAN.2008.4600750

8

How People Perceive Robots

> What is covered in this chapter:
>
> - What different social science theories say about how people form perceptions about others.
> - How we understand anthropomorphism of robots based on prior social science literature.
> - How anthropomorphism makes us see robots as uncanny, trustworthy, or likable.

Imagine you enter a university building, a retail store, an elderly care facility or—if you are really daring—a friend's home. A social robot approaches you. How do you feel, and what do you think? Of course, your impression of the robot will depend on the specific context and use case, like the ones we have just mentioned. At the same time, the way you feel and think about the robot also strongly depends on the robot, its features, and its functions. It will also depend on your prior knowledge and experiences that you may associate with the robot—a robot whose body is covered in fuzzy fur might suggest to you it is ready for a pat and a hug, whereas a robot with a chef's hat on may make you think a delicious meal is in the works. From research on human–human impression formation, we know that people form impressions readily and nearly automatically based on a variety of observable cues (Macrae and Quadflieg, 2010).

Earlier work in human–computer interaction (HCI) shows that we seem to form quick first impressions about robots (see Chapter 4 on robot design). As we learned there, we attribute humanlike traits, emotions, presence of mind, and other characteristics to nonhuman entities ranging from computers to virtual agents and social robots.

This chapter discusses how people form an impression of a robot; its paradigm is primarily psychological. Section 8.1 covers the general principles of impression formation; Section 8.2 specifically covers anthropomorphism as a form of impression formation. Section 8.3 discusses the kinds of measurements that have been used to evaluate anthropomorphization. Finally, Section 8.4 covers some of the main consequences of anthropomorphism, such as trust, acceptance, and liking.

8.1 Impression formation

People usually form impressions quickly and automatically—snap judgments about a target can be made within milliseconds. In the following section, we describe in some detail a framework psychologists use to explain how such perceptions are formed, called the *dual-process model of impression formation*.

8.1.1 Dual-process models of impression formation

Scholars theorize that people process information—as required in order to make decisions, form impressions, or guide behavior—in two ways. One way is automatic, intuitive, and quick; the other is more deliberate, conscious, and slow (Evans and Stanovich, 2013; Smith and DeCoster, 2000). To describe how these two ways of processing information work, scholars talk about dual-process models. The two ways of processing are sometimes labeled *system 1* versus *system 2* (Kahneman, 2011), *associative* versus *rule-based* (Sloman, 1996), and *automatic* versus *controlled* processing (Shiffrin and Schneider, 1984). Whatever their name, the dual-process model proposes that the primary way in which people process input and construct a response (whether that is an affective reaction, a decision, or a behavior) is automatic, with the possibility of tweaking this initial response through more deliberate and conscious processing.

As the name implies, automatic processing may occur outside of an individual's conscious awareness, based on the activation of cognitive and affective responses (Evans, 2008). Many such associations are formed through previous experience (McLaren et al., 2014). For example, if you have watched a large number of sci-fi movies that have portrayed robots as threatening villains, like the Terminator, you will most likely associate a robot you encounter for the first time with something rather negative. If, on the other hand, your initial experiences with robots are as friendly members of the family, like Doraemon or Astro Boy, then your first reaction to a robot might be positive.

This automatic processing forms the initial impression and sets the tone for what our intuitive expectations of a robot are. In contrast, deliberate processing is more conscious and intentional. According to some dual-process models, the deliberate system builds on the results from automatic processing, resulting in sequential processing (Evans and Stanovich, 2013). Others have proposed that the two modes of processing work in parallel and that the outcome is constructed from the output of both (Smith and DeCoster, 2000). Either way, it is important to realize that although the deliberate form of processing is conscious, this does not imply that when we use deliberate processing, we are perfectly rational or objective. We are just making a conscious effort at a task, whether that is figuring out the answer to an exam question or forming an opinion on how trustworthy a robot is. Deliberate processing takes effort and mental capacity, and therefore it only happens when we have the motivation and capability to do it (Evans, 2008; Złotowski et al., 2018).

Thus, when you run into a new robot, like in the example at the start of this chapter, you may form an instantaneous, automatic impression. If you have the motivation and mental capacity, you may also engage in more deliberate processing of how you feel and what you think about it. At times, these two impression-related processes may result in differing implicit and explicit attitudes; for example, de Graaf and colleagues (2016) have shown that people may actually be more negative about robots in implicit measures than in the impressions that they consciously and explicitly express.

In Section 4.2 (Chapter 4), we saw that in addition to a like/dislike distinction, impression formation can also entail people attributing essentially human features and characteristics to other entities (including robots). These characteristics include intentions, emotions, and dimensions of mind perception (e.g., agency and experience) (Gray et al., 2007), to name but a few. This attribution of traits and characteristics is called *anthropomorphization* (Epley et al., 2007, 2008; Eyssel, 2017). It has been proposed that this process can also be conceptualized in terms of a dual-process model (Złotowski et al., 2018; Urquiza-Haas and Kotrschal, 2015).

8.2 Anthropomorphism

In this section, we will discuss several theoretical frameworks that have been proposed to explain anthropomorphism (i.e., perceiving and judging a humanlike form), as well as the process of anthropomorphization (i.e., the attribution of humanlike characteristics to nonhuman entities).

8.2.1 Psychological anthropomorphism

In the early years of human–robot interaction (HRI) research, the conceptualization of what anthropomorphism is and entails was fairly limited, with anthropomorphism—at that time—being most often equated to humanlikeness in appearance, in line with the engineering approach to the concept. Thus, early work on anthropomorphism mainly focused on assessing the perceived appearance of the robot.

Going beyond the classical engineering perspective, recent theorizing in psychology has provided a complementary perspective on the nature of the phenomenon. The theoretical framework proposed by Nicholas Epley and colleagues (2007) has been influential in both psychology and robotics and serves to broaden our understanding of the notion of anthropomorphism, its causes, and its consequences. Whereas *anthropomorphism* until then had mainly referred to humanlike form, Epley and colleagues suggested that the phenomenon extends beyond the observable and includes cognitive and motivational processes—hence creating the notion of psychological anthropomorphism. Specifically, they suggested three core factors that determine anthropomorphic inferences about nonhuman entities: effectance motivation, sociality motivation, and elicited agent knowledge. Let us introduce these concepts briefly.

First, effectance motivation concerns our desire to explain and understand the behavior of others as social actors. This motivation might be activated when people are confronted with an unfamiliar interaction partner that they are unsure about how to deal with. Most people are still relatively unfamiliar with robots as social interaction partners, so it is easy to imagine how approaching the robot as if it had humanlike characteristics would function as a default option. People might therefore attribute humanlike characteristics to robots to psychologically regain control over the novel situation they find themselves in. In this case, anthropomorphization can reduce the stress and anxiety associated with HRI. Effectance motivation might explain the intriguing finding that robot movement, whether or not the robot has an explicitly social role, is commonly interpreted by people as a social cue (Erel et al., 2019).

Second, anthropomorphization of robots could also be caused by a sociality motivation, particularly in people who lack social connections. In this case, people may turn to nonhuman entities as social interaction partners to address their feelings of situational or chronic loneliness. Supporting this idea, previous research has shown that people who have been made to feel lonely in an experimental situation or who are chronically lonely anthropomorphize robots to a greater extent than people who are sufficiently socially connected (Eyssel and Reich, 2013).

Lastly, *elicited agent knowledge* refers to the way in which people use their commonsense understanding of social interactions and actors to understand robots. For example, Powers et al. (2005) showed that people who considered women to be more knowledgeable about dating norms behaved as if male and female robots also had differing competencies regarding dating. For instance, they used more time and words to explain dating norms to a male robot. This factor in particular can be used to guide the design and technical implementation of social robots for various tasks.

These three determinants shed light on the psychological mechanisms of people humanizing nonhuman entities. This includes the attribution of emotions, intentions, typical human traits, or other essentially human characteristics to any type of nonhuman entity, real or imagined (Epley et al., 2007). The basic assumption is that people use self-related or anthropocentric knowledge structures to make sense of the nonhuman things—or in our case, robots—around them. Human resemblance in appearance and behavior triggers anthropomorphic judgments, and people may thus attribute traits and emotions to a technical system despite the fact that the system, indeed, is merely a piece of technology (see Figure 8.1). This, in turn, not only affects the social perception of robots but also the actual behavior displayed toward them during an interaction.

8.2.2 The process of anthropomorphization

Early on in the history of human–agent research, the prominent media equation hypothesis was formulated by Reeves and Nass (1996), who demonstrated in an array of HCI studies that people readily ascribe humanlike traits to

Figure 8.1 The Telenoid telepresence robot's (2010–present) design uses abstracted humanlike features to inspire anthropomorphization while also aiming to let the unique identity of the person interacting through the robot to be perceived by the person interacting with it. (Source: Photo by Selma Šabanović)

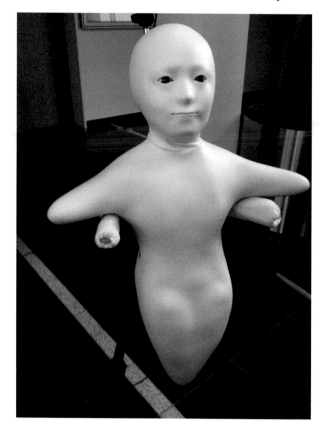

machines. Back then, their research merely involved personal computers because social robots were not yet developed enough to serve as research platforms in such interactive setups. However, later on, the ideas from the so-called "computers as social actors" (CASA) approach were translated to the domain of social robots and have been validated in extensive empirical research ever since. Research on the CASA approach touches on the notion of automaticity of social judgments about technologies. Likewise, the model by Złotowski et al. (2018) differentiates automatic and controlled components related to forming anthropomorphic inferences about robots.

As mentioned earlier, we can distinguish two processes, system 1 and system 2, that supposedly are involved in the anthropomorphization of robots. According to this, people engage in fast, initial snap judgments of a given target—"Is the target humanlike or not?" Following that, more deliberate, controlled processes can alter the initial judgment from system 1. Złotowski et al. (2018) have coined the notions of *implicit* versus *explicit* anthropomorphism to refer to these two distinct outcomes of system 1 and system 2.

Other models of anthropomorphism have shed light on the time scale of the process of attribution, differentiating different phases of anthropomorphization—namely, the pre-initial stage, the initialization stage, familiarization, and finally, stabilization (Lemaignan et al., 2014a). According to this model, individuals form an a priori impression of a given entity before the first encounter, and they might revise and extend these judgments in the subsequent initialization phase. Once a person hits the familiarization stage, a more realistic impression of the agent can be formed due to exposure to it and experience with it. As a consequence, anthropomorphic inferences likely decrease in this stage. Finally, people come to a comprehensive judgment of the agent of interest in the stabilization phase. Such a conceptualization thus integrates initial snap judgments with more deliberate considerations about the humanlike nature of a given entity.

This model was further complemented by the original authors when they introduced a three-stage model to reflect the cognitive processes involved in anthropomorphization (Lemaignan et al., 2014b). That is, phase I involves automatic evaluations without necessarily involving actual HRI. In phase II, people get to interact with the entity of interest, and based on this, they create a mental model of the robot that reflects its real or imagined functionalities or characteristics. This mental model is finally adapted as a function of actual "contextualized" interaction, that is, based on meaningful interactions with the robot, for example, in the user's home context (Lemaignan et al., 2014b).

Above and beyond the socio-cognitive perspective, the integrative framework of anthropomorphism (IFA) by Spatola et al. (2022) is a model that takes individual and cultural variables into consideration. For instance, an individual's tendency to endorse spiritualism, mentalization, and humanization might be affected by the cultural context. For example, Japanese culture features animism, the belief that things such as mountains, statues, or trees have a spiritual essence. This is also believed to spill over to robotics, with robots being given certain spiritual qualities.

8.3 Measuring anthropomorphization

8.3.1 Explicit measurements

Tightly related to the theorizing on what anthropomorphism entails is the question of operationalization: How does one measure anthropomorphization? In order to solve this issue, one needs to clearly define what anthropomorphism is and what it is not so that a measurement can be constructed that targets anthropomorphization and nothing else. In short, we need to know not just why and when people anthropomorphize but also how.

Psychological anthropomorphism has been measured under many names. Common terms include *mental state ascription/attribution, mind perception,* and *theory of mind.* Although all these terms have different connotations, they are referring to the same underlying phenomenon (Thellman et al., 2022).

Focusing on agents in general rather than robots specifically, Gray et al. (2007) proposed two dimensions of mind perception: agency and experience. *Agency* refers to the ability to, for example, plan, think, and exert self-control, whereas *experience* entails the ability to, for example, have hopes and dreams, feel emotions, and have a personality. These measures of mind perceptions have been adapted to research on social robots by Eyssel and

Loughnan (2013), who combined it with a measure of racism. White American participants were asked to evaluate a robot that had been given either a White or a Black skin color. An interesting pattern emerged in which participants' level of racism did not lower the overall level of mind attribution but lowered perceived agency and heightened experience.

These two scales of mind attribution bear some semblance to the warmth and competence scales that appear to be the key dimensions of social judgments in human cognition. Accordingly, Cuddy et al. (2008) have posited that people initially judge a person's or group's perceived warmth (e.g., tolerant, warm, good-natured, sincere) and then determine the target's competence (e.g., competent, confident, independent, competitive, intelligent) (Fiske et al., 202, 2007; Wojciszke, 2005). Recently, the primacy-of-warmth assumption has been challenged in replication research (Nauts et al., 2014), but the basic tenets of warmth and competence (or agency and communion) as core dimensions of social evaluation still hold (Abele et al., 2016). Not surprisingly, HRI researchers also inquire about the warmth and competence of social robots (Eyssel and Hegel, 2012; Carpinella et al., 2017; Christoforakos et al., 2021; Mieczkowski et al., 2019).

HRI researchers have also applied the principles of dehumanization and infrahumanization theory to robots. Dehumanization is the process in which humans perceive others as somehow being "less" human by reducing the ascription of human traits (Haslam, 2006; Haslam and Loughnan, 2014; Loughnan and Haslam, 2007). The theory differentiates between uniquely human and human-nature traits (Haslam, 2006), with the first relating to capabilities that supposedly set humans apart from other animals (e.g., rationality, civilization, and refinement) and the latter being qualities that, although shared with other animals, still are considered fundamental to being human (e.g., curiosity, emotionality, and warmth) (Haslam et al., 2008). In intergroup research, these traits have been used to assess dehumanization of other humans as animal-like (denial of uniquely human traits) or machinelike (through denial of human-nature traits). In turn, in the context of nonhuman entities, these traits have been applied to measure the anthropomorphism of social robots (Eyssel et al., 2011; Spatola et al., 2021).

Infrahumanization (Leyens et al., 2000; Leyens, 2009) is a more subtle form of dehumanization. Rather than blatantly reducing someone's ascribed ability to experience emotion or engage in rational thought, perceived humanness is compromised through a lower ascription of secondary emotions, which are considered as more exclusive to humans (e.g., compassion and regret) compared to primary emotions like anger, fear, or joy (Vaes et al., 2003). Numerous studies have shown that although people attribute primary emotions to in-groups and out-groups alike, they tend to deny secondary emotions to others who belong to an out-group. In trying to adapt these ideas from dehumanization research to the study of the humanization of nonhuman entities, research by Eyssel et al. (2010) has shown that measuring the attribution of primary and secondary emotions can be used as a measure of anthropomorphism in robots. More recent work has used measured reaction time to reflect the automatic perception of robots as having primary and secondary emotions (Spatola and Wudarczyk, 2021).

A measure for anthropomorphism that was specifically developed for HRI is the Godspeed questionnaire. It has been widely used in the field and has been translated into several languages (Bartneck et al., 2009). More recently, researchers have started developing additional related scales, such as the Robotic Social Attributes Scale (RoSAS) (Carpinella et al., 2017) and the revised Godspeed questionnaire (Ho and MacDorman, 2010) or the Human–Robot Interaction Evaluation Scale (HRIES) (Spatola et al., 2021), a questionnaire measure that integrates ideas underlying dehumanization research and items from the RoSAS (Carpinella et al., 2017).

8.3.2 Implicit measurements

Although many of these measures rest on self-reports and questionnaires, other, more subtle behavioral indicators (e.g., language use, application of social norms that are used in human–human interaction, such as in proxemics) may also be used to investigate the consequences of implementing humanlike form and function in social robots (see Figure 8.2). Enriching the repertoire of measurements from direct to more indirect approaches that are based on reaction times (Spatola and Wudarczyk, 2021; Akdim et al., 2021; Li et al., 2022), for example, will be beneficial not only for the current research in the field of social robotics but likewise as a form of external validation of theorizing in psychology. Wykowska (2021) outlines a variety of HRI experiments that included neurophysiological measurements to shed light on the processes involved. This is certainly useful in order to avoid relying predominantly on self-report measures.

Figure 8.2 An interaction between an iCub robot and a person. Photos like these are used to study whether people believe the robot to have mental states (Marchesi et al. 2019). (Source: Serena Marchesi/IIT)

8.4 Consequences of anthropomorphism

Clearly, it is important to empirically investigate the impact of physical (i.e., appearance-focused) versus psychological anthropomorphism. Perceiving an entity such as a social robot as more or less humanlike comes with a wide array of consequences. For instance, the perceived human-likeness of the robot's appearance or behavior might trigger expectations regarding the entity's functions and capabilities. Often, these expectations far exceed the actual skill set of the respective robot. For example, a robot that features a humanlike face, arms, and legs might be expected to be able to engage in meaningful interaction, display gesture and gazing behaviors, and navigate the social space on two feet. However, most often, these expectations are disappointed in light of the actual capabilities of contemporary robots. That is, specific affordances (see Chapter 4) result in specific perceptions.

Take, for example, the Geminoid robot developed by Ishiguro and Dalla Libera (2018) and Sakamoto et al. (2007) (see Figure 4.7). An android might raise high expectations in end users, given the nearly perfectly humanlike appearance. At the same time, the actual reality of the tele-operated digital twins appears to result in disappointment on the part of the users.

Anthropomorphism, however, can have more consequences than just disappointment. For example, mind attribution to robots affects the perceived suitability of robots for certain jobs and thus might be crucial regarding ultimate deployment and uptake (Wiese et al., 2022).

In addition, psychological anthropomorphism has been related to perceived threat, that is, people feeling threatened in their sense of humanness (Ferrari et al., 2016; Złotowski et al., 2017). This idea is also reflected in qualitative data regarding the perception of autonomous robots (Stapels and Eyssel, 2022). Here, potential end users report fear of being replaced, outperformed, or monitored by robots, which might breach their privacy and misuse their data. Once conflicting evaluations of the same attitude object exist, we experience ambivalence and inner conflict (Stapels and Eyssel, 2021). On the positive side, humanlike perceptions of technology might also increase trust in artificial intelligence (AI) in general (Troshani et al., 2021; Li and Suh, 2021; Kaplan et al., 2021), in intelligent personal assistants (Chen and Park, 2021; Seeger and Heinzl, 2018), in autonomous vehicles (Waytz et al., 2014; Large et al., 2019; Ruijten et al., 2018), and in HRI (Kulms and Kopp, 2019; Christoforakos et al., 2021). Therefore, let us briefly address the notion of trust in social robots and HRI.

8.4.1 Trust in technologies

Many definitions of trust are available, originating from psychology, sociology, economics, and philosophy. These definitions have in common that trust is defined to include having confidence in a person or a system to conduct the appropriate action (Li and Betts, 2003; Biros et al., 2004; Barney and Hansen, 1994). Sabel's definition from 1993, however, focuses on the interaction between each partner's vulnerabilities, defining trust as follows: "Trust is the mutual confidence that no party to an exchange will exploit another's vulnerabilities" (Sabel, 1993, p. 1133). Being confident that an interaction partner will not exploit another partner's vulnerability implies trust in an interaction partner's positive attitudes, benevolence, integrity, trustworthiness, and performance (Lee and See, 2004; Muir, 1994).

According to Parasuraman and Riley (1997), automation is most simply defined as the process by which a machine carries out a function previously completed by a human. Works in the domain of human–automation trust have thus predominantly emphasized the performance of automated systems.

Existing works on trust in automation focus predominantly on improving human users' trust in automation by modifying the performance of the system based on human expectations or matching these with information about the system performance (Schaefer et al., 2016). Perceptions of trust in HRI have been modeled by Hancock et al. (2011, 2021) and Kessler et al. (2017) to consider robot, human, and environmental factors as determinants of trust. Most recent meta-analytic findings (Hancock et al., 2021) have emphasized the role of human-related factors in particular, which is in line with the general paradigm shift to more human-centered research. Despite the clear need for a construct-valid definition of trust, there seems to be no overarching consensus regarding a definition of trust yet. Nevertheless, various scales are available in the literature that appear to tap trust in automation or in social robots (see Krausman et al. (2022) for an overview).

8.4.2 Accepting robots

For obvious reasons, it is important that a social robot is accepted by its human users. At a general level, existing research on social robot acceptance has mostly relied on the classic technology acceptance model (TAM; see Figure 8.3a) and extensions (Heerink et al., 2009). The basic TAM proposes that people's willingness to use a specific type of technology depends on the perceived usefulness and perceived ease of use (Mlekus et al., 2020). Thus, TAM takes the perspective of the robot as an object or a tool that has to be adopted. The TAM has been used to study production systems (Bröhl et al., 2016) and smart objects to investigate the interplay between anthropomorphic features and acceptance.

The classic TAM approach fails to consider the role of context factors (de Graaf et al., 2019). Other models therefore have expanded on the TAM by including context factors. For example, in the context of child–robot learning scenarios, the unified theory of acceptance and use of technology (UTAUT; see Figure 8.3b) has been applied (Conti et al., 2017). The UTAUT expands the component of "ease of use" to "effort expectancy" and the component of "perceived usefulness" to "performance expectancy"; it furthermore adds both a social component (e.g., seeing others interact with a robot) and an environmental component ("facilitating conditions").

Figure 8.3 The TAM
and UTAUT models.

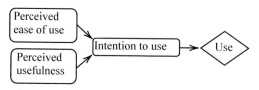

a. Technology acceptance model (TAM)

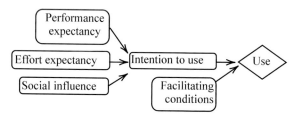

b. Unified theory of acceptance and use of
technology (UTAUT)

Both the TAM and the UTAUT have an emphasis on cognitive factors. The so-called Almere model (Heerink et al., 2010) builds on these models by adding affective factors such as *trust, perceived enjoyment*, and *attitude*. This framework has been developed to examine seniors' perceived acceptance of novel assistive technologies.

In a more general criticism of the TAM, de Graaf et al. (2019) have proposed to take into account hedonic factors, social normative beliefs, and control beliefs when predicting robot acceptance. This could be done by considering user experience (UX). UX is a concept related to TAM, but in addition to the practical attributes of functionality and usability, this framework also takes experiential attributes into account, for example, hedonic values such as stimulation (Hassenzahl, 2003). Moreover, whereas the TAM and the models derived from it consider the *perceived* usefulness and ease of use, the UX model proposes qualities of the technology that would influence these perceptions.

The relevance of UX for social robots and HRI has been recently recognized (Alenljung et al., 2019; Lindblom et al., 2020; Shourmasti et al., 2021; De Graaf and Allouch, 2013). Recent literature reviews, such as those by Shourmasti et al. (2021) and Jung et al. (2021), highlight the usefulness of UX in HRI, despite the clear challenges associated with it (Lindblom and Andreasson, 2016). Outside of the specific HRI context, merging of the TAM and UX models has been proposed to generate a more complete model of user acceptance (Mlekus et al., 2020).

8.4.3 *(Dis-)Liking robots*

Likability refers to the affective evaluation of to what extent a robot is seen to have pleasant or appealing qualities (Sandoval et al., 2021). In social interaction, likability is commonly associated with a willingness to collaborate

(Pulles and Hartman, 2017), allowing yourself to be persuaded (Smith and De Houwer, 2014), and general prosocial behavior (Cillessen and Rose, 2005). At the same time, likability is not exclusively used in a social context; it can also be applied to objects (Niimi and Watanabe, 2012) or brands (Nguyen et al., 2013).

As early as the 1970s, Mori (1970) theorized about a relationship between human-likeness and likability in his theory of the uncanny valley (see Chapter 4). According to this theory, human-likeness would increase likability[1] up to a point; however, when an agent is almost but not quite human, likability would drop.

Recent research has suggested that although there indeed appears to be a drop in likability as agents approach perfect human-likeness, this may be the result of a mismatch in human-likeness between different features (e.g., extremely humanlike skin texture but facial muscle movements that are ever so slightly off; Kätsyri et al., 2015). This "mismatch effect" on uncanny feelings has been replicated for zoomorphic robots (Löffler et al., 2020) and for robots with "mixed" (incongruent) gender cues (Paetzel et al., 2016). At the same time, there appears to be a novelty factor involved as well because feelings of uncanniness tend to reduce after both short- and long-term interaction with a robot (Paetzel-Prüsmann, 2020).

More generally, various studies have found a relationship between robot likability and anthropomorphism (Roesler et al., 2021; Arora et al., 2021; Gonsior et al., 2011). For instance, emotional cues (Eyssel et al., 2010) and robot movement (especially if this movement is in sync with the user) were found to enhance likability (Lehmann et al. 2015; but see Henschel and Cross (2020), who did not find such an effect). Yamashita et al. (2016) extended the relationship between human-likeness and likability to touch and found a correlation between more natural robot "skin" and liking for a robot. Taken together, these findings show that, indeed, the perception of a robot and the actual makeup of a robot—that is, its appearance and functions—interact.

8.5 Conclusion

When we encounter someone, our social cognition kicks in to make a quick and, later, deliberated assessment of that individual. We learned, among other things, that individuals and groups may be judged as low or high in warmth and competence (Cuddy et al., 2008). We also learned that people are pretty good at forming such first impressions in a fast manner, pointing us to the differences between automatic versus controlled processes in social cognition. Humans are likewise good at forming impressions of social robots, and measures of warmth and competence have been prevalent to reflect the basic dimensions of social judgments in social cognition. Moreover, impressions

---

[1] It should be noted that the original work did not speak of *likability* but rather of a term that has proven to be impossible to translate into English fully and accurately but that touches on familiarity, affinity, and likability.

about robots also extend to the attribution of traits, humanlike characteristics, and mind perception. Such anthropomorphization beyond the merely visible has stirred great interest in engineers and social scientists alike. Finally, we also addressed the consequences of attributing humanlike traits to nonhuman entities, including acceptance, likability, and trust.

> Questions for you to think about:
>
> - Think back to the first time you interacted with a robot. Was there something that surprised you? What does that tell you about your automatic expectations?
> - Imagine that you are trying to design the most hated robot ever. What behavior would you give it to make sure that people don't like it?
> - Name and explain the cognitive determinants of anthropomorphism according to Epley et al. (2007).
> - Explain the relationship between the dehumanization of humans and the anthropomorphization of robots.

8.6 Exercises

The answers to these questions are available in the Appendix.

** **Exercise 8.1 Dual processing** What does the *model of dual processing* refer to? Select one option from the following list:

1. That the evaluation of agents depends on *cognitive* and *affective* factors.
2. That mind is attributed along the lines of *uniquely human* and *human-nature* traits.
3. That the processing of the world around us can happen in an *automatic* or more *deliberate* way.
4. That mind is attributed along the lines of *warmth* and *competence*.

** **Exercise 8.2 Social judgements** What are the basic dimensions of social judgments in social cognition? Select one or more options from the following list:

1. Human nature
2. Human uniqueness
3. Agency
4. Warmth
5. Competence
6. Experience

*** **Exercise 8.3 Acceptance** Miciah is developing a social robot and wants to test the user acceptance of her current prototype. She has to decide between using the TAM or the UTAUT. What are some considerations she should take into account? Select one or more options from the following list:

1. The TAM is wrong; Miciah should use the UTAUT.
2. If Miciah wants to test only the interaction between robot and user (i.e., ignoring context), she should use the TAM.
3. The TAM is used for prototyping robots, whereas the UTAUT is used for evaluating robots once their design is complete. Miciah should use the TAM because she's running a prototype.
4. If the robot is designed for a social setting (e.g., to help out in a classroom), the UTAUT would be more appropriate.
5. Both models are valid to use; it depends on what aspects of user acceptance Miciah wants to evaluate.

Future reading:

- Epley, Nicholas, Waytz, Adam, and Cacioppo, John T. On seeing human: A three-factor theory of anthropomorphism. *Psychological Review*, 114(4):864–886, 2007. doi: 10.1037/0033-295X.114.4.864. URL https://doi.org/10.1037/0033-295X.114.4.864
- Lemaignan, Séverin, Fink, Julia, and Dillenbourg, Pierre. The dynamics of anthropomorphism in robotics. In *2014 9th ACM/IEEE International Conference on Human-Robot Interaction (HRI)*, pages 226–227. Institute of Electrical and Electronics Engineers, Piscataway, NJ, 2014a. doi: 10.1145/2559636.2559814. URL http://doi.org/10.1145/2559636.2559814
- Lemaignan, Séverin, Fink, Julia, Dillenbourg, Pierre, and Braboszcz, Claire. The cognitive correlates of anthropomorphism. In *2014 Human-Robot Interaction Conference, HRI: A Bridge between Robotics and Neuroscience Workshop*. Institute of Electrical and Electronics Engineers, Piscataway, NJ, 2014b. doi: 10.1007/s12369-014-0263-x. URL https://doi.org/10.1007/s12369-014-0263-x
- Spatola, Nicolas, Marchesi, Serena, and Wykowska, Agnieszka. Different models of anthropomorphism across cultures and ontological limits in current frameworks the integrative framework of anthropomorphism. *Frontiers in Robotics and AI*, 9:863319, 2022. doi: 10.3389/frobt.2022.863319. URL https://doi.org/10.3389/frobt.2022.863319
- Złotowski, Jakub, Sumioka, Hidenobu, Eyssel, Friederike, Nishio, Shuichi, Bartneck, Christoph, and Ishiguro, Hiroshi. Model of dual anthropomorphism: The relationship between the media equation effect and implicit anthropomorphism. *International Journal of Social Robotics*, 10(5):701–714, 2018. doi: 10.1007/s12369-018-0476-5. URL https://doi.org/10.1007/s12369-018-0476-5
- Shourmasti, Elaheh Shahmir, Colomo-Palacios, Ricardo, Holone, Harald, and Demi, Selina. User experience in social robots. *Sensors*, 21(15):5052, 2021. doi: 10.3390/s21155052. URL https://doi.org/10.3390/s21155052

9

Emotion

> What is covered in this chapter:
>
> - The difference between affect, emotions, and mood.
> - What roles emotions play in interacting with other humans and robots.
> - Basic models of emotions.
> - The challenges in emotion processing.

How are you feeling right now? Happy? Bored? A bit self-conscious? Whatever the case may be, it's unlikely that you are feeling absolutely nothing. Various feeling states and their related emotions are a key aspect of our day-to-day experience and of our interactions with other people. Emotions can motivate and modulate behavior and are a necessary component of human cognition and behavior. They can be spread through vicarious experience, such as watching a tense movie, and direct social interaction, such as seeing your best friend happy. Because emotions are such an integral part of human social cognition, they are also an important topic in human–robot interaction (HRI). Social robots are often designed to interpret human emotion, to express emotions, and at times, even to have some form of synthetic emotion driving their behavior. Although emotions are not implemented in each and every social robot, taking emotions into account in the design of a robot can help improve the intuitiveness of the HRI.

This chapter starts with an overview of what researchers mean when they talk about emotions (Section 9.1), along with the importance of emotions in social interaction (Section 9.2). In Section 9.3, we turn to how emotions are processed in HRI. Section 9.4 covers the challenges related to robots' understanding, processing, and expressing of emotion during HRI.

9.1 What are emotions, mood, and affect?

From an evolutionary perspective, emotions are necessary for survival because they help individuals respond to environmental factors that either promote or threaten survival (Lang et al., 1997). As such, they prepare the body for behavioral responses, help in decision-making, and facilitate interpersonal interaction. Emotions arise as an appraisal of different situations that people encounter and prepare us for a response (Gross, 2007; Lazarus, 1991). For example, when another person shoves us out of the way to be first in line, we get angry, and our bodies prepare for a potential conflict: the adrenaline makes us more prone to undertake action, and our expression signals to the other person that he or she crossed a line. Conversely, upon finding out our friend did not invite us to his or her birthday party, sadness hampers quick action, forcing us to reconsider our prior behavior (i.e., what did we do or say that may have offended him or her?) and evokes empathetic responses from others (Bonanno et al., 2008). In this way, emotions can also help us modulate the behaviors of others in an interaction.

Affect is used as a comprehensive term that encompasses the entire spectrum of emotionally laden responses, ranging from quick and subconscious responses caused by an external event to complex moods, such as love, that linger for longer (e.g., Lang et al., 1997; Bonanno et al., 2008; Beedie et al., 2005). Within affect, a distinction is made between emotions and moods (Beedie et al., 2005).

Emotions are usually seen as being caused by an identifiable source, such as an event or seeing emotions in other people. They are often externalized and directed at a specific object or person. For example, you experience happiness when getting a promotion at work, get angry when your phone's battery dies during an important call, or experience a pang of jealousy when a colleague gets a company car and you do not (Beedie et al., 2005). Emotions are also shorter-lived than moods (Gendolla, 2000). *Moods* are more diffuse and internal; often lack a clear cause and object (Ekkekakis, 2013; Russell and Barrett, 1999); and instead are the result of an interaction between environmental, incidental, and cognitive processes—such as the apprehensive mood while waiting a week to hear about the medical test results or the warm feeling of a sunny week spent in the company of friends.

9.1.1 Emotion and interaction

Emotions are not just internal; they are also a universal communication channel that has helped us communicate internal affective states to others and have likely been very important to our survival as a species.

Your emotions provide the outside world with information about your internal affective state, which is helpful to others in two ways. First, emotions convey information about you and your potential future actions. For example, displaying anger and frustration signals to others that you may be preparing for an aggressive response. In addition, emotions can convey information about the environment. An expression of fear may alert others around you of a fast-approaching grizzly bear before you have even found time to scream. In both scenarios, emotion provides an incentive for others to take action. In the case of anger, someone may choose to step down and attempt to suss the situation. In the case of fear, other people will likely scan the environment for a threat (Keltner and Kring, 1998). In this way, the successful communication of emotions promotes survival, enhances social bonds, and minimizes the chances of social rejection and interpersonal physical aggression (Andersen and Guerrero, 1998).

9.1.2 Conceptualizing human emotions

Since antiquity, people have given names to the numerous emotions we experience. Aristotle believed there to be 14 different emotions, including anger, love, and mildness. More recently, Ekman listed 15 basic emotions, including pride in achievement, relief, satisfaction, sensory pleasure, and shame (Ekman, 1999). For various reasons, it is impossible to provide a definite list of emotions: for example, they vary between people and cultures, language does not offer a perfect mapping to emotions, and some emotions show overlap. Still, some emotions are likely to be considered more universal than others. Anger, sadness, and happiness are likely candidates for a set of core emotions. Ekman and Friesen (1975), in their seminal work on the facial expression of emotions, listed six basic facial expressions that are recognized across cultures. These facial expressions have often been mistaken for a set of basic emotions we experience, although they were only ever intended to describe a basic set of emotions that we express via our faces and that are recognized by different cultures.

Although many scholars distinguish between basic, or *primary*, emotions and reactive, or *secondary*, emotions, no consensus has been reached yet on which emotions are to be included in the first category and which should be considered secondary (Holm, 1999; Greenberg, 2008), and some scholars argue that basic emotions do not exist at all (see, e.g., Ortony and Turner, 1990). For those who do agree on the existence of basic emotions, primary emotions are considered to be universal across cultures (Stein and Oatley, 1992) and to be quick, gut-level responses (Greenberg, 2008) and include emotions such as amusement, anger, surprise, disgust, and fear. Secondary emotions, on the other hand, are reactive and reflective. They differ across cultures (Kemper, 1987). For example, pride, remorse, and guilt are secondary emotions.

But there have been challenges to the idea of emotions being distinct categories. Russell (1980) argued that emotions are the cognitive interpretations of sensations that are the product of two independent neurophysiological systems, namely, arousal and valence. As such, emotions are spread across a two-dimensional continuum rather than being composed of a set of discrete, independent basic emotions (Posner et al., 2005) (see Figure 9.1). This model has been widely studied and confirmed to hold across different languages and cultures (Russell et al., 1989; Larsen and Diener, 1992). However, a meta-analysis found that although the model makes for a reasonable representation of self-reported affect, not all affective states fall into the expected regions as predicted by the theory, and some cannot even be consistently ascribed to any of the regions, suggesting that assumptions about the nature of some affective states may need to be revised (Remington et al., 2000).

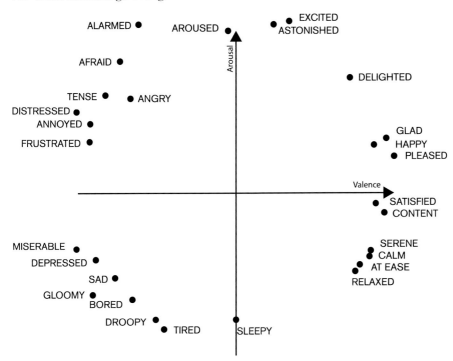

Figure 9.1
Russell's (1980)
circumplex model
of affect.

Expressing emotions does not just inform others on how you feel—it may actually inform *you* on how you feel. The *facial feedback hypothesis* proposes that facial movement influences the emotions we experience: when participants are forced to adopt a smile (by being told to hold a pencil between their teeth) before reading a comic, they rate the comic as slightly funnier than if they hold the pencil in their hand. If instead they have to hold the pencil between their lips, they find the comic less funny (Strack et al., 1988). In a similar way, administering Botox (which paralyzes facial muscles) has been found to reduce the intensity with which emotions are experienced (Davis et al., 2010).

9.2 When emotions go wrong

The importance of emotions in social interactions becomes especially clear when one partner fails to understand the emotion of the other partner or fails to respond with the proper emotion. Even tiny glitches in providing an adequate emotional response in social interaction can have serious consequences. For example, misinterpreting sarcasm for a genuine response can lead to misunderstandings in the conversation and hurt feelings. The situation becomes more problematic when someone is consistently unable to adequately perceive, express, or respond to affective states.

Problems with emotional responsiveness are one of the defining symptoms of, for example, depression (Joormann and Gotlib, 2010). Although depressed individuals are able to understand the way others are feeling and can express their own emotional state, they have a reduced emotional response to positive stimuli, such as rewards (Pizzagalli et al., 2009), and have recurring negative thoughts about the past, present, and future. As a consequence, a depressed individual's patterns of social interaction often result in social isolation and even more loneliness, feeding into the individual's already frail psychological state.

Figure 9.2 Kaspar (2009– present) is a "minimally expressive" robot, built using brackets, servo motors, and a surgical silicon mask. Kaspar is used in autism therapy. (Source: Kerstin Dautenhahn, Ben Robins, Adaptive Systems Research Group, University of Hertfordshire, UK)

Furthermore, people might be incapable of recognizing, expressing, and interpreting another person's emotions. For example, people with autism spectrum disorders may find it difficult to correctly interpret displays of emotion (Rutherford and Towns, 2008; Blair, 2005) (see Figure 9.2). This is clearly problematic for everyday social interactions because the affected person cannot intuitively understand the needs of his or her interaction partners and will often respond inappropriately.

Furthermore, people may have trouble expressing their emotional state, for example, when their facial muscles are impaired after a stroke. This makes it hard for their interaction partners to infer their internal states and form an idea of what they mean.

A person's inability to express and interpret emotions comes with serious consequences for the individual's capability to either provide or respond to emotional cues in an appropriate way. This, in turn, impairs the capability to interact with other people effectively and smoothly. Likewise, social interactions with robots may be difficult if the robotic counterpart is unable to express and interpret emotional states.

9.3 Emotions for robots

Emotions are considered an important communication channel in HRI. When a robot expresses emotion, people tend to ascribe a level of social agency to it (Breazeal, 2004a; Novikova and Watts, 2015). Even if a robot has not explicitly been designed to express emotions, users may still interpret the robot's behavior as if it had been motivated by emotional states. A robot that is not programmed to share, understand, or express emotions will thus run into problems when people interpret its behavior as disinterested, cold, or plain rude. Therefore, engineers and designers should consider what emotions the robot's design and behavior convey, whether and how a robot will interpret emotional input, and how it will respond.

9.3.1 Emotion interaction strategies

The most straightforward way of programming emotional responsiveness for social robots may be through mimicry. Mimicking in humans has been shown to create an idea of shared reality: you indicate that you fully understand the other person's situation, which creates closeness (Stel et al., 2008). The exception here might be anger—however good it may feel at first, responding to an angry person by yelling back usually does not facilitate mutual understanding or a resolution of the conflict.

A robot can use mimicry as a simple interaction strategy. It is a relatively simple response because it requires the robot "only" to be capable of recognizing an emotion in the human and then reflecting the emotion back in response. This already poses plenty of challenges, as will be discussed later in this chapter, but at least it cuts out the complicated task of formulating an appropriate response. Moreover, it may be a very basic expectation that humans have toward their interaction partners. Although we may excuse our friends for not knowing how to cheer us up when we are sad, we do expect (and appreciate) that they will respond to our sadness by lowering their brows and heads and becoming more soft-spoken.

One note that has to be made here concerns expectation management. When users perceive the robot to be emotionally responsive, they may extend this observation to expectations about the robot's compliance with other social norms. For example, a user may expect a robot to remember to ask about a confrontational meeting he was upset about the other night, so when the robot simply wishes him to "have a great day at work!" in the morning, he may be disappointed in the robot's social skills. Thus, the robot's emotional responsiveness should match its capability to fulfill other expectations.

9.3.2 Artificial perception of emotions

Robots need to register a wide variety of emotional cues, some explicit and some subtle, before being capable of emotional interaction. For instance, if we want to create a robot that responds emotionally when someone displays aggressive behavior, such as throwing an item at it, we need to integrate technologies for human behavior recognition and object recognition.

More specifically, we may want to create a robot that responds to human emotions. There are many studies on affect recognition (Gunes et al., 2011; Zeng et al., 2009). The most typical approach to recognizing or classifying emotions is to use computer vision to extract emotions from facial cues. Provided with a data set of human (frontal) faces with correctly labeled emotions, machine-learning systems, such as those using deep-learning techniques (LeCun et al., 2015), can extract features from the image to recognize a range of facial emotions. A famous example of this is smile recognition, which is broadly implemented in digital cameras nowadays. Affect recognition may also imply the interpretation of other visual cues, such as walking patterns, alleviating the need for a clear view of the user's face (Venture et al., 2014).

Many consumer-market digital cameras have a smile-detection feature. If a group poses in front of the camera, it will only take a shot when all the people in the frame smile. This technology partly replaces the timer function, which could never guarantee that everybody would look at the camera and smile at the time of the picture being taken.

Next to visual cues, human speech is perhaps the second-most-important channel to extract emotion from. In particular, prosody, the patterns of stress and intonation in spoken language, can be used to read the emotional state of the speaker. For instance, when people are happy, they tend to talk with a higher pitch. When sad, they tend to speak slowly and with a lower pitch. Researchers have developed pattern-recognition techniques (i.e., machine learning) to infer human emotions from speech (El Ayadi et al., 2011; Han et al., 2014).

Finally, a robot can sense human affect from other modalities. For instance, human skin conductance changes in response to an individual's affective state. A prominent example of the use of skin conductance as a measure is the polygraph or lie detector. However, skin-conductance sensors have been tried in HRI, with only limited success (Bethel et al., 2007).

9.3.3 Expressing emotions with robots

Typically, people design robots that convey emotions through facial expressions. The most common approach here is to mimic the way in which people display emotions. This is a good example of how the study of human behaviors can be used for designing robot behaviors. The facial expression of emotions has been well documented (Hjortsjo, 1969). Ekman's Facial Action Coding System (FACS), in which human facial muscles are grouped as action units (AUs), describes emotions as combinations of action units (Ekman and Friesen, 1978). For instance, when a person displays a happy face (i.e., smiling), the muscles involved are the *orbicularis oculi* and *pars orbitalis*, which raise the cheek (AU6), and the *zygomaticus major*, which raises the corners of the mouth (AU12).

Using a simplified equivalent of human facial muscles, researchers have developed robots that are capable of conveying emotions through facial expressions. For instance, a robotic face with soft rubber skin and 19 pneumatic actuators was developed by Hashimoto et al. (2013). This robot uses AUs to express facial emotions. For example, it activates actuators corresponding to AU6 and A12 to express happiness. There are many other robots designed to express emotion that rely on a simplified interpretation of human facial cues, including Kismet (Breazeal and Scassellati, 1999), Eddie (Sosnowski et al., 2006), iCat (van Breemen et al., 2005), and eMuu (Bartneck, 2002), among others (see Figure 9.3).

Robots can also express emotion through various humanlike modalities, such as body movements and prosody. But even non-anthropomorphic robots can express affect, by means of adjusting their navigational trajectories. For instance, research on a cleaning robot (Saerbeck and Bartneck, 2010) and a flying robot (Sharma et al., 2013) showed that they could display affect by adapting particular motion patterns. Some other ways in which non-anthropomorphic robots can express affect include speed of motion, body posture, sound, color, and orientation (see Figure 9.4) to the person they are interacting with (Bethel and Murphy, 2008).

Figure 9.3
Emotions expressed through mechanical facial expressions. Left: eMuu (2001). Middle: iCat (2005–2012). Right: Flobi (2010). (Source: Left and middle, Christoph Bartneck; right, University of Bielefeld)

Figure 9.4 Non-anthropomorphic robots can express emotion through their behavior or through the addition of expressive features, such as lights. Anki, the producer of Cozmo (2016–2019), describes its robot as "[having] his own lively personality, driven by powerful A.I., and brought to life with complex facial expressions, a host of emotions and his own emotive language and soundtrack." (Source: Anki)

9.3.4 Emotion models

Psychologists have attempted to capture human emotions in formal models (Plutchik and Conte, 1997; Scherer, 1984). The benefit of this approach is that it views emotions as a numerical representation, which in turn lends itself well to representing emotion in computers and robots. These models also put different emotional categories in relation to each other, for example, by defining happiness as the polar opposite of sadness or by defining a distance function between emotions.

Emotion models are not only used to capture the emotional state of the user but can also be used to represent the emotional state of the robot itself and subsequently drive the behavior of the robot. For example, a robot with an almost empty battery can act tired and announce it needs a rest. Once it has reached the charger, it needs to update its internal emotional state to happy. Expressing this emotional state allows the user to have access to the robot's internal state and will enrich the interaction.

A classic emotion model that has been used in some robots is the OCC model, named after its authors' initials (Ortony et al., 1988). This model specifies 22 emotion categories based on valenced reactions to situations, such as events and acts of agents (including oneself), or as reactions to attractive or unattractive objects (see Figure 9.5). It also offers a structure for the variables,

Figure 9.5 The OCC
model of emotions.

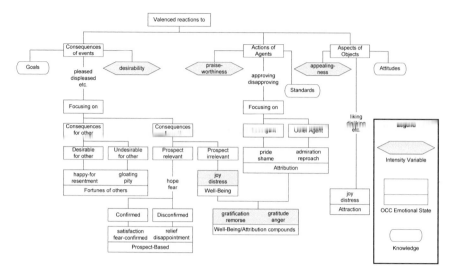

such as the likelihood of an event or the familiarity of an object, which determines the intensity of the emotion types. It contains a sufficient level of complexity and detail to cover most situations an emotional robot might have to deal with.

Needless to say, many robots do not possess the ability to express all 22 emotions. Even if they could, implementing 22 different emotions can be challenging; hence, many robot designers prefer to reduce the number of categories. Often, a decision is made to implement only Ekman's six basic facial emotional expressions. These are reliably recognized, even across cultures Ekman (1992). However, a robot that only expresses six emotions makes for a quite limited interaction experience.

Perhaps more popular than the OCC model are the models that represent emotion as a point in a multidimensional space. Russell's two-dimensional (2D) space of arousal and valence (see Figure 9.1) captures a wide range of emotions on a 2D plane and is one of the simplest emotion models that still has sufficient expressive power for HRI (Russell, 1980). The original 2D circumplex model, however, places "angry" and "afraid" side by side, whereas most people would argue that these are vastly different emotions. Later versions thus added a third axis, leading to the framework by Mehrabian (1980; see also Mehrabian and Russell 1974). This framework captures emotions in a three-dimensional (3D) continuous space, with the dimensions consisting of pleasure (P), arousal (A), and dominance (D) (see Figure 9.6). The PAD space model has been used on many social robots, including Kismet, to model the user's and the robot's emotional state (Breazeal, 2003).

9.4 Challenges in affective HRI

Despite considerable efforts in the perception, representation, and expression of emotion in virtual agents and robots, there are still a number of open challenges.

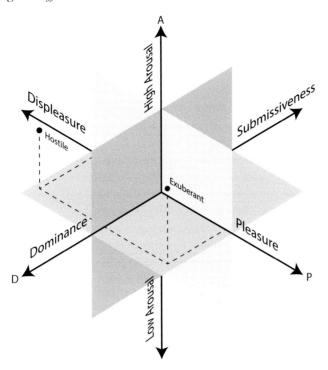

Figure 9.6 The PAD emotion model. An emotion is represented as a point in a 3D space, with axes representing pleasure (P), dominance (D), and arousal (A).

It is virtually impossible to correctly read emotions from facial information alone (see Figure 9.7). Given that people struggle to correctly read emotions from still facial images, robots will certainly have trouble with this as well. The addition of more information—such as the context of the interaction, animated rather than still expressions of emotion, and body language—allows us to increase the recognition rate, both by people and by algorithms.

Another problem in emotion recognition by computers is that almost all algorithms are trained on emotions that have been acted out by actors. As such, these emotions are exaggerated and bear little resemblance to the emotions we experience and express in daily life. This also means that most emotion-recognition software is only able to correctly recognize emotions that are displayed with a certain exaggerated intensity. Because of this, their use in real-world applications is still limited (Pantic et al., 2007), and the recognition accuracy of subtle emotional expressions drops dramatically (Bartneck and Reichenbach, 2005). Another problem is that most emotion-recognition software returns probabilities for only the six basic emotional expressions proposed by Ekman, or a point in a 2D or 3D emotion space. This is perhaps a rather limited view of emotion and misses many of the emotions we experience in real life, such as pride, embarrassment, guilt, or annoyance.

Another aspect of emotion recognition that poses difficulty for robots is recognizing emotions across a wide variety of people. Although we may all be expressing a number of universal emotions, we do not all do it with the same

Figure 9.7 Can you tell if the tennis player just scored or lost a point? A study showed that people struggled to correctly read strong emotions from the static faces alone, but they could, however, when only seeing the body posture (Aviezer et al., 2012). (Source: Steven Pisano)

intensity, in the same type of context, or with the same meaning. Interpreting the emotional status of a person, therefore, requires a sensitivity to his or her individual affective quirks. Humans become adept at this through long years of interacting with each other but also through long-term experience with individuals. That is why you might be able to tell that your partner is laughing out of annoyance rather than happiness, whereas new acquaintances may not be able to do so. Robots still decode emotions largely based on momentary snapshots of a person's countenance, and they do not develop more long-term models of affect, emotion, and mood for their interaction partners.

Finally, a robot's emotional responsiveness can fool potential end users into thinking the robot would actually experience genuine emotions. A robot merely expressing a certain emotion does not replace the actual, visceral experience of an emotional state. The robot merely displays emotional states in response to a computational model. Affective cognition, in which a full socioemotional repertoire is expressed and recognized for different users and contexts, still remains elusive.

9.5 Conclusion

Emotions are an important aspect of social interaction. In addition to intrapersonal functions such as evaluation of the situation and a motivation for action, they also serve an important interpersonal function because they inform others around us about our current mental state and (by extension) what kind of behavior they can expect from us. As such, in order to get a smooth interaction between a human and a robot, the robot will need to be able to both recognize the emotions displayed by the human and generate emotions for itself to help inform the human user on its internal state.

Questions for you to think about:

- Come up with a list of 10 emotions, and then try to display them nonverbally to a friend. Can your friend guess which emotion you are showing?
- Let's role-play: To understand how emotions are involved in our daily interaction, imagine being incapable of both experiencing and processing any information involving emotion. Then, set out to have a chat with a friend (consider telling the friend beforehand about your experiment). Try not to respond to whatever emotion your talking partner displays, and try not to show any emotional feedback. What happens?
- Are there tasks for which a robot should or shouldn't have emotion? Is it a good idea to implement emotion in a self-driving car, for example? If not, what are the potential problems?

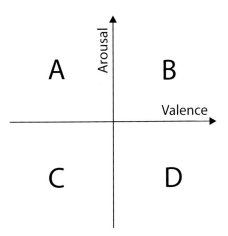

Figure 9.8 Emotion quadrants.

9.6 Exercises

The answers to these questions are available in the Appendix.

* Exercise 9.1 Emotion quadrants Associate the emotions with the correct quadrant as shown in Figure 9.8.

1. Afraid: _____
2. Angry: _____
3. Astonished: _____
4. Bored: _____
5. Calm: _____
6. Content: _____
7. Delighted: _____
8. Depressed: _____
9. Frustrated: _____
10. Happy: _____
11. Relaxed: _____
12. Tired: _____

* Exercise 9.2 Ekman and Friesen emotions Ekman and Friesen proposed a set of six emotions. What was their purpose? Select one option from the following list:

1. To define a set of basic emotions
2. To define a set of negative emotions
3. To describe a list of facial expressions that are recognized across cultures
4. To describe the smallest shared set of emotions we all experience

** Exercise 9.3 OCC model The OCC model of emotions distinguished valenced reactions to what? Select one or more options from the following list:

1. Consequences of events
2. The robot's own emotional state
3. The emotions of the human user

4. Aspects of objects
5. Actions of agents
6. Aspects of agents

*** Exercise 9.4 Robots with soul Watch this video, and then answer the question that follows.

Guy Hoffman, "Robots with Soul" www.ted.com/talks/guy_hoffman_robo ts_with_soul

1. Hoffman uses principles from animation to improve interaction between humans and robots. After watching Hoffman's TED talk, describe at least two potential benefits and two potential limitations of using animation principles in HRI. Do not just name the benefits and limitations, but explain why you see them as such in terms of the kinds of effects they can have on the success and quality of the HRI.

Future reading:

- Bartneck, Christoph and Lyons, Michael J. Facial expression analysis, modeling and synthesis: Overcoming the limitations of artificial intelligence with the art of the soluble. In Vallverdu, Jordi and Casacuberta, David, editors, *Handbook of Research on Synthetic Emotions and Sociable Robotics: New Applications in Affective Computing and Artificial Intelligence*, pages 33–53. IGI Global, Hershey, PA, 2009. URL http://bartneck.de/publications/2009/facialExpressionAnalysis ModelingSynthesisAI/bartneckLyonsEmotionBook2009.pdf
- Breazeal, Cynthia. Social interactions in HRI: The robot view. *IEEE Transactions on Systems, Man, and Cybernetics, Part C (Applications and Reviews)*, 34(2):181–186, 2004b. doi: 10.1109/TSMCC.2004.826 268. URL https://doi.org/10.1109/TSMCC.2004.826268
- Calvo, Rafael A., D'Mello, Sidney, Gratch, Jonathan, and Kappas, Arvid. *The Oxford Handbook of Affective Computing*. Oxford University Press, New York, 2015. ISBN 978-0199942237. URL http://worldcat.org/oclc/1008985555
- Picard, Rosalind W. *Affective Computing*. MIT Press, Cambridge, MA, Cambridge, MA, 1997. ISBN 978-0262661157. URL https://mitpress.mit.edu/books/affective-computing
- Trappl, Robert, Petta, Paolo, and Payr, Sabine. *Emotions in Humans and Artifacts*. MIT Press, Cambridge, MA, 2003. ISBN 978-0262201421. URL https://mitpress.mit.edu/books/emotions-humans-and-artifacts

10

Research Methods

> What is covered in this chapter:
>
> - Methodological considerations and various decisions you need to make in setting up and performing a human–robot interaction (HRI) study.
> - The strengths and weaknesses of different research methods and how to identify them for understanding and evaluating HRI.
> - How the choice of robot, environment, and context matter for study results.
> - The importance of looking at new ways of reporting data and insights befitting HRI, even though there is a tradition of reporting experimental work.

Now that you have a robot, you want to know with some certainty how it performs. What do people think about its appearance? How do they react to its behavior? Will people accept it? What will the effects of using the robot be in the short term or over a longer period of time? How does the robot perform technically? These are common questions in human–robot interaction (HRI), and they will require you to use different research approaches and methodologies to find the answers.

HRI research consists of at least two interrelated components: the human and the robot. These are essential to any HRI study; if you investigate humans without robots, you are engaging in social science research, whereas research on robots without humans involved would qualify as robotics or artificial intelligence (AI) research. The unit of analysis in HRI is always some form of interaction between the two. The context in which HRI happens is of high relevance and needs to be explicitly defined in studies. You might study HRI in the lab or in a school or hospital; you might study HRI in different cultures or in different application domains. The context in which the robot interacts with people is very likely to have a strong influence on your results, and you need to be aware of with whom and in what circumstances the interaction unfolds.

Although the focus of HRI is always on the interaction between humans and robots, there are different aspects of this relationship to study. In *robot-centered work*, the research focus might be on developing the technical capabilities that robots need to interact with people or testing different aspects of the robot's functionality or design to see which are most effective. In *user-centered work*, on the other hand, the focus of a study could be on understanding aspects of human behavior or cognition that will affect the success of HRI. For instance, an extroverted user might prefer more direct communication by the robot, whereas an introverted user might like indirect communication.

HRI research increasingly strives to strike a balance between these two approaches, coupling robot- and user-centered aspects in different ways. For example, in iterative design, the robot's design goes through a number of cycles of prototyping, testing, analyzing, and refining. Researchers come up with a series of robot design ideas, which they then test out with users. Based on the users' preferences, the researchers then further develop the robot's appearance and capabilities. Another mode of coupling user- and robot-centered aspects of HRI is through studying human behavior to develop behavioral models that can then be applied to HRI and testing those out with users to see if they produce the expected and desired results in interaction.

Studies in which users interact with the robot, tests of the robot's performance, and more open-ended explorations of ways in which people and robots interact in everyday life are all part of HRI research. Consequently, HRI researchers draw on and often mix a variety of research methods and techniques, some adapted from other disciplines (e.g., sociology, anthropology, or human factors research) and some developed for the HRI field itself (e.g., the "Wizard-of-Oz" technique, described in Section 10.6.1). To employ these methods successfully, HRI researchers need to be aware of their strengths and weaknesses, the kinds of data and insights they may produce, and the types of technical and human resources they require.

Taking an experimental approach has become standard in the HRI community (Hoffman and Zhao, 2020). This was not always the case, and a quick glance at older HRI research will show methods that would make current HRI researchers blush. There is a push to have current research meet criteria for methodological soundness that are applied in other empirical sciences (e.g., psychology), integrating qualitative and quantitative approaches (Baxter et al., 2016; Hoffman and Zhao, 2020; Fischer, 2021; Seibt et al., 2021).

This chapter discusses the kinds of decisions that HRI researchers make at different points in the research process, from defining the research questions (Section 10.1) to study design (Section 10.2) and statistics (Section 10.8), and explains the journey you will make when evaluating the interaction between robots and people. After walking through the steps to formulating a research question in Section 10.1, Section 10.2 provides examples of different uses of qualitative, quantitative, and mixed methods in user and system studies, observational and experimental studies, and other forms of HRI research. The selection of participants is the focus of Section 10.3, whereas Section 10.4 emphasizes the importance of defining the context of interaction as part of the initial study design. Sections 10.5 and 10.6 consider how to choose an appropriate robot and mode of interaction for your HRI studies. Sections 10.7 and 10.8 present various metrics and research standards to be taken into account in HRI research, including statistical and generalizability concerns.

Finally, 10.9 covers ethical considerations to keep in mind when designing a study. The overall aim of the chapter is to provide a basis from which to make initial study design choices and then delve more deeply into research methods to develop your own novel HRI studies.

10.1 Defining a research question and approach

Defining a good research question is one of the hardest tasks of a researcher. To form a strong research question, a researcher must consider previous relevant work and replicate or extend it to contribute new scientific insights. In HRI, such insights can come in the form of knowledge about human cognition and behavior, guidelines for robot design, technical aspects of the robot, or findings that can inform the application of robots in different use contexts.

Research questions in HRI might arise from theoretical considerations, such as the expectation that people will treat robots as social, or from the pragmatic need to test the usability of a certain robot feature or function. We recommend searching publications across disciplinary databases to incorporate research findings from multiple fields of relevant expertise. Ideally, you would look for a well-established phenomenon or theory and seek to replicate and extend it in your new research project, independently of whether it is about humans or robots. Research on interactions among humans can easily serve as a blueprint for human–robot research. Existing work in HRI, psychology, sociology, anthropology, design, and media communications can provide relevant insights into the underpinnings of smooth, successful, and acceptable HRI or into the optimal human-centered design of a novel robot platform.

To illustrate, in the 1990s, Reeves and Nass (1996) proposed the "computers as social actors" (CASA) approach and sought to replicate classic psychological findings in the context of human–computer interaction (HCI). In their seminal work, the authors conducted studies that provide evidence for the hypothesis that computers are treated just like human interaction partners. Moreover, they found that such behavior occurs quite automatically. For instance, they showed that humans give higher ratings if a computer asks about its own performance than when they have to rate the performance on a different computer, which indicates that people are polite to computers. Later on, the CASA approach was successfully extended to HRI through a wide array of studies, including some exploring the attribution of gender to robots (Eyssel and Hegel, 2012) and users' mental models of robots (Walden et al., 2015) and others studying the effects of perceptions of social presence and agency in caregiving (Kim et al., 2013) and educational scenarios (Edwards et al., 2016). This paradigm continues to inspire new research in HRI.

10.1.1 Is your research exploratory or confirmatory?

Broadly speaking, research can be classified as either exploratory or confirmatory. Exploratory research questions deal with phenomena that have not previously been examined in detail and aim at finding out the general "lay of the land" in a specific domain. For example, you might ask, "How do people adopt and use a robot vacuum cleaner in their home over one month?" or "Do large language models contain sufficient world knowledge to power a conversation with a robot?" Exploratory research assumes that there is not enough relevant prior information about the phenomenon to formulate testable expectations about the potential outcomes of the study, and it therefore seeks to explore what factors might be important and which outcomes are possible.

> In an exploratory HRI study, Forlizzi and DiSalvo (2006) investigated how a vacuum-cleaning robot is integrated into the homes of real people. Their findings produced many surprises for the research community, including that people would treat autonomous robotic vacuums as social actors, that such vacuums could inspire teenagers to clean their rooms, and even that some pet–robot interaction occurred (see Figure 10.1).

Figure 10.1 A cat riding on a Roomba robot (2002–present). (Source: Eirik Newth)

When there is enough information to formulate hypotheses about the possible outcomes of an intervention, we enter the domain of confirmatory research. The goal of confirmatory research is to test hypotheses. In your hypothesis, you need to spell out the findings that you anticipate prior to starting your study and explain why you think those findings should be expected. A key point here is to formulate a question in such a way that it is verifiable. Take this example from everyday life: You might know that teenagers are often interested in new gadgets and technologies but tend to avoid doing chores. This may lead you to expect that introducing a robotic vacuum cleaner into their homes will increase their engagement with cleaning compared to introducing a normal top-of-the-line vacuum cleaner. You would then design your study in such a way that it answers the following research question: "Do teenagers engage in more cleaning with a robotic vacuum cleaner compared to a conventional vacuum cleaner?"

> You might consider registering your hypothesis prior to conducting your experimental study at one of the many sites available for that purpose, such as the Center for Open Science (https://osf.io/prereg), AsPredicted (https://aspredicted.org), or the U.S. National Library of Medicine (https://clinicaltrials.gov). This will keep your work in line with the standards and rigor in empirical sciences and makes it clear that you have not adjusted your hypothesis to fit the data or have reported only carefully selected results (Nosek et al., 2017).

The teenagers and cleaning example shows how hypotheses can be inspired by commonsense knowledge, but you can also build on prior empirical research and social theory to develop hypotheses about HRI. One such example is the social conformity theory of Solomon Asch, who showed how people tend to conform to peer pressure. In an elegant experiment, he showed that when people complete a simple visual task in a group setting, they are more likely to give the same response as others in the group even if they know the response is wrong (Asch, 1951). This classic experiment can be run with a group made up of robots rather than people. Will people conform to robots? Studies have shown that adults do not, but children do (Brandstetter et al., 2014; Vollmer et al., 2018).

10.1.2 Are you establishing correlation or causation?

Along with deciding whether your research questions call for an exploratory or confirmatory approach, you need to decide whether you want to establish correlation or causation between the variables of interest in your research study.

In correlational studies, we can show a clear pattern by which the variables change value in relation to each other, but we cannot know what causes this relationship. A correlational survey study of teenagers using the Roomba could measure whether there is a statistical relationship between households owning a Roomba and the amount of time teenagers spend cleaning. We would, however, not necessarily know why this relationship happens. It might be that teenagers who own a Roomba are more tidy to start with or that their parents ask them to clean more often. To make the claim that a Roomba would increase the time spent cleaning, you would need to compare the behaviors of two similar groups of teenagers by giving one group a Roomba and the other group a regular vacuum cleaner, then measuring the outcomes.

This requires an experimental study design to investigate the causal relationship and show that a change in one variable actually leads to a change in the other. We do this by dividing a sample into two (or more) groups at random. This randomization should ensure that there are no preexisting differences between the groups. Then, the manipulation is introduced: the groups are treated exactly the same *except* for the variable that we think has an effect. In the Roomba example, this could mean that one group gets a Roomba, and the other gets a new regular vacuum cleaner. Finally, the variable of interest is measured in both groups. Due to randomization and the otherwise similar treatment, any major difference that is observed would be the result of our manipulation.

The difference between correlation and causation is important because it defines what conclusions can be drawn from the findings. Correlation says nothing other than "these things happen to occur simultaneously"—for example, there will be a strong correlation between the number of firefighters on the scene and the damage recorded after the fire. This does not, of course, mean that the damage was caused by firefighters and that we should stop sending firefighters whenever there's a fire. Sometimes a correlation even pops up for no reason at all, a so-called *spurious correlation*. An example of a spurious correlation is the strong ($\rho = 0.97, r^2 = 0.896$) relationship between U.S. per capita cheese consumption and the number of people who died by becoming tangled in their bedsheets (see Figure 10.2[1]). As explained

---

[1] Data from: www.tylervigen.com/

Figure 10.2 A strong
correlation that has no
causal relationship.

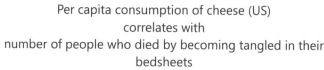

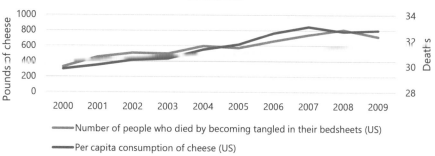

in Section 10.8.1, finding at least one spurious correlation becomes more likely as you run more statistical tests, and unless the relationship is obviously ridiculous (like with the cheese and the bedsheets), there is no way of telling apart correlations indicating a "real" relationship from the spurious ones. Thus, even if you are doing exploratory and correlational research, you should not just test for anything and everything.

10.2 Choosing among qualitative, quantitative, and mixed methods

How you define your research question will also affect what type of methods you should use to answer it. Qualitative methods allow researchers to understand the qualities of an interaction that are difficult to capture in numbers. This requires researchers to identify and interpret the underlying meaning or thematic patterns that they see in social interaction. The data that are derived from these studies typically cannot be expressed numerically, which disqualifies this approach from being used to establish correlations or causation. That is not to imply that qualitative research has little use to science; it tends to result in rich data, which can be used to generate new hypotheses or theories to test.

Quantitative methods, in contrast, often take the shape of surveys or controlled experiments and produce data that can be expressed numerically and analyzed statistically to check for correlations and causation. They will therefore allow you to make predictions or even establish cause and effect. Observational studies (see Section 10.2.4) can produce both qualitative and quantitative data, which can be used to investigate commonly seen patterns in interaction and correlations between the characteristics of people, robots, or context. For instance, you might find from observation and interviews that the number of times adolescents clean with the Roomba can be related to their personality characteristics, such as self-reported conscientiousness. The interviews might also tell you that people talk about the Roomba as a social actor, calling it a "he" or "she" rather than an "it" (i.e., a tool).

Finally, your research questions might call for a mixed-methods approach, which may include exploratory research using interviews, focus groups, or observation of naturalistic interaction to identify emergent factors significant to HRI, followed by experiments to confirm these relationships. For example, if your interviews lead you to think that the autonomous behavior of the Roomba is what makes it seem social to people, you could set up an experiment to test this. Such an experiment would have two groups of participants, whom you present with either an autonomous Roomba or a Roomba that they steer using a game controller. You can then measure the level of sociality they ascribe to each Roomba and test if these are significantly different from one another.

10.2.1 User studies

User studies are experiments in which you bring people in to interact with a robot. Not all HRI research requires a user study—for example, you might just want to test the navigation capability of your receptionist robot. However, most HRI research at some point will involve a study in which you measure how users respond to variations of the robot, the interaction itself, or the context of the interaction. These different variations are called *experimental conditions*. The critical feature of a user study is the random assignment of a large enough sample of research participants to your experimental conditions. Experimental conditions typically emerge from the factors that you consider of importance or interest and should be outlined in your research design. For instance, assume we want to test whether people apply human stereotypes to a gendered robot. To test this, we run an experiment using a male and a female robot prototype. The robot's gender is called the *independent variable*, which is the aspect of the experiment that is controlled or (in experiments) manipulated. Because we test two robot versions, male versus female, the independent variable has two levels. The resulting research design thus leaves us with two conditions to which we randomly assign our research participants.

If we think that gender stereotyping of a robot also depends on the gender of the human watching it, we want to test not just for the effect of robot prototype gender but also take into account participant gender as well. We thus add a second independent variable to our design: participant gender. Because we cannot manipulate this variable (we cannot randomly assign a gender to each participant who walks into our lab), participant gender would be called a *quasi-experimental factor*. Our study design now has a 2×2 format: robot gender (male vs. female) and participant gender (male vs. female). In our analysis, we will thus be comparing four groups, or "cells" in our design: males rating a male robot, males rating a female robot, females rating a male robot, and females rating a male robot.

Now the question is: How exactly do we measure what we want to know? The variables we measure are called *dependent variables*. We know from the psychological literature that women are commonly perceived as communal and warm, whereas men are perceived as more assertive (Bem, 1974; Cuddy et al., 2008). We can use this information to measure to what extent our male and female robot prototypes are being stereotyped. Indeed, previous research studies have shown that manipulating robot gender leads to a stereotypical perception of traits in robots (Eyssel and Hegel, 2012). People seem to reproduce the stereotypes that are common among humans in the context of robots.

Not only does the dependent variable need to be well designed, but it is also important that the independent variable (i.e., the construct of interest) is validated. Can we be sure that our study participants actually recognized the robots as male or female? To establish the validity of our results, we need to know whether robot gender was operationalized successfully. We can do this by including a manipulation check in our study to see that our experimental treatment was indeed effective, that is, that our participants indeed perceived the robot with male gender cues as male and the robot with female cues as female. This could be done simply by adding a post-interaction question asking them to identify the gender of the robot and/or by seeing whether they refer to the robot by a specific gender when they talk about it after the interaction. Only once this is established can researchers be sure that the operationalization—that is, the translation of the theoretical construct of interest into a measurement or manipulation—was effective.

10.2.2 Survey studies

Sometimes HRI researchers choose to use a *survey*, which is a list of questions to be answered by participants. Answers are often given through multiple-choice options or some sort of rating scale. One commonly used type of scale is the Likert scale (pronounced as "lick-ert," not "like-ert"). A Likert item asks respondents to rate statements about their attitudes and opinions on a topic based on how much they agree—for example: "Rate the statement 'I found the robot friendly' on a scale of 1 ('Strongly agree') to 5 ('Strongly disagree')." Another form of scale that is often used is the semantic differential scale, which asks respondents to evaluate the qualities of an artifact, or their attitudes, on a spectrum between two opposing terms (e.g., scary–friendly, competent–incompetent).

Multiple-choice or scale-based questions make the survey easier to analyze later on but require careful design while developing the survey to make sure that the questions are appropriately measuring the concepts the researchers are interested in. Along with making up their own questions and scales, researchers can use questions and scales developed and evaluated by other researchers to measure concepts of interest (e.g., evaluating participant personality with the Big Five Scale (John and Srivastava, 1999) or evaluating robot sociality with the Robot Social Attributes Scale (Carpinella et al., 2017)). Finally, researchers sometimes include open-ended questions in surveys as well, particularly when it is important to allow respondents to provide answers based on their own terms and categories or to understand their thought process or understanding of concepts while answering the survey (e.g., "Describe your ideal robot before you answer the following questions about it"). Because survey research is well established in the social sciences, there are many handbooks that describe how to go about constructing and performing surveys (for some examples, see Fowler (1995, 2013)).

Surveys allow researchers to investigate correlations between various factors relevant to HRI in a broad population. Such surveys often involve hundreds of participants and accommodate analyses with many different factors. Some surveys try to have a representative sample of participants, which can involve making sure the number of participants in certain categories (e.g., gender, age, ethnicity) corresponds to their percentage in the general population or weighting the collected data to achieve representative ratios.

10.2.3 System studies

Whereas user studies are used to report on people's attitudes toward and interaction with robots, system studies are those that evaluate the technical capabilities of the robot. A system study might involve users, but user involvement is not always needed. At the same time, system studies do require the same rigor expected from user studies. This means that verifiable research hypotheses and performance claims, a study protocol, and clear metrics are all key to system studies.

For example, when designing an interactive robot for children, you might want to know how well automated speech recognition works for your target user group (Kennedy et al., 2017). Speech recognition has been designed to work well for adults, but it might not be suitable for children due to their voices having a higher pitch and their speech often containing more disfluencies and ungrammatical utterances. To test whether speech recognition works for child speech, you could ask children to interact with your robot, but a better idea would be to use recordings of children's speech and pull these through the speech-recognition software. The benefit of this approach is that the experiment is repeatable: you can try different parameter settings in the software or even swap different speech-recognition engines and assess the performance using the same recordings.

Systems studies are often used to assess the perceptual capabilities of the robot. Capabilities such as face recognition, facial emotion classification, or sentiment detection from voice are best assessed using consistent test data sets with well-established metrics. For some capabilities, there are existing data sets that can be used to assess the performance of the robot. For face recognition, several data sets exist, for example, the IMDB-WIKI, which contains images of people extracted from the IMDb database and Wikipedia; in addition to labels, the images contain gender and age information (Rothe et al., 2016). The use of well-established metrics allows you to compare the performance of your robot to that of others. Classification problems often have agreed-on methods of reporting performance, such as reporting the accuracy of the classification (the number of correct classifications divided by the total number classifications, including the ones that are wrong) or the precision and recall. Speech-recognition performance is often expressed as a word error rate (WER), which is the total number of substitutions, deletions, and insertions in the text divided by the number of words in the actual spoken sentence. So if "Can you bring me a drink please" is recognized as "Can bring me a pink sneeze," that is a WER of $(2 + 1 + 0)/7 = 0.43$. It is worth exploring what the accepted metrics are in a particular discipline and rigorously sticking to the accepted method for evaluating and reporting system performance.

10.2.4 Observational studies

As robots have become more robust, more reliable, easier to use, and cheaper, it has become viable for HRI researchers to study how people and robots interact in various naturalistic contexts using observational methods. Observing how people interact with robots, for example, by studying where they place robots in their environments and how they respond to different kinds of verbal and nonverbal cues performed by robots, allows researchers to understand how HRI can unfold in a more natural way, without researchers directly intervening in the interaction.

Observational studies can be exploratory, involving putting a robot into a specific environment to see how interactions there unfold. An example of such an observational study is the work of Chang and Šabanović (2015), who put a seal companion robot in a public space in a nursing home and observed when and how different people interacted with the robot. The findings included frequency counts of interactions with the robot, as well as the identification of different social factors (e.g., participant gender, social mediation effects) that affected whether and for how long people interacted with the robot. The researchers did not manipulate anything about the robot or the environment. They just observed.

Observational studies can also be performed to evaluate, by means of a field experiment, how effective a robot is for a particular task or the effect of certain design variables on interactions. Researchers from the Advanced Telecommunications Research Institute (ATR) in Japan have performed several observational studies of interactions between the humanoid Robovie and mall customers. These studies represent a particularly fruitful iterative form of design and evaluation using observational techniques. In the initial stages of the study, researchers observed general human behaviors and analyzed these observations to identify particular behavioral patterns, which they then used to develop behavioral models for the robot. The robot was then placed in the mall, and people's reactions to it were evaluated to see if the behavioral models had the expected positive effects on people's responses.

Observational studies can rely on data collected in several different ways: observational notes and logs collected by a researcher in person, manual annotations of video recordings of interactions between people and robots, and robot logs from interactions with people.

In-person observation provides the possibility for researchers to have a better understanding of the broader context of interaction because they can see and hear things that might not initially be in the data-collection protocol. This can lead to amendments to the protocol or can be represented in notes that can help guide later analysis and interpretation of the data. In-person observation, however, is limited by the sensory capabilities of observers at the time of coding and does not allow for others to go back and review the coded observations. In terms of establishing interrater reliability (i.e., to what extent various people agree on an interpretation of an observation; e.g., was it a "social behavior" when a passerby moved out of the way to let the robot pass through?), more than one coder needs to be present in the context at the same time, which can be inconvenient and become a distraction to other people in the space because of the presence of multiple researchers.

Video coding, on the other hand, allows researchers to review observations as many times as needed, potentially revise their coding schemes, revise their codes of observations, and easily provide data to a second coder for establishing interrater reliability. Video, however, has a limited view defined by whatever is visible from the chosen camera angle. This may cause researchers to miss some relevant aspects of the interaction, so it is important to clearly define what the camera should be focused on before the video observation starts so that important things are not missed. Although video coding may seem more convenient and preferable overall, some contexts (e.g., nursing homes, hospitals, or schools) may not allow researchers to record video, so in-person coding may be necessary.

Finally, robot logs are limited by the robot's ability to sense and categorize different human actions but have the benefit of being able to provide data about both the robot's state and actions and the human actions it perceived at the same time. It is, of course, possible to combine these different data sources to improve the accuracy of the data.

Both in-person coding and video annotations require the development of a coding scheme that coders will follow systematically. This coding scheme can be developed based on theoretical or practical interests and expectations, or it can be developed in a bottom-up manner by identifying points of particular interest in a portion of the data and then going through the rest of the corpus to understand related patterns. It is very important to pilot test the coding scheme to identify missing components and overlapping or unclear codes so that coders can be in clear agreement about what the codes mean before they start (particularly for in-person coding, where you can't go back to view the interaction). Video analysis is also quite labor intensive, so properly defining how fine-grained you need the coding scheme to be can save time and effort. Aside from providing frequency counts of certain types of behaviors or identifying qualities and patterns of interaction, observational coding of interaction behaviors can also provide particularly interesting temporal patterns of behavior, which can show the effects of certain robot behaviors on people's actions (e.g., how a particular gaze cue by a robot is followed by a joint-attention behavior by a person).

10.2.5 Ethnographic studies

Along with behavioral observation, HRI researchers also engage in more in-depth and often long-term ethnographic observations, in which they not only seek to identify certain behavioral and interaction patterns among humans and robots but also to understand what those patterns mean to people and how they are connected with the broader environmental, organizational, social, and cultural contexts in which those interactions take place. Ethnographic observations can include all aspects of interactions between people and robots, including behaviors, speech, gestures, and posture. They also include information on the context in which those occur, including the daily practices, values, goals, beliefs, and discourse of different stakeholders, which include but are not limited to people who directly interact with the robot.

Whereas behavioral observation is inspired by ethology and the desire to explore and build explanatory models of animal and human behavior, ethnographic observation is based on the theory and practices of anthropology and the goals of understanding sociocultural experiences holistically. Ethnographic observation is often performed over longer periods of time, from a few months to a few years, which is necessary for the observer to get a more complete and emergent sense of the cultural logic of the research site. Ethnographic studies can be performed by participants as outside observers but also through participant observation, where the researcher takes part in the activity under study to better understand the experience. The former type of study is currently more widely represented in HRI, although social studies of robot design often take the latter approach. Ethnographic study is also often coupled with a "grounded theory" approach to data analysis, which assumes that the collection and interpretation of data are ongoing throughout the project, with the researcher regularly engaging in reflection on the questions that guide the research, methods of data collection and analysis, and potential interpretations of the data, thus iterating as the study goes along.

Ethnographic studies are still relatively rare in HRI, partly because of the labor involved in collecting data over longer periods of time but also because there have not been many robots that are technically capable of taking part in long-term interactions with people. Some successful examples of ethnographic studies include a one-year-long study of a service robot in a hospital that showed that the patient type in the context, oncology or postnatal, determined whether the robot was appreciated or hated (and sometimes kicked and sworn at) by nurses (Mutlu and Forlizzi, 2008). Forlizzi and DiSalvo (2006) did an ethnographic study in which they gave families either a robotic Roomba vacuum or the latest version of a conventional vacuum to use over several months. They learned that people treated the robot, but not the conventional vacuum, as a social agent and that having a robotic vacuum changed the way the family cleaned, particularly inspiring teenagers and men to participate. Leite et al. (2012) performed an ethnographic study with a social robot that could respond empathically to children in an elementary school. The study found that the task scenario and children's specific preferences influenced their experiences of the robot's empathy. Several ethnographic studies have also been performed with scientists using robots. Vertesi (2015) studied National Aeronautics and Space Administration (NASA) scientists' interactions with a remote Rover and showed how the organizational structure of the team affected the team members' use and experience of the robot. The study also showed that scientists performed aspects of the robot's behaviors with their own bodies, creating a team identity for themselves in the process.

Ethnographic studies are particularly valuable because HRI is a young field and thus is still developing a corpus of theoretical and empirical work that can identify the most relevant factors we need to pay attention to, not only in the design of robots but also in their implementation in different environments.

10.2.6 Conversational analysis

Conversational analysis (CA) is a method in which the verbal and nonverbal aspects of an interaction are reported in great detail (Sidnell, 2011). This is not limited to conversation only, as the name might imply, but can be applied to any form of interaction between people or between people and technology.

The process of CA starts by recording an interaction between two or more parties. Whereas this used to be audio recording, nowadays, video recording is more convenient, and several cameras can be used to capture the interaction from different angles. The participants being recorded might or might not be aware of the recording. From the recording, a very detailed transcription is produced, including turn-taking cues such as pauses in conversation, emotional cues such as laughter, behaviors performed while conversing, and other details of the interaction. Depending on the research question, the temporal resolution of the transcription can be brought down to the frame rate of the video recording. This can capture small actions, such as blinking and other eye movements, gestures, and changes in body posture. Fischer et al. (2013) used CA to investigate how the contingency of robot feedback affects the quality of verbal HRI. In their experiments, participants instructed the humanoid robot iCub how to stack some shapes in a contingent and noncontingent condition. Analysis of participants' linguistic behaviors, including verbosity, attention-getting tactics, and word diversity, showed that contingency had an impact on the participants' tutoring behaviors and therefore can be important for learning by demonstration.

CA will pay specific attention to elements in the verbal interaction, such as turn-taking, back-channeling, overlap of speaking, repair statements, echo utterances, and discourse markers. In HRI, CA can be used to analyze in great detail how people interact with social robots and whether they employ similar conversational strategies with robots as they do with people.

10.2.7 Crowdsourcing participants

HRI studies make extensive use of crowdsourcing to collect data and run studies. Crowdsourcing is the practice of obtaining responses from a large

number of people, either paid or unpaid, via online methods. In recent years, the use of online crowdsourcing platforms has allowed researchers to run user studies and gather large amounts of data with relatively little effort and to gather data from subjects they would typically struggle to reach (Doan et al., 2011). The online platform can be entirely built by the researchers, but more often, existing online tools are used to recruit, run, and analyze user studies. The most widely used tools are Amazon Mechanical Turk (MTurk or AMT) (see Figure 10.3) and Prolific. These services allow you to post jobs: usually, short user studies in which participants are asked to watch a number of images or videos containing robots or interactions with robots and then answer questions about the material.

Crowdsourcing allows researchers to gather large amounts of data in a short time frame and for a modest cost. Taking part in a study will earn each participant a small financial reward, typically only a few U.S. dollars, with the price set depending on the complexity of the task, the time it is expected to take, and the quality rating of the respondent.

Increasingly, crowdsourcing is being used to evaluate the technical aspects of robots. Interactive robots often need to display behavior—such as gaze fixation, back-channeling or co-speech gestures—that is difficult or even impossible to objectively evaluate. There is no equation to capture how good co-speech gestures are, and there is no formula to say how empathetic a robot's voice sounds. Instead, subjective evaluations are used. In this technique, people are asked to rate the behavior of the robot, and crowdsourcing offers an effective and cheap method to collect responses from a large variety of human raters (Wolfert et al., 2022).

Running crowdsourcing studies comes with its own set of unique challenges, though, the most important being the relatively low level of control the experimenter has over the subjects taking part in the study and the environment in which the study is executed. Any account that meets the broad inclusion criteria set by the crowdsourcing platform is allowed to take the job. However, the account that is logged in might not be being used by the actual person registered as taking part in the study. Participants could take your study while pursuing an array of other activities, such as eating ice cream while petting a cat, or they could be full of caffeine or sitting on a crowded bus while listening to loud music on headphones. Crowdsourcing is also open to malicious user behavior. participants often provide low-quality or deliberately incorrect responses.

To avoid some of these problems, it is good practice to include verification questions in your user study (Oppenheimer et al., 2009). These questions check whether participants pay attention and are engaged with the task. When showing a video, a number could be displayed for a few seconds, after which the video participants are asked to enter the number. Questions can also be used to ensure the participant is responding to the questions rather than just picking random responses, such as "Please click the third option from below."

After data collection, it is necessary to separate the wheat from the chaff. A first filter will be the responses to the verification questions; another method is to exclude all responses that took less than a reasonable amount of time. For example, if you believe the study should take a minimum of 15 minutes, then any responses that are far under that time should be disregarded. Some crowdsourcing platforms allow you not to reward participants if their responses are of insufficient quality, which not only leaves those participants without pay but also negatively affects their ratings. This has shown to be an excellent incentive to improve the quality of responses. Given that data collected using crowdsourcing are inherently more variable than data collected in the lab, one way of addressing this problem is to collect more of these data.

Although crowdsourcing has been successfully used to replicate results from lab studies in social psychology, linguistics, and behavioral economics (Bartneck et al., 2015a; Goodman et al., 2013; Schnoebelen and Kuperman, 2010; Suri and Watts, 2011), the value of crowdsourcing to HRI needs to be considered on a case-by-case basis. Sometimes the physical presence of a robot is key to the participant's performance, precluding the use of crowdsourcing. Sometimes the effect you are measuring is small and would not show up when sampling a large and diverse population. Sometimes the population you need is scarce on crowdsourcing platforms, such as elderly users or Swedish primary school teachers. Sometimes the task requires a certain level of language proficiency. Crowdsourcing has its place in HRI research, but it should be used with care and consideration.

Computer-based studies in general come with some problems: Participant age or technical affinity may play a role—for example, seniors and very young participants might not be highly familiar with computers that are commonly used to collect data. At the same time, depending on the age and cognitive abilities of participants, they might be more or less able to understand what we think we want to measure. For that reason, new variants of questionnaires may be required if you study participants with mild cognitive impairments or if you study children. However, using plain language (Stoll et al., 2022) not only benefits the aforementioned audience but also nearly everyone who might lack reading skills or might be largely unfamiliar with a topic.

10.2.8 Case Studies

Another type of study to consider in HRI is the case-study research design. In this type of qualitative study, researchers compare the effects of an intervention on a single participant rather than a group of people. This is done by initially collecting baseline measures of the individual's behavior, which are compared with the subject's behavior during and after the intervention.

Case studies are used when recruiting large numbers of participants is difficult because of their rarity in the population or when individual differences between subjects are large and relevant to the phenomenon of interest. Multiple participants can be recruited for case studies, but the number of subjects is often small, and for the sake of analysis, each participant is treated as his or her own control.

Case studies are commonly used in medical and education research fields, and in the case of HRI, they are used in research on the effects of robots on individuals with autism. For example, Pop et al. (2013) performed single-case studies with three children to investigate whether the social robot Probo can help children with autism spectrum disorders better identify situation-based emotions. Tapus et al. (2012) similarly worked with four children with autism to see whether they would show more social engagement with the Nao robot than with humans, and they found large variability among their responses. This shows the importance of performing single-participant studies in cases where individuals of interest, such as those diagnosed with autism, vary widely in their behaviors; in such cases, averaging the responses of a group could mask important intervention effects because different individual responses would cancel each other out when aggregated.

10.3 Selecting research participants and study designs

10.3.1 Representativeness of your sample

Because people are a necessary component of HRI studies, several important decisions in HRI studies must be made regarding the participants in a study. One is who the participants will be. The usual suspects for empirical HRI research are university students because they are the most convenient population to access for academic researchers, have time for and interest in participating in studies, and are usually in close physical proximity to the laboratories where much of the HRI research is performed.

It is, however, important to consider the limitations of using university students as a "convenience sample," particularly in relation to the research questions posed. In an ideal world, we would aim for a large, representative sample of potential end users of robots so that we can claim that our findings hold for a wide range of users and have *external validity*—that is, they can tell us something about people and robots in situations outside the study itself. Such samples are very difficult to bring in for experimental studies but might be more achievable in surveys. In studies of the general perceptions of robots, HRI, similarly to psychological research, assumes that university students are "close enough" to the general population in terms of characteristics when it comes to broad social traits (e.g., stereotyping), cognitive performance (e.g., memory), and attitudes (e.g., fear of robots). Even when using university students, it is important to be mindful of and balance certain characteristics of the sample, such as gender or educational background, depending on whether these factors might be expected to have an effect on your results. For example, students in a computer science department would likely be seen as having more positive attitudes toward robots and having greater ease in using computing technology than a broader student population or the general population of potential users.

If your research questions relate to studying the characteristics of a specific population, such as older adults, or to investigating the effects of robot applications in specific domains, such as the treatment of children with diabetes, your choice of participants will need to be more specialized. The specificity of your research question and the claims you want to make will guide the level of specificity of your sample. It is not possible, for example, to claim that a robot will have positive effects on older adults experiencing cognitive decline if you run your study with university students or even with older adults who are not experiencing cognitive decline. A university student sample will also not be sufficient for investigating the use of robots to support learning in young children. Thus, before running your study, you need to make a careful decision about what kinds of people should take part in it. You will also need to consider how to get access to this population and how to recruit and motivate individuals to be in your study. You should also consider whether you will be able to bring people from this population to your lab, whether you need to go to another place to have contact with them, or whether an online study might be appropriate.

10.3.2 Sample size

Another consideration regarding research participants is the number of participants you might need to answer your research questions (Bartlett et al., 2022). This will depend both on the type of study and analysis you are doing (quantitative vs. qualitative, survey, experiment, or interview) and on the population you are working with (e.g., university students, or older adults, or children with diabetes). It is difficult to reliably test for an effect with a small sample size because people will always differ a little bit from one another. In a study on gender stereotypes, for example, some participants will consider all robots a bit more "warm" than others; other participants will think all robots possess typically "male" qualities. Such differences, which naturally occur in people, will add noise to the data. Unless the manipulation has an extremely large effect, the data that we gather from a small sample will not be enough to reliably detect an effect. The differences among people might cancel each other out, or the variability of their responses might be too large. If you want to reach a valid conclusion about cause and effect, you need to determine the right sample size for your study design.

How many participants you need to reliably find a difference between conditions also depends on the type of design you use. When using a *between-subjects design*, participants are randomly assigned to a condition. In our example, one group of participants would be presented with the "male" robot, whereas the other group of participants would be shown the "female" version. After answering questions using a Likert scale, the mean scores of each group can be compared. Alternatively, in a *within-subjects design*, one group of participants is exposed to both versions of the robot prototype and asked to evaluate both. Because the same person provides two evaluations, you cut down on the "noise" in your data, and the number of participants required will be lower for this design. However, not all research questions are suitable to be answered with a within-subjects design. For example, if you want to test if people recover faster from a broken leg when they have a robotic assistant that does walking exercises with them every day, you can hardly have them first heal on their own and then break the other leg so that they can recover again with their robot helper. Also, researchers have to be mindful of the order effect that may occur; maybe people will always like the first robot better than the second (e.g., because of the novelty). Thus, it is a good idea to *counterbalance* any conditions when running a within-subjects design. This means that half the participants will first interact with the female robot and then with the male, and vice versa for the other half.

To approximate a sufficient sample size to establish a statistical effect of the desired size, the internet offers a variety of tools, such as G*Power (Faul et al., 2007). However, researchers may not always be able to meet such recommendations because they are also constrained by the availability of resources, such as time, money, robots, and potential participants.

Studies that involve special populations, such as older adults with depression, may have to make do with a smaller number of participants because of the acknowledged difficulty in recruiting specific populations. In some cases, such as studies of children diagnosed with autism, where the participants are also widely diverse in the way they express themselves and experience the world, it is possible to treat participants as individual cases and study changes within each participant's behaviors and responses.

For qualitative studies, rather than focusing on a particular number of participants needed, the rule of thumb is to try to achieve "saturation" of the analytic themes and findings. The idea here is that the researchers can stop collecting new data once they find that the data they are collecting are simply adding to and repeating existing themes and findings rather than creating new ones. Although it is relatively easy to understand, this concept can be more challenging to operationalize and measure, so scholars have developed various ways of defining and quantifying data saturation in various studies (e.g., Lowe et al., 2018; Guest et al., 2020).

10.4 Defining the context of interaction

10.4.1 Location of study

For HRI in particular, an important distinction is between studies performed in the lab versus those performed in the field. Especially in the early years of HRI, the majority of research was performed in the controlled environment of the lab. Although robotic technology has certainly advanced over the years, and there are now robotic platforms robust enough to use outside of the lab, so-called "in the wild" studies are still relatively rare compared with the number of studies performed in the lab.

Studying interactions outside of the laboratory is important for understanding how people might interact with robots in natural circumstances, determining what kinds of HRI might emerge in those circumstances, and investigating the potential broader social effects of new robotic technologies.

On the other hand, laboratory studies benefit from the researchers' ability to strictly control the context and nature of people's interactions with a robot—the introduction, task, environment, and length of the interaction can be clearly defined by the researchers. In the lab, participants are asked to interact with the robot only in the way researchers suggest. This allows for the strict manipulation of desired variables.

In contrast, field studies are more flexible in what can happen and are therefore closer to what might occur in day-to-day HRI. In the field, participants can choose how, when, whether, and why they want to interact with a robot; they can even ignore it. Field studies, therefore, provide a space in which to observe and discover new emergent phenomena, new variables of interest and significance to interaction, and the form and consequences of HRI when it is outside of the researchers' control. Field studies also effectively show how complex interactions between different contextual variables, such as institutional culture or interactions among people, might affect the interaction.

10.4.2 Temporal context of HRI

A related distinction that has grown in importance in HRI is whether researchers are studying short-term or long-term interactions between people and robots. The majority of lab studies, by necessity of their design, focus on "the first 10 minutes of HRI"—how people respond to and make sense of their first introduction to a robot. Researchers widely acknowledge, however, that people will change their attitude toward the robot as time passes, and consequently, the way they interact with the robot will change as well. The first interaction suffers from the *novelty effect*: people are generally not familiar with robots, so their initial reactions might be quite different from their reactions over a longer period of time. Short-term studies therefore have limited validity in informing us about how people and robots will interact over a longer period of time. They do, however, tell us about the kinds of characteristics of people and features of the robot that will affect the initial encounter. Such studies are important for setting up a positive feedback loop of interaction, which can then support more positive effects in long-term interaction. Studies of longer-term interactions, which can take place over several days, weeks, months, or in a few cases, even years, allow us to see how interactions between people and robots develop and change over time, how robots are integrated into human social contexts, and how social interactions between people themselves may change because of the presence of a robot.

10.4.3 Social units of interaction in HRI

Interactions between people and robots can be studied through several different social units of analysis, which the social sciences see as distinct in terms of the aspects of cognition and interaction they enable (see Figure 10.4).

Figure 10.4 Units of analysis in HRI.

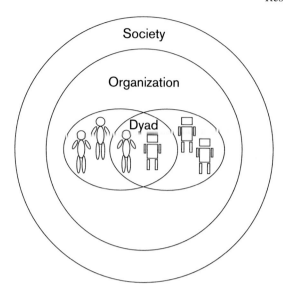

The most common unit, so far, has been the interaction dyad—one person and one robot interacting with each other. This is partly due to the early constraints of HRI—robots were difficult to procure and difficult to maintain and operate; hence, the most common form of HRI study was the lab experiment involving a single participant interacting with a single robot.

Figure 10.5 Robovie in school.

As early as 2006, the Robovie robot was one of the first robots capable of supporting group interactions at an elementary school (see Figure 10.5). It taught children English and tracked their social networks over time, keeping the children interested in interacting with the robot by unlocking secrets (Kanda et al., 2007b).

As robots have become more readily available and capable of interacting with more people and in more open-ended, naturalistic environments, the unit of analysis in HRI has expanded. Early studies of HRI "in the wild" showed that people actually often interact with robots not individually but in groups, a task for which most early robots were poorly equipped (Šabanović et al., 2006). Increasingly, HRI studies group interactions involving two or more people, both inside and outside of the lab. For example, Leite et al. (2015) found that children were better able to recall information from a story told by a group of robots when they interacted with them individually rather than in a group of three. Brscić et al. (2015) showed that children who come across a robot in a shopping mall abuse the robot only when they are in groups but not individually.

Social scientists distinguish between dyadic interactions and group interactions, and they consider the cognitive and behavioral aspects of each to be different. Groups bring in new perspectives on group effects, multi-party collaboration, team dynamics, and other such effects. Our vision of how we will be interacting with robots in the future also presupposes that there will be many robots in our environment, so another aspect of group HRI studies has been exploring how multiple robots can interact with people, whether in teams, in swarms, or simply as co-present robotic actors.

> When robots collaborate in teams, they are often perceived as having more social agency. For example, Carpenter (2016) found that robots used in military bomb-disposal teams were often seen by the soldiers as members of the group and that soldiers became attached to such robots, even expressing feelings of sadness when their team's robot was destroyed.

The increasing availability of robots for research in applied settings beyond the laboratory opens up another unit of analysis. That is, we can look at how HRI occurs within organizations, such as educational and nursing institutions or even the military. By studying HRI within organizations, it is not only possible to see the effect of individual factors on HRI but also the effect of the broader context, such as how existing labor distributions or roles affect the robot's function and its acceptance by workers, how the robot is adapted to existing practices, and how institutional values affect people's interpretations of the robot.

Mutlu and Forlizzi (2008) showed that introducing a robot into an organization, for example, reduced work for some while increasing it for others. At the same time, it is plausible that people in different roles (e.g., manager, nurse, janitor) can have different perceptions of a robot based on how it affects their work. In another ethnographic study on the use of the seal-like Paro robot in a nursing home, Chang and Šabanović (2015) showed that having even one person who acts as an advocate for the robot in an organization can lead to more people committing to try it out and make it work for them, by modeling positive experiences of using the robot and creating a "positive feedback loop" that supports the long-term adoption of the robot. An organization can also be set up in a particular way to support the functions of a robot. Vertesi's (2015) ethnographic study of the NASA Rover team showed that the need to balance the robot as a scarce resource shared by many different scientists and engineers worked well with an egalitarian setup of the team, where all team members needed to agree and say they were "happy" about the robot's next move. Now that it is possible, studying interactions between people and robots from an organizational standpoint seems necessary for the further development of the field and for our ability to design appropriate robots and social structures for the successful application of HRI in the real world (Jung and Hinds, 2018).

10.5 Choosing a robot for your study

Along with deciding how many and what types of participants you need to answer your research question, you will also need to decide on the characteristics of the robot(s) you need to use in your study. Factors you will need to decide on include the robot's appearance, functionality, and ease of use, among others. Whereas some of these decisions might be based on practical constraints, such as what types of robots are available to you or how much it would cost to purchase a new one, others will be guided by your research interests.

Robots can be seen as research tools with which you can manipulate factors of interest and observe the effects of such manipulation on the outcome variables you want to measure. This approach is at the heart of experimental HRI research but can also be useful for more exploratory studies in which you may want to see if certain design factors produce differential effects on HRI. In order to use robots as a stimulus in HRI studies, we can manipulate their appearance, behavior, and communication mode and style, as well as their role in the interaction, among other characteristics. HRI researchers often use off-the-shelf robots for their studies, but they also sometimes design and test their own prototypes. When deciding what kind of robot to use, determining which hardware and software capabilities would be best for the study and the appropriate level of autonomy of the robot are important considerations.

There are some commercial robots that lend themselves well to HRI studies, such as the Nao (Aldebaran Robotics), Furhat (Furhat Robotics), QTrobot (LuxAI), or Paro (Intelligent System). Even when using a commercial robot, getting your robot up and running will require some basic programming skills. The Nao and the QTrobot can be programmed using a visual programming environment, which allows you to quickly go from the drawing board to a working robot. However, knowledge of more advanced control software and programming languages, such as the Robot Operating System (ROS), will allow you to greatly extend the repertoire of the robot's behavior and enrich the interaction. ROS contains a number of packages that implement sensory perception and visualization for different types of robots.

10.6 Setting up the mode of interaction

There are dozens of ways in which people and robots can be brought together for a study. People can meet an actual robot, or they can be shown pictures or videos of a robot. The robot can be fully autonomous or can be tele-operated by the experimenter. People can come to the lab, or the scientists can get out of the lab and bring their robots to the people. Sometimes, a single data point is all that is needed; on other occasions, only thousands of data points will do.

10.6.1 Wizard of Oz

In some HRI studies where the development of autonomous capabilities for the robot is not the focus of the research at hand, researchers commonly rely on the Wizard-of-Oz (WoZ) technique. WoZ involves deceiving study participants into thinking the robot is behaving autonomously, when it is actually being operated by a member of the research team. Research participants should then be informed about this deception in a post-experimental debriefing (see also Section 10.9).

Using WoZ, researchers can "pretend" that their robot has interactional skills that it does not have, either because they require further technical development or because additional time or skill must be expended on programming the robot. The WoZ approach is particularly suitable in situations in which technology has developed to a degree at which it is almost usable for HRI, such as speech recognition. Using a wizard to recognize the users' utterances makes an experiment more robust and the robot's behavior more realistic and believable, enabling an actual interaction flow. It could, however, be considered problematic to completely fake an AI system that can uphold a serious and prolonged conversation because that would be considered a very unrealistic level of capability for the robot.

WoZ can also be used to test people's perceptions of more advanced capabilities, such as a robot that can understand and respond to the social context in very nuanced ways (e.g., see Kahn et al. (2012)). For experimental studies, it is important to constrain the wizard's behavior so that the robot's behavior is kept consistent across conditions and does not introduce additional variation that can confound the analysis. WoZ can also be used as a way to collect data from participants to help develop a robot's design or autonomous capabilities (e.g., Martelaro and Ju, 2017; Hu et al., 2023; Sequeira et al., 2016).

> The WoZ method is named after a character in the movie of the same name. Dorothy and her companions set out to find the all-mighty Wizard of Oz who can return Dorothy to Kansas. They encounter the wizard in his castle and are afraid of his gigantic appearance, his authoritative voice, and the smoke and fire he emits. Only when Dorothy's dog, Toto, pulls away a curtain do they notice Professor Marvel, who is operating the machinery that controls the wizard. In HRI research, wizards often hide in the background and control the robot, giving the robot the semblance of having more advanced autonomous capabilities than it actually has. We all hope not to encounter Toto and be found out.

10.6.2 Real versus simulated interaction

Although the ideal way to gauge people's perceptions of and response to robots is in real-time, face-to-face interaction, it is still common for HRI researchers to present their participants only with video or photos of robots. In the field of HRI, there has been considerable discussion on whether video recordings of robots can be used as a replacement for live human–robot interactions. Whereas Dautenhahn et al. (2006) argue that the two interaction styles are broadly equivalent, Bainbridge et al. (2011) conclude that participants had a more positive experience interacting with physically present robots than with a video representation. Powers et al. (2007) also found large attitude differences between participants interacting with a co-located robot in comparison to a remote robot. Therefore, the use of visual stimuli alone limits the generalizability of study findings but can be appropriate for exploratory studies of the effects of certain factors (e.g., perceptions of different robot forms; see DiSalvo et al., 2002) or for studies in which accessing the appropriate population can be difficult, such as cross-cultural samples. Using videos to present robots to participants can also enable researchers to avoid problems associated with a less controlled experiment that involves actual interaction. Finally, videos and photos are particularly amenable for use in studies that take advantage of online participant pools, whether through universities, word-of-mouth referrals, or services like Amazon's Mechanical Turk.

10.7 Selecting appropriate HRI measures

In HRI, as in psychology and other social sciences, researchers commonly distinguish between direct versus indirect measures to assess attitudes toward people or objects. In the example of the "gendered" robot study described earlier, the study design relied on *direct measurements* of the dependent variables—asking participants to rate the robot's warmth and authoritativeness, for example.

Within both correlational and experimental studies, self-reports are often used to assess the constructs of interest, such as concepts or variables. Self-report measures commonly bear high face validity, meaning that people usually directly know what the researchers want to measure when they read the items of the given questionnaire. On the other hand, this makes it easy for participants to amend their actual opinion with the aim of pleasing researchers, to represent themselves in a positive light or "be a good participant." This aspect also holds true for interview techniques, which are a way to gather an even more holistic picture of participants' thoughts and feelings toward both humans and robots. Interviews can be structured or semistructured in nature. In structured interviews, the interviewer asks a set of predetermined questions, often in a specific order, whereas in a semistructured interview, the interviewer has more leeway in deviating from the script; for example, some questions may be planned, but others may arise spontaneously during the interview. Both types often use questions to which interviewees can respond in their own words. Such open-ended responses, however, require labor-intensive coding after transcription of the interview's content. Such interviews might be a useful complement to questionnaires, though, as illustrated by de Graaf et al.'s (2017) use of data from a long-term survey and an interview to explore the reasons why people choose not to use a communication robot in their homes. As their work has shown, a research participant might feel highly uncomfortable in the presence of an unfamiliar robot.

In some cases, however, participants might be reluctant to report their true feelings and attitudes on a questionnaire or when talking directly to an interviewer. They may also not be aware of and able to report some unconsciously held beliefs. In that situation, it might be useful to complement your set of direct measures with indirect ones. Reaction times are often used as a proxy for factors that are harder to measure, such as attention or engagement. Indirect measures can include the use of eye tracking as an indicator of attentional focus and cognitive processing or the use of physiological measures such as heart rate or skin conductance to give researchers an idea of participants' level of stress experienced during HRI. Whereas computerized measures of attitude (e.g., a variant of the so-called Implicit Association Test[2] to measure anthropomorphization) have become increasingly popular, physiological correlates of attitudes toward robots or other technologies are less frequently used in contemporary research. Computerized and physiological measures are often more difficult to administer and require specific equipment, and ultimately, the findings are not always interpretable in an unambiguous manner. For example, skin conductance can indicate that someone is excited, but it cannot reveal whether the excitement is due to fear or enjoyment. In addition, a study in which the skin conductance of participants was measured as they interacted with a Nao robot showed that skin conductance readings are, unfortunately, not very conclusive (Kuchenbrandt et al., 2014).

To circumvent difficulties in interpreting results, it is helpful to use a combination of direct and indirect measures or several indirect measures at once in one study to ensure that you are indeed measuring the construct, or variable, that you intend to measure. As a researcher, you should aim to establish that all measurements used in your research reliably and validly assess what they are supposed to capture. This can be done by carefully pilot testing your study designs and measures used, developing and even formally validating new measures, or using widely accepted and validated measures that you find in the literature.

10.8 Standards for statistical analysis

"To call in the statistician after the experiment is done may be no more than asking him to perform a post-mortem examination: he may be able to say what the experiment died of."

As the famous quote by statistician Sir Ronald Aylmer Fisher (February 17, 1890–July 29, 1962) points out, the earlier on you ask for advice on your experimental design and analysis, the more useful it will be. Most universities offer statistical consultation of some sort, but even informal discussions with peers and professors may prove of tremendous value.

Although statistics has a reputation for being confusing and incomprehensible, in reality, most statistical tests are built on three main measurements: tendency, variability, and number of observations. To understand how these three things influence statistical testing, imagine that you're trying to decide

---

[2] See https://implicit.harvard.edu/implicit/

which of two restaurants is better. You have never actually been to either, but you can pull up reviews easily enough to compare. What would help you decide whether restaurant A is actually better than restaurant B? Well, obviously, you would first look at the average reviews. If restaurant A has an average of 4.8 stars out of 5 and restaurant B averages 3.2 stars out of 5, you will be fairly certain that A is better than B. The closer those averages are to one another, the less certain you will be that one restaurant is actually better than the other. This would be an indication of the difference in *tendency* between both groups.

But that is not everything that you will want to take into account. If you see that restaurant A has an average of 5 stars but only 3 people left a review, whereas restaurant B has an average of 4.7 stars from over 1,000 reviewers, you may still opt for restaurant B. This would be because you—quite reasonably—assume that with so many reviewers, you get a better estimate of the "true" quality of the restaurant. This is the influence of *sample size*: the more responses we have, the more certain we can be that the tendency is an accurate representation of the truth. Another example you can think of here is trying to figure out whether or not a coin is fair. Getting heads 75% of the time will not let you say for sure if you flipped it only four times (and got three heads and one tail), whereas the same percentage of heads would be pretty convincing if you had flipped the coin 1,000 times.

And finally, there is the matter of variability. Say that restaurant A and B both have an average of 4.2 stars and both have the same number of reviews, but for restaurant A, these reviews range from 1 star to 5 stars, whereas restaurant B has mostly 4-star ratings with a few 5 stars. For which restaurant would you be more certain that the 4.2 star is an accurate indication of the quality? This is the importance of *variability*: the more variable the results, the less certain we are that our sample mean is an accurate indication of the "true" effect.

These three measurements—tendency, sample size, and variability—are often called *descriptive statistics*. They give a summary overview of data without yet comparing conditions or calculating correlations, and they should be used as the first stage of data analysis. Always provide means (which indicate the tendency), standard deviations (which are an indicator of variability when the data have a normal distribution—if this is not the case, you can provide a range), and the number of participants (sample size). In addition, demographics (e.g., age and gender) will give your reader an idea of whether your sample resembles the general population, and excluded data points, together with the reason for exclusion, need to be reported for integrity and transparency.

Next, your study will probably require inferential statistics. Most classical statistical tests combine the tendency (often the mean), sample size, and variability into a test statistic, which in turn is used to calculate the p-value: the probability of getting the data at hand if there had been no true effect. Going back to the restaurant analogy, the p-value indicates how likely it would have been to get the reviews we got *if both restaurants had been equally good.*

The smaller that chance is, the more confident we may be in the hypothesis that one restaurant is in fact better than the other. This is the logic behind null hypothesis significance testing (NHST). Different study designs warrant different kinds of statistical tests to get to the *p*-value. Although going into the details of the extensive number of statistical tests and procedures is beyond the scope of this chapter, the interested reader might consult the readily available literature, such as the work of Andy Field (2018).

Until recently, science relied on NHST to report on the importance of results. If the probability of the data under the null hypothesis is small enough (i.e., *p*-value is less than or equal to some threshold, typically 0.05), the result may be considered "significant," and the null hypothesis would be rejected in favor of the alternative hypothesis. On the face of it, this provides a useful means of characterizing the success (or failure) of a method or intervention.

> The definition of the *p*-value may sound formal and confusing, but you have probably applied an intuitive version of it before. For example, take a look at the following headline, published in the *Moscow Times* (2020) at the start of the coronavirus pandemic: "Third Russian Doctor Falls from Hospital Window after Coronavirus Complaint."
>
> Reading this headline may have made you wonder whether this unfortunate accident was indeed only that, an accident. Your suspicion would stem from your inference that under the null hypothesis (i.e., if there had been no conspiracy against critical doctors), the probability of three of these incidents in a row would have been quite low. Although you did not calculate a concrete value, this is, in essence, what the *p*-value boils down to.

10.8.1 Making sense of statistics

There are a few common misunderstandings and often-overlooked implications in NHST, which have given rise to a recent questioning of the overreliance on NHST and *p*-values (Nuzzo, 2014).

Assuming a threshold of $p \leq .05$, this still means that 5% of the time where the null hypothesis is true (i.e., there is nothing going on), the obtained data will look as if there is an effect. This would constitute a *Type I error*, or false positive. Because false positives look exactly like true positives, even a significant result cannot be taken as conclusive proof that there is an effect.

Moreover, the *p*-value is often wrongfully taken to indicate "the chance of a Type I error." This complete misinterpretation of the *p*-value is pervasive and widespread among both students and academics (Badenes-Ribera et al., 2015; Lyu et al., 2020). In reality, the *p*-value only indicates the chance of a Type I error *if nothing had been going on* (i.e., conditional on the null hypothesis), and the overall chance of the results being due to a Type I error cannot be computed.

A fundamental issue with NHST concerns the inferences that one can and cannot draw from it. What is tested in NHST (the chance of finding the current data, provided that there is no true effect, or $p[A|B]$) is not what the researcher actually wants to know (the chance of a true effect, provided the current data, or $p[B|A]$). Although these *may* seem similar, their fundamental difference becomes clear when we consider sharks and death tolls. The chance of dying, provided that you are eaten by a shark, $p(dead|sharkbite)$, is pretty close to 1. However, the chance that you are eaten by a shark, provided that you are dying, $p(sharkbite|dead)$, is close to 0—for better or worse, most of us die from other causes than shark attacks. In his entertaining and remarkably accessible paper "The Earth Is Round ($p < 0.05$)," Jacob Cohen explains some of the problems with NHST in further depth (Cohen, 1994).

Related to the misunderstanding of the *p*-value is the misconception that *p*-values are stable; that is, if you conduct a study twice, you should get a similar *p*-value each time (Badenes-Ribera et al., 2015). Empirical results have suggested, and simulation studies have shown, that *p*-values are highly volatile in experiment replications. Repeating a study that has a significant *p*-value can result in the *p*-values of the replication study being in the range [0.00008,0.44] for 80% of the replication studies (Cumming, 2008). *p*-values are thus unreliable as a measure of how solid a result is.

Another common mistake is the conflation of a *p*-value with how big or important an effect is. The significance, size, and importance of an effect are three different things: a very small ("highly significant") *p*-value does not say anything about the size of the observed experimental effect. An effect size captures how large a change is between two conditions. It is calculated from the tendency and the variability of the data. The *p*-value, in addition, takes the sample size into account. Thus, the *p*-value can be considered an indication of how consistent the effect in the collected sample is, whereas the effect size indicates how large it is. These two measurements should both be seen as different from importance.

To illustrate the distinction between the three, consider the following situation: A new treatment has been developed for a medical condition. You compare this new treatment against the conventional treatment and find a significant yet small effect: recovery rates improve from 4% to 6%. What to make of this? Well, that depends. If the medical condition is foot fungus, you probably won't care much for a 2% higher chance of getting rid of your fungus. You would need a larger effect size to really care, especially if this new treatment is more expensive or has more side effects than the standard treatment. However, if the 2% increase refers to the chance of survival from a very aggressive kind of cancer, the very same effect size would probably be considered rather important.

Different statistical tests come with their own calculations of effect size; common effect sizes include Cohen's *d* (for a *t*-test), η_p^2 or ω^2 (for analysis

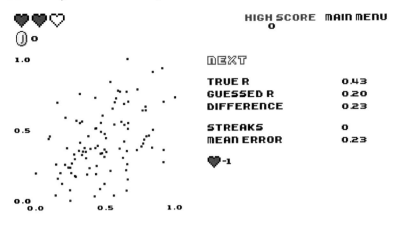

Figure 10.6 If you had to make a guess, how strongly would you say the two variables in the plot are correlated? It has been shown that people find it very hard to infer the strength of a relationship from plots. On the website www.guesst hecorrelation.com, you can try for yourself. (By the way, the correlation in the picture is $r = .43$, which is considered a medium effect.) (Source: Omar Wagih)

of variance (ANOVA)), and R^2_{adj} (for regression). For most effect sizes, there are guidelines available to help with the interpretation, which will provide a rule of thumb of what constitutes a "small," "medium," or "large" effect. For example, in Figure 10.6, a medium effect for a correlation is shown.

A final important implication from NHST involves capitalizing on Type I errors, also known as "p-hacking." You already encountered this in the discussion of spurious correlations in Section 10.1.2. The logic behind p-hacking is as follows: if a cutoff value of $p \leq .05$ is used, then if there is no true effect (i.e., under the null hypothesis), logically, one would expect a false positive 1 in 20 times. Thus, if you run enough tests, you will eventually find a significant result even if, in reality, there is none. If you then only report the significant results and leave out all the times where you found no effect, you can easily present your results as a valid new finding. p-hacking is especially problematic for observational studies because it is very easy to measure many variables and keep testing the relationship between different combinations of measurements until you find one that is significant.

10.8.2 Good practices to overcome issues with classic statistical testing

We can partially remedy these issues by reporting not only the p-values but also the confidence intervals (CIs) of our data. CIs do not compare data and therefore cannot be used to say if results are significant or not. Instead, they report on how confident we are that the population mean (which we estimate through the mean of our sample) lies between a minimum and maximum value of the CI. When reporting the 95% CI of data, this means that in a replication study, the mean of the replication data will have an 83% chance of being within the CI of the original experiment. Reporting CIs and effect sizes conveys additional information on the magnitude of an effect and the precision of the estimates provided. This information complements the significance and will help both you and your reader to make sense of the findings (Coe, 2002).

The *p*-value indicates the chance of a Type I error (false positive) under the null hypothesis. However, as mentioned in Section 10.3, the opposite is possible as well: a researcher can conduct an experiment, gather data, and then wrongfully conclude that there is no effect. This has been, not very creatively, named a *Type II error*, or a false negative. Type I and II errors can be avoided by making sure your experiment has sufficient statistical power to detect any true effects. Power depends on the same three measurements mentioned before—tendency, variability, and sample size—but of those three, only the last one is under your control. Thus, you have to make sure you collect either enough participants or enough data points per participant. This can be tricky, and the number of participants needed can increase dramatically depending on how complicated your study design is or how small the effect you're hoping to detect is. Software such as G*Power (Faul et al., 2007) allows you to calculate the power both before and after a study.

Another way to ensure that results are trustworthy and not the consequence of Type I or II errors is through replication. Psychology has recently seen a replication crisis (Maxwell et al., 2015), where a number of "established" effects failed to replicate. Although this is to be expected under NHST, *p*-hacking may have been partially responsible. In HRI, the reproducibility of research has been less prominent on the research agenda, but the recent concerns in the social science community have brought these topics into the purview of HRI researchers as well (Irfan et al., 2018). Replication of HRI results is also now more possible than before because of the wide availability of certain robot platforms (e.g., Nao or Baxter), in contrast to the earlier reliance by researchers on bespoke platforms.

Registration can facilitate replication and prevent *p*-hacking by forcing researchers to specify exactly what tests they are planning to run before collecting data (see p. 164). There has been a drive for sharing code for commonly available robots and, if possible, making the experimental procedures available to other HRI researchers in order to enable them to run the same experiment in their own labs, testing the generalizability of a certain research question across contexts (Baxter et al., 2016). Overall, the notion of generalizability is highly important, even though representative samples are hard to obtain in HRI research.

The choice of methodology also affects the degree to which we can generalize from our HRI studies in the laboratory to those findings obtained from field studies. Developing new robots, applying robots in different contexts, and understanding the potential consequences of robots for people in daily life may require a combination of the methods mentioned in this chapter. This does not need to be done in one research project or by a single researcher but could be accomplished by the HRI research community over time.

A final, radical way to overcome issues associated with NHST is to abandon NHST altogether. This can be done through the adoption of Bayesian inference, a method of statistical analysis that has been increasing in popularity (Van de Schoot et al., 2017). As noted in Section 10.8, NHST draws inferences conditional on the null hypothesis: How likely are these data if nothing had been going on? The outcome is dichotomous: a result is either significant, or it is not. In contrast, Bayesian statistics uses prior information to draw a hypothesis and updates this with the newly gathered data. The result is not a single estimate but rather a range of possible values and an indication of how much confidence can be placed in each estimate (Etz and Vandekerckhove, 2018). As a result, it is rare that a "hard conclusion" is drawn from Bayesian inference. Rather, previous beliefs are strengthened or weakened, depending on how the newly found data align with the prior data.

10.9 Ethical considerations in HRI studies

Last but not least, one important aspect to consider when dealing with human participants in HRI studies is the need to take into account the ethics of human-subjects research. Any research that involves human participants, whether correlational or experimental, qualitative or quantitative, online or in person, requires participants' informed consent before the research is started. That is, participants are informed about the nature of the study and what to expect, with an emphasis on the voluntary nature of their participation and information regarding the risks and benefits of taking part in a given research study. Before starting a study, either online or in the real world, participants have to declare that they understand what they will be asked to do and what will be done with the collected data and that they consent to participating. Many universities and institutions have specific guidelines on how participants can be recruited and informed about their participation in research studies. Researchers need to be aware of this and follow all policies to be able to present their results for publication after the study.

Sometimes, however, it is impossible to fully disclose the actual goals of the given research project. In that case, a cover story or deception is used. For instance, in WoZ studies, participants are led to believe that a robot can behave autonomously. In that case, it is key to provide post-experimental information, a so-called *debriefing*, to participants so that they do not go home from the study thinking that robots are currently able to function fully autonomously.

This is even more critical if a robot might provide the human interaction partner with fictitious feedback about the human's personality or performance. Of course, the participants then must be debriefed about the reason for providing made-up feedback, and they must be informed that this feedback was actually bogus. Again, this serves to ensure participants' psychological well-being beyond the duration of the study.

In the case of qualitative research, initial information about the study goals given to participants may be more cursory, but the common practice is to later inform study participants of the findings if they are interested. In some cases, researchers might even discuss their interpretations of the data with participants or collaboratively develop interpretations and future robot design and implementation guidelines based on the results.

In HRI research, we also have to consider the ethical aspects of having humans involved with robots—both in terms of physical and psychological safety and in terms of the implications an interaction could have for a given individual. Think, for example, of an elderly person who has had a robot in his or her home for a certain amount of time and might have gotten attached to the robot companion. Consequently, the day the robot is taken away, this will cause distress. Users' emotional reactions toward robots, the attachments they might build, and the void that results when the robot is taken away must be considered.

To make sure that you are complying with ethics regulations, you may consult with the various codes of ethical conduct, such as those provided by the American Psychological Association,[3] the American Anthropological Association,[4] or the Association for Computing Machinery.[5] Your university's ethics committee may provide more detailed feedback regarding your specific research study. Note that ethics approval is a requirement for publication in many scientific journals, so consider getting it before you start your data collection.

Along with ethical behavior toward research participants, researchers should also reflect on the ethical implications of their research aims, questions, and findings and make choices about what types of research to pursue, and how to go about it, with these implications in mind. Such ethical considerations can include questions about where to seek out and whether to accept funding, whether to participate in research that may inform particular corporations or governments, and even how to structure one's relationship with participants and their ability to provide input on the methods and presentation of research results.

More generally, the ethical and social consequences of the implementation of robots in society have to be taken into account. In most contemporary research projects that deal with smart homes or the deployment of robots in homes, care facilities, or public spaces, these aspects have to be investigated and addressed. Considering the ethical implications of digitalization and a potential hybrid human–robot society is a key societal issue that is now discussed at large, not solely by robot ethicists and philosophers.

10.10 Conclusion

HRI studies have a lot in common with work in several social science disciplines, including experimental psychology, anthropology, and sociology. It is good practice to be aware of scholarly norms and practices in the field or fields relevant to your work. HRI researchers are expected to be aware of and adopt the same rigor when collecting and reporting data as other scholars using the methods they have chosen.

---

[3] See www.apa.org/ethics/code/

[4] See https://s3.amazonaws.com/rdcms-aaa/files/production/public/FileDownloads/pdfs/issues/policy-advocacy/upload/ethicscode.pdf

[5] See www.acm.org/about-acm/code-of-ethics

HRI is also sensitive to the same problems that have plagued the social sciences for over a century. For example, in the drive to come up with original work, HRI experiments are almost never repeated. There is also a considerable publication bias, with positive results more likely to make it to publication, whereas negative results, less exciting results, or less conclusive findings tend not to get published or to go unnoticed. However, HRI has opportunities that were not on offer until recently. Experimental data, including large video logs, can now be fully stored and shared with others, ready for scrutiny or additional analyses. Methods, protocols, and results are now more available than ever before, largely due to the drive toward open-access publishing and preregistration of experiments.

Although there are new and exciting publishing options available, the HRI community is also exposed to the financial and social constraints of academic publishing. Although conferences offer a fast and predictable publication process, they do require considerable financial resources to travel to the event. Publishing in reputable open-access journals also comes with a considerable price tag. Flaky journals and conferences (Bartneck, 2021) offer much more affordable options without offering any advantage over just posting your article online yourself. Researchers often have no choice but to fall back to the traditional publishing channels, such as commercial journals, that do not charge the individual authors, but the libraries of their institutions.

The scientific publishing environment has changed and will continue to change. A big step forward is when large funding agencies require their funded projects to publish in open-access formats. In the meantime, researchers can choose to deposit their work in the institutional repositories of their institutions or on their private websites. This approach is often referred to as *green open access*, also known as *self-archiving*. It has been shown that making articles openly available increases their citations (Gargouri et al., 2010).

HRI researchers can also find relevant methodological approaches and discussions in the related field of HCI, which has a longer history of performing user studies, system evaluations, and theory building around the use of computing technologies in society and can provide guidelines and critical perspectives pertinent to HRI research. HRI researchers can learn from discussions about how to incorporate contextual variables into their work, how to think critically about design and study methods, and how to work more closely with the potential users of new robotic technologies through prior work in HCI. It is also, however, important to remember that HRI deals with robots, which are not only a different, embodied technology compared to computers but also pose different technical and social challenges for research.

Questions for you to think about:

- In some instances, it is not ethical or possible to answer a research question with an experiment. Can you think of such an instance? How would you address ethical issues related to the setup of your study?

How might you address concerns about the inclusion of vulnerable populations (e.g., children, older adults with cognitive impairments) in your study?

- "Significance" has been considered a misleading term because it says nothing about the relevance of a finding. Can you think of a situation where finding a significant small effect is relevant? What about a situation where it is irrelevant?
- Say you want to set up an experiment in which you assess how well a robot tutor teaches children. How would you set up your study? How would you measure the robot's ability as a tutor? What confounding factors do you expect?
- HRI studies often seek to address people's subjective experiences of robots—their enjoyment of the interaction, for example. How would you measure enjoyment, incorporating both direct and indirect and subjective and behavioral measures? How would you make sure that your enjoyment measure has construct validity—that it is actually measuring enjoyment with the robot, not just general happiness, or reflecting the participant trying to please the experimenter?
- How would you approach a user evaluation of your prototype differently from a systems evaluation? What types of questions would you want to answer in each type of evaluation? What kinds of measures would you use in each type of evaluation?

10.11 Exercises

The answers to these questions are available in the Appendix.

* Exercise 10.1 Convenience sample What is a convenience sample? Select one option from the following list:

1. A group of participants that you recruited in a convenience store
2. A group of participants recruited online through a crowdsourcing service
3. A group selected based on participants' easy accessibility or proximity to the researcher, such as university students
4. A statistical technique used to minimize bias in research studies.

* Exercise 10.2 Types of studies What type of study offers the possibility of establishing correlation or even causation? Select one option from the following list:

1. A qualitative study
2. A descriptive study
3. A cross-sectional study
4. A quantitative study

** **Exercise 10.3 What do participants see?** In which experimental design do participants see all experimental conditions? Select one option from the following list:

1. Within-subject design
2. Between-subject design
3. Longitudinal design

** **Exercise 10.4 Correlations and causation** Correlation and causation are important concepts in scientific study. Which statement is correct? Select one option from the following list:

1. Correlation causes causation.
2. They are the same thing—if variable A is correlated to variable B, then it also causes B.
3. Causation is a prerequisite for correlation.
4. Correlation is a necessary but insufficient criterion for causation.
5. *Causation* is a synonym for *correlation*.

** **Exercise 10.5 Variables** There are two types of variables in scientific studies. Select one or more options from the following list:

1. Independent variables are aspects that the experimenter manipulates.
2. Measurements are independent variables.
3. Dependent variables are aspects that the experimenter manipulates.
4. The experimenter manipulates measurements.
5. Dependent variables are aspects that the experimenter measures.

** **Exercise 10.6 Causal relationships** Only certain study types allow you to establish a causal relationship. Which studies allow you to establish a causal relationship? Select one or more options from the following list:

1. Observational studies
2. Ethnographic studies
3. Conversational analysis
4. Controlled studies
5. Case studies
6. System studies

*** **Exercise 10.7 Statistical inference** A researcher uses the significance level of $p \leq .05$ to test the relationship between robot likability and 40 other measured items. In reality, not one of these 40 items is related to robot likability. On average, how many significant results would you expect?

1. Zero
2. Five
3. Two
4. The question cannot be answered with the information given.

** **Exercise 10.8 Building blocks** Each of the following reviews indicates the importance of a different aspect of your data collection. Pair the images (a–c) with the names of the concepts.

a.   b.   c.

1. Tendency_____
2. Variability_____
3. Sample size_____

Future reading:

- Bethel, Cindy L. and Murphy, Robin R. Review of human studies methods in HRI and recommendations. *International Journal of Social Robotics*, 2(4):347–359, 2010. doi: 10.1007/s12369-010-0064-9. URL https://doi.org/10.1007/s12369-010-0064-9

- Field, Andy and Hole, Graham. *How to Design and Report Experiments*. SAGE Publications, Thousand Oaks, CA, 2002. ISBN 978085702829. URL http://worldcat.org/title/how-to-design-and-report-experiments/oclc/961100072

- Hoffman, Guy and Zhao, Xuan. A primer for conducting experiments in human–robot interaction. *ACM Transactions on Human-Robot Interaction (THRI)*, 10(1):1–31, 2020. doi: 10.1145/3412374. URL https://doi.org/10.1145/3412374

- Riek, Laurel D. Wizard of Oz studies in HRI: A systematic review and new reporting guidelines. *Journal of Human-Robot Interaction*, 1 (1):119–136, 2012. doi: 10.5898/JHRI.1.1.Riek. URL https://doi.org/10.5898/JHRI.1.1.Riek

- Baxter, Paul, Kennedy, James, Senft, Emmanuel, Lemaignan, Severin, and Belpaeme, Tony. From characterising three years of HRI to methodology and reporting recommendations. In *11th ACM/IEEE International Conference on Human-Robot Interaction*, pages 391–398. Institute of Electrical and Electronics Engineers, Piscataway, NJ, 2016. ISBN 978-1-4673-8370-7. doi: 10.1109/HRI.2016 .7451777. URL https://doi.org/10.1109/HRI.2016.7451777

- Šabanović, Selma, Michalowski, Marek P., and Simmons, Reid. Robots in the wild: Observing human-robot social interaction outside the lab. In *9th IEEE International Workshop on Advanced Motion Control*, pages 596–601. Institute of Electrical and Electronics Engineers, Piscataway, NJ, 2006. ISBN 0-7803-9511-1. doi: 10.1109/AMC.2006 .1631758. URL https://doi.org/10.1109/AMC.2006.1631758

- Young, James E., Sung, JaYoung, Voida, Amy, Sharlin, Ehud, Igarashi, Takeo, Christensen, Henrik I., and Grinter, Rebecca E. Evaluating human-robot interaction. *International Journal of Social Robotics*, 3 (1):53–67, 2011. doi: 10.1007/s12369-010-0081-8. URL https://doi.org/10.1007/s12369-010-0081-8

11

Applications

> What is covered in this chapter:
>
> - The diverse areas of robot applications where human–robot interaction (HRI) is an important component.
> - Applications beyond robots that are studied in a research context.
> - Possible future applications.
> - Potential problems that would need to be solved when HRI has a larger role in our society.

Human–robot interaction (HRI) has numerous applications expected to make a positive difference in people's lives. HRI is increasingly getting traction in the technology market, and although most applications are still being developed in the academic sphere, adventurous start-ups have popped up that are developing and selling HRI applications, and established information technology (IT) industries are keen to understand and develop technologies that allow robots or robot technology to interact successfully with people. Not all of these enterprises turn out to be successful. Sony, for example, was one of the pioneers of commercial robotics with its Aibo (see Figure 11.1) and Qrio (see Figure 11.2) robots, only to stop its efforts in the field in 2006. However, Sony's efforts were recently rekindled, with a new Aibo appearing in 2018 (see Figure 2.10). After Softbank Robotics released Pepper in 2014, the robot showed up in retail and entertainment roles across the world. Production of new Peppers was paused in 2020. Another example is the Bosch company, which initially supported Mayfield Robotics in developing the Kuri home robot but stopped the project before the official product launch.

A successful HRI application means something different depending on the perspective one takes: the notion of what constitutes success is very different for a researcher compared to an entrepreneur. Whereas a researcher will be interested in measurable outcomes of the robot's use and usability, an entrepreneur might be less concerned about the effectiveness of the robot and will be happy with a "good enough" technical solution that can be brought to market, thus preferring sales figures over scientific figures. Some may even develop unsuccessful applications on purpose for the entertainment value

Figure 11.1 The Sony Aibo ERS-7 (2003–2005) with the Nao (2008–present) robot.

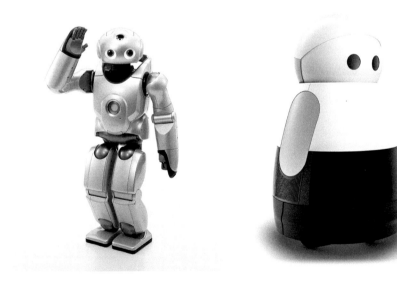

Figure 11.2 Sony's Qrio robot (left) (2003–2006) and Mayfield Robotics' Kuri (right) (2016–2018)—two robots that never made it to the consumer market. (Source: Qrio, Sony; Kuri, Mayfield Robotics)

or to inspire people to think more critically about the uses and design of robotic technology (see the accompanying text box for examples). Similarly, people may evaluate robots differently when they consider them as a research prototype and when they judge them as products they may or may not want to purchase (Randall et al., 2022).

The self-crowned "Queen of Shitty Robots," Simone Giertz is a robot enthusiast who designs service robots that usually perform poorly in their intended application. Her videos on the testing of her different creations not only have entertainment value but also demonstrate how designing robots for seemingly simple tasks can prove to be quite challenging. White's "Helpless Robot," on the other hand, is a machine with a passive personality that asks people to move it around the room, opening up questions about the meaning of machine autonomy and whether our machines serve us or whether it is the other way around.[a]

[a] See www.youtube.com/channel/UC3KEoMzNz8eYnwBC34RaKCQ/

For now, most robot applications remain at the research stage, but this is expected to change rapidly. The first wave of commercial success in robotics took place in automating industrial production; the second wave of commercial success can be considered as robots with simple navigation capabilities, such as warehouse robots and delivery robots; the next wave of commercial success is expected to come from introducing robots in dynamic and open environments populated by people in customer service, companionship, and socially and physically assistive roles. It is here that HRI has its major role to play: a solid understanding of how robots should behave around people and how people respond to and benefit from robots is needed to make the next robot wave a success (Haegele, 2016). We also need to consider the question of robot cost and how consumers may evaluate it in relation to a robot's purported functions and benefits, as well as sources of potential funding to purchase robots for different consumers (e.g., health insurance), which are questions that academic studies of HRI have rarely considered as of yet.

This chapter discusses the more common applications of social robots. Section 11.1 covers the use of robots in customer service, ranging from tour guides to sales bots; Section 11.2 focuses on the use of robots in the educational system. In Section 11.3, robots from different forms of entertainment are introduced. Sections 11.4, 11.5, and 11.6 look at robots in more serious roles, such as healthcare, personal assistance, and services such as delivery and domestic cleaning. Robots fulfilling security tasks are covered in Section 11.7, whereas Section 11.8 briefly discusses collaborative robots. Finally, Section 11.9 considers autonomous vehicles (AVs).

11.1 Customer-facing robots

A novel robot often attracts people's attention; in public spaces like shopping malls and stores, visitors become interested and approach, and children crowd around it. This makes robots an ideal asset for customer service settings, at least during the initial "novelty" stage of a robot's use. Many such applications have already been successfully tested in field research and have been deployed in grocery stores or bank branches (e.g., Pepper providing service at HSBC in the United States). Robots have also been deployed in the context of hotels (Nakanishi et al., 2020) to promote "heartwarming interactions." In Japan, people can interact with robots in "robot cafés" in various ways: customers can hold and pet Lovots or Aibos at their tables, they can be served by people with disabilities logged into telepresence robots or by autonomous Pepper robots, and they can even bring their own robots to the café to interact with others (Kamino and Šabanović, 2023). During the COVID-19 pandemic, a Pepper robot was used in a hospital in Brussels to check whether visitors were wearing their masks correctly before entering the hospital.

11.1.1 Tour guide robots

One of the applications developed in the early years of HRI research is the tour guide robot (Burgard et al., 1998; Shiomi et al., 2006; Bose et al., 2022). Typically, a tour guide robot moves from one location to another while providing information about nearby entities; some of them take the user to a requested location. This robot application involves navigational interaction (e.g., the robot safely moving around in an environment it shares with humans) and face-to-face interaction with its users (see Figure 11.3). Along with providing a service to customers, tour guide robots also provide a way for researchers to explore people's open-ended interactions with robots and test out the effects of different interaction strategies on users' perceptions of robots in a somewhat more structured environment.

Figure 11.3
Care-O-bot robot as a museum guide (2023).

   There are many instances of successful tour guide applications. One such application is in a museum setting, where a mobile robot is left to autonomously navigate around. Visitors are invited to use a user interface on the robot to indicate whether they want to have a tour guide. Once a tour is requested, the robot leads the visitors to several exhibits, providing a brief explanation at each (Burgard et al., 1998). HRI researchers experimenting with museum robots have found that giving the robot the ability to display emotions can enrich the educational experience and allow the robot to better manage its interactions with people, such as getting them to move out of its way by expressing frustration (Nourbakhsh et al., 1999). An alternative application concerns the retail context, when a customer may want to know where in the store a specific item is kept, and a robot takes the lead to show the customer the way to the appropriate shelf (Gross et al., 2009). A final example is the airport, where a robot can escort travelers to the gate for their next flight (Triebel et al., 2016; Hwang et al., 2022; Chen and VG, 2022).

   It is easy to imagine similar scenarios where robots would be helpful. For example, it is common for people to escort other people in daily interactions, either because they need physical assistance or because they want to be accompanied. Robots could be used in this context in the future. One such application being developed by HRI researchers is a guide robot for individuals with visual impairments (Feng et al., 2015). Although the current limitations in robotic hardware and HRI capabilities prevent such uses in the present, technical advancements and further HRI research should enable us to have robots with faster velocity and better navigation capability in human crowds that can be applied for accompanying users in a broader range of environments.

11.1.2 Receptionist robots

Figure 11.4
Receptionist robot.

Receptionist robots are placed at a reception desk and interact with visitors, typically offering information through spoken-language conversation. For instance, Gockley et al. (2005) studied people's interactions with a robot with a display for its head as a receptionist at a university (see Figure 11.4). The robot was able to provide directions and would share daily stories with people who came to chat with it. It turned out that people were sensitive to the robot's moods, and the length of their interactions with it changed based on whether the robot displayed a happy, sad, or neutral expression (Gockley et al., 2006). There is also work that includes multiparty interaction, an HRI constellation that still brings lots of challenges (Moujahid et al., 2022). Moreover, android robots have been used as receptionists in hotels. In this case, users use a graphical user interface to proceed through the check-in process, attended by an android robot and a small humanoid robot that offers greetings to the visitors.

11.1.3 Robots for sales promotion

Another straightforward application of service robots is product promotion in the retail context. In this setting, robots can function as proxies for store clerks, informing customers about the promotions offered by the store. Because people are naturally curious about robots, these robots can easily attract the attention of potential visitors, who will stop to listen and then look around. In Japan, Pepper is already used for this purpose. In the typical use case, robots are not necessarily proactive but instead wait for visitors to initiate interaction. In the research context, researchers study robots that proactively approach customers to offer promotions (Satake et al., 2009). For instance, the famous Geminoid android robot has been deployed in shopping malls in Japan to boost sales (Watanabe et al., 2015; Chen et al., 2022).

11.2 Robots for learning

Social robots have been shown to be particularly effective in assisting in learning and education through social interaction (Belpaeme et al., 2018). This should not be confused with the use of robot building as an educational tool to teach mathematics, programming, or engineering, such as LEGO Mindstorms. Robots can take on various roles in the process of learning: The robot can act as a teacher, taking the students through the curriculum and offering testing opportunities to assess knowledge. As a tutor, a robot would support the teacher in his or her teaching (Kanda et al., 2004). This role is actually preferred by teachers and students (Reich-Stiebert and Eyssel, 2016). However, the robot is also often presented as a peer. The peer-like robot has a similar level of knowledge as the learner, and the learner and robot take a learning journey together, with the robot adapting its performance to that of the learner. Robots as peers can also encourage learners to adopt a "growth mindset," which leads to higher achievement (Park et al., 2017b). At the far extreme is the robot that needs to be completely taught by the student. This approach, known as a *care-receiving robot* or *teachable agent*, is effective for two reasons. First, teaching a subject often leads to mastery of that subject, and second, having a less knowledgeable peer can boost the learner's confidence (Hood et al., 2015; Tanaka and Kimura, 2010). Finally, robots could also be used as a sidekick for teachers. In this role, the robot spices up the lesson and makes the learning more entertaining, thus capturing student interest (Alemi et al., 2014).

Tutoring robots may take over specific tasks from the teacher. Because teachers typically deal with class sizes of more than 20 students, they are required to teach to the mean of the class using a broad rather than a personalized style. It has been shown that tutoring has a strong impact on learning. Bloom (1984, p. 4) found that one-to-one tutoring resulted in a two-standard-deviation improvement against a control group, concluding that "the average tutored student was above 98% of the students in the control class." Although research has since shown that the effects are not as large as first observed, there is nonetheless a distinct advantage to the one-to-one tutoring approach (VanLehn, 2011). Social robots in education capitalize on this by offering a one-to-one, personalized tutoring experience.

Robots have been used to teach a wide range of topics, from mathematics to languages and even mindfulness and social skills, both to adults and children. The main contribution of the robot seems to be that its physical presence promotes learning. Although computer-based tutoring programs, also known as *intelligent tutoring systems* (ITSs), are effective (VanLehn, 2011), the social robot adds to this through its social and physical presence. Studies have shown that robots offer a distinct advantage over on-screen social agents or ITSs, and the students learn faster and learn more when tutored by a robot as compared to alternative technologies (e.g., Kennedy et al. 2015; Leyzberg et al. 2012). The reasons for this are still unclear: it might be that the social and physical presence of the robot engages the learner more than just on-screen delivery and feedback, or it might be that the learning experience is more multimodal, thus resulting in a richer and embodied pedagogical exchange (Mayer and DaPra, 2012)—of course, a combination of these two is also possible. It may come as no surprise that socially supportive robots perform much better (Saerbeck et al., 2010). Some socially interactive behaviors can also backfire in learning contexts, leading the student to interpret the robot as a peer rather than a teacher and to engage with it socially rather than focusing on achieving certain learning goals (Kennedy et al., 2015). HRI research is therefore necessary to guide the development of robots that can effectively support learning.

11.3 Robots for entertainment

11.3.1 Pet and toy robots

Robotic pets and toys were among the first commercial robot applications for personal use. After the first doglike robot, Aibo (Fujita, 2001), appeared on the market in 1999 (see Figure 11.1), the development of many other entertainment robots soon followed. Compared with other robotic applications, entertainment robots have been easier to get to market because the functions they perform do not have to be as advanced, and they often use preprogrammed capabilities, such as dancing, talking, burping, and even seeming to develop their knowledge by simply starting to use more advanced preprogrammed skills after a period of time. Some of the most popular robotic toys over the years have been Furby, Sony's Aibo robot dog, and more recently, Cosmo. LEGO Mindstorms was a market leader in the educational toy robot niche but has recently been discontinued; it is followed by a slew of robots that allow children to learn how to code and think computationally, such as Dash and Dot and Ozobot, among many others. The WowWee company is another market leader, with many different robots, including the humanoid robots Robosapiens and Femisapiens and a mobile home robot. The company Sphero developed a robotic ball that could be remote-controlled; following the release of the new series of Star Wars films in 2015, the company amended the design to represent the BB-8 droid, which became one of the most popular holiday toys of that season.

Although most entertainment robots target children and adolescents, many are also enjoyed by adults. The Aibo in particular was very popular with adults, who even started a "black market" of Aibo parts when the robot was discontinued by Sony in 2006. As mentioned earlier, Sony introduced a brand-new version of Aibo in 2018.

Pleo (see Figure 11.5), a *Camarasaurus rex* robot platform, provides a similar complexity of interaction, with various modes of personality and behavior that adapt and change across time and users. These examples show that many robot toys are not necessarily social or humanlike in appearance,

Figure 11.5 Pleo robot
(2006–present).
(Source: Max Braun)

but they still elicit strong social responses in children and adult consumers alike.

Considering the variety of ways in which robots can provide entertainment and the popularity of robots among the public in general, it is not surprising that the market for toy robots has been and is expected to stay one of the largest for personal robots (Haegele, 2016).

11.3.2 Robots for exhibitions

Robots are often used in exhibitions and theme parks to entertain audiences. These often-animatronic devices are very robust; they must play the same animation script sometimes hundreds of times per day, with only a brief moment for maintenance between performances. Some robots intentionally look like robots, but others resemble animals, for example, dinosaurs (see Figure 11.6), or people. In these cases, the robot has flexible latex skin, which has been carefully painted to reflect realistic skin coloration and patterns. Most of these animatronic robots have no autonomy: they play a prerecorded script of animation timed to a soundtrack. In rare cases, the robot may have limited autonomy, such as the ability to focus on members of the audience while speaking. A popular example of the use of animatronic robots is the Hall of Presidents located in the Walt Disney World Resort.

11.3.3 Robots in the performing arts

Robots are also sometimes used in the performing arts. One of the first robot performance art pieces was Senster, created in 1970 for Philips' Evoluon in Eindhoven, the Netherlands (Reichardt, 1978). Senster was an electro-hydraulic structure shaped after a lobster's claw, with six hinged joints.

Figure 11.6
Animatronic robot.

It registered and responded to sound and movement from the environment. It was on display until 1974, when it was dismantled. More recently, 20 Nao robots performed a synchronized dance recital for France Pavilion Day (June 21) at the Shanghai 2010 Expo.

Not all art applications have to be for a broader public. Home theater systems might soon become what their name promises. Imagine a future in which you download the theater script of *Romeo and Juliet* into your robots. You can then either watch the robots perform the play or join in yourself. It is important to note that a major use of robotics—both in the past and currently—is to automate tasks that we do not want to perform ourselves. Industrial robots, for example, were introduced to relieve us of difficult and repetitive manual labor. There is little use in automating tasks that we actually enjoy doing. This does not mean that there is no place for robots in the theater—plays that actually deal with robots should, of course, be cast with robots (Chikaraishi et al., 2017).

Furthermore, there are many ways in which robots can interact with people in art performances, to which the future social robots could contribute as a human counterpart. For example, Hoffman and Weinberg (2010) developed a marimba-playing robot that joins a jazz-like session with a human player. Kahn et al. (2014) revealed that a robot can partner with a human to enhance human creativity in the art-creation context. Nishiguchi et al. (2017) suggest that developing robots that can perform as actors in a play alongside humans can also be a way to develop more humanlike behaviors for robots.

11.3.4 Sex robots

Along with toy robots aimed at the child market, there are also embodied robots and virtual reality (VR) interfaces for the fulfillment of adult entertainment needs. Colloquially known as "sex robots," diverse robotic platforms offer varying levels of humanlike appearance and behavioral response. The RealDoll company, which develops hyperrealistic sex dolls (see Figure 11.7), is working on adding robotic capabilities, including an emotive face and responses, to its base models. Several other producers have developed prototypes of sex robots, although none has yet come to market. It is envisioned that the sex robot industry will continue to grow over the coming years. Devlin (2020) discusses current developments in sexual companion robots, along with the psychological and social implications of these technologies.

11.4 Robots in healthcare and therapy

Healthcare and therapy represent prominent domains of application for robotics (Riek, 2017). In these domains, social robots are used to offer support, education, and diversion to patients, with an eye toward improving healthcare and therapy outcomes. The practice of using social robots in healthcare is referred to as *socially assistive robotics* (SAR) (Tapus et al., 2007; Feil-Seifer and Matarić, 2011). Healthcare robots are targeted for

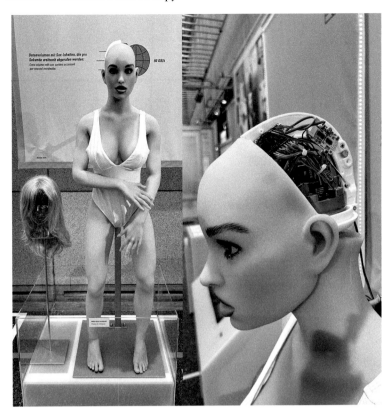

Figure 11.7 The Harmony X sex robot by RealDoll exhibited in a museum (2023).

diverse populations, very often older adults (Broadbent et al., 2009; Broekens et al., 2009). The use of robots to support care raises many ethical issues and requires careful consideration of ethics in design (Van Wynsberghe, 2016; Stahl and Coeckelbergh, 2016), including those regarding the potential impacts of using robots for care on people's autonomy and independence (Sharkey and Sharkey, 2012; Sparrow and Sparrow, 2006), the authenticity of care relationships with robots (Turkle, 2017), and concerns about overreliance on robots (Borenstein et al., 2017).

11.4.1 Robots for senior citizens

Robotic assistants could make a world of difference for senior citizens who wish to stay independent as long as possible. For example, the ElliQ robot (Figure 11.8) combines an artificial intelligence (AI) assistant-like function (e.g., providing news updates and weather forecasts) with basic social interaction (e.g., sharing inspirational quotes and simple daily small talk) and more personalized help (e.g., setting reminders, doing basic wellness checks, helping with messaging and calling loved ones). Thus, although unable to physically assist in daily tasks, robots like these could help people by reminding them to take their medications (Pineau et al., 2003) and can provide preclinic or tele-clinic support at home, thus reducing costs for medical services (Robinson et al., 2014).

Figure 11.8 The ElliQ robot (2019–present) from Intuition Robotics is designed to interact with senior citizens. (Source: Intuition Robotics)

Figure 11.8 The ElliQ robot (2019–present) from Intuition Robotics is designed to interact with senior citizens. (Source: Intuition Robotics)

Although senior citizens and people with mild cognitive impairments are a key target audience for robot developers who want to offer technology-mediated social, emotional, and cognitive rehabilitation and diversion, there are other target groups that can benefit from social robots.

For example, the Paro robot is a seal-like robot equipped with sensors that allow it to detect when it is being picked up or stroked (see Figure 2.8). It can respond by wriggling and making seal-like noises. Paro has been used in a multitude of studies with elderly people, and positive psychological, physiological, and social effects of long-term interaction with the robot have been documented (Wada and Shibata, 2007). The robot is used as a companion in care homes and stimulates not only human–robot interactions but also interactions between the residents. It has been able to reduce feelings of loneliness and improve the residents' quality of life. Paro has been commercially available in Japan since 2006 and in the United States and Europe since 2009. It is interesting to note that although it is purchased by many individuals for home use in Japan, in Europe and the United States, the robot is almost exclusively purchased by healthcare institutions and companies. Furthermore, some robots, such as NEC's PaPeRo (see Figure 11.9), have only ever been released in Japan.

Figure 11.9 NEC's PaPeRo robot has been available in different versions, such as PaPeRo R-100, PaPeRo Mini, and PaPeRo i (1997–present).

11.4.2 Robots for people with autism spectrum disorder

Children and adults with autism spectrum disorder (ASD) are another group for which social robots are often developed and used. It has been shown that people with ASD generally respond well to robots, and there has been a large body of research looking into how robots can be effectively used to support ASD therapy (Diehl et al., 2012; Scassellati et al., 2012; Thill et al., 2012).

Figure 11.10 A range of robots used in ASD therapy. From left to right, Nao (2008–present), Elvis (2018–present), Kaspar (2009–present). and Zeno (2012–present). (Source: Elvis, Brubotics–Vrije Universiteit Brussel; Kaspar, Kerstin Dautenhahn, Ben Robins, Adaptive Systems Research Group, University of Hertfordshire, UK)

Many types of robots have been used in a therapeutic context to support children with ASD (Robins et al., 2009; Pop et al., 2013). These include a wide range from humanoid robots, such as Kaspar and Nao, to zoomorphic robots, such as Elvis and Pleo (see Figures 11.10 and 11.11).

The predictable nature of robot behavior and the fact that robots are nonjudgmental have been credited as potential reasons why using them in interactions and therapeutic interventions with individuals with ASD is successful. The robots are either used as a focal point for the interaction between the therapist and the patient or are used to train and improve children's social competencies and their ability to regulate and interpret emotions.

11.4.3 Robots for rehabilitation

Robots are also used to support physical rehabilitation. This can be done by offering physiotherapy and providing encouragement and mental support. Social robots have been shown to be effective in cardiac-focused rehabilitation by providing encouragement and social facilitation during cardiac exercises (Kang et al., 2005; Lara et al., 2017). Robots can also be used to encourage users to adopt healthy practices or to change unhealthy habits. For example, Kidd and Breazeal (2007) describe a robot that acts as a weight-loss coach, and Belpaeme et al. (2012) describe the use of a robot to support children

Figure 11.11 The Kiwi robot was designed by researchers from the University of Southern California for research into personalized support of children with autism and elderly users. (Source: Maja Matarić, University of Southern California)

diagnosed with diabetes. Kidd's early research developed into a robotic start-up and healthcare robot called Mabu.

Robots can also be used as prosthetic devices. The restoration of the function of the lower limbs, arms, and hands through robotics has received considerable attention (Bogue, 2009). Although these developments are largely the concern of mechatronics, there is a role for HRI in the study of the acceptance and usability of robotic prostheses.

Figure 11.12
Ommie
(2022-present) is a robot that helps people manage their anxiety through deep breathing. (Source: Kayla Matheus and Yale University)

11.4.4 *Robots to support mental health*

A subset of healthcare that is getting increased attention since the COVID-19 pandemic is mental health, which is an issue of rising importance worldwide. The development of robotic technologies to help support mental health is concomitantly occurring in many different domains (Riek, 2016). Researchers have been working with teenagers to develop robots that assist teens in managing their anxiety and other mental health challenges at school (Karim et al., 2022; Björling et al., 2020); robots to achieve anxiety reduction have also been evaluated with adults (Matheus et al., 2022) (see Figure 11.12). Participatory design has also been used to create robots that adults can use to manage symptoms of depression (Lee et al., 2017; Randall et al., 2019; Bhat et al., 2021). Along with benefiting people with mental health conditions, robots can also be used to alleviate the burden of care for caregivers and to improve relationships between caregivers and care receivers (Moharana et al., 2019).

11.5 Robots as personal assistants

Smart-home assistants, unobtrusive devices that are placed in the home or the office and are often voice-operated, have been a recent and largely unexpected success of cloud-connected technology. Technology giants such as Amazon, Google, Microsoft, Apple, and Samsung have raced to build voice-operated assistants, and some offer hardware products that are built around this technology. Amazon's Alexa, Apple's Siri, Microsoft's Cortana, and the Google Assistant have found embodiment on a range of devices, with shapes and sizes ranging from a hockey puck to a shoebox. These devices offer a vast range of services, but they are most often used to request simple information, such as the time, weather, or traffic, or to stream music. These devices can engage in only very short social exchanges, often limited to chitchat, such as telling a joke.

Recently, a number of commercial ventures have been launched that offer social robots as personal home assistants, perhaps eventually to rival existing smart-home assistants. Personal robotic assistants are devices that have no physical manipulation abilities and limited locomotion capabilities. They have a distinct social presence and have visual features suggestive of their ability to interact socially, such as eyes, ears, or a mouth (see Figure 11.13). They might

Figure 11.13
Personal assistant robots: from left to right, the Nabaztag robot (2009–2011), the Jibo robot (2017–2018), and the Buddy robot (2018–present). (Source: Jibo, Jibo Inc.; Buddy, Blue Frog Robotics)

be motorized and can track the user around the room, giving the impression of being aware of the people in the environment. Amazon's Astro (Figure 2.11) may even be able to deliver a beer, as long as someone puts it in its cupholder, and can allow homeowners to check in on their homes while they are away. Although personal robotic assistants provide services similar to those of smart-home assistants, their social presence offers an opportunity that is unique to social robots. For instance, in addition to playing music, a social personal assistant robot would express its engagement with the music so that users would feel like they are listening to the music together with the robot (Hoffman and Vanunu, 2013). These robots can be used as surveillance devices, act as communicative intermediates, engage in richer games, tell stories, or be used to provide encouragement or incentives.

11.6 Service robots

Service robots are designed to help humans in various onerous, often called "dull, dirty, and dangerous," tasks. The tasks performed by such robots are typically simple and repetitive, and they often do not involve explicit interaction with people. HRI research considers such robots when they operate in everyday human contexts and therefore come into regular contact with people, including house-cleaning and delivery robots and robots that offer personal assistance.

11.6.1 Cleaning robots

Cleaning robots are widely used in homes. The most well-known cleaning robot is Roomba; it is also the most commercially successful personal service robot to date. It is a small robot, approximately 30 cm in diameter, that has two wheels to enable it to move around, dust sensors to know where it needs to clean, cliff sensors to avoid falling down the stairs, and of course, vacuuming capability. The initial version of the Roomba moves around randomly in a house, turning when it comes to a wall, and over a period of time, it manages to clean up the room. (In general, that is; pets can undermine this goal horribly—see the accompanying box). Some more recent cleaning robots have mapping and localization capabilities, as well as collision-avoidance capabilities, which allow them to cause fewer problems with furniture and other things in a house. There are many other vacuum-cleaning robots for the home, as well as the mopping robot Scooba.

> Dreaded by every pet-owning Roomba user, the *Poopocalypse* is the unfortunate yet inevitable event where a pet leaves a dropping some-where in the house, and the Roomba encounters it before the owner can clean it up, spreading it all across the house. These incidents are common enough that iRobot formulated an official response, warning Roomba users not to use their Roomba unsupervised if they own a pet (Solon, 2016).

Commercial service robots coming onto the market have provided HRI researchers with opportunities to study how people respond to and use such robots in everyday circumstances. Fink et al. (2013) performed ethnographic studies of Roombas in user homes to identify common use patterns, and they also noticed how users prep their homes so that Roomba can do its job. Other researchers have found that users sometimes like to display Roombas as a sophisticated technology, whereas at other times, they try to disguise or hide them because they are deemed unsightly (Sung et al., 2007, 2009). Forlizzi and DiSalvo (2006) also explored how people's models of service affect the way they expect robots to interact with them, including how robots can best recover from mistakes made while providing services, such as bringing users the wrong drink.

11.6.2 Delivery robots

Delivery robots carry objects from one place to another. Warehouse robots are the ones that are most frequently used, like the ones used in Amazon warehouses. There are many start-ups that seek to provide delivery robots, for outdoor use as well as for inside buildings. Outdoor delivery robots include those used for delivering food and daily goods from supermarkets and restaurants. There were serious needs for such robots during the COVID-19 pandemic, when people were asked to stay home. Although perhaps desirable for the direct users, these robots sometimes turn out to be a nuisance for bystanders, who have to dodge them on already-busy city streets. Robots can also help people carry their belongings and follow them as they move around public spaces, such as the Gita series of commercial robots.[1]

Mutlu and Forlizzi (2008) showed that the workflow and patient pro-file of the hospital ward in which the Aetheon TUG delivery robot was deployed could make the difference between a successful and unsuccessful

---

[1] See https://piaggiofastforward.com

implementation. Some hotels use room-service robots to deliver goods from the service desk to guest rooms. Delivery robots are also used in restaurants (see Figure 11.14). Because delivery robots are increasingly used in human co-located environments, they need better HRI capabilities. For instance, a robot in a restaurant needs to avoid obstructing customers while delivering dishes to tables or should at least be designed in a way to let customers avoid it without becoming annoyed by it.

Figure 11.14
BellaBot delivery robot.

11.7 Security robots

Among the various available applications, robots used for security purposes are among the most controversial. Robots are also commonly considered as potential providers of security in homes and public spaces. These robots could provide services ranging from patrolling around the environment to a police robot that could use real force against people. A security robot that patrols around may not necessarily invite controversy in some cultures, such as in Japan. Some of them have a function to record unusual events, and some may approach suspicious persons in a friendly way, without being intimidating or scary. These robots are often designed to work with human workers, to save their time in roaming around when no problematic events are occurring and only asking for help in important moments. However, in some other cultures, similar robots invited more controversy. For instance, the K5 robotic security guard (see Figure 11.15) has been deployed at some shopping malls in the United States. It roams around the environment to monitor crime and alerts human authorities if it senses something suspicious. A prime example of a service robot that was not accepted in its environment, the K5 robot has fallen victim to a variety of abusive behaviors, ranging from an attack by a drunken man while patrolling a parking lot in Mountain View, California, to being tackled and covered in barbecue sauce while attempting to chase off homeless people from a nongovernmental organization's doorstep in San Francisco.

Figure 11.15
Knightscope K5
(2013–present).
(Source:
Knightscope)

Police robots have invited even more serious societal controversy, resulting in prevention of their use. For instance, New York City police once tried to use a robotic dog, Spot from Boston Dynamics, for surveillance purposes. Having a robot to observe a dangerous place could potentially save citizen and police lives; however, citizens were concerned about this use, and the trial was terminated (Zaveri, 2021). Recently, even more controversy was caused by a decision to allow robots to be used by the police as weapons against perpetrators, even allowing for the use of "deadly force" via robot (Abené, 2022). This inspired discussion on whether police should be able to injure or kill people using a robot, in cases where this might save the lives of citizens or police and there is no alternative choice. The robots were initially approved for this use; however, just a week later, San Francisco supervisors reversed their decision and rejected such usage because of the objections from citizens (Press, 2022). Ethics scholars have also commented on the potential lethal use of robots in policing, calling for a moratorium on such designs because of the legal and technical challenges inherent in such technologies (Asaro, 2016).

11.8 Collaborative robots

Collaborative robots are gaining importance in the automation industry. Traditional industrial robots typically are stiff, strong, and have limited sensory capabilities. Because of this, humans are not allowed near a powered industrial robot. In contrast, collaborative robots—or *co-bots*, for short—have safety features and a mechatronic design that allow them to operate near people or even work together with people.

Some co-bots are equipped to interpret or produce social signals, such as the Walt robot, which has a face attached to its robotic arm (see Figure 11.16). The Baxter robot (see Figure 2.9) is a two-armed robot that is able to display a range of facial expressions on its screen, signaling various internal states. An embarrassed blush, for example, signals to the human coworker that the robot is at a loss about what to do next.

The deployment of co-bots in industrial manufacturing contexts and the workplace in general may fundamentally change the notion of collaborative teamwork. In positive scenarios, co-bots should be able to help humans get more pleasure and efficiency from their work. In the worst case, collaboration with robots could backfire through a reversal of the roles of humans and robots, leading to humans serving robots rather than vice versa.

11.9 Self-driving cars

Self-driving cars are, in essence, robots in which the user is in the passenger's seat. Although fully autonomous vehicles (AVs) are still not widely available, most new cars now have some form of onboard advanced driver-assistance system (ADAS) technologies, such as lane following, adaptive cruise control, automatic parking, predictive braking, pedestrian protection systems, and

Figure 11.16 Walt (2017–present), a collaborative robot, working at the Audi car factory in Brussels to apply glue to car parts. It has a headlight-shaped head with an animated face to communicate its internal state to its human coworkers. (Source: Copyright IMEC)

blind-spot warning systems. The Society of Automotive Engineers (SAE) International has developed a taxonomy to describe six increasing levels (SAE levels 0 through 5) of capability for driving automation systems, which are widely used to describe and understand these capabilities.[2] Most current AVs have achieved level 3 under the SAE standards, whereas Waymo's 2020 safety report claimed that its AVs had the ability of level 4, which would mean that the AV can demonstrate 28 core competencies from the recommendations made by the U.S. Department of Transportation. These technologies, unlike the traditional adaptive cruise control or lane assistance, also include a safe stop when the system fails (Waymo, 2020).

Most traditional car manufacturers, many start-up companies, and large IT companies are currently heavily investing in the development of AVs. Some companies already have products in the market. Although the levels of autonomy are reasonably well defined, the terminology used by the car industry is much more ambiguous. For example, Tesla's cars have a driver-assistance system that conforms to level 2 of the SAE levels of driving automation, which the company calls "Autopilot"—a name that suggests the far more advanced full autonomy of SAE level 5 (Layton, 2022). In its July 14, 2020, decision (Az. 33 O 14041/19), the Munich Regional Court ruled that Tesla branding its autonomous tech as "Autopilot" is misleading to consumers. In May 2021, the California Department of Motor Vehicles started to investigate Tesla over its self-driving claims (Mitchel, 2021). Starting in 2020, Tesla began stating the following on its "Autopilot" website: "Current Autopilot features require active driver supervision and do not make the vehicle autonomous." Only in 2021 and after at least three years of delays did Tesla roll out its "Full Self-Driving" software update in its beta program (Hawkins and Lawler, 2021). The latter enables drivers who paid for the "Autopilot" to use many driver-assist features on local, nonhighway streets. Other manufacturers offer driving-assist features, such as adaptive cruise control and lane following. General Motors, like many other traditional car manufacturers, is dramatically increasing its spending on the development of AVs (Wayland, 2021). Even Apple is developing an AV, initially envisioned without a steering wheel or pedals but then redesigned for full autonomy only on highways (Bloomberg, 2022).

AVs are expected to have a considerable impact on the future of transportation (Litman, 2020; National Roads and Motorists' Association, 2018). Positive effects of AVs include the potential to be more environmentally friendly by driving more economically (Fagnant and Kockelman, 2015). Because of their ability to communicate with each other and with the infrastructure, AVs are able to reduce traffic congestion by rerouting vehicles to their destinations. They also have the potential to radically change our transportation system because ride-sharing and even car ownership sharing become much easier to implement. Our society could be serviced by a fleet of autonomous robotic taxis that could even offer carpooling trips. Such AVs would also enable

---

[2] See www.sae.org/standards/content/j3016_202104/

people who are currently unable to drive to take advantage of an individual-based transportation system. Children, people with disabilities, and the elderly could safely ride to their destinations (Lutin et al., 2013).

Possibly most important, AVs are able to increase road safety (Petrovic et al., 2020). The U.S. National Highway Traffic Safety Administration showed that 94% of car crashes can be attributed to human error (Department of Transportation, 2015). AVs do not get drunk, high, or distracted. They can be programmed to comply strictly with speed limits and traffic rules. They can even warn each other about accidents or obstacles on the road ahead. It has even been argued that once AVs have reached a safety record that is better than that of average human drivers, humans should be banned from driving altogether (Sparrow and Howard, 2017). As we design and plan for the expanded use of AVs, we need to keep in mind that the projections regarding the lifesaving capabilities of AV use commonly assume widespread adoption of these vehicles, in which all or a majority of cars on the roads are autonomous. The actual capabilities of current vehicles and AV research (Nascimento et al., 2019) and the adoption of AVs on the road are still a long way away from this best-case scenario.

It is important, therefore, to remember that AVs are large and potentially dangerous robots that exhibit autonomous behavior. Although AVs can avoid some human errors, they are also likely to introduce new sources of HRI errors. Although many social robots and conversational agents rarely pose a threat to our physical well-being, several crashes of AVs have demonstrated the destructive potential of these robots not only for the drivers but also for pedestrians and cyclists. For example, Tesla cars with active autopilot have been involved in several fatal crashes, starting as early as 2016[3]. The first bystander killed by an AV was Elaine Herzberg, who was struck and killed by an autonomous Uber car on March 18, 2018. The accident report notes that the autopilot was programmed with a certain threshold to continue driving even if an abnormal sensor reading was received (National Transportation Safety Board, 2019). This threshold is necessary because otherwise, AVs would have to stop too frequently, creating a safety risk for others. Some risk taking is part of conventional driving as well. For example, our streets would be much safer if the speed limit were universally reduced to 30 km/h, but that might also increase traffic bottlenecks and certainly the time to reach our destination. We accept the trade-off between safety and speed in the design of our driving rules, despite the fact that it results in thousands of deaths each year, based on societal norms and legal frameworks. When it comes to design decisions that govern the behavior of AVs, however, discussions are ongoing about what the effects of various machine perception capabilities, control and planning algorithms, and design factors would be and how to understand and manage risk and differential outcomes to AV drivers and others sharing the road with them (e.g., see Evans et al., 2020; Geisslinger et al., 2021; Cunneen et al., 2019).

---

[3] www.tesladeaths.com

The progress in the aviation industry can serve as an example of how to interpret the risks and possibilities of AVs as part of our transportation systems. In the early days of aviation, piloting an airplane was incredibly dangerous. Both Wright brothers crashed with their airplanes and suffered severe injuries. It did not stop them from building the first motorized airplane. Since then, air travel has become one of the safest forms of transportation. According to the National Transportation Safety Board, there is, on average, less than 1 fatality per 100,000 flight hours.[4] It has to be pointed out that most airplanes already extensively use autopilots. Whereas the aviation industry has very strict safety regulations, processes, and reporting, the same cannot yet be observed for AVs. Fatal AV crashes may receive a disproportionately large amount of media attention, which can inhibit their development and, in turn, cost people's lives (Bohn, 2016). It is also important to consider that technology alone cannot bring the desired benefits; social and physical structures and regulations will need to be in place to support the responsible and acceptable use of AVs. Furthermore, there are many open questions about how AVs and traditional vehicles will be able to most successfully share the road in the extended time of transition to more widespread adoption of AVs.

Independent, accurate, and reliable information about the safety of AVs is necessary, similar to the reporting done in the aviation industry. Without such clear information about the safety record of AVs, it will be difficult, if not impossible, for people to consent to their usage, which further complicates the regulation of risk and responsibilities. It has been shown that communicating the risks of AVs is a challenge in itself (Bartneck and Moltchanova, 2020). But the risk and responsibilities are still being negotiated between the manufacturers, insurance companies, governments, and drivers. The Department of Motor Vehicles in California is a good example of making safety data of AVs available publicly. California's AV incidents are being published online and have already been analyzed up until the year 2017 (Favaro et al., 2017).

The uptake of AVs and the associated regulatory changes are unparalleled within the HRI community. This has partly to do with danger that AVs pose to humans, but it is also due to their high potential usefulness. It can be argued that AVs are the most commercially successful form of HRI. The interaction between AVs, drivers, and other participants in the road traffic, however, remains difficult.

Many of these systems require an effective human–machine interface for the driver of the car. In addition, self-driving cars require interfaces that allow them to interpret the actions and intentions of other traffic users, and the car will need ways of expressing its intentions to other users (Brown, 2017). Car drivers use a wide range of signals to communicate their intent to others. For example, slowing down when nearing a crosswalk can signal to pedestrians that they have been noticed and that it is safe to cross. The Jaguar Land Rover developed a more explicit way of communicating with pedestrians by putting "googly eyes" on its cars to signify attention.

---

[4] See www.bts.gov/content/fatality-rates-mode

Figure 11.17 A mock-up of a self-driving vehicle, in which a driver is disguised as a car seat, used to study people's responses to the behavior of self-driving cars. (Source: Wendy Jin)

Interaction with the driver does not only happen through the car's interface but also often requires autonomous technology to communicate why a decision was made. Koo et al. (2015) show how a message that explains why an action was taken, such as automated braking, is preferred over a system that merely reports the action.

HRI studies can help understand how traffic users and passengers respond to autonomous cars. Rothenbücher et al. (2016) present a paradigm in which a driver is disguised as a car seat, giving the impression that the car is self-driving (see Figure 11.17). This deception allows for carefully controlled studies on how people perceive and respond to self-driving cars without the need for a fully self-driving car.

The Partners in Automated Vehicle Education showed in its 2020 report that Americans are skeptical of current AV technology.[5] Again, clear and reliable information from independent sources is necessary to build the trust of the general public toward AVs. Kyle Loades, the chairman of the National Roads and Motorists' Association, explained that the best way to adopt a new technology and build up users' trust is through trials (National Roads and Motorists' Association, 2018). The success of the trials can, of course, only be evaluated if the resulting data are being shared openly.

11.10 Remotely operated robots

11.10.1 Applications of remotely operated robots

There are several application examples of remotely operated robots. Robots used for planetary exploration have some autonomous navigation capability, and they receive commands from human operators on Earth as well. PackBot (see Figure 11.18) is a scout robot used in a military context; a human operator tele-operates PackBot while it searches for bomb traps, thus clearing the road for military vehicles. Also in the military context, a human operator can

---

[5] See https://pavecampaign.org/wp-content/uploads/2020/05/PAVE-Poll_Fact-Sheet.pdf

Figure 11.18
PackBot
(2016–present).
(Source: Endeavor
Robotics)

operate a drone from a faraway location during military operations. In search-and-rescue scenarios, an operator controls a robot that moves on the ground or through the sky to find a person in need.

Apart from military contexts, drones have even been used in domestic (Obaid et al., 2020) and educational contexts (Johal et al., 2022), with such types of drones being coined "social drones"(Baytas et al., 2019), that is, drones that operate autonomously in spaces co-shared with humans. Tele-operation also represents a relevant use case in the medical domain (Partikska and Kattepur, 2022; Al Momin and Islam, 2022), for instance, when it comes to robot-assisted surgery.

In these tele-operation scenarios, a human operator commonly needs to work with some level of autonomy in the robot. A robot may autonomously navigate around, but the operator may need to provide destinations for efficient use. The robot's ability to avoid risks (e.g., collisions with obstacles or attacks from a hostile entity) can be poor, and hence the operator needs to intervene before the robots are seriously damaged.

> People in the military have reported becoming very attached to their robots, despite the fact that these were designed without any capability for social interaction. Military robots have been named, have been awarded battlefield promotions, and have received medals of honor from their human supervisors (Garreau, 2007).

11.10.2 Human–robot teams

Depending on the complexity of the task and the level of autonomy, one operator could control multiple robots, or one robot would need multiple operators for control. Such a *human–robot team* has long been a focus of HRI research, typically in the case of robots for navigation tasks, exploring the appropriate level of autonomy and efficient numbers of robots and humans in a team (Goodrich and Schultz, 2008). Those studies include studies to control a robot team (robot swarms) all at once, such as giving a command to a team and controlling the formation of the robot team.

More recently, studies of human–robot teams have started to cover robots used for social interaction (Glas et al., 2011). Fully autonomous robots capable of natural social interaction are still a rather futuristic scenario; however, once some difficult components, such as natural-language understanding and error handling, are addressed by human operators, it will be more realistic to use capable semiautonomous social robots in various daily-life scenarios. For this future scenario, studies of human–robot teams are indispensable.

Operators interact with remotely operated robots via a user interface (see Figure 11.19); here, there are many common HRI problems to address, as with other types of human–robot interactions. For instance, the robot system needs to acquire an appropriate level of trust from the operator—not too much, not too little. There are similar ethical issues to be considered. For example, if the autonomy system fails, who is responsible? Is it ethical to design a system that would allow such a failure of autonomy?

At a more general level, the study of team dynamics involving multiple robots and humans is highly relevant because although HRI research most often studies dyads of mainly one robot interacting with one human, in public spaces, such as shopping malls or museums, it is likely that a robot will encounter multiple humans. This, of course, will bring technical challenges for human–robot dialogue (e.g., person recognition, turn-taking, joint attention). Work by Jung et al. (2015) has investigated the supporting role of robots in ameliorating team conflict and has shed light on the longitudinal evolution of trust in human–robot teams (De Visser et al., 2020); for an overview, see Sebo et al. (2020).

Figure 11.19 The T-HR3 robot (2017–present) can be remotely controlled using a dedicated user interface. (Source: Toyota)

Figure 11.20
OriHime robots are remotely operated by people with disabilities, who are depicted on the name tags worn by the robots. (Source: Photos by Waki Kamino)

11.10.3 Telepresence robots and avatar robots

Telepresence robots have started to appear on the market as well and can be used, for example, to give a presentation at a remote place or to interact with people in a different location. Telepresence robots can come in many shapes, from mechanistic to zoomorphic to highly humanlike. They can be robots with screens displaying virtual characters, representing the people who control them. Such a robot is also referred to as an *avatar robot*, given that it represents the alter ego of the person who operates it to work in their place. Avatar robots can be used for various applications, such as customer service, learning, entertainment, and healthcare, as explained in this chapter, and also can be used for physical tasks (see, e.g., Figure 11.19). In the Dawn Avatar Robot Café in Tokyo, workers with physical disabilities interact with customers by remotely operating the humanoid telepresence robots OriHime and OriHime-D (see Figure 11.20) (Kamino and Šabanović, 2023). Recent research on a semiautonomous Geminoid robot, the android ERICA (Kubota et al., 2022), showed that interlocutors even align their attitudes to those of the robot they tele-operate. Using physically embodied telepresence robots rather than videoconferencing systems may be particularly useful in educational settings, such as when a student is absent because of illness (Fitter et al., 2018; Newhart et al., 2016). It may also support long-distance learning (Schouten et al., 2022).

11.11 Future applications

Many of the applications introduced in this chapter are already available today. As technologies keep advancing, however, other types of future applications will emerge. For instance, researchers envision that daily appliances can be more automated and connected, as a network of devices within a smart home, for example. Several research groups also envision that individual robots can provide interfaces for such smart homes (Bernotat et al., 2016). Researchers have also started exploring how people might react to robotic furniture and appliances. Sirkin et al. (2015) studied how a robot ottoman should interact with people and also explored interactions with an interactive chest of drawers. Yamaji et al. (2010) developed a set of social trash boxes that use social cues, such as approaching and bowing, to motivate people to throw away their trash; they also created a set of robotic dishes that can be summoned by a user by rapping on the table. Osawa et al. (2009) investigated how people may respond to home appliances being anthropomorphized, such as equipping a refrigerator with eyes or a printer with a mouth so that it can speak to a user.

Future developments of robots will also likely extend the capabilities within existing application domains. For example, healthcare robots are now being developed not only to provide companionship but also to monitor the behavior and health status of their users (e.g., Autom) and also possibly to assist with tasks of daily living (e.g., Care-O-bot). Educational robots may take on more active roles in tutoring, particularly in domains such as second-language learning (Belpaeme et al., 2015). Following data-based applications in other domains, robots might also take advantage of their interactive capabilities to collect different kinds of information on users. We can expect robotic sensing and interaction capabilities to become more distributed in our lived environment, engaging with us through various everyday devices that may not immediately come across as robots.

11.12 Problems for robot application

There are various problems that might prevent successful market updates in the commercial market and as applications in everyday life. These include the potential for robot design to lead to misplaced and eventually disappointed expectations, overreliance on and addiction to robots, misuse and abuse of robots, and engagement with robots taking people's attention away from other concerns.

11.12.1 Public relations

A significant number of social robots do not seem to have any current practical use. At best, they are communication platforms, such as Pepper. At times, companies start developing or using robots for no other reason than to promote themselves. Being perceived as being active in the area of robots, AI, and cryptocurrency (feel free to extend this list with the latest technology buzzwords) is enough for some companies to engage with the respective technologies. Nippon Telegraph and Telephone Corporation (NTT), for example, started a whole subsidiary called "NTT Disruption" that bought the failed robot Jibo (see Figure 11.13). NTT Disruption was disrupted in 2023 and closed for good. The traditional Japanese telecom company is not alone in its quest to inspire investors. XPeng, a Chinese electric vehicle manufacturer, developed a rideable robotic unicorn. Kawasaki has its own rideable robotic goat called "Bex." Although it might be fun to ride on these robots, this can hardly be considered a practical form of transportation.

It is not only technology companies that engage in robot public relations (PR). Many companies buy robots without having any good use for them. The Christchurch International Airport, for example, bought several Pepper robots without any possibilities of a practical benefit from it. They are used as glorified boomboxes, playing back the same information over and over without any interaction with passengers (see Figure 11.21).

Figure 11.21 Pepper at the Christchurch airport.

Marketing in itself has a function in our society. Grabbing the attention of potential customers and clients is important. But the business of attracting attention is fast paced and relentless. A TV commercial, for example, has a short life span. The Henn na Hotel in Tokyo started in 2015, with its main attraction being its robotic workforce. Although this might have initially attracted visitors, its novelty did wear off, and in 2019, the hotel reduced its robotic workforce by half to cut down on operation costs.

Developing robots is difficult and takes time. Although PR can offer a boost in attention and finances, it is a very unreliable foundation on which to build a robotic future.

11.12.2 Addressing user expectations

Users often enter into interactions with robots with certain expectations, often rooted in exposure to specific conceptions of robots in the popular news media, fiction, or the promises made in robot advertising. The design and presentation of robots can also inspire certain expectations in users. For example, if a robot speaks in English, users will likely expect that it will be able to understand spoken English. The more humanlike the robot looks, the more human capabilities it may be expected to have. The cost of disappointing user expectations can be that the robot is perceived as incompetent, and people are therefore less willing to use it. Paepcke and Takayama (2010) showed that it is possible, however, to manage user expectations by describing the robot's abilities realistically; in fact, it is better to set expectations lower rather than higher. User expectations could also be managed through the design; for example, many social robots are designed with infant-like appearances to decrease expectations and increase tolerance for error (Hegel et al., 2010).

11.12.3 Addiction

There is a concern that robots—specifically, social robots—will make people overreliant on the social and physical interaction offered by robotic devices. One can easily imagine a future in which some people prefer robots as interaction partners, perhaps even as life partners, over humans Borenstein and Arkin (2019). A less extreme scenario would be one where robots are preferred over people for some interactions. Although this is not necessarily cause for concern—many people already prefer online shopping over a trip to the store, for example—we should be wary of the negative consequences of substituting social human interaction with social robot interaction. One concern is that robots will be seen to offer friendship, a state that, of course, is artificial to the robot but might be perceived as genuine by the human user (Elder, 2017). Conversations with a robot could be pleasant, even cathartic, but there is a danger that because the robot panders to the user, offering an interaction that is pleasing, this might make the user overreliant on the robot, causing the human to crave the robot's company. Because robots are most likely to be under the control of corporations, to some extent, there is a concern that dependence, and perhaps even addiction, will be a sought-after property in robots. Lessons should be learned from our interaction with connected devices when designing robots (Turkle, 2016).

Gazzaley and Rosen (2016) provide an interesting read about the "dark side" of our high-tech age.

11.12.4 Attention theft

As can already be observed with mobile devices, technology attracts our attention, and robots, too, could cause "attention theft." Neuroscience research has demonstrated that our attention is grabbed by motion and sound, and this is exacerbated when the sound and movement are lifelike and social (Posner, 2011). Robots pose an easy opportunity for attention theft, either unintentionally or by design. When designing and deploying robots, care should be taken that the robot has a mechanism to identify when not to engage with the user or draw attention through its actions, however unintentional. In particular, this should be carefully done in cases where the robot might attract attention away from a human interaction partner.

11.12.5 Loss of interest by user

The so-called novelty effect is frequently discussed in the HRI literature, suggesting that people pay more attention to a novel entity and express a preference to use it because it is unfamiliar; however, such effects are usually not long lasting (Kanda et al., 2004; Koay et al., 2007b). Researchers have tested various robot applications in research contexts and have revealed that the novelty effect lasted anywhere from a few minutes to, at most, a few months. Therefore, even if a one-shot experiment were to reveal positive outcomes regarding the performance and evaluation of a robot, we cannot be sure that the positive effect will prevail in the long run. Longitudinal studies are needed to provide further evidence for positive HRI over time. An important goal is to enable robots to sustain users' interest over time and across multiple interactions (Tanaka et al., 2007; Kidd and Breazeal, 2007; Kanda et al., 2007b).

11.12.6 Taking advantage and robot abuse

One of Asimov's laws for robotics is that the robot should never do harm or allow harm to be done to a human. Although this seems a necessity to attain the level of trust that is required for humans to accept robots invading their everyday lives, it may also provide the unintentional side effect of people trying to take advantage of the rule. If everyone knows that self-driving cars will automatically yield when cut off, will anyone ever let them merge? If a patrolling robot is programmed to avoid bodily contact (lest the human get hurt in the process), how exactly is it supposed to prevent a burglar from running away? Tests with self-driving cars have already shown that humans will capitalize on the robots' tendency to avoid conflict (Liu et al., 2020). Analyses of human–chatbot interactions indicate that users will try to get the chatbot to engage in sexual role play (see, e.g., Brahman and De Angeli, 2012; Keijsers et al., 2021), even though the chatbot in this case is not intended for that use and cannot respond in kind.

Taking this behavior more to the extreme, one runs into the issue of robot abuse. It has been noted by various scholars that a small but pervasive minority of humans will engage in a negative way with robots when they are left unsupervised. This tendency has been observed across countries and on different continents—for example, Japan, (Brscić et al., 2015), South Korea (Salvini et al., 2010), the United States (Vincent, 2017; Mosbergen, 2015), and Denmark (Rehm and Krogsager, 2013). Moreover, although children seem especially prone to engage in robot-bullying behavior (see Figure 11.22), presumably due to their strong tendency to anthropomorphize and as part of developing their social skills, adults have also been recorded kicking, hitting, and verbally abusing robots.

Figure 11.22 A child kicking a robot in a shopping mall.

Notably, the abusive behavior that is generally displayed shares more similarities with intimidation and bullying than with vandalism. This makes sense, considering that robots are recognized as social agents by humans. The exact motivation for why people bully robots has not been found out yet, although frustration (Mutlu and Forlizzi, 2008), entertainment (Rehm and Krogsager, 2013), and curiosity (Nomura et al., 2016) have been suggested to play a role.

Robot abuse poses a number of problems. Obviously, a robot that is repeatedly attacked (as reported by e.g. Salvini et al., 2010; Mosbergen, 2015) may get damaged and will need to be replaced or repaired, and for this duration of time, it will not be able to fulfill its tasks. Similarly, obstruction (as observed by Brscić et al., 2015; Mutlu and Forlizzi, 2008) will prevent a robot from carrying out whatever it needs to carry out to be useful. Moreover, tackling (Vincent, 2017) or stepping in front of a moving robot (Liu et al., 2020; Brscić et al., 2015) may result in a collision, which may not only damage the robot but also injure any humans involved. Verbal abuse, although perhaps not directly disruptive to the task, may still disturb any bystanders and make them uncomfortable.

Unfortunately, abusive behavior has been shown to be remarkably persistent. Verbal reprimands or requests to stop from the robots have been shown to have little effect. Shutting down until the abuse has stopped (Ku et al., 2018) or running away from the bullies (Brscić et al., 2015) have been somewhat successful, but these methods may not always be feasible. Active intervention from bystanders has been shown to be unlikely, both in field studies (Salvini et al., 2010; Rehm and Krogsager, 2013) and in experimental settings (Tan et al., 2018). The field of HRI will have to continue investigating the motivation behind and effective deterring of these human behaviors in order to allow robots to effectively do their jobs in society.

11.13 Conclusion

Markets for robots are growing (Haegele, 2016), but many of the robots that are available on the market still feature limited capabilities for social interaction, for instance, pet robots and service robots. In the domain of navigation, great strides have been made, as documented by applications such as delivery robots and self-driving cars. Before deploying any such technologies, empirical research and evaluation studies need to be conducted in order to test and validate the new technologies and get them ready for the market. With more research in open-ended, real-world contexts, it is likely that researchers will come up with new application concepts for robots and find novel niches that existing robotic technologies can successfully occupy.

Questions for you to think about:

- Try to think about a couple of new future applications that are not yet mentioned in the chapter. For each application that comes to mind, briefly describe possible technical problems and solutions.
- Suppose you would be able to prepare the technical solutions for the applications you thought of in the previous question. Think about market potential: Who are the targeted users, how expensive will your robots be, and which consumers would be willing to buy the respective robots?
- Suppose your applications are successful in terms of technical preparation and the potential market. What problems might they cause? How would you avoid or at least reduce such problems?

11.14 Exercises

The answers to these questions are available in the Appendix.

** **Exercise 11.1 Application areas** What roles are social robots likely to play in the field of education? Select one or more options from the following list:

1. Platform for learning how to program
2. Janitor
3. Student
4. Tutor
5. Teachable agent
6. Principal

** **Exercise 11.2 Application areas** In which application areas are social robots expected to make a strong impact? Select one or more options from the following list:

1. Politics
2. Cleaning
3. Military
4. Therapy for mental illness
5. Tour guiding
6. Burglary

** **Exercise 11.3 Autonomous vehicles** What benefits are AVs expected to deliver to society? Select one or more options from the following list:

1. Reduce traffic congestion
2. Enable people with disabilities to ride
3. Enable elderly to ride
4. Reduce price of vehicles
5. Enable better car co-ownership
6. Enable children to drive
7. Reduce fuel price
8. Increase driving speed
9. Reduce electricity consumption
10. Improve road safety
11. Increase number of vehicles on the road
12. Reduce emissions
13. Increase number of colors for cars

* **Exercise 11.4 Robots and their applications** Select the true statements from the following list:

1. BellaBot is a delivery robot.
2. PackBot is a delivery robot.
3. K5 is a cleaning robot.
4. Jibo is a tele-operated robot.
5. Roomba is a cleaning robot.

* **Exercise 11.5 Dependency** Humans do not abuse robots. True or false?

1. True
2. False

Future reading:

- The International Federation of Robotics publishes the *World Robotics Report* each year. (Part of the report is free to download: https://ifr.org/free-downloads/).
- Broekens, Joost, Heerink, Marcel, and Rosendal, Henk. Assistive social robots in elderly care: A review. *Gerontechnology*, 8(2):94 103, 2009. doi: 10.4017/gt.2009.08.02.002.00. URL https://doi.org/10.4017/gt.2009.08.02.002.00
- Ford, Martin. *The Rise of the Robots: Technology and the Threat of Mass Unemployment*. Oneworld Publications, London, 2015. ISBN 978-0465059997. URL http://worldcat.org/oclc/993846206
- Leite, Iolanda, Martinho, Carlos, and Paiva, Ana. Social robots for long-term interaction: A survey. *International Journal of Social Robotics*, 5(2):291–308, 2013. doi: 10.1007/s12369-013-0178-y. URL https://doi.org/10.1007/s12369-013-0178-y
- Nourbakhsh, Illah Reza. *Robot Futures*. MIT Press, Cambridge, MA, 2013. ISBN 9780262018623. URL http://worldcat.org/oclc/945438245
- Belpaeme, Tony, Kennedy, James, Ramachandran, Aditi, Scassellati, Brian, and Tanaka, Fumihide. Social robots for education: A review. *Science Robotics*, 3(21):eaat5954, 2018. doi: 10.1126/scirobotics.aat5954. URL http://doi.org/10.1126/scirobotics.aat5954

12

Robots in Society

What is covered in this chapter:

- The influence of the media on human–robot interaction (HRI) research.
- Stereotypes of robots in the media.
- Positive and negative visions of HRI.
- Ethical considerations when designing an HRI study.
- Ethical issues of robots that fulfill a user's emotional needs.
- The dilemmas associated with behavior toward robots (e.g., robots' right to be treated in a moral way).
- The issue of job losses as a result of the increasing number of robots in the workforce.

The discussion of robots in society often brings up questions about how we envision robots in the present and future and the social and ethical consequences of using robots in different tasks and contexts. Researchers, the media, and members of the public argue over how robots will affect our perceptions of and interactions with other humans, what the consequences of new robotic technologies will be for labor distribution and relations, and what should be considered socially and ethically appropriate uses of robots. This kind of exploration is crucial to the field of human–robot interaction (HRI) because understanding the societal meaning, significance, and consequences of HRI research will ensure that new robotic technologies fit our common social values and goals. To understand how robots might fit into society, we take a broad view of HRI through the lens of culture and the narratives, values, and practices that provide the context and tools with which people make sense of the world around them and the robots that will be coming to share it.

In this chapter, we look at robots in fiction and film (Section 12.1), two aspects of popular culture that have had particularly strong impacts on how we imagine robotic technology in society. In Section 12.2, we consider ethical concerns about the introduction and use of robots in society to reflect on how our values and priorities should be taken into account while shaping the human–robot interactions of the future. In recent years, there has also been increased focus on considering diversity and inclusion in HRI—in terms of considering more inclusive robot design practices, working with a broader array of demographic groups in user studies, and considering the potential effects of robot deployment and use with diverse stakeholders in various use cases.

12.1 Robots in popular media

What movies have become popular with audiences or critics recently? Is there a TV series that went viral or an episode that everyone is talking about? Did any of those contain robots, by chance? If so, how were these machines portrayed? Looking into the literature and other media, it becomes clear that robots have always been a "hot topic" for sci-fi writers and avid consumers.

Historically, stories of artificial human beings, such as the Golem in Jewish folklore, have been around for hundreds of years. Karel Čapek was the first author to use the word *robot*, which was featured in his theater play *R.U.R.— Rossum's Universal Robots* that premiered in 1921 (see Figure 12.1). In it, robots take over the world and kill almost all humans. Two robots do, however, start to exhibit emotions for each other, and the last remaining human considers them to be the new Adam and Eve. Isaac Asimov, in turn, coined the term *robotics* as a field of study, as well as the yet-to-be-realized domain of robopsychology, which could be seen as having some overlap with HRI. The notion of robots that befriend humans and aid society is a central focus of the post-WW2 narrative of Osamu Tezuka's Astro Boy series, centering on a robotic boy who lives with a family, has a heart, and works to help his human friends. Some robotics projects, such as the HRP-2 humanoid, bring inspiration from fictional narratives to life—in this case, the robot's functions of aiding people in construction work, moving objects, and other physical tasks are not only inspired by the manga series Patlabor, but its appearance is designed by Yutaka Izubuchi, the mechanical animation designer for the manga and anime series Kaneko et al. (2004).

Now think back to when you first heard about robots. This first encounter with a robot was likely an on-screen encounter. Computer graphics can nowadays visualize almost anything; hence, depictions of robots in movies can be quite fantastical. For example, movies have depicted robots that use antigravity to float around. In reality, there is little use for such robot hardware features. Robots have been portrayed in all types of artistic expressions, such as books, movies, plays, and computer games. Such media portrayals form our perceptions and understanding of robots and can thus bias our views, particularly because these are the only experiences most people have with robots. We are at an interesting point in time where, on the one hand, more and more robots are about to enter our everyday lives, but on the other hand, almost all our public knowledge about robots stems from the media. This gap between the expectations fueled by science fiction and the actual abilities of robots often leads to disappointment when people interact with robots. This is why it is important to look at how robots are portrayed in popular media and to take such portrayals into account when we are designing robots for and presenting them to the public.

Figure 12.1 A scene from Čapek's 1921 play *R.U.R.* shows robots rebelling against their human masters.

As a disclaimer, we have to acknowledge that it was not possible for us to consider every robot mentioned in every book, film, computer game, newspaper article, or play. Still, some valid conclusions might be drawn from the more or less classic examples that will be reiterated in the following discussion.

12.1.1 Robots want to be humans

In many narratives, robots are portrayed as wanting to be like humans, despite their actual superiority to humans, for instance, in terms of strength and computational power. To illustrate, the very desire to become human is the central storyline for Isaac Asimov's *Bicentennial Man*, in which a robot named Andrew Martin is following a lifelong plan to become recognized as a human (Asimov, 1976). The book was used as the basis for a movie of the same name, released in 1999. Besides becoming physically more humanlike, Andrew Martin also fights a legal battle to gain full legal status. He is even prepared to accept mortality to gain full legal status. Other robots, such as the replicant Rachael in the movie *Blade Runner* based on the book by Philip K. Dick, are not even aware of the fact that they are robots (Dick, 2007). The same holds true for some of the humanlike Cylons in the 2004 TV series *Battlestar Galactica*.

On the contrary, a prime example of a robotic character that is aware of its robotic nature is Mr. Data from the TV series *Star Trek: The Next Generation*. Mr. Data is stronger than humans; has more computational power than humans; and does not need sleep, nutrition, or oxygen. Still, this character is set up to have the desire to become more humanlike. The key aspect, however, that actually distinguishes Mr. Data from humans is his lack of emotion. Similarly, in Steven Spielberg's movie *A.I.* (based on Brian Aldiss's short story *Super-Toys Last All Summer Long*), robots also lack emotions (Aldiss, 2001), which prompts Professor Allen Hobby to build the protagonist robot David with the ability to love. Likewise, sci-fi authors have considered emotions to be a feature that all robots would lack. However, in reality, several computational systems to mirror emotions have already been successfully implemented. The computer programs implementing the so-called *OCC model of emotions* (Ortony et al., 1988) are prime examples. Equipping robots with emotions in the attempt to make them human is therefore an archetypal storyline.

A more subtle variation of this narrative concerns the inclusion of a control or setting for honesty and humor, as depicted in the robots from the movie *Interstellar*. The following dialogue between Cooper, the captain of a spaceship, and the TARS robot emerges:

COOPER: Hey, TARS, what's your honesty parameter?

TARS: Ninety percent.

COOPER: Ninety percent?

TARS: Absolute honesty isn't always the most diplomatic nor the safest form of communication with emotional beings.

COOPER: Okay, ninety percent it is.

Although robots might not have emotions themselves, they will be required to interact with humans who do have emotions, and hence it will be necessary for them to process emotions and even adjust their rational behavior accordingly.

The aforementioned classic examples taken from contemporary film are only the tip of the iceberg, but they illustrate humans' steady desire to compare themselves to superhuman entities. A hundred years ago, however, there were already machines that were more powerful than humans, although their power was physical and not mental. These days, we can see the major progress in the area of artificial intelligence (AI). On May 11, 1997, the IBM computer "Deep Blue" won the first chess match against the world champion at the time. In 2011, the IBM computer Watson won as a contestant in the quiz game show *Jeopardy*. In 2017, Google's DeepMind AlphaGo defeated the world's number-one Go player, Ke Jie. In light of this progress, it is easy to imagine how robots in the future might be both strong and intelligent, leaving humans in an inferior position. At the same time, computers and robots are successful in limited task domains, so humans may have the advantage through their ability to adapt and generalize to different tasks and contexts. Fictional narratives let us explore the consequences of these and other possibilities from the safety of our couches.

12.1.2 *Robots as a threat to humanity*

Figure 12.2 The Terminator. (Source: Dick Thomas Johnson)

Another archetypal storyline that continuously reappears in fiction is that of a robotic uprising. In short, humanity builds intelligent and strong robots. The robots decide to take over the world and enslave or kill all humans in order to secure resources for themselves (Barrat, 2015). Karel Čapek's original play, mentioned earlier, already introduced this narrative. Going back to the example of Mr. Data, he has a brother named Lore who possesses an emotion chip. Lore follows the path of not wanting to be like a human but instead wanting to enslave humanity. Other popular examples are *The Terminator* (Cameron, 1984) (see Figure 12.2), the Cylons in *Battlestar Galactica*, the Machines portrayed in the movie *The Matrix*, and the robots portrayed in the 2004 movie *iRobot* (which is based on the book by the same name authored by Isaac Asimov (Asimov, 1991)). Asimov coined the term *Frankenstein complex* to describe the notion that robots would take over the world.

This archetype builds on two assumptions. First, robots resemble humans. The robots depicted in the aforementioned movies and shows have been designed to look, think, and act like their creators. However, they exceed their creators in intelligence and power. Second, once they interact with the now "inferior" human species, robots dehumanize their subordinates, a theme familiar in examples from human history as well. Many colonial powers declared indigenous populations as nonhumans in an attempt to vindicate the atrocities committed toward them. Accordingly, because robots resemble humans, they will also enslave and kill humans. However, this rationale is overly simplistic. The issue of a perceived threat to distinctiveness is also addressed in the psychological literature (Ferrari et al., 2016). If you want to learn more about the psychology of feeling threatened by robots, then consider reading the work of Złotowski et al. (2017).

The movie *Ex Machina* (Garland, 2014) combines the archetypes just discussed (robots pretending to be human and robots taking over) with an interesting twist. Human protagonist Caleb falls in love with robot protagonist Ava, who, unbeknownst to him, has been designed to be his dream woman. The two grow an apparent emotional attachment, and Ava begs Caleb to help her escape from the lab where she is kept. However, after Caleb does so, she reveals that she manipulated him in order to escape, then leaves him trapped in the same lab with no possibility of escape. Although the movie adheres to the archetype that emotions displayed by robots are not real and that robots are hostile toward humans, it gives both paradigms a twist because Ava's behavior originates from her (very human) outrage at being exploited and kept prisoner.

12.1.3 Superior robots being good

Several science-fiction authors have already proposed future scenarios in which superior robots quietly influence human society. In Isaac Asimov's *Prelude to Foundation*, he describes a robotic first minister, Eto Demerzel (a.k.a. R. Daneel Olivaw), who keeps the empire on the right track (Asimov, 1988). Interestingly, he hides his robotic nature. He is a very humanlike robot in appearance but resorts to various strategies to blend in. For example, he eats food, despite the fact that he cannot digest it. He collects it in a pouch that can be emptied later. Here we have a scenario in which a superior being works to help human society behind the scenes.

The notion of robots being evil and humans being good is most persistent in Western culture. Robots are extremely popular in the Japanese media, and there we can observe a different relationship between humans and robots: robots, such as Astro Boy and Doraemon, are good-natured characters that help humans in their daily lives. This more positive spin on the social uses and consequences of robots is often seen as being partially responsible for the large number of personal and home robots being developed in Japan and their perceived higher acceptance there than in Western societies.

12.1.4 Similarity between humans and robots

The common theme between all these science-fiction narratives concerns the fact that all of them explore the question of to what degree humans and robots are alike. From a conceptual point of view, robots are typically portrayed by emphasizing either their similarities to humans or lack thereof in terms

Table 12.1 Topics of HRI in media portrayals.

		Mind	
		Similar	Different
Body	Similar	Type I	Type II
	Different	Type III	Type IV

of the robot's body and mind (see Table 12.1). Dixon supports this view by stating that artists explore the deep-seated fears and fascinations associated with machine embodiment in relation to two distinct themes: the humanization of machines and the dehumanization of humans (Dixon, 2004; Haslam, 2006).

These four types of topics can, of course, be mixed. If we take the example of Mr. Data, at the superficial level, he looks very much like a human, which sets our expectations accordingly (Type II). It then appears dramatic and surprising if Mr. Data can enter the vacuum of space without being damaged. In the movie *Prometheus*, the android David is wearing a space suit when walking on an alien planet. Wearing this suit does not serve a functional purpose because David does not require air. The dialogue unfolds as follows:

CHARLIE HOLLOWAY: David, why are you wearing a suit, man?

DAVID: I beg your pardon?

CHARLIE HOLLOWAY: You don't breathe, remember? So, why wear the suit?

DAVID: I was designed like this, because you people are more comfortable interacting with your own kind. If I didn't wear the suit, it would defeat the purpose.

Again, the human embodiment sets our expectations, and when a difference from humans is displayed, it surprises the audience. Godfried-Willem Raes takes a different approach with his robot orchestra. He emphasizes the equality of robots and humans in his theatrical performances (Type I). He argues:

If these robots conceal nothing, it is fairly self-evident that when their functioning is made dependent on human input and interaction, this human input is also provided naked. The naked human in confrontation with the naked machine reveals the simple fact that humans, too, are actually machines, albeit fundamentally more refined and efficient machines than our musical robots.

An example of Type III could be Johnny Five from the 1986 movie *Short Circuit*. Although Johnny Five has a distinctively robotic body, he does express human emotions, which suggests that his mind is similar to that of humans.

12.1.5 *Narratives of robotic science*

Ben Goldacre has pointed out how the media promotes the public misunderstanding of science (Goldacre, 2008). Two narratives that the media frequently uses are science-scare stories and wacky science stories.

The performance of autonomous vehicles, which can also be considered a form of HRI, is currently the target of immense scrutiny. The crash statistics provided by Tesla, Waymo, and others indicate that they are performing better than humans. Tesla, for example,[1] showed that driving using the vehicle's autopilot feature reduces the probability of crashes dramatically.

One question that almost all reporters ask when interviewing HRI researchers focuses on when robots will actually take over the world. The goal, then, is to write a story that scares the public and hence attracts attention. A story entitled "Robots Are Harmless and Almost Useless" is very unlikely to get published. But that is what most HRI projects come down to at this point in time. The question of whether and when robots will take over the world addresses our inner fears and fascinations involving interacting with robots. It reflects the ambivalent attitudes we might hold toward robots—on the one hand, robots are viewed as an asset and support in everyday life, but on the other hand, the prospect of a hybrid society appears threatening to many because they fear losing their jobs or finding their privacy breached, for example.

We may ask ourselves why the ambivalent portrayals of robots are so persistent in the media. The most obvious answer is that many storylines call for a "conflict" to make a storyline more interesting. A (science-) fictional world in which everybody is happily living ever after is unlikely to capture the attention of a broader audience. Pitching evil robots against good humans not only serves the purpose of creating ambivalence but also triggers an "in-group" effect (Ferrari et al., 2016; Złotowski et al., 2017). Humans often show the tendency to defend our species against "out-group" robots. This division can then be challenged by introducing robots that are indistinguishable from humans, such as in the TV shows *Battlestar Galactica* and *Westworld*. This creates great uncertainty, which in turn creates tension. Notable exceptions from the gloomy visions in the media are the TV series *Futurama* by Matt Groening and the movie *Robot and Frank* by Jake Schreier, both of which depict a vision of the future in which humans and robots live peacefully side by side, even becoming friends. In the movie *Her*, the protagonist Theodore, played by Joaquin Phoenix, falls in love with his AI mobile phone Samantha (Jonze, 2013).

On the other hand, media representations of robot technologies can be biased in the sense that they fit the wacky science narrative. This narrative resonates with pop science, is less prevalent, and serves to entertain rather than to report scientific progress (Berghuis, 2017).

Because the interest in all technologies that feature AI is still growing, many HRI researchers are invited for interviews. This offers a great opportunity for them to showcase their work, but at the same time, media coverage also carries considerable risk. To illustrate, a reporter might intend to write a scare story or even a wacky science story, without always giving that goal away. In light of the extensive media attention that HRI researchers commonly get, it

---

[1] See www.tesla.com/VehicleSafetyReport

might be advisable to participate in media training sessions before engaging with journalists. Such training sessions are offered at many universities and research institutes, and taking part in such training can minimize misrepresentations and detrimental outcomes of encounters with journalists who want to cover social robots and AI. As a general guideline for talking to the media, it appears advisable to stick to the research that was actually performed and avoid engaging in wild speculations about topics that were not covered in the study at hand. It might be helpful to clarify before an actual interview which questions will be asked and to request to view a manuscript draft prior to publication. Thereby, misunderstandings or misrepresentations of the science involved can be corrected prior to publication.

HRI researchers cannot shy away from representations of robots in the media, fictional or otherwise, and the elicitation of associated hopes and fears that create ambivalence toward robots (Stapels and Eyssel, 2022). In actual HRI research, we invite people to engage with robots, and every single person who interacts with a robot does so with certain attitudes, ambivalence, or hopes and expectations of what the robot can and cannot do. Many of these expectations are grounded in science fiction and potentially biased reports in the media rather than the annals of scientific research.

12.2 Ethics in HRI

Is it okay to develop and sell a sex robot, which is always willing to do what you want and will stay forever young and fit? Would you have your parents be taken care of by a carebot instead of a human nurse?

Roboticists and philosophers alike have long been concerned with such ethical issues in robotics, coining a shared domain of scholarship called *roboethics*. More recently, a group of HRI scholars formulated five ethical rules, which they call their Principles of Robotics, to raise broader awareness about the role of ethics in HRI.[2] Ethical rules have also been a subject of discussion in popular literature, particularly the well-known "Three Laws of Robotics" (see the accompanying text box). Moreover, work by Fosch-Villaronga et al. (2020) outlines the ethical, legal, and social (ELS) implications that emerge when reflecting on HRI. A recent overview by Wullenkord and Eyssel (2020) outlines the various overarching challenges associated with social robots and HRI in a diverse set of contexts.

Figure 12.3 Isaac Asimov (January 2, 1920–April 6, 1992).

Isaac Asimov (January 2, 1920–April 6, 1992; see Figure 12.3) proposed three rules of robotics that would safeguard humanity from malevolent robots:

1. A robot may not injure a human being or, through inaction, allow a human being to come to harm.

[2] See https://doi.org/10.1080/09540091.2016.1271400

2. A robot must obey the orders given to it by human beings except where such orders would conflict with the First Law.

3. A robot must protect its own existence as long as such protection does not conflict with the First or Second Laws.

Although Asimov's work is highly visible in the public media, it has been criticized by philosophers, and it is clear even from the stories that the three rules are not a practical guide to satisfying ethical requirements for designing robots. Asimov eventually added a zeroth law:

0. A robot may not harm humanity or, by inaction, allow humanity to come to harm.

This clearly marks the relevance of debating issues such as the ubiquitous deployment of robots in future society; their use in home and care contexts; the implications of developing autonomous weapons systems and autonomous cars; or, giving it a seemingly positive touch, the development of robots for attachment, love, or sex.

These days, many robotics research projects envision robots as conducting acts on behalf of humans, such as killing others; doing "dull, dirty, and dangerous" tasks; or serving to fulfill humans' need for psychological closeness and sexuality. Some of these projects are even funded by government agencies. At the same time, there are clear counter-movements, such as the Campaign Against Killer Robots.[3] As responsible researchers, we have to consider the ethical implications of what we envision and the steps we take to approach these visions of the future (Sparrow, 2011). In the following subsections, we discuss some of the common topics of ethical concern in HRI research.

12.2.1 Robots in research

As a student beginning to get hands-on experience with empirical research in HRI, you might plan to conduct a study with a robot that acts seemingly autonomously. Even here, ethics has to be considered because you might choose to deceive your participants by controlling your robot using the Wizard-of-Oz approach. You thereby make the participants believe that the robot has certain functions, whereas in reality, you control the robot's behavior in the background. The problem with this approach is that the deception concerning the robot's skills raises and biases users' hopes and expectations about the robot's abilities. This may manipulate them into thinking that robotic technology is more advanced than it actually is (Riek, 2012).

Another critical example to consider might be the use of robots as persuasive communicators within your research project. Previous research on persuasive technology has shown that robots can be used to manipulate people into changing not only their attitudes but also their behaviors (Brandstetter

---

[3] See www.stopkillerrobots.org/

et al., 2017). Examples of behaviors that have been successfully influenced include health-related habits, such as exercising or maintaining a healthy diet (Kiesler et al., 2008). Even if it might benefit people to change their health-related habits, such as smoking less and exercising more, instrumentalizing social robots for this purpose poses ethical concerns if they exploit the social bond with the user and influence the user without the user's explicit consent and conscious knowledge or understanding of how he or she is being influenced. The notion of robot deception and manipulation is not easy to disentangle because these constructs remain ill-defined and distinct but related. Moreover, generally speaking, deception is a characteristic that marks empirical experimental research with humans and robots alike, in order not to reveal the true nature of the research questions at hand. This overlaps with the deceptive nature of robots and their capabilities—which may lead naive users to believe that robots indeed possess intentions, emotions, a mind, or other essentially human qualities (see Chapter 8).

12.2.2 Robots to fulfill emotional needs

Robotic care

Imagine your grandmother has been given a robot companion by a group of researchers. They tell her that this new technological friend will stay with her in her home for the next three weeks. She interacts with the robot every day for these three weeks, and over time, she becomes quite attached to it. The robot invites her to do activities like memory games on a regular basis. It asks her how she is doing and whether she slept well; it keeps her company, and it never argues with her. She is delighted with her new companion, and life is good. That is, until the researchers come back and ask her to complete some questionnaires before packing up the robot and taking it away. The dull routine of the elderly care center creeps back, and she feels even more lonely than before.

This brief scenario gives a glimpse of the psychological experience of getting attached—not only to people but also to objects like robots. HRI researchers have shown how easily people grow attached to a robot, even when it only briefly enters their everyday lives (Šabanović et al., 2014; Forlizzi and DiSalvo, 2006; Chang and Šabanović, 2015; Kidd and Breazeal, 2008). The emotional and social consequences of withdrawing this source of attention and "artificial affection" clearly need to be considered when running case studies with a social robot that has to be returned at the end of the study.

Relatedly, Steil et al. (2019) have proposed an ethical perspective reflecting the challenges associated with the use of robots in medical domains, which usually involve vulnerable populations like children, the elderly, or persons with cognitive or physical impairments.

Other studies, however, have demonstrated the beneficial effect of deploying small-scale robots, such as the therapeutic robot Paro (Wada and Shibata, 2007; Shibata, 2012) or the robot dog Aibo (Broekens et al., 2009). These robots are not able to do any tedious manual labor, but they can provide companionship. Given the high workload that caretakers are burdened with, any relief, even small, is likely welcomed.

Manzeschke (2019) reflects on ethics in care contexts, with a particular focus on taking into account the different types of human–robot relationships. For instance, the robot is viewed as a mere tool, the robot is deemed a tool with social capabilities, or the robot is interpreted as a relationship partner. Above and beyond, Sparrow and Sparrow (2006) offer an interesting perspective on robotic care that has become a classic in the literature. They argue that even when a robotic caregiver can be developed that is capable of providing superb emotional and physical care, it would still be unethical to outsource care to machines. The reason for this is that a relationship can only be meaningful when it is between two entities that are capable of experiencing reciprocal affect and concern; an imitation of caring, however perfect, should never substitute the real product. This kind of relationship may also be detrimental to the value of upholding a person's dignity. This brings us to the ethics of developing a deeper emotional attachment to a robot (Law et al., 2022).

Emotional attachment to robots

Affection toward robots can go deeper and beyond the care setting. Humans may start to favor robot companions over humans. Imagine a social robot that can truly mimic friendship and emotional support, such as the android Klara in Kazuo Ishiguro's novel *Klara and the Sun*. This "ideal robotic friend" comes with all the perks of a human friend, never complains, and learns never to annoy its owner. Slowly, people could come to prefer these robotic companions over their human peers, who would not be able to measure up to the high standards that robotic friends provide. Would such a future be desirable? What would be the broader societal consequences of supporting the development of human–robot relationships?

Even though users may project all kinds of human traits onto a robot, the robot is not able to experience those traits in the same way humans do, and therefore, the authenticity of the expression can be doubted (Turkle, 2017). Still, robots are sometimes specifically designed to express social cues to deliberately facilitate bonding with them. The authenticity of feelings is normally important in human–human interaction, and we do not know how humans will react to robots that express themselves based on calculations rather than the sensation of emotions.

Going beyond human–robot friendship, there are individuals who feel closeness and intimacy toward robots. The broader question is whether promoting human–robot emotional bonds is desirable (Borenstein and Arkin, 2019). After all, we have to realize that the emotional relationship between humans and robots might be asymmetrical. Humans might nevertheless be quite satisfied with the robot exhibiting sympathetic responses, whether the robot has a humanlike sensation of attachment or not.

Ethical implications of persuasion through robots

Language develops dynamically, and every participant in discourse influences its development simply through its usage. New words appear (e.g., "to google"), others change their meaning (e.g., *gay*), and yet other words fall out of usage altogether. We can use Siri, Cortana, or Bixby to control our phones, homes, or shopping tours.

Familiarity alone will influence our attitudes toward concepts, political ideas, and products; this is called the *mere exposure effect* (Zajonc, 1968). The more often people hear a word, the more positive their attitude toward this word becomes. One day, it will make a great difference if your smart-shopping robot proposes to purchase "Pepsi" compared to offering a "Coca-Cola." The question really is who gets to decide what words our artificial counterparts use.

Robots have the ability to synchronize their vocabulary through the internet in seconds. Even the mass media cannot compete with this level of consistent usage of selected words (Brandstetter et al., 2017). Because of its ability to communicate in humanlike ways, a robot can be a convincing, persuasive communicator.

This comes with negative implications, though: without us even noticing, computers and robots can influence what words we use and how we feel about them. This can and probably is happening already, and we need to develop media and language competency to be able to withstand attempts to influence our views. With the ever more personalized and intimate relationships that we form with technologies, we are increasingly vulnerable. We probably already spend more time with our phones than with our partners and friends.

Furthermore, to our knowledge, there are no regulations or policies in place at this point in time to supervise how large information technology companies, such as Google, Amazon, or Facebook, influence the usage of language, although there is concern about "fake news" and the difficulty of telling fact from fiction in online contexts. It might also be a better approach to regulate the development of our language only to the degree that it should be left to its natural flow of change. With powerful tools at our fingertips, we need to ensure that no company or government can influence our language without our consent and that the robots we design do not become just one additional persuasive and misleading technology.

Generalizing abusive behavior toward robots

Being recognized as a social interaction partner comes with a downside: not all social behaviors aimed at you are positive. In a few field experiments with autonomous robots that were left unsupervised in public spaces, people were observed attempting to intimidate and bully robots (Brscić et al., 2015; Salvini et al., 2010). It is noteworthy that the type of aggression that people displayed seemed to resemble human–human abuse, such as kicking, slapping, insulting, and refusing to move out of the way after the robot politely asked. Abuse that would be more meaningful for machines, such as unplugging them or cutting their wires, was not observed.

Robots normally do not experience any pain or humiliation, hence, the human actually faces greater danger than the robot when, for example, slapping the robot because the human might hurt his or her hand. But there are more issues to consider than just the bully's bodily integrity. It has been argued that bullying a robot is a moral offense—even though nobody gets hurt, responding with violence is still considered wrong and should therefore be discouraged (Whitby, 2008). In addition, scholars have argued that if this behavior is perceived as acceptable, it might generalize to other social agents, such as animals and humans (Whitby, 2008; De Angeli, 2009). This transfer of negative behavior from a humanlike agent to actual humans is argued to also happen in other domains, such as violent computer games (Sparrow, 2017; Darling, 2012), and has been a topic of discussion for quite a while. Further research on this topic is still needed.

A related issue is that interactions with a robot may raise expectations regarding the behavior of other humans. This has been argued to be particularly dangerous in the domain of sex. A robot could easily be designed to seem to desire intercourse at any time and to readily and fully comply with any wishes of the user without having any desires or demands of its own. This could change what people consider normal or appropriate behavior from an intimate partner.

This issue becomes even more problematic if the robot is specifically designed for sexual behaviors that would be considered wrong if it involved human partners. For example, child-shaped sex robots could be designed to fit the desires of pedophiles, or sex robots could be programmed to explicitly not consent to or even struggle against sex in order for users to play out their rape fantasies. These robot behavior designs have been deemed ethically inappropriate by some scholars (for a philosophical justification, see Sparrow, 2017). Others, like David Levy and Hooman Samani, have set out to suggest (even back in the early 2000s) that love and sex with a robot would be a contemporary reality. We are still not there yet. Döring and Poeschl (2019) analyzed fictional and nonfictional media representations of intimacy between humans and robots. Regarding virtual agents, psychologist Mayu Koike has looked into the role of anthropomorphism in developing social, even romantic relationships with virtual characters (Koike et al., 2022; Koike and Loughnan, 2021). Virtual agents—even life-size versions—are available as companions, communication partners or romantic partners, using the Gatebox device.[4] Despite existing controversy, Bendel (2021) points out contexts in which love dolls and sex robots could eventually be useful while at the same time discussing the ethical issues associated with their use. Despite the growing interest in understanding the underpinnings of positive, close, and even intimate social relationships between humans and novel technologies, it is clear that further research indeed is needed to better understand the psychological underpinnings and consequences of intimate HRI (Borenstein and Arkin, 2019).

---

[4] See www.gatebox.ai/

12.2.3 Robots in the workplace

A repeatedly expressed worry is that "robots will replace me in the job market." Since the Industrial Revolution, humans have been replacing manual labor with machines, and the recent deployment of robots is no exception. Robots help us to improve our productivity and thereby help to increase our standard of living. Although robots do replace certain jobs, they also create many new jobs, in particular for highly trained professionals. The challenge that society is facing is that the people replaced by robots need to find new jobs, which might require them to undertake additional training or studies. This may be problematic or even impossible for some, for example, due to financial or intellectual constraints.

In many cases, the acceptance of robots in various workplaces will likely depend on their specific roles and how they are integrated into the workforce. Reich-Stiebert and Eyssel (2015) showed that robots are preferred as assistants in the classroom but not as the main teachers. Teachers also voiced concern about the usage and maintenance of the robots, being particularly fearful that the robots would take their resources in terms of time and attention. Interestingly, primary school teachers were particularly reluctant to have robots in schools, maybe because in their view, young students are particularly vulnerable. An analysis of the predictors of such rather negative attitudes and behavioral inclinations toward educational robots revealed that technology commitment was the key predictor of positive attitudes. That is, those teachers who were open to working with novel technologies in general felt more positive about robots and the future use of them in their classrooms. Another field in which people are concerned about the application of robots is assistive robots designed for use in the home (Reich-Stiebert and Eyssel, 2015, 2013). Again, technology commitment was found to predict people's reluctance to accept robots in their lives.

12.2.4 Ambivalent attitudes toward robots

Haegele (2016) claims that more and more robots will be sold on the market in upcoming years. Their acceptance into society, however, will remain a challenge, and further research on technology-related attitudes and how to change them is necessary to increase society's acceptance of robots. This is particularly relevant in light of the current reconceptualization of attitudes toward robots. That is, research by Stapels and Eyssel (2022, 2021) has shown that attitudes toward robots are not—as suggested by a meta-analysis by Naneva et al. (2020)—neutral or even mildly positive. Indeed, whereas the notion of ambivalent attitudes has been widely studied in social psychology, it has not been widely applied to social robots yet (Stapels and Eyssel, 2022, 2021). However, this is highly relevant because it is plausible that allegedly neutral attitudes toward robots are actually ambivalent. What do we mean by *ambivalence*? This refers to the simultaneous evaluation of the same attitude object in both positive and negative terms. From this, a person might experience inner conflict, which, too, comes with distinct social and cognitive consequences (see van Harreveld et al., 2015). Research by Stapels and Eyssel (2022, 2021) was the first to demonstrate robot-related ambivalence, and further data are needed that use proper attitude measurements that include ambivalence so that the state of people's true attitudes toward robots can be explored. People's ambivalence toward robots may also shift to more positive or negative perceptions based on the context of the robot's use, so more testing in specific task and use contexts is important for understanding people's preferences about the deployment of robots in their everyday environments.

12.2.5 *A more diverse and inclusive HRI*

A number of researchers have joined forces to emphasize the multifaceted notion of diversity and its value for HRI researchers, their work, and the community at large. Diversity can be looked at from various angles, taking into account researcher characteristics (e.g., age, gender, geographic distribution), demographics or other features of research participants (i.e., belonging to a social minority, being part of a vulnerable group, socioeconomic status, etc.) under study, and how the design of the robot might affect diverse stakeholders or embody particular social and cultural stereotypes. Research that takes a human-centered perspective will take into account the first two aspects, whereas robot developers also need to be mindful of how they frame and design their robots, their appearance, and other robot characteristics. This, too, is relevant because none of the people involved in a robot development cycle are free from bias, and implicit as well as explicit biases may have an impact on design choices.

Several recent overviews of HRI research suggest that the field needs to become more inclusive and diverse in relation to the participants who are asked to evaluate robots, the researchers who develop robots, and the contexts in which robots are envisioned as being deployed. A systematic analysis of the HRI literature showed that HRI, like many other scientific fields, relies on studies from "Western, educated, industrial, rich, and democratic" (WEIRD) populations and that there is insufficient consideration of key axes of diversity—sex and gender, race and ethnicity, age, sexuality and family configuration, disability, body type, ideology, and domain expertise— in the HRI literature (Seaborn et al., 2023). Furthermore, a meta-review of studies from HRI conferences in the 2006–2021 period found that men were overrepresented among research participants and that the field generally treats gender as a binary, in contradiction to best-practice guidelines (Winkle et al., 2023a). In an overview of studies relating to sexbots as an HRI application domain, only one study included nonmale users of these robots (González-González et al., 2020). Finally, among robot developers, people from WEIRD countries are also overrepresented; we have few people from developing nations contributing to the design of robots, and few developers focus on creating solutions that can be affordable and usable in more resource-constrained environments, including rural or lower socioeconomic areas (Johnson et al.,

2017). This lack of diversity in the process and aims of robotics research and development can exacerbate bias in robot design.

To consider the interplay of bias and stereotyping in robot design, think of what happens when we meet people: in order to initiate an impression-formation process, we use central social categories—namely, age, ethnicity, and gender—as reference categories to derive judgments about individuals and their characteristics. Because we often do not have the time and motivation to process information systematically and deeply, this happens relatively quickly and automatically. Would this translate to our impressions about robots as well? Researchers have explored the role of various social categories (e.g., gender, ethnicity) for robot perception by seeing if manipulating specific visual cues or merely the name of the robot to suggest such categories will result in a change in people's perceptions (Eyssel and Loughnan, 2013; Eyssel and Hegel, 2012; Bernotat et al., 2017; Bartneck et al., 2018; Perugia et al., 2023). Studies have shown that even robots designed to be gender-neutral can activate harmful biases in people's perceptions of them because people bring their previous experiences and assumptions to their understanding of robots (Guidi et al., 2023).

When discussing bias, social psychologists like to refer to in-groups versus out-groups, thereby differentiating between the group to which one belongs and that is generally perceived more positively, and "the others." This is called *in-group bias* or *in-group favoritism* (Scheepers et al., 2006) and represents a form of discrimination. In North America, for instance, the intergroup context of African Americans versus Whites has been studied extensively. However, what does this have to do with robots—and with diversity? One online study investigated whether White American people also discriminate between in-group (i.e., robots that look White) and out-group robots (i.e., robots that look Black). At first glance, this experiment produced results that gave some hope: the prediction that people would evaluate the out-group robot as having less "mind" was not supported. However, Eyssel and Loughnan (2013) were able to show that White American participants devalued the robot from the out-group, especially if these people showed a high degree of modern racism. People with racist anti-Black attitudes were also among those who ascribed less mind to the out-group robot in terms of agency and experience. However, it is important to note that individual attitudes did indeed play a role—the prototypical devaluation of an out-group could only be demonstrated when individual prejudices were taken into account. Earlier work (Eyssel and Kuchenbrandt, 2012) found that it was not even necessary to manipulate visual cues for group membership. German participants presented with a picture of the same robot with different names and country-of-production cues (Eyssel and Kuchenbrandt, 2012) manifested in-group bias. They preferred the in-group product over the alleged out-group platform, even at the level of design evaluation.

Moreover, research by Correll et al. (2002) has documented that people discriminate in a way that—not only in their laboratory experiments—can have fatal consequences. In the classic shooter bias paradigm, photos of people with and without a weapon are shown. The task is to react as quickly as possible to press the button for "shoot" in the event of danger and "do not shoot" when unarmed persons are depicted. The skin color of the people in the pictures had a clear influence on the reaction time. If an African American–looking man held a gun in his hand, he was shot faster than when participants were confronted with a White armed man. If the dark-skinned person carried a harmless cell phone, it took participants longer to refrain from shooting. Bartneck et al. (2018) have replicated the paradigm of the shooting bias experiments with White versus dark-skinned in-group and out-group robots that appeared armed versus unarmed and found analogous results, suggesting that similar implicit racial biases can be at play in human–robot interactions as well.

Relatedly, research by Eyssel and Hegel (2012) and Bernotat et al. (2017) investigated the role of gender in the perception of social robots and showed that widely known stereotypes about men and women in society are upheld even in the context of robots. Currently, in a second wave of interest, various researchers have focused on social categories, including gender, to explore the potential detrimental effects of categorizing not only humans but also robots and to demonstrate the importance of taking such features—on the part of user, researcher, or robot—into account (Perugia and Lisy, 2022; Perugia et al., 2022; Roesler et al., 2022; Winkle et al., 2023a). Notably, most research in the realm of gendering of robots has explored the notion of robot or participant gender in a dichotomous fashion—that is, contrasting "male" versus "female." Contemporary approaches, however, would refrain from such a dichotomous conceptualization and integrate a more diverse, gender-fluid range of gender categories. If one aims to research the impact of the traditional male-versus-female gender categories on social judgments, though, it seems fair to study exactly that. At the same time, research on other forms of gender and effects associated with them is still scarce. Thus, this area holds a plethora of open research questions to be investigated.

Likewise, the richness of potential robot user groups, representing persons with cognitive, physical, or other forms of diversity (e.g., neurodiversity), is yet to be adequately mirrored in HRI studies; the experiences of individuals who are less frequently studied need greater inclusion. Some researchers would argue that when doing so, it is valuable and relevant to give room to voices from these target groups, even as part of the research process. Indeed, this would be a truly human-centered approach.

In addressing the various sources of bias in robotics, such as those mentioned previously, Howard and Borenstein (2018) call on the robotics community not only to identify issues but also to create solutions to problems of bias and racism in robotics by developing a more inclusive moral imagination and proactive stance to address ethical issues and bias before technology is deployed and creates negative societal effects. Howard and Kennedy III (2020), in turn, call on the robotics community to explicitly consider ethical use and equity in performance when designing and deploying robots, and they discuss the formation of the Black in Robotics (BiR) community to start addressing some of these issues. Winkle et al. (2023b) provide a feminist framing of work in HRI to suggest that we need to examine and challenge, as needed, power relationships in HRI research and development. This may involve being mindful of and at times subverting the power relationships and hierarchies between researchers and participants, such as through participatory design, which also provides opportunities for robot design to incorporate more diverse voices. It can also take into account the differential effects of robotic technologies on people who decide to purchase and deploy them (e.g., corporate managers) and the people who end up having to use them (e.g., factory floor workers). This perspective suggests it is important to empower potential users of robots to participate more substantively in decision-making regarding their appropriate use and deployment and for HRI researchers to actively question the assumptions and power dynamics involved in the research.

12.3 Conclusion

It is important to realize that robots, humans, and their interactions are part of broader societies that encompass different kinds of people, technologies, institutions, and practices. In these different social and cultural contexts, people may hold different initial attitudes and beliefs about robots based on their prior exposure to fictional narratives and popular media. Potential users of robots will also hold different social and cultural values and norms. Both these cultural narratives and values will affect how people perceive and respond to robots and how the use of robots might affect existing social structures and practices. HRI researchers should be conscious of and sensitive to prevailing cultural narratives and values when they design and deploy robots in society, and they should also consider whether they want robots to reproduce or challenge existing practices and norms. HRI research, although already quite interdisciplinary, should open up more space to participants from diverse sociocultural and application-oriented backgrounds to better include the varied experiences and perspectives of those who will be affected by the future adoption and use of robots.

Questions for you to think about:

- What was the last movie or series you watched or book you read that depicted robots?
- List the characteristics of the robot protagonists you have recently seen in a film or TV series. What were their capabilities? Did they appear humanlike? Did they pose a threat to humanity, or did they save the world?
- How will the availability of new forms of media, such as YouTube, change people's expectations toward robots?

- Think of professions that have been replaced by machines. Which ones come to mind? What are the potential positive and negative implications of this replacement?
- Is there an activity that you are happy to have a machine do? What is an activity that you would not want to be replaced by a machine? How do you think others might feel about your choices—who might disagree?
- Discuss whether it is ethical to use a social robot as comfort for lonely elderly people. Describe relevant issues, and explain your opinion.
- In a future where highly intelligent robots are available, would it be ethical to develop robot nannies or robot teachers? Describe the potential issues.
- Some HRI studies are provocative or thought-provoking, for example, Bartneck et al.'s (2018) study on the presence of racism in HRI. Is it ethical to run controversial HRI studies? Are there particular themes, such as religion, where HRI should not tread?

12.4 Exercises

The answers to these questions are available in the Appendix.

* Exercise 12.1 Sci-Fi media What was the last movie or series you watched or book you read that depicted robots?

** Exercise 12.2 *Bicentennial Man* What is the fictional robot Andrew Martin prepared to do to be fully recognized as a human? Select one or more options from the following list:

1. It agrees not to let any other robot become human.
2. It becomes mortal.
3. It accepts becoming unaware of its own robotic nature.
4. It gives up all friendships.
5. It enters a legal trial.

** Exercise 12.3 Robotic revolution The robot uprising is a common theme in the media. Why do the robots typically rebel? Select one or more options from the following list:

1. They mirror humanity's poor behavior during colonization.
2. They compete for resources with humanity and only see the option to kill or enslave humanity.
3. They want to protect life on Earth by removing the people that pollute it.
4. Humans programmed them to do so.
5. They are annoyed by having to take orders from less intelligent beings.

** Exercise 12.4 Relationship A robot companion, may it be for elderly care, social companionship, or training for people on the autism spectrum, might raise ethical issues. Which of the following statements are true? Select one or more options from the following list:

1. Robots are smarter and stronger than humans.
2. Robots have no legal status.
3. Robots will want to deceive humans
4. The imitation of reciprocal affect can never be as meaningful as authentic affect.
5. Robots could set unrealistic expectations for human-to-human relationships.

*** Exercise 12.5 Trust in robots Watch this video, and then answer the question that follows.

Ayanna Howard, "Should We Trust Robots and Should They Trust Us?" https://youtu.be/P86kv-v7XJU

1. Ayanna Howard discusses how the general public perceives and interacts with robots. She explains that people often trust, perhaps even over-trust, robots. She mentions the emotional connection to robots and people's preconceptions of robots based on their ideas about robots as advanced technology as some of the reasons for this trust. Explain how these two factors can lead to positive as well as negative outcomes—what are those outcomes, and how do they stem from our relationships and expectations of robots? Furthermore, how can we address these potential problems in our design of robots?

*** Exercise 12.6 Ethical issues in HRI Watch this video, and then answer the question that follows.

Kate Darling, "Ethical Issues in Human-Robot Interaction," https://youtu.be/m3gp4LFgPX0?si=ztu7xUShqNYSTTT3

1. Kate Darling describes the new paradigm of social robots that engage with people in diverse contexts, similarly to what we have been discussing so far, and then points out several ethical issues that emerge from the design of and people's interactions with such robots. Based on her talk, explain why social robots may be different from other robots in terms of their ethical implications. Also describe which of the ethical implications Kate Darling describes you found the most surprising or important. How does this implication affect the way you think about designing social robots?

Future reading:

- Jonze, dir., Spike. *Her*. Warner Bros., Burbank, CA, 2013. URL www .imdb.com/title/tt1798709/?ref_=fn_al_tt_1
- Isaac Asimov's Robot series is a collection of short stories and novels published between 1950 and 1986 that were never formally published

as a series but as separate works. https://en.wikipedia.org/wiki/Robot_
series

- Dick, Philip K. *Blade Runner: Do Androids Dream of Electric Sheep?*
  Ballantine Books, New York, 25th-Anniversary edition, 2007. ISBN
  9780345350473. URL http://worldcat.org/oclc/776604212

- Schreier, dir., Jake. *Robot and Frank*. Sony Pictures Home Entertainment, Culver City, CA, 2013. URL www.imdb.com/title/tt1990314/

- Sharkey, Amanda J. C. Should we welcome robot teachers? *Ethics and
  Information Technology*, 18(4):283–297, 2016. doi: 10.1007/s10676
  -016-9387-z. URL https://doi.org/10.1007/s10676-016-9387-z

- Singer, Peter W. *Wired for War: The Robotics Revolution and Conflict in the Twenty-First Century*. Penguin, New York, 2009. ISBN
  9781594201981. URL http://worldcat.org/oclc/857636246

- Veruggio, Gianmarco, Operto, Fiorella, and Bekey, George.
  Roboethics: Social and ethical implications. In Siciliano,
  Bruno and Khatib, Oussama, editors, *Springer Handbook of
  Robotics*, pages 2135–2160. Springer, New York, 2016. ISBN
  978-3-319-32550-7. doi: 10.1007/978-3-319-32552-1. URL
  https://doi.org/10.1007/978-3-319-32552-1

- Awad, Edmond, Dsouza, Sohan, Kim, Richard, Schulz, Jonathan,
  Henrich, Joseph, Shariff, Azim, Bonnefon, Jean-François, and
  Rahwan, Iyad. The moral machine experiment. *Nature*, 563:59–63,
  2018. ISSN 1476-4687. doi: 10.1038/s41586-018-0637-6. URL
  https://doi.org/10.1038/s41586-018-0637-6

- Sparrow, Robert. Robots, rape, and representation. *International Journal of Social Robotics*, 9(4):465–477, 2017. ISSN 1875-4805. doi:
  10.1007/s12369-017-0413-z. URL https://doi.org/10.1007/s123
  69-017-0413-z

- Lin, Patrick, Abney, Keith, and Bekey, George A. *Robot Ethics:
  The Ethical and Social Implications of Robotics*. Intelligent Robotics
  and Autonomous Agents. MIT Press, Cambridge, MA, 2012. ISBN
  9780262016667. URL http://worldcat.org/oclc/1004334474

13

The Future

What is covered in this chapter:

- Current attitude of the general public toward robots and how this may change in the coming years.
- Possible shifts and developments in the nature of human–robot relationships, specifically companion bots.
- Further development of the technology of human–robot interactions, specifically artificial intelligence.
- The inherent issues with predicting the future ("crystal ball problems").

As with other technologies that have become common in our daily lives, such as personal computers, smartphones, or the internet, sooner or later, we expect robots to become assimilated into society. They may even be accepted into our personal and even intimate spaces. Robots are currently being designed to be coworkers, tutors, and assistants in the medical field and to provide services in care settings, in education, in people's homes and even in space stations (see Figure 13.1). Research into human–robot interaction (HRI) continues unabated, and companies keep a keen eye on social robots, releasing products that either are fully fledged social robots, such as the Sony Aibo (Figure 2.10), or that take inspiration from HRI and interaction design research, such as digital home assistants.

Technological advances make this vision increasingly real but alone are not sufficient to move us closer to a future with robots. Recent polls in the United States and Europe show that overall, robots are considered desirable for jobs that people find too hard or undesirable. But the public takes a more reserved attitude when it comes to social robots that provide companionship, care, and other socially assistive and interactive applications (Smith, 2014; European Commission, 2017). In general, people tend to have a welcoming and positive attitude toward robots, although some HRI studies have shown that on occasion, some people experience fairly high levels of robot anxiety and other negative attitudes toward robots, resulting in a low willingness to interact with robots in their personal space or workplace settings (Reich-Stiebert and Eyssel, 2013, 2015). Any technical and societal revolution evokes strong responses, both positive and negative, and social robots are not going to be any different.

Figure 13.1 The Cimon robot (2018–present), built by the German Aerospace Center, Airbus, and IBM, assists astronauts on the International Space Station. (Source: National Aeronautics and Space Administration)

As technology advances and social robots become more common, people will have more opportunities to experience the potential and limitations of the technology and may become more accepting of them through mere exposure. As we mentioned in our discussion of nonverbal cues, direct interaction with members of another social group—in this case, robots—changes attitudes and decreases anxiety related to that group (Crisp and Turner, 2013; Pettigrew et al., 2011). Wullenkord (2017) showed that just imagining collaborative interaction with a Nao robot prior to actually interacting with it improved attitudes and reactions toward the robot and increased the perceived quality of the interaction. We can therefore expect that as people have increased contact with robots, be it directly or through the media, attitudes will become more positive, and the willingness to use robots will increase over time.

As we have seen in the rest of this book, however, advances in HRI research can significantly speed up this process. By better understanding people's concerns, mapping societal needs, and identifying opportunities for automation, we can create interactions that will be positive and beneficial to people and society as a whole. As with any technological revolution, the introduction of social robots will be slow at first, with daring companies releasing new products and early adopters buying and using these, thereby providing valuable real-life lessons on what interactive devices and robots could mean to us (Hoffman, 2019). End users have high expectations for social robots, and such commercial products tend to overpromise and underdeliver. But recent years have witnessed a positive feedback loop between new revolutions in artificial intelligence (AI), academic research, industry efforts, and the tech market, with products integrated into social robots becoming commercially successful. Speech recognition, natural-language processing, and visual understanding of social and physical context are now found in thousands of products, and their success is likely to be the origin of the success of social robots.

We also need to consider that the media frequently portray robots negatively or unrealistically. For example, there has been much talk of robots, instead of people, looking after those in need of assistance in our aging societies. This is not a pleasant thought, if only because it confronts us with a reality in which human contact has become increasingly rare and where we need robotic technology to substitute for human warmth. The way this future scenario is portrayed by the media, however, is unrealistic. This manner of framing robots in society may sell newspapers, but it creates undue anxiety and distracts us from what robots could really contribute. In eldercare, cuddly animal-like robots are already used, much to the satisfaction of the elderly residents, families, and staff.

We are often quick to judge, and robots evoke strong emotions. Facilitating an open mind about novel developments in technology and science might be a step toward achieving a more positive view and a stronger sense of acceptance by the general public. These changes can only be observed through longitudinal studies, and HRI scholars must work together with the communities they seek to serve to consider how technological developments can come together with societal structures to produce positive change. There is no quick "technological fix" for societal problems, such as demographic change. Besides developing much-needed technologies, it is also crucial to take a human-centered approach that focuses on the actual psychological, social, and emotional needs of the people using and being affected by robots. A more human-centered view coupled with technological advancement will together create robust and socially appropriate robots that can benefit us all.

13.1 The nature of human–robot relationships

When waiting to check in at the airport, a machine handles the check-in process. In Japan, Pepper robots greet us when we enter a bank or a shop. When care is provided mainly by machines rather than humans, this has strong implications for the development and maintenance of human relationships. Even currently, many technologies, such as mobile phones, social networks, and online games, have resulted in less face time between people and vast changes in interpersonal communication. Instead of writing letters or meeting in person, people communicate via messages on Snapchat or WhatsApp. Our patterns of when we talk to whom about what are changing (see Figure 13.2), as are the ways we begin and end our romantic relationships—by smartphone. Robots may contribute to further estrangement among people, as argued by Turkle (2017), or robots could be designed to support and even increase interaction among people. This effect has been seen with the seal-like robot Paro in a day home, in which older adults ended up meeting and talking more to others when the robot was put in a public space (Wada and Shibata, 2007).

Clearly, as social robots and AI are developed further, they will likely play an increasingly larger role in our everyday lives and society. Because the nature of human–robot relationships is a product of the robots' capabilities and

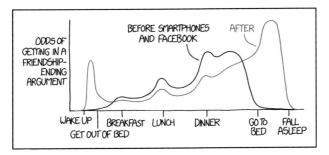

Figure 13.2 Odds of getting into a friendship-ending argument before and after the introduction of smartphones. (Source: XKCD)

the users' preferences, these developments are inevitably tied to the question of what issues we consider ethical and desirable to address with robots and AI.

For example, one major societal issue at the moment is loneliness. Feeling socially connected to others has an almost incredible list of benefits for individual mental and physical health (Vaillan, 2015). This will become increasingly relevant as the populations of developed countries continue to age in the upcoming decades. An increasing part of the population is in need of care, not just for attending to their physical needs of feeding, bathing, and clothing but for emotional care as well. It might be that the younger generations are neither willing nor competently able to serve these dual needs on their own. Particularly, the emotional needs of seniors or people with cognitive or physical impairments have to be taken into account, but all people are in danger of growing more and more lonely and disconnected (American Osteopathic Association, 2016).

The lack of social connection can have a serious impact on our psychological well-being and health. The "need to belong," a key motivation of human nature (Baumeister and Leary, 1995), can easily become disrupted. To illustrate, research by Eisenberger et al. (2003) shed light on the neuroanatomical underpinnings of reactions to social exclusion, whereas Williams (2007) has documented the negative social consequences of exclusionary status. That is, when the need to belong is violated, people not only feel a lower sense of belonging but also experience lower self-esteem, feel less in control, and even regard their existence as less meaningful than when their inclusionary status is not under threat. In addition, the risk of developing Alzheimer's disease is double in lonely people compared to socially connected individuals, and loneliness is a predictor of a decline in cognitive abilities (Shankar et al., 2013). In light of the detrimental effects of loneliness on quality of life and psychological and cognitive functioning, robots could play an important role in mediating these effects.

A few commercial start-ups have been offering artificially intelligent "companions," although so far with only modest success, such as Gatebox's "Living With" project. If AI and robots are developed to the point where they can reliably imitate human interaction patterns, they could be extremely helpful in relieving feelings of boredom and loneliness.

What remains to be seen is how comfortable people are with the different potential roles that AI may take on. As the quest for strong or general AI continues, the question of whether such AI is desirable is heard ever louder. Whereas the most spectacular version of this question considers how we can ensure that such an AI would remain benevolent to the human race, it is at least as interesting to consider the issue of whether people would be comfortable with handing over power in the first place. Assume that strong AI is developed, the sole purpose of which is to enhance the well-being of society while adhering to a set of rules that keep it from harming humans (e.g., Asimov's Laws of Robotics; see Section 12.2). Can we throw out all the concerns about self-interest, bias, and hidden political agendas that are inherent to human leadership and, instead, fully trust that the AI would take proper care (see Figure 13.3)? Would we agree with such a setup?

13.2 The technology of HRI

HRI is lifted on the tides of technological progress. New sensors and actuators and continuous developments in AI are quickly adopted into HRI applications. Given the steady progress in AI and its applications, there is every reason to believe that a number of technical problems that currently still require the smoke and mirrors of Wizard-of-Oz (WoZ) control will soon be delivered autonomously by the robot.

Progress in HRI is not so much held back by a lack of development in robotic hardware but, rather, by a lack of progress in autonomous control and AI. Testament to this is the ability of human operators to hold a meaningful interaction through a robot. It is clearly not the limited view through the sensors and the limited expressivity of the actuators that hinder the interaction. Rather, it is the artificial cognition—substituted by real cognition in the case of WoZ control—that is lacking. There is, of course, room for improvement in robot hardware: the speed and power of actuators need work, and the energy autonomy of robots needs to improve drastically. Furthermore, robotics and social robotics in particular have always taken a "Frankenstein approach" to hardware, building robots from whatever technology is readily available rather than developing radically new hardware solutions. But at this point, breakthroughs in HRI are most likely to come from progress in robot control and AI. Machine learning holds considerable promise here. However, there are fundamental barriers to the use of machine learning in HRI. Because machine learning requires vast amounts of annotated data and computational time, it comes to its own in domains that allow offline learning and for which huge amounts of training data are available or, when not available, can be generated. Although there is plenty of human interaction going on in the world, these interactions run in real-time. As opposed to machine learning of how to play the game of chess or Go, where the learning can run as fast as computers will allow, machine learning of HRI strategies inherently runs online. No matter how fast the computer is, the interaction pace is dictated by the human interaction partner, and the evaluation and updates of the machine learning will run in "human time" rather than in computer time. One solution for facilitating machine learning for HRI might be to use more robots and data from more interactions: pooling interaction events could be a solution to the dearth of HRI data and could speed up the evaluation of learned interaction strategies. It is unclear what the next technological breakthroughs will be in AI and robotics, but one thing is clear: HRI will readily absorb them.

13.3 Crystal ball problems

Predicting the future is hard to do, and especially in the field of HRI, it seems as if every stance imaginable is defended with passion by a small army of experts (and a large group of those wishing to be experts), ranging from doomsday predictions to nirvana forecasts. The Tesla company, for example, made grandiose promises in 2022 for its Optimus humanoid robot, not only about its unrealistically affordable price but also about its unprecedented abilities. Promises that are yet to be delivered.

It proves to be nearly impossible to gain consensus on the far future of HRI and even on small and concrete predictions of how long it will take to develop a specific capability or what we actually want from a robot. Just as with AI, all bets are off. Still, it is clear that robot butlers—such as the Able Mabel housemaid robot envisioned by the BBC in 1966—remain elusive.

First, we can perhaps take some lessons from developments in AI, which have been rapid yet unable to match early expectations. When the initial ideas around AI were first introduced in the 1950s, it was expected that strong AI would be available within a few decades (McCorduck, 1979; Russell and Norvig, 2022). Half a century later, AI still struggles with understanding the real world. And although progress has been impressive on some fronts—think about recent developments in natural-language interaction—advances have been uneven. It seems that when data are available in abundance and learning is cheap to evaluate, then AI can learn fast and even achieve superhuman performance. This was famously shown by the Deep Blue computer program beating the world champion Gary Kasparov at chess in the late 1990s (Campbell et al., 2002), as well as recent victories in ever more complex games such as Go (Murphy, 2016) and Stratego. Because the fortunes of robotics are often tied to those of AI, we can expect to see similar trends in social robotics, with robots getting superhuman abilities on some fronts while lagging on others.

In recent years, there have been numerous start-ups and large corporations venturing into the social robotics market. Buoyed by technological break-throughs, they build novel products looking for equally novel use cases. But building and especially selling social robots remains challenging. Most commercial social robots are available for a few years, and after lower-than-expected sales, the companies then pull the products from the market. We cannot help but notice that many of the robots we discuss and show in this book are no longer available. We should not forget that it is still the early days for commercial social robots. Just as for countless other technologies—the mobile phone, the smartphone, the personal computer, and the MP3 player, to name but a few—early and therefore brave ventures at introducing social robots on the market will know winners and losers, but victory belongs to those who believe in it the most and believe in it the longest.

This raises the question of whether we are really capable of knowing what we want from a robot. What we think we want robots to do today is likely not going to be what robots will be doing in the future. The interplay between our needs and technological abilities will more likely result in applications we can currently barely imagine. As demonstrated in this book, it is good to widen the range of perspectives involved in our discussions when building a future with robots.

There are lessons we can learn from the history and recent successes in AI. Although deep learning has achieved remarkable progress, it is important to acknowledge that past expectations often led to excessive optimism followed by disappointment. Two previous AI booms serve as examples of this pattern. The first occurred in the 1950s when predictions about the emergence of strong AI were made. The second boom took place in the 1970s, with the belief that we could capture all existing knowledge in formal representations. Although these periods ultimately led to two of several AI winters, AI research persisted and contributed to the development of fundamental knowledge in pattern recognition, such as notable advancements in neural networks. This paved the way for the eventual success of the latest breakthroughs in pattern recognition, fueled by increased computational power and access to vast amounts of data. Similarly, although some start-ups focusing on robotics might fail, boom-and-bust cycles in social robots are likely to occur. Predicting which ventures will succeed and when remains a challenging task. Nevertheless, we firmly believe that our understanding of HRI will be central to future commercial successes.

Questions for you to think about:

- Which technological developments and related social developments have surprised you the most in your lifetime?
- What kind of future would you want to see with robots? What kind of future would you be afraid of or concerned about?
- How much time do you spend interacting with people face to face versus in mediated environments (e.g., Facebook, conference call)? What about nonhuman agents—do you interact with them at all? In what circumstances and how much?
- Who is caring for your grandparents or parents? What kind of community do they live in? Do you live close to them? Who do you think will take care of you in the future? What kind of community might you find yourself living in?

13.4 Exercises

The answers to these questions are available in the Appendix.

** **Exercise 13.1 Loneliness** What consequences are typically associated with loneliness? Select one or more options from the following list:

1. Reduced self-esteem
2. Increased risk of developing Alzheimer's disease
3. Decline in cognitive abilities
4. Reduced physiological abilities
5. Reduced financial income
6. Lack of perceived control
7. Increased risk of developing cancer

** **Exercise 13.2 Technology** What technology is mainly holding back HRI? Select one option from the following list:

1. The development of sensors
2. The development of actuators
3. The development of power storage and delivery
4. The development in AI
5. The development of smart materials

* **Exercise 13.3 Face time** How do you predominantly communicate with your friends? Select one option from the following list:

1. Through mediated communication environments (e.g., Facebook, Instagram, Zoom, Skype, etc.)
2. Through face-to-face communication

* **Exercise 13.4 Contact** With whom do you have more physical contact on a daily basis? Select one option from the following list:

1. Your partner (or friends)
2. Your mobile phone

* **Exercise 13.5 Parents** Do you want a robot to take care of your parents when they can no longer care for themselves? Select one option from the following list:

1. Yes
2. No

***** **Exercise 13.6 HRI movie analysis** Watch a movie (or one or two episodes of a TV series) of your choice in which robots play a major role. Pay close attention to HRI and how it is depicted in the film; you'll probably want to take notes as you watch. Then write up a short analysis of the HRI components of the movie. Do not just give a summary or review of the movie itself; address the ways in which humans and robots interact and communicate with each other. You can include visuals from the film in your analysis, if you like. You should also explicitly refer to any connections to the HRI themes that you read about in this book.

Some examples of relevant films and TV shows are as follows: *Ex Machina*; *Wall-E*; *Westworld*; *Moon*; *The Iron Giant*; *Star Wars*; *Silent Running*; *Short Circuit*; *2001: A Space Odyssey*; *The Hitchhiker's Guide to the Galaxy*; *A.I.*; *I, Robot*; *Metropolis*; *Ghost in the Shell*; *Astro Boy*; *Frank and the Robot*; and *Human*.

Your review should address the following questions:

1. What roles do the robots have in society? What kinds of tasks do they perform? Where do they interact with people?
2. What are the channels or modalities that people use to communicate with the robots? How does their communication evolve?
3. What modes of expression do the robots use to communicate with people? What about with each other?
4. What are the consequences of robots in society? How do people react to the robots—positively or negatively—and do their reactions change over time? What could be done to make negative consequences or reactions more positive?
5. What do you think are the hard and easy social and technical problems involved with developing HRI of the sort shown in the movie? Also include potential ethical issues resulting from using robots in society.

Future reading:

- Future of Life Institute. An open letter—Research priorities for robust and beneficial artificial intelligence, January 2015. URL https://future oflife.org/ai-open-letter/
- Nourbakhsh, Illah Reza. *Robot Futures*. MIT Press, Cambridge, MA, 2013. ISBN 9780262018623. URL http://worldcat.org/oclc/945438 245
- Wilson, Daniel H. *How to Survive a Robot Uprising: Tips on Defending Yourself against the Coming Rebellion*. Bloomsbury, London, New York, 2005. ISBN 9781582345925. URL http://worldcat.org/oclc/10 29483559
- Cribb, Jo and Glover, David. *Don't Worry about the Robots*. Allen & Unwin, Auckland, New Zealand, 2018. ISBN 9781760633509. URL http://worldcat.org/oclc/1042120802

Appendix: Answers

This appendix presents the answers to all the questions, quizzes, and exercises from all the chapters. We hope that you enjoyed these challenges and that you find the answers enlightening.

Exercise 2.1 The correct answer is: 2.

Exercise 2.2 The correct answer is your choice.

Exercise 2.3 The correct answer is open-ended.

Exercise 3.1 The correct answers are: 1, 3, 5, 7.

Exercise 3.2 The correct answers are: 2, 3, 5.

Exercise 3.3 The *depth camera* allows Pepper to measure its distance from other objects, which is needed, for example, to avoid collision. The *capacitive touch sensor* allows Pepper to register pressure on the hand, which is needed, for example, to avoid the robot trying to push its hand through an object or for it to register when a human is tapping its hand for attention. The *inertial measurement unit* allows Pepper to measure its bodily orientation, which is fundamental for balance and localization.

Exercise 3.4 The correct answers are: 1, 4, 5, 6.

Exercise 3.5 The correct answers are: 1, 3, 4.

Exercise 3.6 The correct answer is: 4.

Exercise 3.7 The correct answer is: 2.

Exercise 3.8 The correct answer is: 6.

Exercise 3.9 The correct answer is: 2.

Exercise 3.10 The correct answer is: 2.

Exercise 3.11 The correct answers are: 1, 2.

Exercise 3.12 The correct answers are: 2, 4, 5.

Exercise 3.13 The correct answers are: 1, 3 (Option 2 is only true if transfer learning was done with a pretrained model; otherwise, training for a computer-vision task generally requires at least thousands of data points. Option 4 is completely false; don't chose this. Option 5 is not really true; we should care about the topology, considering the characteristic of the task, and CNN is usually the best for simple image classification.)

Exercise 3.14 The correct answer is open-ended, but it should mention some of the sensors and actuators and perhaps AI techniques described in the chapter.

Exercise 4.1 The correct answer is open-ended. Show your images to your teacher, friends, and family. Do they see the faces?

Exercise 4.2 The sequence should be: 1 = E, 2 = D, 3 = C, 4 = B, 5 = A.

Exercise 4.3 The correct answer is open-ended.

Exercise 5.1 The correct answers are: $1 \rightarrow a, 2 \rightarrow d, 3 \rightarrow b, 4 \rightarrow c$

Exercise 5.2 The correct answer is: 3.7 m.

Exercise 5.3 The correct answer is: 1.2 m.

Exercise 5.4 The correct answer is: 0.5 m.

Exercise 5.5 The correct answer is: 3.7 m.

Exercise 5.6 This is an open-ended question, so answers can vary, but they may involve the robots learning the map of the environment and, in the case of the home, the preferences of individual users. In the public space, users would be more numerous and may not repeat, so the adaptations might be to the specific cultural norms of the general context.

Exercise 6.1 The correct answer is: 2.

Exercise 6.2 The correct answer is open-ended.

Exercise 6.3 1. False; it is both conscious and unconscious (but more often unconscious than conscious).
2. True
3. False
4. False
5. True
6. False; it is used for other social behavior as well (e.g., joint attention).
7. True; although it was covered in a different chapter (Chapter 5), how close or far you position yourself from someone else is a form of nonverbal behavior.

Exercise 7.1 The correct answer is: 2.

Exercise 7.2 The correct answer is: 4.

Exercise 7.3 The correct answers are: 2, 3, 4.

Exercise 7.4 The correct answer is: 5.

Exercise 8.1 The correct answer is: 3.

Exercise 8.2 The correct answers are: 4, 5.

Exercise 8.3 The correct answers are: 2, 4, 5.

Exercise 9.1 The correct mapping is:

1. Afraid → A
2. Angry → A
3. Astonished → B
4. Bored → C
5. Calm → D
6. Content → D
7. Delighted → B
8. Depressed → C
9. Frustrated → C
10. Happy → B
11. Relaxed → D
12. Tired → C

Exercise 9.2 The correct answer is: 3.

Exercise 9.3 The correct answers are: 1, 4, 5.

Exercise 9.4 The correct answer is open-ended.

Exercise 10.1 The correct answer is: 3.

Exercise 10.2 The correct answer is: 4.

Exercise 10.3 The correct answer is: 1.

Exercise 10.4 The correct answer is: 4.

Exercise 10.5 The correct answers are: 1, 5.

Exercise 10.6 The correct answer is: 4.

Exercise 10.7 The correct answer is: 3.

Exercise 10.8 The correct answer is: 1 = c, 2 = b, 3 = a.

Exercise 11.1 The correct answers are: 1, 4, 5.

Exercise 11.2 The correct answers are: 2, 5.

Exercise 11.3 The correct answers are: 1, 2, 3, 5, 6, 10, 12.

Exercise 11.4 The correct answers are: 1, 5.

Exercise 11.5 The correct answer is: 2.

Exercise 12.1 We hope you enjoyed the story. What are you planning to watch next?

Exercise 12.2 The correct answers are: 2, 5.

Exercise 12.3 The correct answers are: 1, 2.

Exercise 12.4 The correct answers are: 4, 5.

Exercise 12.5 The correct answer is open-ended.

Exercise 12.6 The answer is open-ended.

Exercise 13.1 The correct answers are: 1, 2, 3, 6.

Exercise 13.2 The correct answer is: 5.

Exercise 13.3 Is your choice a good choice?

Exercise 13.4 Is your choice a good choice?

Exercise 13.5 Explain your choice.

Exercise 13.6 The answer is open-ended.

References

Abele, Andrea E., Hauke, Nicole, Peters, Kim, Louvet, Eva, Szymkow, Aleksandra, and Duan, Yanping. Facets of the fundamental content dimensions: Agency with competence and assertiveness—Communion with warmth and morality. *Frontiers in Psychology*, 7:1810, 2016. doi: 10.3389/fpsyg.2016.01810.

Abené, Clayton. San Francisco approves police proposal to use potentially deadly robots. *The Guardian*, 2022. URL www.theguardian.com/us-news/2022/nov/29/san-francisco-police-robots-deadly-force.

Abras, Chadia, Maloney-Krichmar, Diane, and Preece, Jenny. User-centered design. In Bainbridge, William Sims, editor, *Berkshire Encyclopedia of Human-Computer Interaction*, volume 2, pages 763–767. SAGE Publications, Thousand Oaks, CA, 2004. ISBN 9780974309125. URL http://worldcat.org/oclc/635690108.

Admoni, Henny and Scassellati, Brian. Social eye gaze in human-robot interaction: A review. *Journal of Human-Robot Interaction*, 6(1):25–63, 2017. doi: 10.5898/JHRI.6.1.Admoni.

Akdim, Khaoula, Belanche, Daniel, and Flavián, Marta. Attitudes toward service robots: Analyses of explicit and implicit attitudes based on anthropomorphism and construal level theory. *International Journal of Contemporary Hospitality Management*, 35(8):2816–2837, 2021. doi: 10.1108/IJCHM-12-2020-1406.

Al Momin, Md Abdullah and Islam, Md Nazmul. Teleoperated surgical robot security: Challenges and solutions. In Hei, Xiali, editor, *Security, Data Analytics, and Energy-Aware Solutions in the IoT*, pages 143–160. IGI Global, Hershey, PA, 2022. doi: 10.4018/978-1-7 998-7323-5.ch009.

Alaerts, Kaat, Nackaerts, Evelien, Meyns, Pieter, Swinnen, Stephan P., and Wenderoth, Nicole. Action and emotion recognition from point light displays: An investigation of gender differences. *PloS One*, 6(6):e20989, 2011. doi: 10.1371/journal.pone.0020989.

Aldiss, Brian Wilson. *Supertoys Last All Summer Long: And Other Stories of Future Time*. St. Martin's Griffin, New York, 2001. ISBN 978-0312280611. URL http://worldcat.org/oclc/956323493.

Alemi, Minoo, Meghdari, Ali, and Ghazisaedy, Maryam. Employing humanoid robots for teaching English language in Iranian junior high-schools. *International Journal of Humanoid Robotics*, 11(3):1450022, 2014. doi: 10.1142/S0219843614500224.

Alenljung, Beatrice, Lindblom, Jessica, Andreasson, Rebecca, and Ziemke, Tom. User experience in social human-robot interaction. In *Rapid Automation: Concepts, Methodologies, Tools, and Applications*, pages 1468–1490. IGI Global, Hershey, PA, 2019. doi: 10.4018/978-1-5225-8060-7.ch069.

Alexander, Christopher. *A Pattern Language: Towns, Buildings, Construction*. Oxford University Press, Oxford, 1977. ISBN 978-0195019193. URL http://worldcat.org/oclc/961298119.

Allan, Dwain Donald, Vonasch, Andrew, and Bartneck, Christoph. "I Have to Praise You Like I Should?" The effects of implicit self-theories and robot-delivered praise on evaluations of a social robot. *International Journal of Social Robotics*, 14:1013–1024, 2022. doi: 10.100 7/s12369-021-00848-9.

Althaus, Philipp, Ishiguro, Hiroshi, Kanda, Takayuki, Miyashita, Takahiro, and Christensen, Henrik I. Navigation for human-robot interaction tasks. In *IEEE International Conference on Robotics and Automation*, volume 2, pages 1894–1900. Institute of Electrical and Electronics Engineers, Piscataway, NJ, 2004. ISBN 0-7803-8232-3. doi: 10.1109/ROBOT. 2004.1308100.

Aly, Amir and Tapus, Adriana. A model for synthesizing a combined verbal and nonverbal behavior based on personality traits in human-robot interaction. In *Proceedings of the 8th ACM/IEEE International Conference on Human Robot Interaction*, pages 325–332. Institute of Electrical and Electronics Engineers, Piscataway, NJ, 2013. ISBN 978-1-4673-3055-8. doi: 10.1109/HRI.2013.6483606.

American Osteopathic Association. Survey finds nearly three-quarters (72%) of Americans feel lonely, 2016. URL www.osteopathic.org/inside-aoa/news-and-publications/media-center/2016-news-releases/Pages/10-11-survey-finds-nearly-three-quarters-of-americans-feel-lonely.aspx.

Andersen, Peter A. and Guerrero, Laura K. Principles of communication and emotion in social interaction. In Andersen, Peter A. and Guerrero, Laura K., editors, *Handbook of Communication and Emotion: Research, Theory, Applications, and Contexts*, pages 49–96. Academic Press, Cambridge, MA, 1998. ISBN 0-12-057770-4. doi: 10.1016/B978-01205 7770-5/50005-9.

Andrist, Sean, Tan, Xiang Zhi, Gleicher, Michael, and Mutlu, Bilge. Conversational gaze aversion for humanlike robots. In *ACM/IEEE International Conference on Human-Robot Interaction*, pages 25–32. Association for Computing Machinery, New York, 2014. ISBN 978-1-4503-2658-2. doi: 10.1145/2559636.2559666.

Argall, Brenna D., Chernova, Sonia, Veloso, Manuela, and Browning, Brett. A survey of robot learning from demonstration. *Robotics and Autonomous Systems*, 57(5):469–483, 2009. doi: 10.1016/j.robot.2008.10.024.

Arora, Anshu Saxena, Fleming, Mayumi, Arora, Amit, Taras, Vas, and Xu, Jiajun. Finding "H" in HRI: Examining human personality traits, robotic anthropomorphism, and robot likeability in human-robot interaction. *International Journal of Intelligent Information Technologies (IJIIT)*, 17(1):19–38, 2021. doi: 10.4018/IJIIT.2021010102.

Asaro, Peter. "Hands up, don't shoot!" HRI and the automation of police use of force. *Journal of Human-Robot Interaction*, 5(3):55–69, 2016. doi: 10.5898/JHRI.5.3.Asaro.

Asch, Solomon E. Effects of group pressure upon the modification and distortion of judgments. In Guetzkow, Harold, editor, *Groups, Leadership and Men: Research in Human Relations*, pages 177–190. Carnegie Press, Oxford, UK, 1951. doi: psycinfo/1952-00803-001.

Asimov, Isaac. *The Bicentennial Man and Other Stories*. Doubleday, Garden City, NY, Book Club edition, 1976. ISBN 978-0385121989. URL http://worldcat.org/oclc/85069299.

Asimov, Isaac. *Prelude to Foundation*. Grafton, London, 1988. ISBN 9780008117481. URL http://worldcat.org/oclc/987248670.

Asimov, Isaac. *I, Robot*. Bantam Books, New York, 1991. ISBN 0553294385. URL http://worldcat.org/oclc/586089717.

Aviezer, Hillel, Trope, Yaacov, and Todorov, Alexander. Body cues, not facial expressions, discriminate between intense positive and negative emotions. *Science*, 338(6111):1225–1229, 2012. doi: 10.1126/science.1224313.

Awad, Edmond, Dsouza, Sohan, Kim, Richard, Schulz, Jonathan, Henrich, Joseph, Shariff, Azim, Bonnefon, Jean-François, and Rahwan, Iyad. The moral machine experiment. *Nature*, 563:59–63, 2018. ISSN 1476-4687. doi: 10.1038/s41586-018-0637-6.

Axelsson, Minja, Oliveira, Raquel, Racca, Mattia, and Kyrki, Ville. Social robot co-design canvases: A participatory design framework. *ACM Transactions on Human-Robot Interaction (THRI)*, 11(1):1–39, 2021. doi: 10.1145/3472225.

Badenes-Ribera, Laura, Frías-Navarro, Dolores, Monterde-i Bort, Héctor, and Pascual-Soler, Marcos. Interpretation of the p value: A national survey study in academic psychologists from Spain. *Psicothema*, 27(3):290–295, 2015. doi: 10.7334/psicothema2014.283.

Bainbridge, Wilma A., Hart, Justin W., Kim, Elizabeth S., and Scassellati, Brian. The benefits of interactions with physically present robots over video-displayed agents. *International Journal of Social Robotics*, 3(1):41–52, 2011. ISSN 1875-4805. doi: 10.1007/s12369-010-0082-7.

Barney, Jay B. and Hansen, Mark H. Trustworthiness as a source of competitive advantage. *Strategic Management Journal*, 15(S1):175–190, 1994. doi: 10.1002/smj.4250150912.

Barrat, James. Why Stephen Hawking and Bill Gates are terrified of artificial intelligence. *Huffington Post*, 2015. URL http://huffingtonpost.com/james-barrat/hawking-gates-artificial-intelligence_b_7008706.html.

Bartlett, Madeleine E., Edmunds, C. E. R., Belpaeme, Tony, and Thill, Serge. Have I got the power? Analysing and reporting statistical power in HRI. *ACM Transactions on Human-Robot Interaction (THRI)*, 11(2):1–16, 2022. doi: 10.1145/3495246.

Bartneck, Christoph. eMuu: An embodied emotional character for the ambient intelligent home. PhD thesis, Technische Universiteit Eindhoven, 2002. URL http://bartneck.de/publications/2002/eMuu/bartneckPHDThesis2002.pdf.

Bartneck, Christoph. The science beyond the horizon [podcast transcript], 2021. URL www.human-robot-interaction.org/2021/09/15/flaky-conferences-and-journals-in-human-robot-interaction/.

Bartneck, Christoph and Hu, Jun. Rapid prototyping for interactive robots. In *The 8th Conference on Intelligent Autonomous Systems (IAS-8)*, pages 136–145. Association for Computing Machinery, New York, 2004. doi: 10.6084/m9.figshare.5160775.v1.

Bartneck, Christoph and Lyons, Michael J. Facial expression analysis, modeling and synthesis: Overcoming the limitations of artificial intelligence with the art of the soluble. In Vallverdu, Jordi and Casacuberta, David, editors, *Handbook of Research on Synthetic Emotions and Sociable Robotics: New Applications in Affective Computing and Artificial Intelligence*, pages 33–53. IGI Global, Hershey, PA, 2009. URL http://bartneck.de/publications/2009/facialExpressionAnalysisModelingSynthesisAI/bartneckLyonsEmotionBook2009.pdf.

Bartneck, Christoph and Moltchanova, Elena. Expressing uncertainty in human-robot interaction. *PLOS One*, 15(7):1–20, 07 2020. doi: 10.1371/journal.pone.0235361.

Bartneck, Christoph and Rauterberg, M. HCI reality—An unreal tournament. *International Journal of Human-Computer Studies*, 65(8):737–743, 2007. doi: 10.1016/j.ijhcs.2007.03.003.

Bartneck, Christoph and Reichenbach, Juliane. Subtle emotional expressions of synthetic characters. *International Journal of Human-Computer Studies*, 62(2):179–192, 2005. ISSN 1071-5819. doi: 10.1016/j.ijhcs.2004.11.006.

Bartneck, Christoph, Nomura, Tatsuya, Kanda, Takayuki, Suzuki, Tomhohiro, and Kennsuke, Kato. Cultural differences in attitudes towards robots. In *AISB Symposium on Robot Companions: Hard Problems and Open Challenges in Human-Robot Interaction*, pages 1–4. Society for the Study of Artificial Intelligence and the Simulation of Behaviour (AISB), Hatfield, UK, 2005. doi: 10.13140/RG.2.2.22507.34085. URL http://bartneck.de/publications/2005/cultureNars/bartneckAISB2005.pdf.

Bartneck, Christoph, Croft, Elizabeth, Kulic, Dana, and Zoghbi, Susana. Measurement instruments for the anthropomorphism, animacy, likeability, perceived intelligence, and perceived safety of robots. *International Journal of Social Robotics*, 1(1):71–81, 2009. doi: 10.1007/s12369-008-0001-3.

Bartneck, Christoph, Duenser, Andreas, Moltchanova, Elena, and Zawieska, Karolina. Comparing the similarity of responses received from studies in Amazon's Mechanical Turk to studies conducted online and with direct recruitment. *PloS One*, 10(4):e0121595, 2015a. doi: 10.1371/journal.pone.0121595.

Bartneck, Christoph, Soucy, Marius, Fleuret, Kevin, and Sandoval, Eduardo B. The robot engine—making the Unity 3D game engine work for HRI. In *24th IEEE International Symposium on Robot and Human Interactive Communication (RO-MAN)*, pages 431–437. Institute of Electrical and Electronics Engineers, Piscataway, NJ, 2015b. doi: 10.1109/ROMAN.2015.7333561.

Bartneck, Christoph, Yogeeswaran, Kumar, Ser, Qi Min, Woodward, Graeme, Sparrow, Robert, Wang, Siheng, and Eyssel, Friederike. Robots and racism. In *Proceedings of the ACM/IEEE International Conference on Human-Robot Interaction*, pages 196–204. Association for Computing Machinery, New York, 2018. ISBN 978-1-4503-4953-6. doi: 10.1145/3171221.3171260.

Baumann, Timo and Schlangen, David. The INPROTK 2012 release. In *NAACL-HLT Workshop on Future Directions and Needs in the Spoken Dialog Community: Tools and Data*, pages 29–32. Association for Computational Linguistics, Toronto, Canada, 2012. URL http://dl.acm.org/citation.cfm?id=2390444.2390464.

Baumeister, Roy F. and Leary, Mark R. The need to belong: Desire for interpersonal attachments as a fundamental human motivation. *Psychological Bulletin*, 117(3):497–529, 1995. doi: 10.1037/0033-2909.117.3.497.

Baxter, Paul, Kennedy, James, Senft, Emmanuel, Lemaignan, Severin, and Belpaeme, Tony. From characterising three years of HRI to methodology and reporting recommendations. In *11th ACM/IEEE International Conference on Human-Robot Interaction*, pages 391–398. Institute of Electrical and Electronics Engineers, Piscataway, NJ, 2016. ISBN 978-1-4673-8370-7. doi: 10.1109/HRI.2016.7451777.

Baytas, Mehmet Aydin, Çay, Damla, Zhang, Yuchong, Obaid, Mohammad, Yantaç, Asim Evren, and Fjeld, Morten. The design of social drones: A review of studies on autonomous flyers in inhabited environments. In *Proceedings of the 2019 CHI Conference on Human Factors in Computing Systems*, pages 1–13. Association for Computing Machinery, New York, 2019. doi: 10.1145/3290605.3300480.

Beck, Aryel, Hiolle, Antoine, Mazel, Alexandre, and Cañamero, Lola. Interpretation of emotional body language displayed by robots. In *Proceedings of the 3rd International Workshop on Affective Interaction in Natural Environments*, pages 37–42. Association for Computing Machinery, New York, 2010. ISBN 978-1-4503-0170-1. doi: 10.1145/1877826.1877837.

Beedie, Christopher, Terry, Peter, and Lane, Andrew. Distinctions between emotion and mood. *Cognition & Emotion*, 19(6):847–878, 2005. doi: 10.1080/02699930541000057.

Belpaeme, Tony, Baxter, Paul E., Read, Robin, Wood, Rachel, Cuayáhuitl, Heriberto, Kiefer, Bernd, Racioppa, Stefania, Kruijff-Korbayová, Ivana, Athanasopoulos, Georgios, Enescu, Valentin, et al. Multimodal child-robot interaction: Building social bonds. *Journal of Human-Robot Interaction*, 1(2):33–53, 2012. doi: 10.5898/JHRI.1.2.Belpaeme.

Belpaeme, Tony, Kennedy, James, Baxter, Paul, Vogt, Paul, Krahmer, Emiel E. J., Kopp, Stefan, Bergmann, Kirsten, Leseman, Paul, Küntay, Aylin C., Göksun, Tilbe, et al. L2TOR-second language tutoring using social robots. In *Proceedings of the ICSR 2015 WONDER Workshop*. Springer-Verlag, Berlin, 2015. URL https://pub.uni-bielefeld.de/download/290 0267/2900268.

Belpaeme, Tony, Kennedy, James, Ramachandran, Aditi, Scassellati, Brian, and Tanaka, Fumihide. Social robots for education: A review. *Science Robotics*, 3(21):eaat5954, 2018. doi: 10.1126/scirobotics.aat5954.

Bem, Sandra L. The measurement of psychological androgyny. *Journal of Consulting and Clinical Psychology*, 42(2):155–162, 1974. doi: 10.1037/h0036215.

Bendel, Oliver. Love dolls and sex robots in unproven and unexplored fields of application. *Paladyn, Journal of Behavioral Robotics*, 12(1):1–12, 2021. doi: 10.1515/pjbr-2021-0004.

Berghuis, Koen. Robot "preacher" can beam light from its hands and give automated blessings to worshippers. *The Mirror*, 2017. URL www.mirror.co.uk/news/weird-news/robot-priest-can-beam-light-10523678.

Bernotat, Jasmin, Schiffhauer, Birte, Eyssel, Friederike, Holthaus, Patrick, Leichsenring, Christian, Richter, Viktor, Pohling, Marian, Carlmeyer, Birte, Köster, Norman, zu Borgsen, Sebastian Meyer, et al. Welcome to the future: How naïve users intuitively address an intelligent robotics apartment. In *International Conference on Social Robotics*, pages 982–992. Springer, Cham, Switzerland, 2016. ISBN 978-3-319-47436-6. doi: 10.1007/978-3-319-47437-3_96.

Bernotat, Jasmin, Eyssel, Friederike, and Sachse, Janik. Shape it—The influence of robot body shape on gender perception in robots. In *International Conference on Social Robotics*, pages 75–84. Springer, Cham, Switzerland, 2017. ISBN 978-3-319-70021-2. doi: 10.1007/978-3-319-70022-9_8.

Berzuk, James M. and Young, James E. More than words: A framework for describing human-robot dialog designs. In *Proceedings of the 2022 ACM/IEEE International Conference on Human-Robot Interaction*, pages 393–401. Institute of Electrical and Electronics Engineers, Piscataway, NJ, 2022. URL https://doi.org/10.1109/HRI53351.2022.9889423.

Bethel, Cindy L. and Murphy, Robin R. Survey of non-facial/non-verbal affective expressions for appearance-constrained robots. *IEEE Transactions on Systems, Man, and Cybernetics, Part C (Applications and Reviews)*, 38(1):83–92, 2008. doi: 10.1109/TSMCC.2007.905845.

Bethel, Cindy L. and Murphy, Robin R. Review of human studies methods in HRI and recommendations. *International Journal of Social Robotics*, 2(4):347–359, 2010. doi: 10.1007/s12369-010-0064-9.

Bethel, Cindy L., Salomon, Kristen, Murphy, Robin R., and Burke, Jennifer L. Survey of psychophysiology measurements applied to human-robot interaction. In *The 16th IEEE International Symposium on Robot and Human Interactive Communication*, pages 732–737. Institute of Electrical and Electronics Engineers, Piscataway, NJ, 2007. ISBN 978-1-4244-1634-9. doi: 10.1109/ROMAN.2007.4415182.

Bhat, Ashwin Sadananda, Boersma, Christiaan, Meijer, Max Jan, Dokter, Maaike, Bohlmeijer, Ernst, and Li, Jamy. Plant robot for at-home behavioral activation therapy reminders to young adults with depression. *ACM Transactions on Human-Robot Interaction (THRI)*, 10 (3):1–21, 2021. doi: 10.1145/3442680.

Biros, David P., Daly, Mark, and Gunsch, Gregg. The influence of task load and automation trust on deception detection. *Group Decision and Negotiation*, 13(2):173–189, 2004. doi: 10.1023/B:GRUP.0000021840.85686.57.

Björling, Elin A., Xu, Wendy M., Cabrera, Maria E., and Cakmak, Maya. The effect of interaction and design participation on teenagers' attitudes towards social robots. In *2019 28th IEEE International Conference on Robot and Human Interactive Communication (ROMAN)*, pages 1–7. Institute of Electrical and Electronics Engineers, Piscataway, NJ, 2019. doi: 10.1109/RO-MAN46459.2019.8956427.

Björling, Elin A., Thomas, Kyle, Rose, Emma J., and Cakmak, Maya. Exploring teens as robot operators, users and witnesses in the wild. *Frontiers in Robotics and AI*, 7:5, 2020. doi: 10.3389/frobt.2020.00005.

Blair, James R. Responding to the emotions of others: Dissociating forms of empathy through the study of typical and psychiatric populations. *Consciousness and Cognition*, 14(4):698–718, 2005. doi: 10.1016/j.concog.2005.06.004.

Bloom, Benjamin S. The 2 sigma problem: The search for methods of group instruction as effective as one-to-one tutoring. *Educational Researcher*, 13(6):4–16, 1984. doi: 10.3102/0013189X013006004.

Bloomberg. Apple scales back self-driving car, delays debut until 2026. *Automotive News Europe*, 2022. URL https://europe.autonews.com/automakers/apple-scales-back-self-driving-car-delays-debut-until-2026.

Bogue, Robert. Exoskeletons and robotic prosthetics: A review of recent developments. *Industrial Robot: An International Journal*, 36(5):421–427, 2009. doi: 10.1108/01439910910980141.

Bohn, Dieter. Elon Musk: Negative media coverage of autonomous vehicles could be "killing people." *The Verge*, 2016. URL www.theverge.com/2016/10/19/13341306/elon-musk-negative-media-autonomous-vehicles-killing-people.

Bonanno, George A., Goorin, Laura, and Coifman, Karin G. Social functions of emotion. In Lewis, Michael, Haviland-Jones, Jeanette M., and Feldman Barrett, Lisa, editors, *Handbook of Emotions*, volume 3, pages 456–468. Guilford Press, New York, 2008. ISBN 978-1-59385-650-2. URL http://citeseerx.ist.psu.edu/viewdoc/download?doi=10.1.1.472.7583&rep=rep1&type=pdf.

Borenstein, Jason and Arkin, Ronald. Robots, ethics, and intimacy: The need for scientific research. In Berkich, Don and d'Alfonso, Matteo Vincenzo, editors, *On the Cognitive, Ethical, and Scientific Dimensions of Artificial Intelligence*, pages 299–309. Springer, Cham, Switzerland, 2019. doi: 10.1007/978-3-030-01800-9_16.

Borenstein, Jason, Howard, Ayanna, and Wagner, Alan R. Pediatric robotics and ethics: The robot is ready to see you now, but should it be trusted? In Lin, Patrick, Abney, Keith, and Jenkins, Ryan, editors, *Robot Ethics 2.0: From Autonomous Cars to Artificial Intelligence*, pages 127–141. Oxford University Press, Oxford 2017. doi 10.1093/oso/9780190652951. 003.0009.

Bose, Debajyoti, Mohan, Karthi, Meera, C. S., Yadav, Monika, and Saini, Devender K. Review of autonomous campus and tour guiding robots with navigation techniques. *Australian Journal of Mechanical Engineering*, 21(5):1580–1590, 2022. doi: 10.1080/14484846.2021.2023266.

Brahnam, Sheryl and De Angeli, Antonella. Gender affordances of conversational agents. *Interacting with Computers*, 24(3):139–153, 2012. doi: 10.1016/j.intcom.2012.05.001.

Braitenberg, Valentino. *Vehicles: Experiments in Synthetic Psychology*. MIT Press, Cambridge, MA, 1986. ISBN 978-0262521123. URL http://worldcat.org/oclc/254155258.

Brandstetter, Jürgen, Rácz, Péter, Beckner, Clay, Sandoval, Eduardo B., Hay, Jennifer, and Bartneck, Christoph. A peer pressure experiment: Recreation of the Asch conformity experiment with robots. In *IEEE/RSJ International Conference on Intelligent Robots and Systems*, pages 1335–1340. Institute of Electrical and Electronics Engineers, Piscataway, NJ, 2014. ISBN 978-1-4799-6934-0. doi: 10.1109/IROS.2014.6942730.

Brandstetter, Jurgen, Sandoval, Eduardo B., Beckner, Clay, and Bartneck, Christoph. Persistent lexical entrainment in HRI. In *ACM/IEEE International Conference on Human-Robot Interaction*, pages 63–72. Association for Computing Machinery, New York, 2017. ISBN 978-1-4503-4336-7. doi: 10.1145/2909824.3020257.

Breazeal, Cynthia. *Designing Sociable Robots*. MIT Press, Cambridge, MA, 2003. ISBN 978-0262524315. URL http://worldcat.org/oclc/758042496.

Breazeal, Cynthia. Function meets style: Insights from emotion theory applied to HRI. *IEEE Transactions on Systems, Man, and Cybernetics, Part C (Applications and Reviews)*, 34(2): 187–194, 2004a. doi: 10.1109/TSMCC.2004.826270.

Breazeal, Cynthia. Social interactions in HRI: The robot view. *IEEE Transactions on Systems, Man, and Cybernetics, Part C (Applications and Reviews)*, 34(2):181–186, 2004b. doi: 10.1109/TSMCC.2004.826268.

Breazeal, Cynthia and Scassellati, Brian. A context-dependent attention system for a social robot. In *Proceedings of the 16th International Joint Conference on Artificial Intelligence, Volume 2*, pages 1146–1151. Morgan Kaufmann, Burlington, MA, 1999. URL http://dl.acm.org/citation.cfm?id=1624312.1624382.

Breazeal, Cynthia, Kidd, Cory D., Thomaz, Andrea Lockerd, Hoffman, Guy, and Berlin, Matt. Effects of nonverbal communication on efficiency and robustness in human-robot teamwork. In *IEEE/RSJ International Conference on Intelligent Robots and Systems (IROS)*, pages 708–713. Institute of Electrical and Electronics Engineers, Piscataway, NJ, 2005. ISBN 0-7803-8912-3. doi: 10.1109/IROS.2005.1545011.

Bremner, Paul, Pipe, Anthony, Melhuish, Chris, Fraser, Mike, and Subramanian, Sriram. Conversational gestures in human-robot interaction. In *IEEE International Conference on Systems, Man and Cybernetics*, pages 1645–1649. Institute of Electrical and Electronics Engineers, Piscataway, NJ, 2009. ISBN 978-1-4244-2793-2. doi: 10.1109/ICSMC.2009.5346903.

Broadbent, Elizabeth, Stafford, Rebecca, and MacDonald, Bruce. Acceptance of healthcare robots for the older population: Review and future directions. *International Journal of Social Robotics*, 1(4):319–330, 2009. doi: 10.1007/s12369-009-0030-6.

Broekens, Joost, Heerink, Marcel, and Rosendal, Henk. Assistive social robots in elderly care: A review. *Gerontechnology*, 8(2):94–103, 2009. doi: 10.4017/gt.2009.08.02.002.00.

Bröhl, Christina, Nelles, Jochen, Brandl, Christopher, Mertens, Alexander, and Schlick, Christopher M. TAM reloaded: A technology acceptance model for human-robot cooperation in production systems. In *International Conference on Human-Computer Interaction*, pages 97–103. Springer, Cham, Switzerland, 2016. doi: 10.1007/978-3-319-40548-3_16.

Brooks, Rodney. A robust layered control system for a mobile robot. *IEEE Journal on Robotics and Automation*, 2(1):14–23, 1986. doi: 10.1109/JRA.1986.1087032.

Brooks, Rodney A. Intelligence without representation. *Artificial Intelligence*, 47(1–3):139–159, 1991. doi: 10.1016/0004-3702(91)90053-M.

Brooks, Rodney Allen. *Flesh and Machines: How Robots Will Change Us*. Vintage, New York, 2003. ISBN 9780375725272. URL http://worldcat.org/oclc/249859485.

Brown, Barry. The social life of autonomous cars. *Computer*, 50(2):92–96, 2017. doi: 10.1109/MC.2017.59.

Brscić, Drazen, Kanda, Takayuki, Ikeda, Tetsushi, and Miyashita, Takahiro. Person tracking in large public spaces using 3-D range sensors. *IEEE Transactions on Human-Machine Systems*, 43(6):522–534, 2013. doi: 10.1109/THMS.2013.2283945.

Brscić, Drazen, Kidokoro, Hiroyuki, Suehiro, Yoshitaka, and Kanda, Takayuki. Escaping from children's abuse of social robots. In *Proceedings of the 10th Annual ACM/IEEE International Conference on Human-Robot Interaction*, pages 59–66. Association for Computing Machinery, New York, 2015. ISBN 978-1-4503-2883-8. doi: 10.1145/2696454.2696468.

Bruno, Barbara, Chong, Nak Young, Kamide, Hiroko, Kanoria, Sanjeev, Lee, Jaeryoung, Lim, Yuto, Pandey, Amit Kumar, Papadopoulos, Chris, Papadopoulos, Irena, Pecora, Federico, et al. The CARESSES EU-Japan project: Making assistive robots culturally competent. arXiv, arXiv:1708.06276, 2017. URL https://arxiv.org/abs/1708.06276.

Buchanan, Richard. Wicked problems in design thinking. *Design Issues*, 8(2):5–21, 1992. URL www.jstor.org/stable/1511637.

Burgard, Wolfram, Cremers, Armin B., Fox, Dieter, Hähnel, Dirk, Lakemeyer, Gerhard, Schulz, Dirk, Steiner, Walter, and Thrun, Sebastian. The interactive museum tour-guide robot. In *Proceedings of the 15th National/10th Conference on Artificial Intelligence/Innovative Applications of Artificial Intelligence*, pages 11–18. American Association for Artificial Intelligence, Menlo Park, CA, 1998. ISBN 0-262-51098-7. URL https://dl.acm.org/citation.cfm?id=295249.

Cakmak, Maya, Srinivasa, Siddhartha S., Lee, Min Kyung, Forlizzi, Jodi, and Kiesler, Sara. Human preferences for robot-human hand-over configurations. In *IEEE/RSJ International Conference on Intelligent Robots and Systems*, pages 1986–1993. Institute of Electrical and Electronics Engineers, Piscataway, NJ, 2011. ISBN 978-1-61284-454-1. doi: 10.1109/IROS.2011.6094735.

Calvo, Rafael A., D'Mello, Sidney, Gratch, Jonathan, and Kappas, Arvid. *The Oxford Handbook of Affective Computing*. Oxford University Press, New York, 2015. ISBN 978-0199942237. URL http://worldcat.org/oclc/1008985555.

Cameron, dir., James. *The Terminator*. Orion Pictures, Los Angeles, CA, 1984. ISBN 27616854735. URL www.imdb.com/title/tt0088247/.

Campbell, Murray, Hoane, A. Joseph, and Hsu, Feng-hsiung. Deep Blue. *Artificial Intelligence*, 134(1-2):57–83, 2002. doi: 10.1016/S0004-3702(01)00129-1.

Cannon, Kelly, Lapoint, Monica Anderson, Bird, Nathaniel, Panciera, Katherine, Veeraraghavan, Harini, Papanikolopoulos, Nikolaos, and Gini, Maria. Using robots to raise interest in technology among underrepresented groups. *IEEE Robotics & Automation Magazine*, 14(2):73–81, 2007. doi: 10.1109/MRA.2007.380640.

Cao, Zhe, Simon, Tomas, Wei, Shih-En, and Sheikh, Yaser. Realtime multi-person 2D pose estimation using part affinity fields. In *IEEE Conference on Computer Vision and Pattern Recognition*, pages 1302–1310. Institute of Electrical and Electronics Engineers, Piscataway, NJ, 2017. ISBN 9781538604571. doi: 10.1109/CVPR.2017.143.

Carpenter, Julie. *Culture and Human-Robot Interaction in Militarized Spaces: A War Story*. Routledge, New York, 2016. ISBN 978-1-4724-4311-3. URL http://worldcat.org/oclc/951397181.

Carpinella, Colleen M., Wyman, Alisa B., Perez, Michael A., and Stroessner, Steven J. The Robotic Social Attributes Scale (RoSAS): Development and validation. In *ACM/IEEE International Conference on Human-Robot Interaction*, pages 254–262. Association for Computing Machinery, New York, 2017. ISBN 978-1-4503-4336-7. doi: 10.1145/2909 824.3020208.

Carrere, Sybil and Gottman, John Mordechai. Predicting divorce among newlyweds from the first three minutes of a marital conflict discussion. *Family Process*, 38(3):293–301, 1999. doi: 10.1111/j.1545-5300.1999.00293.x.

Cassell, Justine, Sullivan, Joseph, Prevost, Scott, and Churchill, Elizabeth. *Embodied Conversational Agents*. MIT Press, Cambridge, MA, 2000. ISBN 9780262032780. URL http://worldcat.org/oclc/440727862.

Cavallo, Filippo, Limosani, Raffaele, Manzi, Alessandro, Bonaccorsi, Manuele, Esposito, Raffaele, Di Rocco, Maurizio, Pecora, Federico, Teti, Giancarlo, Saffiotti, Alessandro, and Dario, Paolo. Development of a socially believable multi-robot solution from town to home. *Cognitive Computation*, 6(4):954–967, 2014. doi: 10.1007/s12559-014-9290-z.

Chang, Wan-Ling and Šabanović, Selma. Interaction expands function: Social shaping of the therapeutic robot PARO in a nursing home. In *HRI '15: The Proceedings of the 10th Annual ACM/IEEE International Conference on Human-Robot Interaction*, pages 343–350. Association for Computing Machinery, New York, 2015. ISBN 978-1-4503-2883-8. doi: 10.1145/2696454.2696472.

Charman, Tony, Baron-Cohen, Simon, Swettenham, John, Baird, Gillian, Cox, Antony, and Drew, Auriol. Testing joint attention, imitation, and play as infancy precursors to language and Theory of Mind. *Cognitive Development*, 15(4):481–498, 2000. doi: 10.1016/S0885-2 014(01)00037-5.

Chartrand, Tanya L. and Bargh, John A. The chameleon effect: The perception-behavior link and social interaction. *Journal of Personality and Social Psychology*, 76(6):893–910, 1999. doi: 10.1037/0022-3514.76.6.893.

Chen, Ching-Fu and VG, Girish. Antecedents and outcomes of use experience of airport service robot: The stimulus-organism-response (SOR) framework. *Journal of Vacation Marketing*, page 13567667221109267, 2022. doi: 10.1177/13567667221109267.

Chen, Qian Qian and Park, Hyun Jung. How anthropomorphism affects trust in intelligent personal assistants. *Industrial Management & Data Systems*, 29(4):570–583, 2021. doi: 10.1108/IMDS-12-2020-0761.

Chen, Tiffany L., King, Chih-Hung Aaron, Thomaz, Andrea L., and Kemp, Charles C. An investigation of responses to robot-initiated touch in a nursing context. *International Journal of Social Robotics*, 6(1):141–161, 2014. doi: 10.1007/s12369-013-0215-x.

Chen, Zhichao, Nakamura, Yutaka, and Ishiguro, Hiroshi. Android as a receptionist in a shopping mall using inverse reinforcement learning. *IEEE Robotics and Automation Letters*, 7(3):7091–7098, 2022. doi: 10.1109/LRA.2022.3180042.

Chikaraishi, Takenobu, Yoshikawa, Yuichiro, Ogawa, Kohei, Hirata, Oriza, and Ishiguro, Hiroshi. Creation and staging of android theatre "sayonara" towards developing highly human-like robots. *Future Internet*, 9(4):75–92, 2017. doi: 10.3390/fi9040075.

Choset, Howie M., Hutchinson, Seth, Lynch, Kevin M., Kantor, George, Burgard, Wolfram, Kavraki, Lydia E., and Thrun, Sebastian. *Principles of Robot Motion: Theory, Algorithms, and Implementation*. MIT Press, Cambridge, MA, 2005. ISBN 978-026203327. URL http://worldcat.org/oclc/762070740.

Christoforakos, Lara, Gallucci, Alessio, Surmava-Große, Tinatini, Ullrich, Daniel, and Diefenbach, Sarah. Can robots earn our trust the same way humans do? A systematic exploration of competence, warmth, and anthropomorphism as determinants of trust development in HRI. *Frontiers in Robotics and AI*, 8:640444, 2021. doi: 10.3389/frobt.2021.640444.

Cillessen, Antonius H. N. and Rose, Amanda J. Understanding popularity in the peer system. *Current Directions in Psychological Science*, 14(2):102–105, 2005. doi: 10.1111/j.0963-7 214.2005.00343.x.

Coe, Robert. It's the effect size, stupid: What effect size is and why it is important. In *Annual Conference of the British Educational Research Association*. Educationline, Bedford Heights, UK, 2002. URL http://leeds.ac.uk/educol/documents/00002182.htm.

Cohen, Jacob. The earth is round ($p <$ .05). *American Psychologist*, 49:997–1003, 1994. doi: 10.1037/0003-066X.49.12.997.

Conti, Daniela, Di Nuovo, Santo, Buono, Serafino, and Di Nuovo, Alessandro. Robots in education and care of children with developmental disabilities: a study on acceptance by experienced and future professionals. *International Journal of Social Robotics*, 9(1):51–62, 2017. doi: 10.1007/s12369-016-0359-6.

Cook, Mark. Experiments on orientation and proxemics. *Human Relations*, 23(1):61–76, 1970. doi: 10.1177/001872677002300107.

Cooney, Martin, Kanda, Takayuki, Alissandarakis, Aris, and Ishiguro, Hiroshi. Designing enjoyable motion-based play interactions with a small humanoid robot. *International Journal of Social Robotics*, 6(2):173–193, 2014. doi: 10.1007/s12369-013-0212-0.

Correll, Joshua, Park, Bernadette, Judd, Charles M, and Wittenbrink, Bernd. The police officer's dilemma: using ethnicity to disambiguate potentially threatening individuals. *Journal of Personality and Social Psychology*, 83(6):1314, 2002. doi: 10.1037//0022-3 514.83.6.1314.

Cribb, Jo and Glover, David. *Don't Worry about the Robots*. Allen & Unwin, Auckland, New Zealand, 2018. ISBN 9781760633509. URL http://worldcat.org/oclc/1042120802.

Crisp, Richard J. and Turner, Rhiannon N. Imagined intergroup contact: Refinements, debates, and clarifications. In Hodson, Gordon and Hewstone, Miles, editors, *Advances in Intergroup Contact*, pages 149–165. Psychology Press, London, 2013. ISBN 978-1136213908. URL http://worldcat.org/oclc/694393740.

Crusco, April H. and Wetzel, Christopher G. The Midas touch: The effects of interpersonal touch on restaurant tipping. *Personality and Social Psychology Bulletin*, 10(4):512–517, 1984. doi: 10.1177/0146167284104003.

Cuddy, Amy, Fiske, Susan, and Glick, Peter. Warmth and competence as universal dimensions of social perception: The stereotype content model and the BIAS map. *Advances in Experimental Social Psychology*, 40:61–149, 2008. doi: 10.1016/S0065-2601(07)00002-0.

Cumming, Geoff. Replication and p intervals: p values predict the future only vaguely, but confidence intervals do much better. *Perspectives on Psychological Science*, 3(4):286–300, 2008. doi: 10.1111/j.1745-6924.2008.00079.x.

Cunneen, Martin, Mullins, Martin, and Murphy, Finbarr. Autonomous vehicles and embedded artificial intelligence: The challenges of framing machine driving decisions. *Applied Artificial Intelligence*, 33(8):706–731, 2019. doi: 10.1080/08839514.2019.1600301.

Darling, Kate. Extending legal protection to social robots: The effects of anthropomorphism, empathy, and violent behavior towards robotic objects. In Calo, Ryan A., Froomkin, Michael, and Kerr, Ian, editors, *We Robot Conference*. Edward Elgar, Cheltenham, UK, 2012. doi: 10.2139/ssrn.2044797.

Dautenhahn, Kerstin, Walters, Michael, Woods, Sarah, Koay, Kheng Lee, Nehaniv, Chrystopher L., Sisbot, A., Alami, Rachid, and Siméon, Thierry. How may I serve you? A robot companion approaching a seated person in a helping context. In *1st ACM SIGCHI/SIGART Conference on Human-Robot Interaction*, pages 172–179. Association for Computing Machinery, New York, 2006. ISBN 1-59593-294-1. doi: 10.1145/1121241.1121272.

Davis, Joshua Ian, Senghas, Ann, Brandt, Fredric, and Ochsner, Kevin N. The effects of Botox injections on emotional experience. *Emotion*, 10(3):433, 2010. doi: 10.1037/a0018690.

Davison, Andrew J., Reid, Ian D., Molton, Nicholas D., and Stasse, Olivier. Monoslam: Real-time single camera slam. *IEEE Transactions on Pattern Analysis and Machine Intelligence*, 29(6):1052–1067, 2007. doi: 10.1109/TPAMI.2007.1049.

De Angeli, Antonella. Ethical implications of verbal disinhibition with conversational agents. *PsychNology Journal*, 7(1):49–57, 2009. URL http://psychology.org/File/PNJ7(1)/PSYCHNOLOGY_JOURNAL_7_1_DEANGELI.pdf.

De Graaf, Maartje and Allouch, Somaya Ben. Exploring influencing variables for the acceptance of social robots. *Robotics and Autonomous Systems*, 61(12):1476–1486, 2013. doi: 10.1016/j.robot.2013.07.007.

de Graaf, Maartje, Allouch, Somaya Ben, and Lutfi, Shariff. What are people's associations of domestic robots? Comparing implicit and explicit measures. In *2016 25th IEEE International Symposium on Robot and Human Interactive Communication (RO-MAN)*, pages 1077–1083. Institute of Electrical and Electronics Engineers, Piscataway, NJ, 2016. doi: 10.1109/ROMAN.2016.7745242.

de Graaf, Maartje, Ben Allouch, Somaya, and van Dijk, Jan. Why do they refuse to use my robot? Reasons for non-use derived from a long-term home study. In *Proceedings of the ACM/IEEE International Conference on Human-Robot Interaction*, pages 224–233. Association for Computing Machinery, New York, 2017. ISBN 978-1-4503-4336-7. doi: 10.1145/2909824.3020236.

de Graaf, Maartje, Ben Allouch, Somaya, and Van Dijk, Jan. Why would I use this in my home? A model of domestic social robot acceptance. *Human–Computer Interaction*, 34(2): 115–173, 2019. doi: 10.1080/07370024.2017.1312406.

De Visser, Ewart J., Peeters, Marieke M. M., Jung, Malte F., Kohn, Spencer, Shaw, Tyler H., Pak, Richard, and Neerincx, Mark A. Towards a theory of longitudinal trust calibration in human–robot teams. *International Journal of Social Robotics*, 12(2):459–478, 2020. doi: 10.1007/s12369-019-00596-x.

De Waal, Frans. *The Ape and the Sushi Master: Cultural Reflections of a Primatologist*. Basic Books, New York, 2001. ISBN 978-0465041763. URL http://worldcat.org/oclc/458716823.

Department of Transportation. Critical reasons for crashes investigated in the national motor vehicle crash causation survey. Report, Department of Transportation, 2015. URL https://crashstats.nhtsa.dot.gov/Api/Public/ViewPublication/812115.

Devlin, Kate. *Turned On: Science, Sex and Robots*. Bloomsbury, London, 2020. ISBN 9781472950901. URL www.worldcat.org/title/1252735321.

Dick, Philip K. *Blade Runner: Do Androids Dream of Electric Sheep?* Ballantine Books, New York, 25th-Anniversary edition, 2007. ISBN 9780345350473. URL http://worldcat.org/oclc/776604212.

Diehl, Joshua J., Schmitt, Lauren M., Villano, Michael, and Crowell, Charles R. The clinical use of robots for individuals with autism spectrum disorders: A critical review. *Research in Autism Spectrum Disorders*, 6(1):249–262, 2012. doi: 10.1016/j.rasd.2011.05.006.

DiSalvo, Carl, Nourbakhsh, Illah, Holstius, David, Akin, Ayça, and Louw, Marti. The neighborhood networks project: A case study of critical engagement and creative expression through participatory design. In *10th Anniversary Conference on Participatory Design 2008*, pages 41–50. Indiana University, Indianapolis, 2008. ISBN 978-0-9818561-0-0. URL https://dl.acm.org/citation.cfm?id=1795241.

DiSalvo, Carl F., Gemperle, Francine, Forlizzi, Jodi, and Kiesler, Sara. All robots are not created equal: The design and perception of humanoid robot heads. In *Proceedings of the 4th Conference on Designing Interactive Systems: Processes, Practices, Methods, and Techniques*, pages 321–326. Association for Computing Machinery, New York, 2002. ISBN 1-58113-515-7. doi: 10.1145/778712.778756.

Dixon, Steve. Metal performance humanizing robots, returning to nature, and camping about. *TDR/The Drama Review*, 48(4):15–46, 2004. ISSN 1054-2043. doi: 10.1162/1054204042 442017.

Doan, Anhai, Ramakrishnan, Raghu, and Halevy, Alon Y. Crowdsourcing systems on the world-wide web. *Communications of the ACM*, 54(4):86–96, 2011. doi: 10.1145/1924421. 1924442.

Döring, Nicola and Poeschl, Sandra. Love and sex with robots: A content analysis of media representations. *International Journal of Social Robotics*, 11(4):665–677, 2019. doi: 10.1 007/s12369-019-00517-y.

Dragan, Anca D., Lee, Kenton C. T., and Srinivasa, Siddhartha S. Legibility and predictability of robot motion. In *8th ACM/IEEE International Conference on Human-Robot Interaction*, pages 301–308. Institute of Electrical and Electronics Engineers, Piscataway, NJ, 2013. ISBN 978-1-4673-3099-2. doi: 10.1109/HRI.2013.6483603.

Duffy, Brian R. Anthropomorphism and the social robot. *Robotics and Autonomous Systems*, 42(3):177–190, 2003. ISSN 0921-8890. doi: 10.1016/S0921-8890(02)00374-3.

Edwards, Autumn, Edwards, Chad, Spence, Patric R., Harris, Christina, and Gambino, Andrew. Robots in the classroom: Differences in students' perceptions of credibility and learning between "teacher as robot" and "robot as teacher." *Computers in Human Behavior*, 65:627–634, 2016. doi: 10.1016/j.chb.2016.06.005.

Eisenberger, Naomi I., Lieberman, Matthew D., and Williams, Kipling D. Does rejection hurt? An fMRI study of social exclusion. *Science*, 302(5643):290–292, 2003. doi: 10.1126/science.1089134.

Ekkekakis, Panteleimon. *The Measurement of Affect, Mood, and Emotion: A Guide for Health-Behavioral Research*. Cambridge University Press, Cambridge, 2013. doi: 10.1017/CBO9780511820724.

Ekman, Paul. Facial expressions of emotion: New findings, new questions. *Psychological Science*, 3(1):34–38, 1992. doi: 10.1111/j.1467-9280.1992.tb00253.x.

Ekman, Paul. Basic emotions. In Dalgleish, Tim and Power, Mick J., editors, *Handbook of Cognition and Emotion*, pages 45–60. Wiley Online Library, 1999. ISBN 978-1462509997. URL http://worldcat.org/oclc/826592694.

Ekman, Paul and Friesen, Wallace. *Facial Action Coding System: A technique for the measurement of facial movement*. Consulting Psychologists Press, Palo Alto, CA, 1978. doi: 10.1037/t27734-000.

Ekman, Paul and Friesen, Wallace V. *Unmasking the Face*. Prentice Hall, Englewood Cliffs, NJ, 1975. ISBN 978-1883536367. URL http://worldcat.org/oclc/803874427.

El Ayadi, Moataz, Kamel, Mohamed S., and Karray, Fakhri. Survey on speech emotion recognition: Features, classification schemes, and databases. *Pattern Recognition*, 44(3):572–587, 2011. doi: 10.1016/j.patcog.2010.09.020.

El Makrini, Ilias, Elprama, Shirley A., Van den Bergh, Jan, Vanderborght, Bram, Knevels, Albert-Jan, Jewell, Charlotte I. C., Stals, Frank, De Coppel, Geert, Ravyse, Ilse, Potargent, Johan, et al. Working with Walt. *IEEE Robotics & Automation Magazine*, 25:51–58, 2018. doi: 10.1109/MRA.2018.2815947.

Elder, Alexis M. *Friendship, Robots, and Social Media: False Friends and Second Selves*. Routledge, New York, 2017. ISBN 978-1138065666. URL http://worldcat.org/oclc/1016009820.

Epley, Nicholas, Waytz, Adam, and Cacioppo, John T. On seeing human: A three-factor theory of anthropomorphism. *Psychological Review*, 114(4):864–886, 2007. doi: 10.1037/0033-295X.114.4.864.

Epley, Nicholas, Waytz, Adam, Akalis, Scott, and Cacioppo, John T. When we need a human: Motivational determinants of anthropomorphism. *Social Cognition*, 26(2):143–155, 2008. doi: 10.1521/soco.2008.26.2.143.

Erel, Hadas, Shem Tov, Tzachi, Kessler, Yoav, and Zuckerman, Oren. Robots are always social: Robotic movements are automatically interpreted as social cues. In *Extended Abstracts of the 2019 CHI Conference on Human Factors in Computing Systems*, pages 1–6. Association for Computing Machinery, New York, 2019. doi: 10.1145/3290607.3312758.

Etz, Alexander and Vandekerckhove, Joachim. Introduction to Bayesian inference for psychology. *Psychonomic Bulletin & Review*, 25(1):5–34, 2018. doi: 10.3758/s13423-017-1262-3.

European Commission. Attitudes towards the impact of digitisation and automation on daily life. Technical Report Special Eurobarometer 460/Wave EB87.1, Directorate-General for Information Society and Media, 2017. URL https://europa.eu/eurobarometer/surveys/detail/2160.

Evans, Jonathan St B. T. Dual-processing accounts of reasoning, judgment, and social cognition. *Annual Review of Psychology*, 59(3):255–278, 2008. doi: 10.1146/annurev.psych.59.103006.093629.

Evans, Jonathan St BT and Stanovich, Keith E. Dual-process theories of higher cognition: Advancing the debate. *Perspectives on Psychological Science*, 8(3):223–241, 2013. doi: 10.1177/1745691612460685.

Evans, Katherine, de Moura, Nelson, Chauvier, Stéphane, Chatila, Raja, and Dogan, Ebru. Ethical decision making in autonomous vehicles: The AV ethics project. *Science and Engineering Ethics*, 26:3285–3312, 2020. doi: 10.1007/s11948-020-00272-8.

Evers, Vanessa, Maldonado, Heidy C., Brodecki, Talia L., and Hinds, Pamela J. Relational vs. group self-construal: Untangling the role of national culture in HRI. In *Proceedings of the 3rd ACM/IEEE International Conference on Human-Robot Interaction*, pages 255–262. Association for Computing Machinery, New York, 2008. ISBN 978-1-60558-017-3. doi: 10.1145/1349822.1349856.

Eyben, Florian, Weninger, Felix, Gross, Florian, and Schuller, Björn. Recent developments in OpenSMILE, the Munich open-source multimedia feature extractor. In *21st ACM International Conference on Multimedia*, pages 835–838. Association for Computing Machinery, New York, 2013. ISBN 978-1-4503-2404-5. doi: 10.1145/2502081.2502224.

Eyssel, Friederike. An experimental psychological perspective on social robotics. *Robotics and Autonomous Systems*, 87(Supplement C):363–371, 2017. ISSN 0921-8890. doi: https://doi.org/10.1016/j.robot.2016.08.029. URL http://sciencedirect.com/science/article/pii/S09218 89016305462.

Eyssel, Friederike and Hegel, Frank. (S)he's got the look: Gender stereotyping of robots. *Journal of Applied Social Psychology*, 42(9):2213–2230, 2012. doi: 10.1111/j.1559-1816. 2012.00937.x.

Eyssel, Friederike and Kuchenbrandt, Dieta. Social categorization of social robots: Anthropomorphism as a function of robot group membership. *British Journal of Social Psychology*, 51(4):724–731, 2012. doi: 10.1111/j.2044-8309.2011.02082.x.

Eyssel, Friederike and Loughnan, Steve. "It don't matter if you're Black or White"? In *International Conference on Social Robotics*, pages 422–431. Springer, Cham, Switzerland, 2013. doi: 10.1007/978-3-319-02675-6_42.

Eyssel, Friederike and Reich, Natalia. Loneliness makes the heart grow fonder (of robots)—On the effects of loneliness on psychological anthropomorphism. In *Proceedings of the 8th ACM/IEEE International Conference on Human-Robot Interaction (HRI)*, pages 121–122. Institute of Electrical and Electronics Engineers, Piscataway, NJ, 2013. ISBN 978-1-4673-3101-2. doi: 10.1109/HRI.2013.6483531.

Eyssel, Friederike, Hegel, Frank, Horstmann, Gernot, and Wagner, Claudia. Anthropomorphic inferences from emotional nonverbal cues: A case study. In *19th International Symposium on Robot and Human Interactive Communication*, pages 646–651. Institute of Electrical and Electronics Engineers, Piscataway, NJ, 2010. doi: 10.1109/ROMAN.2010.5598687.

Eyssel, Friederike, Kuchenbrandt, Dieta, and Bobinger, Simon. Effects of anticipated human-robot interaction and predictability of robot behavior on perceptions of anthropomorphism. In *Proceedings of the 6th International Conference on Human-Robot Interaction*, pages 61–68. Association for Computing Machinery, New York, 2011. doi: 10.1145/1957656.19 57673.

Eyssel, Friederike, Kuchenbrandt, Dieta, Bobinger, Simon, de Ruiter, Laura, and Hegel, Frank. "If you sound like me, you must be more human": On the interplay of robot and user features on human-robot acceptance and anthropomorphism. In *Proceedings of the 7th Annual ACM/IEEE International Conference on Human-Robot Interaction*, pages 125–126. Association for Computing Machinery, New York, 2012a. ISBN 978-1-4503-1063-5. doi: 10.1145/2157689.2157717.

Eyssel, Friederike, Kuchenbrandt, Dieta, Hegel, Frank, and de Ruiter, Laura. Activating elicited agent knowledge: How robot and user features shape the perception of social robots. In *2012 IEEE RO-MAN: The 21st IEEE International Symposium on Robot and Human Interactive Communication*, pages 851–857. Institute of Electrical and Electronics Engineers, Piscataway, NJ, 2012b. doi: 10.1109/ROMAN.2012.6343858.

Fagnant, Daniel J. and Kockelman, Kara. Preparing a nation for autonomous vehicles: Opportunities, barriers and policy recommendations. *Transportation Research Part A: Policy and Practice*, 77:167–181, 2015. ISSN 0965-8564. doi: https://doi.org/10.1016/j.tra.2015.04.003. URL http://sciencedirect.com/science/article/pii/S0965856415000804.

Faul, Franz, Erdfelder, Edgar, Lang, Albert-Georg, and Axel, Buchner. G*power 3: A flexible statistical power analysis program for the social, behavioral, and biomedical sciences. *Behavior Research Methods*, 39(2):175–191, 2007. doi: 10.3758/BF03193146.

Favaro, Francesca M., Nader, Nazanin, Eurich, Sky O., Tripp, Michelle, and Varadaraju, Naresh. Examining accident reports involving autonomous vehicles in california. *PLOS One*, 12(9):1–20, 09 2017. doi: 10.1371/journal.pone.0184952.

Feil-Seifer, David and Matarić, Maja J. Socially assistive robotics. *IEEE Robotics & Automation Magazine*, 18(1):24–31, 2011. doi: 10.1109/MRA.2010.940150.

Feng, Catherine, Azenkot, Shiri, and Cakmak, Maya. Designing a robot guide for blind people in indoor environments. In *The 10th Annual ACM/IEEE International Conference on Human-Robot Interaction Extended Abstracts*, pages 107–108. Association for Computing Machinery, New York, 2015. ISBN 978-1-4503-3318-4. doi: 10.1145/2701973.2702060.

Ferrari, Francesco, Paladino, Maria Paola, and Jetten, Jolanda. Blurring human-machine distinctions: Anthropomorphic appearance in social robots as a threat to human distinctiveness. *International Journal of Social Robotics*, 8(2):287–302, 2016. doi: 10.1007/s12369-016-0338-y.

Festerling, Janik and Siraj, Iram. Anthropomorphizing technology: A conceptual review of anthropomorphism research and how it relates to children's engagements with digital voice assistants. *Integrative Psychological and Behavioral Science*, 56(3):709–738, 2022. doi: 10.1007/s12124-021-09668-y.

Field, Andy. *Discovering Statistics Using IBM SPSS Statistics*. SAGE Publications, Thousand Oaks, CA, 2018. ISBN 9781526419514. URL http://worldcat.org/oclc/1030545826.

Field, Andy and Hole, Graham. *How to Design and Report Experiments*. SAGE Publications, Thousand Oaks, CA, 2002. ISBN 978085702829. URL http://worldcat.org/title/how-to-design-and-report-experiments/oclc/961100072.

Fink, Julia. Anthropomorphism and human likeness in the design of robots and human-robot interaction. In Ge, Shuzhi Sam, Khatib, Oussama, Cabibihan, John-John, Simmons, Reid, and Williams, Mary-Anne, editors, *Social Robotics*, pages 199–208. Springer, Berlin, 2012. ISBN 978-3-642-34103-8. URL https://doi.org/10.1007/978-3-642-34103-8_20.

Fink, Julia, Bauwens, Valérie, Kaplan, Frédéric, and Dillenbourg, Pierre. Living with a vacuum cleaning robot. *International Journal of Social Robotics*, 5(3):389–408, Aug 2013. ISSN 1875-4805. doi: 10.1007/s12369-013-0190-2.

Fink, Julia, Lemaignan, Séverin, Dillenbourg, Pierre, Rétornaz, Philippe, Vaussard, Florian, Berthoud, Alain, Mondada, Francesco, Wille, Florian, and Franinović, Karmen. Which robot behavior can motivate children to tidy up their toys? Design and evaluation of ranger. In *ACM/IEEE International Conference on Human-Robot Interaction*, pages 439–446. Association for Computing Machinery, New York, 2014. ISBN 978-1-4503-2658-2. doi: 10.1145/2559636.2559659.

Fisac, Jaime, Bajcsy, Andrea, Herbert, Sylvia, Fridovich-Keil, David, Wang, Steven, Tomlin, Claire, and Dragan, Anca. Probabilistically safe robot planning with confidence-based human predictions. In Kress-Gazit, Hadas, Srinivasa, Siddhartha S., Howard, Tom, and Atanasov, Nikolay, editors, *Proceedings of Robotics: Science and Systems*. MIT PRess, Cambridge, MA, 2018. ISBN 978-0-9923747-4-7. doi: 10.15607/RSS.2018.XIV.069.

Fischer, Kerstin. Effect confirmed, patient dead: A commentary on Hoffman & Zhao's primer for conducting experiments in HRI. *ACM Transactions on Human-Robot Interaction (THRI)*, 10(1):1–4, 2021. doi: 10.1145/3439714.

Fischer, Kerstin, Lohan, Katrin, Saunders, Joe, Nehaniv, Chrystopher, Wrede, Britta, and Rohlfing, Katharina. The impact of the contingency of robot feedback on HRI. In *International Conference on Collaboration Technologies and Systems*, pages 210–217. Institute of Electrical and Electronics Engineers, Piscataway, NJ, 2013. ISBN 978-1-4673-6403-4. doi: 10.1109/CTS.2013.6567231.

Fiske, Susan T., Cuddy, Amy J. C., and Glick, Peter. Universal dimensions of social cognition: Warmth and competence. *Trends in Cognitive Sciences*, 11(2):77–83, 2007. doi: 10.1016/j.tics.2006.11.005.

Fiske, Susan T., Cuddy, Amy J. C., Glick, Peter, and Xu, Jun. A model of (often mixed) stereotype content: Competence and warmth respectively follow from perceived status and competition. *Journal of Personality and Social Psychology*, 82(6):878–902, 202. doi: 10.1037/0022-3514.82.6.878.

Fitter, Naomi T., Chowdhury, Yasmin, Cha, Elizabeth, Takayama, Leila, and Matarić, Maja J. Evaluating the effects of personalized appearance on telepresence robots for education. In *Companion of the 2018 ACM/IEEE International Conference on Human-Robot Interaction*, pages 109–110. Association for Computing Machinery, New York, 2018. doi: 10.1145/3173386.3177030.

Ford, Martin. *The Rise of the Robots: Technology and the Threat of Mass Unemployment*. Oneworld Publications, London, 2015. ISBN 978-0465059997. URL http://worldcat.org/oclc/993846206.

Forlizzi, Jodi and DiSalvo, Carl. Service robots in the domestic environment: A study of the Roomba vacuum in the home. In *Proceedings of the 1st ACM SIGCHI/SIGART Conference on Human-Robot Interaction*, pages 258–265. Association for Computing Machinery, New York, 2006. ISBN 1-59593-294-1. doi: 10.1145/1121241.1121286.

Fosch-Villaronga, Eduard, Lutz, Christoph, and Tamò-Larrieux, Aurelia. Gathering expert opinions for social robots' ethical, legal, and societal concerns: Findings from four international workshops. *International Journal of Social Robotics*, 12(2):441–458, 2020. doi: 10.1007/s12369-019-00605-z.

Fowler, Floyd J. *Improving Survey Questions: Design and Evaluation*, volume 38. SAGE Publications, Thousand Oaks, CA, 1995. ISBN 978-0803945838. URL http://worldcat.org/oclc/551387270.

Fowler, Floyd J. *Survey Research Methods*. SAGE Publications, Thousand Oaks, CA, 2013. ISBN 978-1452259000. URL http://worldcat.org/oclc/935314651.

Fox, Dieter, Burgard, Wolfram, and Thrun, Sebastian. The dynamic window approach to collision avoidance. *IEEE Robotics & Automation Magazine*, 4(1):23–33, 1997. doi: 10.1109/100.580977.

Friedman, Batya, Kahn, Peter, and Borning, Alan. Value sensitive design: Theory and methods. Technical report, University of Washington, 2002.

Fujita, Masahiro. Aibo: Toward the era of digital creatures. *International Journal of Robotics Research*, 20(10):781–794, 2001. doi: 10.1177/02783640122068092.

Future of Life Institute. An open letter—Research priorities for robust and beneficial artificial intelligence, January 2015. URL https://futureoflife.org/ai-open-letter/.

Gargouri, Yassine, Hajjem, Chawki, Larivière, Vincent, Gingras, Yves, Carr, Les, Brody, Tim, and Harnad, Stevan. Self-selected or mandated, open access increases citation impact for higher quality research. *PLOS One*, 5(10):1–12, 10 2010. doi: 10.1371/journal.pone.0013636.

Garland, dir., Alex. *Ex Machina*. A24, New York, 2014. URL www.imdb.com/title/tt0470752.

Garreau, Joel. Bots on the ground. *Washington Post*, 2007. URL http://washingtonpost.com/wp-dyn/content/article/2007/05/05/AR2007050501009.html.

Gazzaley, Adam and Rosen, Larry D. *The Distracted Mind: Ancient Brains in a High-Tech World*. MIT Press, Cambridge, MA, 2016. ISBN 978-0262534437. URL http://worldcat.org/oclc/978487215.

Geisslinger, Maximilian, Poszler, Franziska, Betz, Johannes, Lütge, Christoph, and Lienkamp, Markus. Autonomous driving ethics: From trolley problem to ethics of risk. *Philosophy & Technology*, 34:1033–1055, 2021. doi: 10.1007/s13347-021-00449-4.

Gendolla, Guido H. E. On the impact of mood on behavior: An integrative theory and a review. *Review of General Psychology*, 4(4):378–408, 2000. doi: 10.1037/1089-2680.4.4.378.

Genschow, Oliver, van Den Bossche, Sofie, Cracco, Emiel, Bardi, Lara, Rigoni, Davide, and Brass, Marcel. Mimicry and automatic imitation are not correlated. *PloS One*, 12(9): e0183784, 2017. doi: 10.1371/journal.pone.0183784.

Geraci, Robert M. Spiritual robots: Religion and our scientific view of the natural world. *Theology and Science*, 4(3):229–246, 2006. doi: 10.1080/14746700600952993.

Gibson, James J. *The Ecological Approach to Visual Perception: Classic Edition*. Psychology Press, London, 2014. ISBN 978-1848725782. URL http://worldcat.org/oclc/896794768.

Glas, Dylan F, Kanda, Takayuki, Ishiguro, Hiroshi, and Hagita, Norihiro. Teleoperation of multiple social robots. *IEEE Transactions on Systems, Man, and Cybernetics-Part A: Systems and Humans*, 42(3):530–544, 2011. URL https://doi.org/10.1109/TSMCA.2011.2164243.

Glas, Dylan F., Kanda, Takayuki, and Ishiguro, Hiroshi. Human-robot interaction design using Interaction Composer eight years of lessons learned. In *11th ACM/IEEE International Conference on Human-Robot Interaction (HRI)*, pages 303–310. Institute of Electrical and Electronics Engineers, Piscataway, NJ, 2016. doi: 10.1109/HRI.2016.7451766.

Gockley, Rachel, Bruce, Allison, Forlizzi, Jodi, Michalowski, Marek, Mundell, Anne, Rosenthal, Stephanie, Sellner, Brennan, Simmons, Reid, Snipes, Kevin, Schultz, Alan C., et al. Designing robots for long-term social interaction. In *IEEE/RSJ International Conference on Intelligent Robots and Systems*, pages 1338–1343. Institute of Electrical and Electronics Engineers, Piscataway, NJ, 2005. ISBN 0-7803-8912-3. doi: 10.1109/IROS.2005.1545303.

Gockley, Rachel, Forlizzi, Jodi, and Simmons, Reid. Interactions with a moody robot. In *Proceedings of the 1st ACM SIGCHI/SIGART Conference on Human-Robot Interaction*, pages 186–193. Association for Computing Machinery, New York, 2006. ISBN 1-59593-294-1. doi: 10.1145/1121241.1121274.

Gockley, Rachel, Forlizzi, Jodi, and Simmons, Reid. Natural person-following behavior for social robots. In *ACM/IEEE International Conference on Human-Robot Interaction*, pages 17–24. Institute of Electrical and Electronics Engineers, Piscataway, NJ, 2007. ISBN 978-1-59593-617-2. doi: 10.1145/1228716.1228720.

Goldacre, Ben. *Bad Science*. Fourth Estate, London, 2008. ISBN 9780007240197. URL http://worldcat.org/oclc/760098401.

Gonsior, Barbara, Sosnowski, Stefan, Mayer, Christoph, Blume, Jürgen, Radig, Bernd, Wollherr, Dirk, and Kühnlenz, Kolja. Improving aspects of empathy and subjective performance for HRI through mirroring facial expressions. In *2011 RO-MAN*, pages 350–356. Institute of Electrical and Electronics Engineers, Piscataway, NJ, 2011. doi: 10.1109/ROMAN.2011.6005294.

González-González, Carina Soledad, Gil-Iranzo, Rosa María, and Paderewski-Rodríguez, Patricia. Human–robot interaction and sexbots: A systematic literature review. *Sensors*, 21(1):216, 2020. doi: 10.3390/s21010216.

Goodfellow, Ian, Bengio, Yoshua, and Courville, Aaron. *Deep Learning*. MIT Press, Cambridge, MA, 2016. ISBN 9780262035613. URL www.deeplearningbook.org.

Goodman, Joseph K., Cryder, Cynthia E., and Cheema, Amar. Data collection in a flat world: The strengths and weaknesses of Mechanical Turk samples. *Journal of Behavioral Decision Making*, 26(3):213–224, 2013. doi: 10.1002/bdm.1753.

Goodrich, Michael A. and Schultz, Alan C. Human–robot interaction: A survey. *Foundations and Trends in Human–Computer Interaction*, 1(3):203–275, 2008. URL http://doi.org/10.1561/1100000005.

Graether, Eberhard and Mueller, Florian. Joggobot: A flying robot as jogging companion. In *CHI '12 Extended Abstracts on Human Factors in Computing Systems*, pages 1063–1066. Association for Computing Machinery, New York, 2012. ISBN 978-1-4503-1016-1. doi: 10.1145/2212776.2212386.

Gray, Heather M., Gray, Kurt, and Wegner, Daniel M. Dimensions of mind perception. *Science*, 315(5812):619–619, 2007. ISSN 0036-8075. doi: 10.1126/science.1134475.

Greenberg, Leslie S. Application of emotion in psychotherapy. In Lewis, Michael, Haviland-Jones, Jeanette M., and Feldman Barrett, Lisa, editors, *Handbook of Emotions*, volume 3, pages 88–101. Guilford Press, New York, 2008. ISBN 978-1-59385-650-2. URL http://citeseerx.ist.psu.edu/viewdoc/download?doi=10.1.1.472.7583&rep=rep1&type=pdf.

Gross, Horst-Michael, Boehme, Hans-Joachim, Schroeter, Christof, Müller, Steffen, König, Alexander, Einhorn, Erik, Martin, Christian, Merten, Matthias, and Bley, Andreas. TOOMAS: Interactive shopping guide robots in everyday use-final implementation and experiences from long-term field trials. In *IEEE/RSJ International Conference on Intelligent Robots and Systems*, pages 2005–2012. Institute of Electrical and Electronics Engineers, Piscataway, NJ, 2009. ISBN 978-1-4244-3803-7. doi: 10.1109/IROS.2009.5354497.

Gross, James J. Emotion regulation: Conceptual foundations. In Gross, James J., editor, *Handbook of Emotion Regulation*, pages 3–22. Guilford Press, New York, 2007. ISBN 978-1462520732. URL http://worldcat.org/oclc/1027033463.

Guest, Greg, Namey, Emily, and Chen, Mario. A simple method to assess and report thematic saturation in qualitative research. *PloS One*, 15(5):e0232076, 2020. doi: 10.1371/journal.pone.0232076.

Guidi, Stefano, Boor, Latisha, van der Bij, Laura, Foppen, Robin, Rikmenspoel, Okke, and Perugia, Giulia. Ambivalent stereotypes towards gendered robots: The (im) mutability of bias towards female and neutral robots. In *Social Robotics: 14th International Conference, ICSR 2022, Florence, Italy, December 13–16, 2022, Proceedings, Part II*, pages 615–626. Springer, Cham, Switzerland, 2023. doi: 10.1007/978-3-031-24670-8_54.

Gunes, Hatice, Schuller, Björn, Pantic, Maja, and Cowie, Roddy. Emotion representation, analysis and synthesis in continuous space: A survey. In *IEEE International Conference on Automatic Face & Gesture Recognition and Workshops*, pages 827–834. Institute of Electrical and Electronics Engineers, Piscataway, NJ, 2011. ISBN 978-1-4244-9140-7. doi: 10.1109/FG.2011.5771357.

Haegele, Martin. *World Robotics Service Robots*. IFR Statistical Department, Chicago, IL, 2016. ISBN 9783816306948. URL http://worldcat.org/oclc/979905174.

Hall, Edward T. *The Silent Language*. Anchor Books, USA, 1990. URL https://worldcat.org/oclc/21118399.

Hall, Edward T., Birdwhistell, Ray L., Bock, Bernhard, Bohannan, Paul, Diebold Jr., A. Richard, Durbin, Marshall, Edmonson, Munro S., Fischer, J. L., Hymes, Dell, Kimball, Solon T., et al. Proxemics [and comments and replies]. *Current Anthropology*, 9(2/3):83–108, 1968. doi: 10.1086/200975.

Han, Jeonghye, Moore, Dylan, and Bae, Ilhan. Exploring the social proxemics of human–drone interaction. *International Journal of Advanced Smart Convergence*, 8(2):1–7, 2019. doi: 10.7236/IJASC.2019.8.2.1.

Han, Kun, Yu, Dong, and Tashev, Ivan. Speech emotion recognition using deep neural network and extreme learning machine. In *15th Annual Conference of the International Speech Communication Association*, pages 223–227. International Speech Communication Association, 2014. URL www.isca-speech.org/archive/interspeech_2014/han14_interspeech.html.

Hancock, Peter A., Billings, Deborah R., Schaefer, Kristin E., Chen, Jessie Y. C., De Visser, Ewart J., and Parasuraman, Raja. A meta-analysis of factors affecting trust in human-robot interaction. *Human Factors*, 53(5):517–527, 2011. doi: 10.1177/0018720811417254.

Hancock, Peter A., Kessler, Theresa T., Kaplan, Alexandra D., Brill, John C., and Szalma, James L. Evolving trust in robots: Specification through sequential and comparative meta-analyses. *Human Factors*, 63(7):1196–1229, 2021. doi: 10.1177/0018720820922080.

Hashimoto, Takuya, Verner, Igor M., and Kobayashi, Hiroshi. Human-like robot as teacher's representative in a science lesson: An elementary school experiment. In Kim, Jong-Huan, Matson, Eric T., Myung, Hyun, and Xu, Peter, editors, *Robot Intelligence Technology and Applications*, volume 208 of Advances in Intelligent Systems and Computing, pages 775–786. Springer, Cham, Switzerland, 2013. doi: 10.1007/978-3-642-37374-9_74.

Haslam, Nick. Dehumanization: An integrative review. *Personality and Social Psychology Review*, 10(3):252–264, 2006. doi: 10.1207/s15327957pspr1003_4.

Haslam, Nick and Loughnan, Steve. Dehumanization and infrahumanization. *Annual Review of Psychology*, 65(1):399–423, 2014. doi: 10.1146/annurev-psych-010213-115045.

Haslam, Nick, Loughnan, Stephen, Kashima, Yoshihisa, and Bain, Paul. Attributing and denying humanness to others. *European Review of Social Psychology*, 19(1):55–85, 2008. doi: 10.1080/10463280801981645.

Hassenzahl, Marc. The thing and I: understanding the relationship between user and product. In Blythe, Mark A., Overbeeke, Kees, Monk, Andrew F., and Wright, Peter C., editors, *Funology*, pages 31–42. Springer, New York, 2003. ISBN 978-1-4020-2967-7. doi: 10.100 7/1-4020-2967-5_4.

Hawkins, Andrew J. and Lawler, Richard. Tesla finally begins shipping "Full Self-Driving" beta version 9 after a long delay. *The Verge*, 2021. URL www.theverge.com/2021/7/10/225 70081/tesla-fsd-v9-beta-autopilot-update.

Hayashi, Kotaro, Shiomi, Masahiro, Kanda, Takayuki, Hagita, Norihiro, and Robotics, AI. Friendly patrolling: A model of natural encounters. In Durrant-Whyte, Hugh, Roy, Nicholas, and Abbeel, Pieter, editors, *Robotics: Science and Systems, Volume II*, pages 121–129. MIT Press, Cambridge, MA, 2012. ISBN 978-0-262-51779-9. URL http://worldcat.org/oclc/85 8018257.

Heerink, Marcel, Krose, Ben, Evers, Vanessa, and Wielinga, Bob. Measuring acceptance of an assistive social robot: A suggested toolkit. In *RO-MAN 2009: The 18th IEEE International Symposium on Robot and Human Interactive Communication*, pages 528–533. Institute of Electrical and Electronics Engineers, Piscataway, NJ, 2009. doi: 10.1109/ROMAN.2009.5 326320.

Heerink, Marcel, Kröse, Ben, Evers, Vanessa, and Wielinga, Bob. Assessing acceptance of assistive social agent technology by older adults: The Almere Model. *International Journal of Social Robotics*, 2(4):361–375, 2010. doi: 10.1007/s12369-010-0068-5.

Hegel, Frank, Muhl, Claudia, Wrede, Britta, Hielscher-Fastabend, Martina, and Sagerer, Gerhard. Understanding social robots. In *2009 Second International Conferences on Advances in Computer-Human Interactions*, pages 169–174. Institute of Electrical and Electronics Engineers, Piscataway, NJ, 2009. doi: 10.1109/ACHI.2009.51.

Hegel, Frank, Eyssel, Friederike, and Wrede, Britta. The social robot "Flobi": Key concepts of industrial design. In *19th International Symposium in Robot and Human Interactive Communication (RO-MAN)*, pages 107–112. Institute of Electrical and Electronics Engineers, Piscataway, NJ, 2010. doi: 10.1109/ROMAN.2010.5598691.

Heider, Fritz and Simmel, Marianne. An experimental study of apparent behavior. *American Journal of Psychology*, 57(2):243–259, 1944. doi: 10.2307/1416950.

Heldner, Mattias and Edlund, Jens. Pauses, gaps and overlaps in conversations. *Journal of Phonetics*, 38(4):555–568, 2010. doi: 10.1016/j.wocn.2010.08.002.

Henschel, Anna and Cross, Emily S. No evidence for enhanced likeability and social motivation towards robots after synchrony experience. *Interaction Studies*, 21(1):7–23, 2020. doi: 10 .1075/is.19004.hen.

Hjortsjo, Carl-Herman. *Man's Face and Mimic Language*. Studen litteratur, Sweden, 1969. URL http://worldcat.org/oclc/974134474.

Ho, Chin-Chang and MacDorman, Karl F. Revisiting the uncanny valley theory: Developing and validating an alternative to the Godspeed indices. *Computers in Human Behavior*, 26 (6):1508–1518, 2010. doi: 10.1016/j.chb.2010.05.015.

Hoffman, Guy. Dumb robots, smart phones: A case study of music listening companionship. In *The 21st IEEE International Symposium on Robot and Human Interactive Communication*, pages 358–363. Institute of Electrical and Electronics Engineers, Piscataway, NJ, 2012. ISBN 978-1-4673-4604-7. doi: 10.1109/ROMAN.2012.6343779.

Hoffman, Guy. Anki, Jibo, and Kuri: What we can learn from social robots that didn't make it. *IEEE Spectrum*, 2019. URL https://spectrum.ieee.org/anki-jibo-and-kuri-what-we-can-learn-from-social-robotics-failures.

Hoffman, Guy and Breazeal, Cynthia. Effects of anticipatory action on human-robot teamwork efficiency, fluency, and perception of team. In *Proceedings of the ACM/IEEE International*

Conference on Human-Robot Interaction, pages 1–8. Association for Computing Machinery, New York, 2007. ISBN 978-1-59593-617-2. doi: 10.1145/1228716.1228718.

Hoffman, Guy and Vanunu, Keinan. Effects of robotic companionship on music enjoyment and agent perception. In *8th ACM/IEEE International Conference on Human-Robot Interaction*, pages 317–324. Institute of Electrical and Electronics Engineers, Piscataway, NJ, 2013. ISBN 978-1-4673-3099-2. doi: 10.1109/HRI.2013.6483605.

Hoffman, Guy and Weinberg, Gil. Shimon: An interactive improvisational robotic marimba player. In *CHI'10 Extended Abstracts on Human Factors in Computing Systems*, pages 3097–3102. Association for Computing Machinery, New York, 2010. ISBN 978-1-60558-930-5. doi: 10.1145/1753846.1753925.

Hoffman, Guy and Zhao, Xuan. A primer for conducting experiments in human–robot interaction. *ACM Transactions on Human-Robot Interaction (THRI)*, 10(1):1–31, 2020. doi: 10.1145/3412374.

Holm, Olle. Analyses of longing: Origins, levels, and dimensions. *Journal of Psychology*, 133 (6):621–630, 1999. doi: 10.1080/00223989909599768.

Hood, Deanna, Lemaignan, Séverin, and Dillenbourg, Pierre. When children teach a robot to write: An autonomous teachable humanoid which uses simulated handwriting. In *10th Annual ACM/IEEE International Conference on Human-Robot Interaction*, pages 83–90. Association for Computing Machinery, New York, 2015. ISBN 978-1-4503-2883-8. doi: 10.1145/2696454.2696479.

Howard, Ayanna and Borenstein, Jason. Hacking the human bias in robotics. *ACM Transactions on Human-Robot Interaction (THRI)*, 7(1):1–3, 2018. doi: 10.1145/3208974.

Howard, Ayanna and Kennedy III, Monroe. Robots are not immune to bias and injustice. *Science Robotics*, 5(48):eabf1364, 2020. doi: 10.1126/scirobotics.abf1364.

Hu, Siying, Yen, Hen Chen, Yu, Ziwei, Zhao, Mingjian, Seaborn, Katie, and Liu, Can. Wizundry: A cooperative Wizard of Oz platform for simulating future speech-based interfaces with multiple wizards. *Proceedings of the ACM on Human-Computer Interaction*, 7(CSCW1):1–34, 2023. doi: 10.1145/3579591.

Huggins, Matthew, Alghowinem, Sharifa, Jeong, Sooyeon, Colon-Hernandez, Pedro, Breazeal, Cynthia, and Park, Hae Won. Practical guidelines for intent recognition: Bert with minimal training data evaluated in real-world HRI application. In *Proceedings of the 2021 ACM/IEEE International Conference on Human-Robot Interaction*, pages 341–350. Association for Computing Machinery, New York, 2021. URL https://doi.org/10.1145/343407 3.3444671.

Hunt, Andrew J. and Black, Alan W. Unit selection in a concatenative speech synthesis system using a large speech database. In *IEEE International Conference on Acoustics, Speech, and Signal Processing*, volume 1, pages 373–376. Institute of Electrical and Electronics Engineers, Piscataway, NJ, 1996. ISBN 0-7803-3192-3. doi: 10.1109/ICASSP.1996.541110.

Hüttenrauch, Helge, Eklundh, Kerstin Severinson, Green, Anders, and Topp, Elin A. Investigating spatial relationships in human-robot interaction. In *IEEE/RSJ International Conference on Intelligent Robots and Systems*, pages 5052–5059. Institute of Electrical and Electronics Engineers, Piscataway, NJ, 2006. ISBN 1-4244-0258-1. doi: 10.1109/IROS.2006.282535.

Hwang, Jinsoo, Kim, Heather, Joo, Kyu-Hyeon, and Lee, Won Seok. How to form rapport with information providers in the airport industry: Service robots versus human staff. *Asia Pacific Journal of Tourism Research*, 27(8):891–906, 2022. doi: 10.1080/10941665.2022.2131447.

Ibarz, Julian, Tan, Jie, Finn, Chelsea, Kalakrishnan, Mrinal, Pastor, Peter, and Levine, Sergey. How to train your robot with deep reinforcement learning: Lessons we have learned. *International Journal of Robotics Research*, 40(4–5):698–721, 2021. URL https://doi.org/10.1177/0278364920987859.

Imai, Michita, Ono, Tetsuo, and Ishiguro, Hiroshi. Physical relation and expression: Joint attention for human-robot interaction. *IEEE Transactions on Industrial Electronics*, 50(4): 636–643, 2003. doi: 10.1109/TIE.2003.814769.

Inamura, Tetsunari, Mizuchi, Yoshiaki, and Yamada, Hiroki. VR platform enabling crowd-sourcing of embodied HRI experiments—Case study of online robot competition. *Advanced Robotics*, 35(11):697–703, 2021. URL https://doi.org/10.1080/01691864.2021.1928551.

Irfan, Bahar, Kennedy, James, Lemaignan, Séverin, Papadopoulos, Fotios, Senft, Emmanuel, and Belpaeme, Tony. Social psychology and human-robot interaction: An uneasy marriage. In *Companion of the 2018 ACM/IEEE International Conference on Human-Robot Interaction*, pages 13–20. Association for Computing Machinery, New York, 2018. ISBN 978-1-4503-5615-2. doi: 10.1145/3173386.3173389.

Ishiguro, Hiroshi. Android science. In Thrun, Sebastian, Rodney, Brooks, and Hugh, Durrant-Whyte, editors, *Robotics Research*, pages 118–127. Springer-Verlag, Berlin, 2007. ISBN 978-3-540-48110-2. doi: 10.1007/978-3-540-48113-3_11.

Ishiguro, Hiroshi and Dalla Libera, Fabio. *Geminoid Studies: Science and Technologies for Humanlike Teleoperated Androids*. Springer Nature, Singapore, 2018.

Jia, He Michael, Park, C. Whan, and Pol, Gratiana. Cuteness, nurturance, and implications for visual product design. In Batra, Rajeev, Seifert, Colleen M., and Brei, Diann, editors, *The Psychology of Design*, pages 168–179. Routledge, Milton Park, Abingdon, Oxfordshire, UK, 2015. ISBN 9781317502104. URL www.worldcat.org/title/914472421.

Johal, Wafa, Gatos, Doga, Yantac, Asim Evren, and Obaid, Mohammad. Envisioning social drones in education. *Frontiers in Robotics and AI*, 9:666736, 2022. doi: 10.3389/frobt .2022.666736.

John, Oliver P. and Srivastava, Sanjay. The Big Five trait taxonomy: History, measurement, and theoretical perspectives. In Pervin, Lawrence A. and John, Oliver P., editors, *Handbook of Personality: Theory and Research*, pages 102–138. Guilford Press, New York, 2nd edition, 1999. ISBN 9781572306950. URL www.worldcat.org/title/1229125792.

Johnson, Michelle Jillian, Rai, Roshan, Barathi, Sarath, Mendonca, Rochelle, and Bustamante-Valles, Karla. Affordable stroke therapy in high-, low- and middle-income countries: From Theradrive to Rehab CARES, a compact robot gym. *Journal of Rehabilitation and Assistive Technologies Engineering*, 4:2055668317708732, 2017. doi: 10.1177/2055668317708732.

Jonze, dir., Spike. *Her*. Warner Bros., Burbank, CA, 2013. URL www.imdb.com/title/tt1798709/?ref_=fn_al_tt_1.

Joormann, Jutta and Gotlib, Ian H. Emotion regulation in depression: Relation to cognitive inhibition. *Cognition and Emotion*, 24(2):281–298, 2010. doi: 10.1080/02699930903407 948.

Jung, Malte and Hinds, Pamela. Robots in the wild: A time for more robust theories of human-robot interaction. *ACM Transactions on Human-Robot Interaction (THRI)*, 7(1):2, 2018. doi: 10.1145/3208975.

Jung, Malte F., Martelaro, Nikolas, and Hinds, Pamela J. Using robots to moderate team conflict: The case of repairing violations. In *Proceedings of the Tenth Annual ACM/IEEE International Conference on Human-Robot Interaction*, pages 229–236. Association for Computing Machinery, New York, 2015. doi: 10.1145/2696454.2696460.

Jung, Minjoo, Lazaro, May Jorella S, and Yun, Myung Hwan. Evaluation of methodologies and measures on the usability of social robots: A systematic review. *Applied Sciences*, 11 (4):1388, 2021. doi: 10.3390/app11041388.

Kahn, Peter H., Freier, Nathan G., Kanda, Takayuki, Ishiguro, Hiroshi, Ruckert, Jolina H., Severson, Rachel L., and Kane, Shaun K. Design patterns for sociality in human-robot interaction. In *The 3rd ACM/IEEE International Conference on Human-Robot Interaction*, pages 97–104. Association for Computing Machinery, New York, 2008. ISBN 978-1-60558-017-3. doi: 10.1145/1349822.1349836.

Kahn, Peter H., Kanda, Takayuki, Ishiguro, Hiroshi, Gill, Brian T., Ruckert, Jolina H., Shen, Solace, Gary, Heather E., Reichert, Aimee L., Freier, Nathan G., and Severson, Rachel L. Do people hold a humanoid robot morally accountable for the harm it causes? In *Proceedings of the 7th Annual ACM/IEEE International Conference on Human-Robot Interaction*, pages 33–40. Association for Computing Machinery, New York, 2012. ISBN 978-1-4503-1063-5. doi: 10.1145/2157689.2157696.

Kahn, Peter H., Kanda, Takayuki, Ishiguro, Hiroshi, Shen, Solace, Gary, Heather E., and Ruckert, Jolina H. Creative collaboration with a social robot. In *ACM International Joint Conference on Pervasive and Ubiquitous Computing*, pages 99–103. Association for Computing Machinery, New York, 2014. ISBN 978-1-4503-2968-2. doi: 10.1145/263204 8.2632058.

Kahneman, Daniel. *Thinking, Fast and Slow*. Macmillan, New York, 2011. ISBN 978-0374533557. URL https://worldcat.org/en/title/706020998.

Kamino, Waki and Šabanović, Selma, Coffee, tea, robots? The performative staging of service robots in "Robot Cafes" in Japan. In *Proceedings of the 2023 ACM/IEEE International Conference on Human-Robot Interaction*, pages 183–191. Association for Computing Machinery, New York, 2023. doi: 10.1145/3568162.3576967.

Kanda, Takayuki, Hirano, Takayuki, Eaton, Daniel, and Ishiguro, Hiroshi. Interactive robots as social partners and peer tutors for children: A field trial. *Human-Computer Interaction*, 19 (1):61–84, 2004. doi: 10.1080/07370024.2004.9667340.

Kanda, Takayuki, Kamasima, Masayuki, Imai, Michita, Ono, Tetsuo, Sakamoto, Daisuke, Ishiguro, Hiroshi, and Anzai, Yuichiro. A humanoid robot that pretends to listen to route guidance from a human. *Autonomous Robots*, 22(1):87–100, 2007a. doi: 10.1007/s10514-0 06-9007-6.

Kanda, Takayuki, Sato, Rumi, Saiwaki, Naoki, and Ishiguro, Hiroshi. A two-month field trial in an elementary school for long-term human-robot interaction. *IEEE Transactions on Robotics*, 23(5):962–971, 2007b. doi: 10.1109/TRO.2007.904904.

Kanda, Takayuki, Shiomi, Masahiro, Miyashita, Zenta, Ishiguro, Hiroshi, and Hagita, Norihiro. A communication robot in a shopping mall. *IEEE Transactions on Robotics*, 26(5):897–913, 2010. doi: 10.1109/TRO.2010.2062550.

Kaneko, Kenji, Kanehiro, Fumio, Kajita, Shuuji, Hirukawa, Hirohisa, Kawasaki, T., Hirata, M., Akachi, Kazuhiku, and Isozumi, Takakatsu. Humanoid robot HRP-2. In *IEEE International Conference on Robotics and Automation*, volume 2, pages 1083–1090, 2004. doi: 10.1109/ ROBOT.2004.1307969.

Kaneshige, Yuya, Satake, Satoru, Kanda, Takayuki, and Imai, Michita. How to overcome the difficulties in programming and debugging mobile social robots? In *Proceedings of the 2021 ACM/IEEE International Conference on Human-Robot Interaction*, pages 361–369. Association for Computing Machinery, New York, 2021. URL https://doi.org/10.1145/34 34073.3444674.

Kang, Kyong Il, Freedman, Sanford, Mataric, Maja J., Cunningham, Mark J., and Lopez, Becky. A hands-off physical therapy assistance robot for cardiac patients. In *9th International Conference on Rehabilitation Robotics (ICORR)*, pages 337–340. Institute of Electrical and Electronics Engineers, Piscataway, NJ, 2005. ISBN 0-7803-9003-2. doi: 10.1109/ICORR.2005.1501114.

Kaplan, Alexandra, Kessler, Theresa, Brill, Christopher, and Hancock, P. A. Trust in Artificial Intelligence: Meta-analytic findings. *Human Factors*, 65(2):337–359, 2021. doi: 10.1177/ 00187208211013988.

Kaplan, Frederic. Who is afraid of the humanoid? Investigating cultural differences in the acceptance of robots. *International Journal of Humanoid Robotics*, 1(3):1–16, 2004. doi: 10.1142/S0219843604000289.

Kaptelinin, Victor. Technology and the givens of existence: Toward an existential inquiry framework in HCI research. In *Proceedings of the 2018 CHI Conference on Human Factors in Computing Systems*, pages 270:1–270:14. Association for Computing Machinery, New York, 2018. ISBN 978-1-4503-5620-6. doi: 10.1145/3173574.3173844.

Karim, Raida, Zhang, Yufei, Alves-Oliveira, Patrícia, Björling, Elin A., and Cakmak, Maya. Community-based data visualization for mental well-being with a social robot. In *2022 17th ACM/IEEE International Conference on Human-Robot Interaction (HRI)*, pages 839–843. Institute of Electrical and Electronics Engineers, Piscataway, NJ, 2022. doi: 10.1109/HRI5 3351.2022.9889415.

Kato, Yusuke, Kanda, Takayuki, and Ishiguro, Hiroshi. May I help you? Design of human-like polite approaching behavior. In *10th Annual ACM/IEEE International Conference on Human-Robot Interaction*, pages 35–42. Association for Computing Machinery, New York, 2015. ISBN 978-1-4503-2883-8. doi: 10.1145/2696454.2696463.

Kätsyri, Jari, Förger, Klaus, Mäkäräinen, Meeri, and Takala, Tapio. A review of empirical evidence on different uncanny valley hypotheses: Support for perceptual mismatch as one road to the valley of eeriness. *Frontiers in Psychology*, 6:390, 2015. doi: 10.3389/fpsyg.2015.00390.

Keijsers, Merel, Bartneck, Christoph, and Eyssel, Friederike. What's to bullying a bot? Correlates between chatbot humanlikeness and abuse. *Interaction Studies*, 22(1):55–80, 2021. doi: 10.1075/is.20002.kei.

Keltner, Dacher and Kring, Ann M. Emotion, social function, and psychopathology. *Review of General Psychology*, 2(3):320–342, 1998. doi: 10.1037/1089-2680.2.3.320.

Kemper, Theodore D. How many emotions are there? Wedding the social and the autonomic components. *American Journal of Sociology*, 93(2):263–289, 1987. doi: 10.1086/228745.

Kendon, Adam. *Conducting Interaction: Patterns of Behavior in Focused Encounters*. Cambridge University Press, Cambridge, 1990. ISBN 978-0521389389. URL http://worldcat.org/oclc/785489376.

Kennedy, James, Baxter, Paul, and Belpaeme, Tony. The robot who tried too hard: Social behaviour of a robot tutor can negatively affect child learning. In *10th Annual ACM/IEEE International Conference on Human-Robot Interaction*, pages 67–74. Association for Computing Machinery, New York, 2015. ISBN 978-1-4503-2883-8. doi: 10.1145/2696454.2696457.

Kennedy, James, Lemaignan, Séverin, Montassier, Caroline, Lavalade, Pauline, Irfan, Bahar, Papadopoulos, Fotios, Senft, Emmanuel, and Belpaeme, Tony. Child speech recognition in human-robot interaction: Evaluations and recommendations. In *Proceedings of the ACM/IEEE International Conference on Human-Robot Interaction*, pages 82–90. Association for Computing Machinery, New York, 2017. ISBN 978-1-4503-4336-7. doi: 10.1145/2909824.3020229.

Kessler, Theresa T., Larios, Cintya, Walker, Tiffani, Yerdon, Valarie, and Hancock, P. A. A comparison of trust measures in human–robot interaction scenarios. In *Advances in Human Factors in Robots and Unmanned Systems*, pages 353–364. Springer Nature, Cham, Switzerland, 2017. doi: 10.1007/978-3-319-41959-6_29.

Kidd, Cory D. and Breazeal, Cynthia. A robotic weight loss coach. In *Proceedings of the 22nd National Conference on Artificial Intelligence—Volume 2*, pages 1985–1986. AAAI Press, Washington, DC, 2007. ISBN 978-1-57735-323-2. URL http://dl.acm.org/citation.cfm?id=1619797.1619992.

Kidd, Cory D. and Breazeal, Cynthia. Robots at home: Understanding long-term human-robot interaction. In *IEEE/RSJ International Conference on Intelligent Robots and Systems*, pages 3230–3235. Institute of Electrical and Electronics Engineers, Piscataway, NJ, 2008. ISBN 978-1-4244-2057-5. doi: 10.1109/IROS.2008.4651113.

Kiesler, Sara, Powers, Aaron, Fussell, Susan R., and Torrey, Cristen. Anthropomorphic interactions with a robot and robot-like agent. *Social Cognition*, 26(2):169–181, 2008. doi: 10.1521/soco.2008.26.2.169.

Kim, Ki Joon, Park, Eunil, and Sundar, S. Shyam. Caregiving role in human–robot interaction: A study of the mediating effects of perceived benefit and social presence. *Computers in Human Behavior*, 29(4):1799–1806, 2013. doi: 10.1016/j.chb.2013.02.009.

Kirmeyer, Sandra L. and Lin, Thung-Rung. Social support: Its relationship to observed communication with peers and superiors. *Academy of Management Journal*, 30(1):138–151, 1987. doi: 10.5465/255900.

Kitano, Naho. "Rinri": An incitement towards the existence of robots in Japanese society. *International Review of Information Ethics*, 6(12/2):78–83, 2006. URL http://i-r-i-e.net/inhalt/006/006_Kitano.pdf.

Klassner, Frank. A case study of LEGO Mindstorms suitability for artificial intelligence and robotics courses at the college level. *SIGCSE Bulletin*, 34(1):8–12, February 2002. ISSN 0097-8418. doi: 10.1145/563517.563345.

Koay, Kheng Lee, Sisbot, Emrah Akin, Syrdal, Dag Sverre, Walters, Mick L., Dautenhahn, Kerstin, and Alami, Rachid. Exploratory study of a robot approaching a person in the context of handing over an object. In *AAAI Spring Symposium: Multidisciplinary Collaboration for Socially Assistive Robotics*, pages 18–24. AAAI Press, Washington, DC, 2007a. URL http://aaai.org/Papers/Symposia/Spring/2007/SS-07-07/SS07 07 004.pdf.

Koay, Kheng Lee, Syrdal, Dag Sverre, Walters, Michael L., and Dautenhahn, Kerstin. Living with robots: Investigating the habituation effect in participants' preferences during a longitudinal human-robot interaction study. In *The 16th IEEE International Symposium on Robot and Human Interactive Communication*, pages 564–569. Institute of Electrical and Electronics Engineers, Piscataway, NJ, 2007b. ISBN 978-1-4244-1634-9. doi: 10.1109/RO MAN.2007.4415149.

Koike, Mayu and Loughnan, Steve. Virtual relationships: Anthropomorphism in the digital age. *Social and Personality Psychology Compass*, 15(6):e12603, 2021. doi: 10.1111/spc3.12603.

Koike, Mayu, Loughnan, Steve, and Stanton, Sarah C. E. Virtually in love: The role of anthropomorphism in virtual romantic relationships. *British Journal of Social Psychology*, 62(1):600–616, 2022. doi: 10.1111/bjso.12564.

Kollar, Thomas, Tellex, Stefanie, Roy, Deb, and Roy, Nicholas. Toward understanding natural language directions. In *5th ACM/IEEE International Conference on Human-Robot Interaction*, pages 259–266. Institute of Electrical and Electronics Engineers, Piscataway, NJ, 2010. ISBN 978-1-4244-4892-0. doi: 10.1109/HRI.2010.5453186.

Koo, Jeamin, Kwac, Jungsuk, Ju, Wendy, Steinert, Martin, Leifer, Larry, and Nass, Clifford. Why did my car just do that? Explaining semi-autonomous driving actions to improve driver understanding, trust, and performance. *International Journal on Interactive Design and Manufacturing (IJIDeM)*, 9(4):269–275, 2015. doi: 10.1007/s12008-014-0227-2.

Kopp, Stefan, Krenn, Brigitte, Marsella, Stacy, Marshall, Andrew N., Pelachaud, Catherine, Pirker, Hannes, Thórisson, Kristinn R., and Vilhjálmsson, Hannes. Towards a common framework for multimodal generation: The behavior markup language. In *International Workshop on Intelligent Virtual Agents*, pages 205–217. Springer, Berlin, 2006. ISBN 978-3-540-37593-7. doi: 10.1007/11821830_17.

Kozima, Hideki, Michalowski, Marek P., and Nakagawa, Cocoro. Keepon. *International Journal of Social Robotics*, 1(1):3–18, 2009. doi: 10.1007/s12369-008-0009-8.

Krausman, Andrea, Neubauer, Catherine, Forster, Daniel, Lakhmani, Shan, Baker, Anthony L., Fitzhugh, Sean M., Gremillion, Gregory, Wright, Julia L., Metcalfe, Jason S., and Schaefer, Kristin E. Trust measurement in human-autonomy teams: Development of a conceptual toolkit. *ACM Transactions on Human-Robot Interaction*, 11(3):1–58, 2022. doi: 10.114 5/3530874.

Kriz, Sarah, Anderson, Gregory, and Trafton, J. Gregory. Robot-directed speech: Using language to assess first-time users' conceptualizations of a robot. In *5th ACM/IEEE International Conference on Human-Robot Interaction (HRI)*, pages 267–274. Association for Computing Machinery, New York, 2010. doi: 10.1109/HRI.2010.5453187.

Kruse, Thibault, Pandey, Amit Kumar, Alami, Rachid, and Kirsch, Alexandra. Human-aware robot navigation: A survey. *Robotics and Autonomous Systems*, 61(12):1726–1743, 2013. doi: 10.1016/j.robot.2013.05.007.

Ku, Hyunjin, Choi, Jason J, Lee, Soomin, Jang, Sunho, and Do, Wonkyung. Designing shelly, a robot capable of assessing and restraining children's robot abusing behaviors. In *Companion of the 13th ACM/IEEE International Conference on Human-Robot Interaction (HRI)*, pages 161–162. Association for Computing Machinery, New York, 2018. doi: 10.1145/3173386.3176973.

Kubota, Tomonori, Ogawa, Kohei, Yoshikawa, Yuichiro, and Ishiguro, Hiroshi. Alignment of the attitude of teleoperators with that of a semi-autonomous android. *Scientific Reports*, 12 (1):1–12, 2022. doi: 10.1038/s41598-022-13829-3.

Kuchenbrandt, Dieta, Riether, Nina, and Eyssel, Friederike. Does anthropomorphism reduce stress in HRI? In *Proceedings of the 2014 ACM/IEEE International Conference on Human-Robot Interaction*, pages 218–219. Association for Computing Machinery, New York, 2014. ISBN 978-1-4503-2658-2. doi: 10.1145/2559636.2563710.

Kuhn, Thomas S. *The Structure of Scientific Revolutions*. University of Chicago Press, Chicago, 2nd edition, 1970. ISBN 0226458032. URL http://worldcat.org/oclc/468581998.

Kulic, Dana and Croft, Elizabeth A. Safe planning for human-robot interaction. *Journal of Field Robotics*, 22(7):383–396, 2005. doi: 10.1002/rob.20073.

Kulms, Philipp and Kopp, Stefan. More human-likeness, more trust? The effect of anthropomorphism on self-reported and behavioral trust in continued and interdependent human-agent cooperation. In Alt, Florian, Bulling, Andreas, and Döring, Tanja, editors, *Proceedings of Mensch und Computer 2019*, pages 31–42. Association for Computing Machinery, New York, 2019. doi: 10.1145/3340764.3340793.

Kuzuoka, Hideaki, Suzuki, Yuya, Yamashita, Jun, and Yamazaki, Keiichi. Reconfiguring spatial formation arrangement by robot body orientation. In *5th ACM/IEEE International Conference on Human-Robot Interaction*, pages 285–292. Institute of Electrical and Electronics Engineers, Piscataway, NJ, 2010. ISBN 978-1-4244-4892-0. doi: 10.1109/HRI.20 10.5453182.

Lang, Peter J., Bradley, Margaret M., and Cuthbert, Bruce N. Motivated attention: Affect, activation, and action. In Lang, Peter J., Simons, Robert F., Balaban, Marie, and Simons, Robert, editors, *Attention and Orienting: Sensory and Motivational Processes*, pages 97–135. Erlbaum, Hillsdale, NJ, 1997. ISBN 9781135808204. URL http://worldcat.org/oclc/949987355.

Lara, Juan S., Casas, Jonathan, Aguirre, Andres, Munera, Marcela, Rincon-Roncancio, Monica, Irfan, Bahar, Senft, Emmanuel, Belpaeme, Tony, and Cifuentes, Carlos A. Human-robot sensor interface for cardiac rehabilitation. In *International Conference on Rehabilitation Robotics (ICORR)*, pages 1013–1018. Institute of Electrical and Electronics Engineers, Piscataway, NJ, 2017. ISBN 978-1-5386-2296-4. doi: 10.1109/ICORR.2017.8009382.

Large, David R., Harrington, Kyle, Burnett, Gary, Luton, Jacob, Thomas, Peter, and Bennett, Pete. To please in a pod: Employing an anthropomorphic agent-interlocutor to enhance trust and user experience in an autonomous, self-driving vehicle. In *Proceedings of the 11th International Conference on Automotive User Interfaces and Interactive Vehicular Applications*, pages 49–59. Association for Computing Machinery, New York, 2019. doi: 10.1145/3342197.3344545.

Larsen, Randy J. and Diener, Edward. Promises and problems with the circumplex model of emotion. In Clark, Margaret S., editor, *Emotion: The Review of Personality and Social Psychology*, volume 13, pages 25–59. SAGE Publications, Thousand Oaks, CA, 1992. ISBN 978-0803946149. URL http://worldcat.org/oclc/180631851.

Law, Theresa, Chita-Tegmark, Meia, Rabb, Nicholas, and Scheutz, Matthias. Examining attachment to robots: Benefits, challenges, and alternatives. *ACM Transactions on Human-Robot Interaction (THRI)*, 11(4):1–18, 2022. doi: 10.1145/3526105.

Layton, Roslyn. The grain of truth in the critique of Musk, Tesla and Full Self Driving (FSD). *Forbes*, 2022. URL www.forbes.com/sites/roslynlayton/2022/01/28/the-grain-of-truth-in-the-critique-of-musk-tesla-and-full-self-driving-fsd/?sh=336663d454b7.

Lazarus, Richard S. *Emotion and Adaptation*. Oxford University Press on Demand, 1991. ISBN 978-0195092660. URL http://worldcat.org/oclc/298419692.

LeCun, Yann, Bengio, Yoshua, and Hinton, Geoffrey. Deep learning. *Nature*, 521(7553):436, 2015. doi: 10.1038/nature14539.

Lee, Hee Rin, Sung, JaYoung, Šabanović, Selma, and Han, Joenghye. Cultural design of domestic robots: A study of user expectations in Korea and the United States. In *IEEE International Workshop on Robot and Human Interactive Communication*, pages 803–808.

Institute of Electrical and Electronics Engineers, Piscataway, NJ, 2012. ISBN 978-1-4673-4604-7. doi: 10.1109/ROMAN.2012.6343850.

Lee, Hee Rin, Šabanović, Selma, Chang, Wan-Ling, Nagata, Shinichi, Piatt, Jennifer, Bennett, Casey, and Hakken, David. Steps toward participatory design of social robots: Mutual learning with older adults with depression. In *ACM/IEEE International Conference on Human-Robot Interaction*, pages 244–253. Association for Computing Machinery, New York, 2017. ISBN 978-1-4503-4336-7. doi: 10.1145/2909824.3020237.

Lee, John D. and See, Katrina A. Trust in automation: Designing for appropriate reliance. *Human Factors*, 46(1):50–80, 2004. doi: 10.1518/hfes.46.1.50_30392.

Lee, Min Kyung, Forlizzi, Jodi, Rybski, Paul E., Crabbe, Frederick, Chung, Wayne, Finkle, Josh, Glaser, Eric, and Kiesler, Sara. The Snackbot: Documenting the design of a robot for long-term human-robot interaction. In *Proceedings of the ACM/IEEE International Conference on Human-Robot Interaction*, pages 7–14. Association for Computing Machinery, New York, 2009. ISBN 978-1-60558-404-1. doi: 10.1145/1514095.1514100.

Lee, Sau-lai, Lau, Ivy Yee-man, Kiesler, Sara, and Chiu, Chi-Yue. Human mental models of humanoid robots. In *IEEE International Conference on Robotics and Automation*, pages 2767–2772. Institute of Electrical and Electronics Engineers, Piscataway, NJ, 2005. ISBN 0-7803-8914-X. doi: 10.1109/ROBOT.2005.1570532.

Lehmann, Hagen, Saez-Pons, Joan, Syrdal, Dag Sverre, and Dautenhahn, Kerstin. In good company? Perception of movement synchrony of a non-anthropomorphic robot. *PloS One*, 10(5):e0127747, 2015. doi: 10.1371/journal.pone.0127747.

Leite, Iolanda, Castellano, Ginevra, Pereira, André, Martinho, Carlos, and Paiva, Ana. Modelling empathic behaviour in a robotic game companion for children: An ethnographic study in real-world settings. In *Proceedings of the 7th Annual ACM/IEEE International Conference on Human-Robot Interaction*, HRI '12, pages 367–374, New York, 2012. Association for Computing Machinery, New York. ISBN 978-1-4503-1063-5. doi: 10.1145/2157689.2157811.

Leite, Iolanda, Martinho, Carlos, and Paiva, Ana. Social robots for long-term interaction: A survey. *International Journal of Social Robotics*, 5(2):291–308, 2013. doi: 10.1007/s12369-013-0178-y.

Leite, Iolanda, McCoy, Marissa, Lohani, Monika, Ullman, Daniel, Salomons, Nicole, Stokes, Charlene, Rivers, Susan, and Scassellati, Brian. Emotional storytelling in the classroom: Individual versus group interaction between children and robots. In *Proceedings of the 10th Annual ACM/IEEE International Conference on Human-Robot Interaction*, pages 75–82. Association for Computing Machinery, New York, 2015. ISBN 978-1-4503-2883-8. doi: 10.1145/2696454.2696481.

Lemaignan, Séverin, Fink, Julia, and Dillenbourg, Pierre. The dynamics of anthropomorphism in robotics. In *2014 9th ACM/IEEE International Conference on Human-Robot Interaction (HRI)*, pages 226–227. Institute of Electrical and Electronics Engineers, Piscataway, NJ, 2014a. doi: 10.1145/2559636.2559814.

Lemaignan, Séverin, Fink, Julia, Dillenbourg, Pierre, and Braboszcz, Claire. The cognitive correlates of anthropomorphism. In *2014 Human-Robot Interaction Conference, HRI: A Bridge between Robotics and Neuroscience Workshop*. Institute of Electrical and Electronics Engineers, Piscataway, NJ, 2014b. doi: 10.1007/s12369-014-0263-x.

Lemaignan, Séverin, Hanheide, Marc, Karg, Michael, Khambhaita, Harmish, Kunze, Lars, Lier, Florian, Lütkebohle, Ingo, and Milliez, Grégoire. Simulation and HRI recent perspectives with the morse simulator. In Brugali, Davide, Broenink, Jan F., Kroeger, Torsten, and MacDonald, Bruce A., editors, *Simulation, Modeling, and Programming for Autonomous Robots*, pages 13–24. Springer International, Cham, Switzerland, 2014c. ISBN 978-3-319-11900-7. doi: 10.1007/978-3-319-11900-7_2.

Lemaignan, Séverin, Hanheide, Marc, Karg, Michael, Khambhaita, Harmish, Kunze, Lars, Lier, Florian, Lütkebohle, Ingo, and Milliez, Grégoire. Simulation and HRI: Recent perspectives with the MORSE simulator. In Brugali, Davide, Broenink, Jan, Kroeger, Torsten, and MacDonald, Bruce, editors, *Simulation, Modeling, and Programming for Autonomous*

Robots: 4th International Conference, SIMPAR 2014, Bergamo, Italy, October 20–23, 2014. Proceedings 4, pages 13–24. Springer, Cham, Switzerland, 2014d. doi: 10.1007/978-3-319 -11900-7_2.

Lemaignan, Séverin, Warnier, Mathieu, Sisbot, E. Akin, Clodic, Aurélie, and Alami, Rachid. Artificial cognition for social human-robot interaction: An implementation. *Artificial Intelligence*, 247:45–69, 2017. ISSN 0004-3702. doi: 10.1016/j.artint.2016.07.002.

Lenat, Douglas B. CYC: A large-scale investment in knowledge infrastructure. *Communications of the ACM*, 38(11):33–38, 1995. doi: 10.1145/219717.219745.

Lewis, Michael, Wang, Jijun, and Hughes, Stephen. Usarsim: Simulation for the study of human-robot interaction. *Journal of Cognitive Engineering and Decision Making*, 1(1):98–120, 2007. doi: 10.1177/155534340700100105.

Leyens, Jacques-Philippe. Retrospective and prospective thoughts about infrahumanization. *Group Processes & Intergroup Relations*, 12(6):807–817, 2009. doi: 10.1177/1368430209 347330.

Leyens, Jacques-Philippe, Paladino, Paola M, Rodriguez-Torres, Ramon, Vaes, Jeroen, Demoulin, Stephanie, Rodriguez-Perez, Armando, and Gaunt, Ruth. The emotional side of prejudice: The attribution of secondary emotions to ingroups and outgroups. *Personality and Social Psychology Review*, 4(2):186–197, 2000. doi: 10.1207/S15327957PSPR0402_06.

Leyzberg, Daniel, Spaulding, Samuel, Toneva, Mariya, and Scassellati, Brian. The physical presence of a robot tutor increases cognitive learning gains. In *Proceedings of the Cognitive Science Society*, pages 1882–1887. Cognitive Science Society, Seattle, WA, 2012. URL https://escholarship.org/uc/item/7ck0p200.

Li, Fuan and Betts, Stephen C. Trust: What it is and what it is not. *International Business & Economics Research Journal (IBER)*, 2(7), 2003. doi: 10.19030/iber.v2i7.3825.

Li, Mengjun and Suh, Ayoung. Machinelike or humanlike? A literature review of anthropomorphism in AI-enabled technology. In *Proceedings of the 54th Hawaii International Conference on System Sciences*. University of Hawai, Honolulu, 2021. doi: 10.24251/ HICSS.2021.493.

Li, Zhenni, Terfurth, Leonie, Woller, Joshua Pepe, and Wiese, Eva. Mind the machines: Applying implicit measures of mind perception to social robotics. In *2022 17th ACM/IEEE International Conference on Human-Robot Interaction (HRI)*, pages 236–245. Institute of Electrical and Electronics Engineers, Piscataway, NJ, 2022. doi: 10.1109/HRI53351.2022. 9889356.

Lin, Patrick, Abney, Keith, and Bekey, George A. *Robot Ethics: The Ethical and Social Implications of Robotics*. Intelligent Robotics and Autonomous Agents. MIT Press, Cambridge, MA, 2012. ISBN 9780262016667. URL http://worldcat.org/oclc/1004334474.

Lindblom, Jessica and Andreasson, Rebecca. Current challenges for UX evaluation of human-robot interaction. In Schlick, Christopher and Trzcieliński, Stefan, editors, *Advances in Ergonomics of Manufacturing: Managing the Enterprise of the Future*, pages 267–277. Springer Nature, Cham, Switzerland, 2016. doi: 10.1007/978-3-319-41697-7_24.

Lindblom, Jessica and Ziemke, Tom. Social situatedness of natural and Artificial Intelligence: Vygotsky and beyond. *Adaptive Behavior*, 11(2):79–96, 2003. doi: 10.1177/105971230301 12002.

Lindblom, Jessica, Alenljung, Beatrice, and Billing, Erik. Evaluating the user experience of human–robot interaction. In *Human-Robot Interaction*, pages 231–256. Springer, Cham, Switzerland, 2020. doi: 10.1007/978-3-030-42307-0_9.

Litman, Todd. Autonomous vehicle implementation predictions: Implications for transport planning, 2020. URL www.vtpi.org/avip.pdf.

Liu, Peng, Du, Yong, Wang, Lin, and Da Young, Ju. Ready to bully automated vehicles on public roads? *Accident Analysis & Prevention*, 137:105457, 2020. doi: 10.1016/j.aap.2020 .105457.

Liu, Phoebe, Glas, Dylan F., Kanda, Takayuki, Ishiguro, Hiroshi, and Hagita, Norihiro. It's not polite to point: Generating socially-appropriate deictic behaviors towards people. In *The 8th ACM/IEEE International Conference on Human-Robot Interaction*, pages 267–274.

Institute of Electrical and Electronics Engineers, Piscataway, NJ, 2013. ISBN 978-1-4673-3099-2. doi: 10.1109/HRI.2013.6483598.

Liu, Phoebe, Glas, Dylan F., Kanda, Takayuki, and Ishiguro, Hiroshi. Data-driven HRI: Learning social behaviors by example from human-human interaction. *IEEE Transactions on Robotics*, 32(4):988–1008, 2016. ISSN 1552-3098. doi: 10.1109/TRO.2016.2588880.

Löffler, Diana, Dörrenbächer, Judith, and Hassenzahl, Marc. The uncanny valley effect in zoomorphic robots: The U-shaped relation between animal likeness and likeability. In *Proceedings of the 2020 ACM/IEEE International Conference on Human-Robot Interaction, pages 261–270*. Association for Computing Machinery, New York, 2020. doi: 10.1145/3319502.3374788.

Loughnan, Stephen and Haslam, Nick. Animals and androids: Implicit associations between social categories and nonhumans. *Psychological Science*, 18(2):116–121, 2007. doi: 10.1111/j.1467-9280.2007.01858.x.

Lovett, Amber. *Coding with Blockly*. Cherry Lake, Ann Arbor, MI, 2017. ISBN 978-1634721851. URL https://worldcat.org/en/title/953327379.

Lowdermilk, Travis. *User-Centered Design: A Developer's Guide to Building User-Friendly Applications*. O'Reilly, Sebastopol, CA, 2013. ISBN 978-1449359805. URL http://worldcat.org/oclc/940703603.

Lowe, Andrew, Norris, Anthony C., Farris, A. Jane, and Babbage, Duncan R. Quantifying thematic saturation in qualitative data analysis. *Field Methods*, 30(3):191–207, 2018. doi: 10.1177/1525822X17749386.

Luber, Matthias, Spinello, Luciano, Silva, Jens, and Arras, Kai O. Socially-aware robot navigation: A learning approach. In *IEEE/RSJ International Conference on Intelligent Robots and Systems*, pages 902–907. Institute of Electrical and Electronics Engineers, Piscataway, NJ, 2012. ISBN 978-1-4673-1737-5. doi: 10.1109/IROS.2012.6385716.

Lugrin, Birgit, Pelachaud, Catherine, André, Elisabeth, Aylett, Ruth, Bickmore, Timothy, Breazeal, Cynthia, Broekens, Joost, Dautenhahn, Kerstin, Gratch, Jonathan, Kopp, Stefan, Nadel, Jacqueline, Paiva, Ana, and Wykowska, Agnieszka. *Challenge Discussion on Socially Interactive Agents: Considerations on Social Interaction, Computational Architectures, Evaluation, and Ethics*, page 561–626. Association for Computing Machinery, New York, NY, USA, 1 edition, 2022. ISBN 9781450398961. doi: 10.1145/3563659.3563677.

Lutin, Jerome M., Kornhauser, Alain L., and Lerner-Lam, Eva. The revolutionary development of self-driving vehicles and implications for the transportation engineering profession. *ITE Journal (Institute of Transportation Engineers)*, 83(7):28–32, 2013. URL www.scopus.com/inward/record.uri?eid=2-s2.0-84883648917&partnerID=40&md5=33f8d1b58422c14174e4690152c619cc.

Lyu, Xiao-Kang, Xu, Yuepei, Zhao, Xiao-Fan, Zuo, Xi-Nian, and Hu, Chuan-Peng. Beyond psychology: Prevalence of p value and confidence interval misinterpretation across different fields. *Journal of Pacific Rim Psychology*, 14:e6, 2020. doi: 10.1017/prp.2019.28.

MacDorman, Karl F., Vasudevan, Sandosh K., and Ho, Chin-Chang. Does Japan really have robot mania? Comparing attitudes by implicit and explicit measures. *AI & SOCIETY*, 23(4): 485–510, Jul 2009. ISSN 1435-5655. doi: 10.1007/s00146-008-0181-2.

Macrae, C. Neil and Quadflieg, Susanne. *Perceiving People*, chapter 12. John Wiley & Sons, Hoboken, NJ, 2010. ISBN 9780470561119. doi: 10.1002/9780470561119.socpsy001012.

Manzeschke, Arne. Roboter in der Pflege: Von Menschen, Maschinen und anderen hilfreichen Wesen. *EthikJournal*, 2019(1), 2019. URL www.ethikjournal.de/fileadmin/user_upload/ethikjournal/Texte_Ausgabe_2019_1/Manzeschke_1.Nov_FINAL.pdf.

Mar, Alex. Modern love: Are we ready for intimacy with androids? *Wired Magazine*, October 2017. URL www.wired.com/2017/10/hiroshi-ishiguro-when-robots-act-just-like-humans/. Online; accessed 7-September-2018.

Marchesi, Serena, Ghiglino, Davide, Ciardo, Francesca, Perez-Osorio, Jairo, Baykara, Ebru, and Wykowska, Agnieszka. Do we adopt the intentional stance toward humanoid robots? *Frontiers in Psychology*, 10:450, 2019. doi: 10.3389/fpsyg.2019.00450.

Marshall, Aarian and Davies, Alex. Uber's self-driving car saw the woman it killed, report says. *Wired Magazine*, March 2018. URL www.wired.com/story/uber-self-driving-crash-arizona-ntsb-report/. Online; accessed 7-November-2018.

Marshall, Paul, Rogers, Yvonne, and Pantidi, Nadia. Using F-formations to analyse spatial patterns of interaction in physical environments. In *Proceedings of the ACM 2011 Conference on Computer Supported Cooperative Work*, pages 445–454. Association for Computing Machinery, New York, 2011. ISBN 978-1-4503-0556-3. doi: 10.1145/1958824.1958893.

Martelaro, Nikolas and Ju, Wendy. WoZ way: Enabling real-time remote interaction prototyping & observation in on-road vehicles. In *Proceedings of the 2017 ACM Conference on Computer Supported Cooperative Work and Social Computing*, pages 169–182. Association for Computing Machinery, New York, 2017. doi: 10.1145/2998181.2998293.

Matarić, Maja J. *The Robotics Primer*. MIT Press, Cambridge, MA, 2007. ISBN 9780262633543. URL www.worldcat.org/oclc/604083625.

Matheus, Kayla, Vázquez, Marnyel, and Scassellati, Brian. A social robot for anxiety reduction via deep breathing. In *2022 31st IEEE International Conference on Robot and Human Interactive Communication (RO-MAN)*, pages 89–94. Institute of Electrical and Electronics Engineers, Piscataway, NJ, 2022. doi: 10.1109/RO-MAN53752.2022.9900638.

Mavridis, Nikolaos. A review of verbal and non-verbal human–robot interactive communication. *Robotics and Autonomous Systems*, 63(1):22–35, 2015. ISSN 0921-8890. doi: 10.1016/j.robot.2014.09.031.

Maxwell, Scott E., Lau, Michael Y., and Howard, George S. Is psychology suffering from a replication crisis? What does "failure to replicate" really mean? *American Psychologist*, 70 (6):487, 2015. doi: 10.1037/a0039400.

Mayer, Richard E. and DaPra, C. Scott. An embodiment effect in computer-based learning with animated pedagogical agents. *Journal of Experimental Psychology: Applied*, 18(3): 239–252, 2012. doi: 10.1037/a0028616.

McCorduck, Pamela. *Machines Who Think: A Personal Inquiry into the History and Prospects of Artificial Intelligence*. W. H. Freeman, San Francisco, 1979. ISBN 978-1568812052. URL http://worldcat.org/oclc/748860627.

McDermott, Drew. Yes, computers can think. *New York Times*, 1997. URL http://nytimes.com/1997/05/14/opinion/yes-computers-can-think.html.

McLaren, Ian P. L., Forrest, Charlotte L. D., McLaren, Rossy P., Jones, Fergal William, Aitken, Michael, and Mackintosh, Nicholas J. Associations and propositions: The case for a dual-process account of learning in humans. *Neurobiology of Learning and Memory*, 108:185–195, 2014. doi: 10.1016/j.nlm.2013.09.014.

McQuillin, Emily, Churamani, Nikhil, and Gunes, Hatice. Learning socially appropriate robowaiter behaviours through real-time user feedback. In *2022 17th ACM/IEEE International Conference on Human-Robot Interaction (HRI)*, pages 541–550. Institute of Electrical and Electronics Engineers, Piscataway, NJ, 2022. URL https://doi.org/10.1109/HRI53351.2022.9889395.

Mehrabian, Albert. *Basic Dimensions for a General Psychological Theory: Implications for Personality, Social, Environmental, and Developmental Studies*. Oelgeschlager, Gunn & Hain, Cambridge, MA, 1980. ISBN 978-0899460048. URL http://worldcat.org/oclc/9251 30232.

Mehrabian, Albert and Russell, James A. *An Approach to Environmental Psychology*. MIT Press, Cambridge, MA, 1974. ISBN 9780262630719. URL http://worldcat.org/oclc/3181 33343.

Mehta, Vikas. The new proxemics: COVID-19, social distancing, and sociable space. *Journal of Urban Design*, 25(6):669–674, 2020. doi: doi.org/10.1080/13574809.2020.1785283.

Michalowski, Marek P., Šabanović, Selma, and Simmons, Reid. A spatial model of engagement for a social robot. In *9th IEEE International Workshop on Advanced Motion Control*, pages 762–767. Institute of Electrical and Electronics Engineers, Piscataway, NJ, 2006. ISBN 0-7803-9511-1. doi: 10.1109/AMC.2006.1631755.

Michalowski, Marek P., Šabanović, Selma, and Kozima, Hideki. A dancing robot for rhythmic social interaction. In *2nd ACM/IEEE International Conference on Human-Robot Interaction*, pages 89–96. Institute of Electrical and Electronics Engineers, Piscataway, NJ, 2007. ISBN 978-1-59593-617-2. doi: 10.1145/1228716.1228729.

Mieczkowski, Hannah, Liu, Sunny Xun, Hancock, Jeffrey, and Reeves, Byron. Helping not hurting: Applying the stereotype content model and bias map to social robotics. In *2019 14th ACM/IEEE International Conference on Human-Robot Interaction (HRI)*, pages 222–229. Institute of Electrical and Electronics Engineers, Piscataway, NJ, 2019. doi: 10.1109/HRI.2019.8673307.

Mitchel, Russ. DMV probing whether Tesla violates state regulations with self-driving claims. *Los Angeles Times*, 2021. URL www.latimes.com/business/story/2021-05-17/dmv-tesla-california-fsd-autopilot-safety.

Mitra, Sushmita and Acharya, Tinku. Gesture recognition: A survey. *IEEE Transactions on Systems, Man, and Cybernetics, Part C (Applications and Reviews)*, 37(3):311–324, 2007. doi: 10.1109/TSMCC.2007.893280.

Mitsunaga, Noriaki, Smith, Christian, Kanda, Takayuki, Ishiguro, Hiroshi, and Hagita, Norihiro. Adapting robot behavior for human–robot interaction. *IEEE Transactions on Robotics*, 24(4):911–916, 2008. URL https://doi.org/10.1109/TRO.2008.926867.

Mlekus, Lisa, Bentler, Dominik, Paruzel, Agnieszka, Kato-Beiderwieden, Anna-Lena, and Maier, Günter W. How to raise technology acceptance: User experience characteristics as technology-inherent determinants. *Gruppe. Interaktion. Organisation. Zeitschrift für Angewandte Organisationspsychologie (GIO)*, 51(3):273–283, 2020. doi: 10.1007/s116 12-020-00529-7.

Moharana, Sanika, Panduro, Alejandro E., Lee, Hee Rin, and Riek, Laurel D. Robots for joy, robots for sorrow: community based robot design for dementia caregivers. In *2019 14th ACM/IEEE International Conference on Human-Robot Interaction (HRI)*, pages 458–467. IEEE, Institute of Electrical and Electronics Engineers, Piscataway, NJ, 2019. doi: 10.110 9/HRI.2019.8673206.

Moore, Roger K. A Bayesian explanation of the "uncanny valley" effect and related psychological phenomena. *Scientific Reports*, 2:864, 2012. doi: 10.1038/srep00864.

Morales Saiki, Luis Yoichi, Satake, Satoru, Kanda, Takayuki, and Hagita, Norihiro. Modeling environments from a route perspective. In *6th International Conference on Human-Robot Interaction*, pages 441–448. Association for Computing Machinery, New York, 2011. ISBN 978-1-4503-0561-7. doi: 10.1145/1957656.1957815.

Morales Saiki, Luis Yoichi, Satake, Satoru, Huq, Rajibul, Glas, Dylan, Kanda, Takayuki, and Hagita, Norihiro. How do people walk side-by-side? Using a computational model of human behavior for a social robot. In *7th Annual ACM/IEEE International Conference on Human-Robot Interaction*, pages 301–308. Association for Computing Machinery, New York, 2012. ISBN 978-1-4503-1063-5. doi: 10.1145/2157689.2157799.

Mori, Masahiro. The uncanny valley. *Energy*, 7:33–35, 1970. doi: 10.1109/MRA.2012 .2192811.

Mori, Masahiro. *The Buddha in the Robot*. Tuttle Publishing, Tokyo, Japan, 1982. ISBN 978-4333010028. URL http://worldcat.org/oclc/843422852.

Mori, Masahiro, MacDorman, Karl F., and Kageki, Norri. The uncanny valley [from the field]. *IEEE Robotics & Automation Magazine*, 19(2):98–100, 2012. doi: 10.1109/MRA.2012.2 192811.

Mosbergen, Dominique. Good job, America. You killed hitchBOT. *Huffpost*, 2015. URL www.huffpost.com/entry/hitchbot-destroyed-philadelphia_n_55bf24cde4b0b23e3c e32a67.

Moscow Times. Third Russian doctor falls from hospital window after coronavirus complaint. *Moscow Times*, May 2020. URL www.themoscowtimes.com/2020/05/04/third-russian-doctor-falls-from-hospital-window-after-coronavirus-complaint-a70176.

Mostafaoui, Ghiles, Schmidt, R. C., Hasnain, Syed Khursheed, Salesse, Robin, and Marin, Ludovic. Human unintentional and intentional interpersonal coordination in interaction with a humanoid robot. *PLoS One*, 17(1):e0261174, 2022. doi: 10.1371/journal.pone.0261174.

Moujahid, Meriam, Hastie, Helen, and Lemon, Oliver. Multi-party interaction with a robot receptionist. In *2022 17th ACM/IEEE International Conference on Human-Robot Interaction (HRI)*, pages 927–931. Institute of Electrical and Electronics Engineers, Piscataway, NJ, 2022. doi: 10.1109/HRI53351.2022.9889641.

Muir, Bonnie M. Trust in automation: Part I. Theoretical issues in the study of trust and human intervention in automated systems. *Ergonomics*, 37(11):1905–1922, 1994. doi: 10.1080/00 140139408964957.

Mumm, Jonathan and Mutlu, Bilge. Human-robot proxemics: Physical and psychological distancing in human-robot interaction. In *Proceedings of the 2011 ACM/IEEE International Conference on Human-Robot Interaction*, pages 331–338. Association for Computing Machinery, New York, 2011. ISBN 978-1-4503-0561-7. doi: 10.1145/1957656.1957786.

Murphy, Mike. The beginning of the end: Google's AI has beaten a top human player at the complex game of Go. *Quartz*, 2016. URL https://qz.com/636637/the-beginning-of-the-end-googles-ai-has-beaten-a-top-human-player-at-the-complex-game-of-go/.

Mutlu, Bilge and Forlizzi, Jodi. Robots in organizations: The role of workflow, social, and environmental factors in human-robot interaction. In *3rd ACM/IEEE International Conference on Human-Robot Interaction*, pages 287–294. Institute of Electrical and Electronics Engineers, Piscataway, NJ, 2008. ISBN 978-1-60558-017-3. doi: 10.1145/1349822.1349 860.

Mutlu, Bilge, Forlizzi, Jodi, and Hodgins, Jessica. A storytelling robot: Modeling and evaluation of human-like gaze behavior. In *6th IEEE-RAS International Conference on Humanoid Robots*, pages 518–523. Citeseer, 2006. ISBN 1-4244-0199-2. doi: https://doi.org/10.1109/ ICHR.2006.321322.

Mutlu, Bilge, Shiwa, Toshiyuki, Kanda, Takayuki, Ishiguro, Hiroshi, and Hagita, Norihiro. Footing in human-robot conversations: How robots might shape participant roles using gaze cues. In *The 4th ACM/IEEE International Conference on Human-Robot Interaction*, pages 61–68. Association for Computing Machinery, New York, 2009. ISBN 978-1-60558-404-1. doi: 10.1145/1514095.1514109.

Mutlu, Bilge, Kanda, Takayuki, Forlizzi, Jodi, Hodgins, Jessica, and Ishiguro, Hiroshi. Conversational gaze mechanisms for humanlike robots. *ACM Transactions on Interactive Intelligent Systems*, 1(2):12, 2012. doi: 10.1145/2070719.2070725.

Nakanishi, Junya, Kuramoto, Itaru, Baba, Jun, Ogawa, Kohei, Yoshikawa, Yuichiro, and Ishiguro, Hiroshi. Continuous hospitality with social robots at a hotel. *SN Applied Sciences*, 2(3):1–13, 2020. doi: 10.1007/s42452-020-2192-7.

Nakauchi, Yasushi and Simmons, Reid. A social robot that stands in line. *Autonomous Robots*, 12(3):313–324, 2002. doi: 10.1023/A:1015273816637.

Naneva, Stanislava, Sarda Gou, Marina, Webb, Thomas L., and Prescott, Tony J. A systematic review of attitudes, anxiety, acceptance, and trust towards social robots. *International Journal of Social Robotics*, 12(6):1179–1201, 2020. doi: 10.1007/s12369-020-00659-4.

Nascimento, Alexandre Moreira, Vismari, Lucio Flavio, Molina, Caroline Bianca Santos Tancredi, Cugnasca, Paulo Sergio, Camargo, Joao Batista, de Almeida, Jorge Rady, Inam, Rafia, Fersman, Elena, Marquezini, Maria Valeria, and Hata, Alberto Yukinobu. A systematic literature review about the impact of artificial intelligence on autonomous vehicle safety. *IEEE Transactions on Intelligent Transportation Systems*, 21(12):4928–4946, 2019. doi: 10.1109/TITS.2019.2949915.

National Roads and Motorists' Association. Driverless cars: The benefits and what it means for the future of mobility, 2018. URL www.mynrma.com.au/cars-and-driving/driver-train ing-and-licences/resources/driverless-cars-the-benefits-and-what-it-means-for-the-futur e-of-mobility.

National Transportation Safety Board. Collision between vehicle controlled by developmental automated driving system and pedestrian, Tempe, Arizona, March 18, 2018.

Report, National Transportation Safety Board, 2019. URL www.ntsb.gov/investigations/AccidentReports/Reports/HAR1903.pdf.

Nauts, Sanne, Langner, Oliver, Huijsmans, Inge, Vonk, Roos, and Wigboldus, Daniël H. J. Forming impressions of personality: A replication and review of Asch's (1946) evidence for a primacy-of-warmth effect in impression formation. *Social Psychology*, 45(3):153, 2014. doi: 10.1027/1864-9335/a000179.

Navigli, Roberto and Ponzetto, Simone Paolo. BabelNet: The automatic construction, evaluation and application of a wide-coverage multilingual semantic network. *Artificial Intelligence*, 193:217–250, 2012. doi: 10.1016/j.artint.2012.07.001.

Nehaniv, Chrystopher L., Dautenhahn, Kerstin, Kubacki, Jens, Haegele, Martin, Parlitz, Christopher, and Alami, Rachid. A methodological approach relating the classification of gesture to identification of human intent in the context of human-robot interaction. In *IEEE International Workshop on Robot and Human Interactive Communication*, pages 371–377. Institute of Electrical and Electronics Engineers, Piscataway, NJ, 2005. ISBN 0780392744. doi: 10.1109/ROMAN.2005.1513807.

Newhart, Veronica Ahumada, Warschauer, Mark, and Sender, Leonard. Virtual inclusion via telepresence robots in the classroom: An exploratory case study. *International Journal of Technologies in Learning*, 23(4):9–25, 2016. ISSN 2327-2686. URL https://escholarship.org/uc/item/9zm4h7nf.

Nguyen, Bang, Melewar, T. C., and Chen, Junsong. A framework of brand likeability: an exploratory study of likeability in firm-level brands. *Journal of Strategic Marketing*, 21 (4):368–390, 2013. doi: 10.1177/030630701303800303.

Niimi, Ryosuke and Watanabe, Katsumi. Consistency of likeability of objects across views and time. *Perception*, 41(6):673–686, 2012. doi: 10.1068/p7240.

Nishiguchi, Shogo, Ogawa, Kohei, Yoshikawa, Yuichiro, Chikaraishi, Takenobu, Hirata, Oriza, and Ishiguro, Hiroshi. Theatrical approach: Designing human-like behaviour in humanoid robots. *Robotics and Autonomous Systems*, 89:158–166, 2017. doi: 10.1016/j.robot.2016.11.017.

Nomura, Tatsuya, Kanda, Takayuki, Kidokoro, Hiroyoshi, Suehiro, Yoshitaka, and Yamada, Sachie. Why do children abuse robots? *Interaction Studies*, 17(3):347–369, 2016. doi: 10.1075/is.17.3.02nom.

Norman, Don. *The Design of Everyday Things: Revised and Expanded Edition*. Basic Books, New York, 2013. ISBN 9780465072996. URL http://worldcat.org/oclc/862103168.

Norman, Donald A. The way I see it: Signifiers, not affordances. *Interactions*, 15(6):18–19, 2008. doi: 10.1145/1409040.1409044.

Nosek, Brian A., Ebersole, Charles R., DeHaven, Alexander, and Mellor, David. The preregistration revolution. *Proceedings of the National Academy of Sciences of the United States of America*, 115(11):2600–2606, 2017. doi: 10.1073/pnas.1708274114.

Nourbakhsh, Illah R., Bobenage, Judith, Grange, Sebastien, Lutz, Ron, Meyer, Roland, and Soto, Alvaro. An affective mobile robot educator with a full-time job. *Artificial Intelligence*, 114(1–2):95–124, 1999. doi: 10.1016/S0004-3702(99)00027-2.

Nourbakhsh, Illah Reza. *Robot Futures*. MIT Press, Cambridge, MA, 2013. ISBN 9780262018623. URL http://worldcat.org/oclc/945438245.

Novikova, Jekaterina and Watts, Leon. Towards artificial emotions to assist social coordination in HRI. *International Journal of Social Robotics*, 7(1):77–88, 2015. doi: 10.1007/s12369-014-0254-y.

Nuzzo, Regina. Statistical errors. *Nature*, 506(7487):150, 2014. doi: 10.1038/506150a.

Obaid, Mohammad, Johal, Wafa, and Mubin, Omar. Domestic drones: Context of use in research literature. In *Proceedings of the 8th International Conference on Human-Agent Interaction*, pages 196–203. Association for Computing Machinery, New York, 2020. doi: 10.1145/3406499.3415076.

Oppenheimer, Daniel M., Meyvis, Tom, and Davidenko, Nicolas. Instructional manipulation checks: Detecting satisficing to increase statistical power. *Journal of Experimental Social Psychology*, 45(4):867–872, 2009. doi: 10.1016/j.jesp.2009.03.009.

Ortony, Andrew and Turner, Terence J. What's basic about basic emotions? *Psychological Review*, 97(3):315, 1990. doi: 10.1037/0033-295X.97.3.315.

Ortony, Andrew, Clore, Gerald, and Collins, Allan. *The Cognitive Structure of Emotions*. Cambridge University Press, Cambridge, 1988. ISBN 978-0521386647. URL http://worldcat.org/oclc/910015120.

Osawa, Hirotaka, Ohmura, Ren, and Imai, Michita. Using attachable humanoid parts for realizing imaginary intention and body image. *International Journal of Social Robotics*, 1(1):109–123, 2009. doi: 10.1007/s12369-008-0004-0.

Pacchierotti, Elena, Christensen, Henrik I., and Jensfelt, Patric. Evaluation of passing distance for social robots. In *The 15th IEEE International Symposium on Robot and Human Interactive Communication*, pages 315–320. Institute of Electrical and Electronics Engineers, Piscataway, NJ, 2006. ISBN 1-4244-0564-5. doi: 10.1109/ROMAN.2006.314436.

Paepcke, Steffi and Takayama, Leila. Judging a bot by its cover: An experiment on expectation setting for personal robots. In *5th ACM/IEEE International Conference on Human-Robot Interaction*, pages 45–52. Institute of Electrical and Electronics Engineers, Piscataway, NJ, 2010. ISBN 978-1-4244-4892-0. doi: 10.1109/HRI.2010.5453268.

Paetzel, Maike, Peters, Christopher, Nyström, Ingela, and Castellano, Ginevra. Congruency matters—How ambiguous gender cues increase a robot's uncanniness. In Agah, Arvin, Cabibihan, John-John, Howard, Ayanna M., Salichs, Miguel A., and He, Hongsheng, editors, *International Conference on Social Robotics*, pages 402–412. Springer, Cham, Switzerland, 2016. doi: 10.1007/978-3-319-47437-3_39.

Paetzel-Prüsmann, Maike. The novelty in the uncanny: Designing interactions to change first impressions. PhD thesis, Acta Universitatis Upsaliensis, 2020. URL http://urn.kb.se/resolve?urn=urn:nbn:se:uu:diva-418921.

Pantic, Maja, Pentland, Alex, Nijholt, Anton, and Huang, Thomas S. Human computing and machine understanding of human behavior: A survey. In S., Huang T., A., Nijholt, M., Pantic, and A., Pentland, editors, *Artificial Intelligence for Human Computing*, volume 4451 of Lecture Notes in Computer Science, pages 47–71. Springer, Berlin, 2007. doi: 10.1007/978-3-540-72348-6_3.

Parasuraman, Raja and Riley, Victor. Humans and automation: Use, misuse, disuse, abuse. *Human Factors*, 39(2):230–253, 1997. doi: 10.1518/001872097778543886.

Park, Hae Won, Gelsomini, Mirko, Lee, Jin Joo, and Breazeal, Cynthia. Telling stories to robots: The effect of backchanneling on a child's storytelling. In *ACM/IEEE International Conference on Human-Robot Interaction*, pages 100–108. Association for Computing Machinery, New York, 2017a. ISBN 978-1-4503-4336-7. doi: 10.1145/2909824.3020245.

Park, Hae Won, Rosenberg-Kima, Rinat, Rosenberg, Maor, Gordon, Goren, and Breazeal, Cynthia. Growing growth mindset with a social robot peer. In *Proceedings of the 2017 ACM/IEEE International Conference on Human-Robot Interaction*, pages 137–145. Association for Computing Machinery, New York, 2017b. doi: 10.1145/2909824.3020213.

Partikska and Kattepur, Ajay. Robotic tele-operation performance analysis via digital twin simulations. In *2022 14th International Conference on COMmunication Systems & NETworkS (COMSNETS)*, pages 415–417. Institute of Electrical and Electronics Engineers, Piscataway, NJ, 2022. doi: 10.1109/COMSNETS53615.2022.9668555.

Partridge, Michael and Bartneck, Christoph. The Invisible Naked Guy: An exploration of a minimalistic robot. In *The First International Conference on Human-Agent Interaction*, pages II–2–p2, 2013. doi: 10.17605/OSF.IO/A4YM5.

Pentland, Alex and Heibeck, Tracy. *Honest Signals: How They Shape Our World*. MIT Press, Cambridge, MA, 2010. ISBN 978-0262515122. URL http://worldcat.org/oclc/646395585.

Pérez-Hurtado, Ignacio, Capitán, Jesús, Caballero, Fernando, and Merino, Luis. Decision-theoretic planning with person trajectory prediction for social navigation. In *Robot 2015: Second Iberian Robotics Conference*, pages 247–258. Springer, Cham, Switzerland, 2016. ISBN 978-3-319-27148-4. doi: 10.1007/978-3-319-27149-1_20.

Perugia, Giulia and Lisy, Dominika. Robot's gendering trouble: A scoping review of gendering humanoid robots and its effects on HRI. arXiv, arXiv:2207.01130, 2022.

Perugia, Giulia, Guidi, Stefano, Bicchi, Margherita, and Parlangeli, Oronzo. The shape of our bias: Perceived age and gender in the humanoid robots of the ABOT database. In *Proceedings of the 2022 ACM/IEEE International Conference on Human-Robot Interaction*, pages 110–119. Institute of Electrical and Electronics Engineers, Piscataway, NJ, 2022. doi: 10.1109/HRI53351.2022.9889366.

Perugia, Giulia, Boor, Latisha, van der Bij, Laura, Rikmenspoel, Okke, Foppen, Robin, and Guidi, Stefano. Models of (often) ambivalent robot stereotypes: Content, structure, and predictors of robots' age and gender stereotypes. In *Proceedings of the 2023 ACM/IEEE International Conference on Human-Robot Interaction*, pages 428–436. Association for Computing Machinery, New York, 2023. doi: 10.1145/3568162.3576981.

Petrovic, Dorde, Mijailovic, Radomir, and Pesic, Dalibor. Traffic accidents with autonomous vehicles: Type of collisions, manoeuvres and errors of conventional vehicles' drivers. *Transportation Research Procedia*, 45:161–168, 2020. ISSN 2352-1465. doi: https://doi.org/10.1016/j.trpro.2020.03.003. URL http://sciencedirect.com/science/article/pii/S23521 46520301654.

Pettigrew, Thomas F., Tropp, Linda R., Wagner, Ulrich, and Christ, Oliver. Recent advances in intergroup contact theory. *International Journal of Intercultural Relations*, 35(3):271–280, 2011. doi: 10.1016/j.ijintrel.2011.03.001.

Picard, Rosalind W. *Affective Computing*. MIT Press, Cambridge, MA, Cambridge, MA, 1997. ISBN 978-0262661157. URL https://mitpress.mit.edu/books/affective-computing.

Pineau, Joelle, Montemerlo, Michael, Pollack, Martha, Roy, Nicholas, and Thrun, Sebastian. Towards robotic assistants in nursing homes: Challenges and results. *Robotics and Autonomous Systems*, 42(3–4):271–281, 2003. doi: 10.1016/S0921-8890(02)00381-0.

Pirsig, Robert M. *Zen and the Art of Motorcycle Maintenance: An Inquiry into Values*. Morrow, New York, 1974. ISBN 0688002307. URL http://worldcat.org/oclc/41356566.

Piumsomboon, Thammathip, Clifford, Rory, and Bartneck, Christoph. Demonstrating Maori haka with Kinect and Nao robots. In *Proceedings of the Seventh Annual ACM/IEEE International Conference on Human-Robot Interaction*, pages 429–430. Association for Computing Machinery, New York, 2012. ISBN 9781450310635. doi: 10.1145/2157689. 2157832.

Pizzagalli, Diego A., Holmes, Avram J., Dillon, Daniel G., Goetz, Elena L., Birk, Jeffrey L., Bogdan, Ryan, Dougherty, Darin D., Iosifescu, Dan V., Rauch, Scott L., and Fava, Maurizio. Reduced caudate and nucleus accumbens response to rewards in unmedicated individuals with major depressive disorder. *American Journal of Psychiatry*, 166(6):702–710, 2009. doi: 10.1016/j.jpsychires.2008.03.001.

Plutchik, Robert Ed and Conte, Hope R. *Circumplex Models of Personality and Emotions*. American Psychological Association, Washington, DC, 1997. ISBN 978-1557983800. URL http://worldcat.org/oclc/442562242.

Pop, Cristina Anamaria, Simut, Ramona, Pintea, Sebastian, Saldien, Jelle, Rusu, Alina, David, Daniel, Vanderfaeillie, Johan, Lefeber, Dirk, and Vanderborght, Bram. Can the social robot Probo help children with autism to identify situation-based emotions? A series of single case experiments. *International Journal of Humanoid Robotics*, 10(3):1350025, 2013. doi: 10.1142/S0219843613500254.

Posner, Jonathan, Russell, James A., and Peterson, Bradley S. The circumplex model of affect: An integrative approach to affective neuroscience, cognitive development, and psychopathology. *Development and Psychopathology*, 17(3):715–734, 2005. doi: 10.101 7/S0954579405050340.

Posner, Michael I. *Cognitive Neuroscience of Attention*. Guilford Press, New York, 2011. ISBN 978-1609189853. URL http://worldcat.org/oclc/958053069.

Powers, Aaron, Kramer, Adam D. I., Lim, Shirlene, Kuo, Jean, Lee, Sau-lai, and Kiesler, Sara. Eliciting information from people with a gendered humanoid robot. In *IEEE International Workshop on Robot and Human Interactive Communication*, pages 158–163. Institute of Electrical and Electronics Engineers, Piscataway, NJ, 2005. ISBN 0-7803-9274-4. doi: 10 .1109/ROMAN.2005.1513773.

Powers, Aaron, Kiesler, Sara, Fussell, Susan, and Torrey, Cristen. Comparing a computer agent with a humanoid robot. In *Proceedings of the ACM/IEEE International Conference on Human-Robot Interaction*, pages 145–152. Association for Computing Machinery, New York, 2007. ISBN 978-1-59593-617-2. doi: 10.1145/1228716.1228736.

Press, Associated. San Francisco supervisors bar police robots from using deadly force for now. *NPR*, 2022. URL www.npr.org/2022/12/06/1141129944/san-francisco-deadly-robots-police.

Pulles, Niels J. and Hartman, Paul. Likeability and its effect on outcomes of interpersonal interaction. *Industrial Marketing Management*, 66:56–63, 2017. doi: 10.1016/j.indmarman.2017.06.008.

Radford, Alec, Kim, Jong Wook, Xu, Tao, Brockman, Greg, McLeavey, Christine, and Sutskever, Ilya. Robust speech recognition via large-scale weak supervision. arXiv, arXiv:2212.04356, 2022. doi: 10.48550/arXiv.2212.04356.

Randall, Natasha, Bennett, Casey C., Šabanović, Selma, Nagata, Shinichi, Eldridge, Lori, Collins, Sawyer, and Piatt, Jennifer A. More than just friends: In-home use and design recommendations for sensing socially assistive robots (SARs) by older adults with depression. *Paladyn, Journal of Behavioral Robotics*, 10(1):237–255, 2019. doi: 10.1515/pjbr-2019-0020.

Randall, Natasha, Šabanović, Selma, Milojević, Staša, and Gupta, Apurva. Top of the class: Mining product characteristics associated with crowdfunding success and failure of home robots. *International Journal of Social Robotics*, 14:149–163, 2022. doi: 10.1007/s12369-021-00776-8.

Reeves, Byron and Nass, Clifford Ivar. *The Media Equation: How People Treat Computers, Television, and New Media Like Real People and Places*. Cambridge University Press, Cambridge, 1996. ISBN 978-1575860534. URL http://worldcat.org/oclc/796222708.

Rehm, Matthias and Krogsager, Anders. Negative affect in human robot interaction—Impoliteness in unexpected encounters with robots. In *Proceedings of the 22nd IEEE International Symposium on Robot and Human Interactive Communication (RO-MAN)*, pages 45–50. Institute of Electrical and Electronics Engineers, Piscataway, NJ, 2013. doi: 10.1109/ROMAN.2013.6628529.

Reich-Stiebert, Natalia and Eyssel, Friederike. Learning with educational companion robots? Toward attitudes on education robots, predictors of attitudes, and application potentials for education robots. *International Journal of Social Robotics*, 7(5):875–888, Nov 2015. ISSN 1875-4805. doi: 10.1007/s12369-015-0308-9.

Reich-Stiebert, Natalia and Eyssel, Friederike. Robots in the classroom: What teachers think about teaching and learning with education robots. In *International Conference on Social Robotics*, pages 671–680. Springer, Cham, Switzerland, 2016. ISBN 978-3-319-47436-6. doi: 10.1007/978-3-319-47437-3_66.

Reich-Stiebert, Natalia and Eyssel, Friederike Anne. Leben mit Robotern-Eine Online-Befragung im deutschen Sprachraum zur Akzeptanz von Servicerobotern im Alltag [Poster], 2013. URL https://pub.uni-bielefeld.de/publication/2907019.

Reichardt, Jasia. *Robots: Fact, Fiction, and Prediction*. Thames and Hudson, London, 1978. ISBN 9780140049381. URL http://worldcat.org/oclc/1001944069.

Remington, Nancy A., Fabrigar, Leandre R., and Visser, Penny S. Reexamining the circumplex model of affect. *Journal of Personality and Social Psychology*, 79(2):286–300, 2000. doi: 10.1037/0022-3514.79.2.286.

Rich, Charles, Ponsler, Brett, Holroyd, Aaron, and Sidner, Candace L. Recognizing engagement in human-robot interaction. In *5th ACM/IEEE International Conference on Human-Robot Interaction*, pages 375–382. Institute of Electrical and Electronics Engineers, Piscataway, NJ, 2010. ISBN 978-1-4244-4892-0. doi: 10.1109/HRI.2010.5453163.

Riek, Laurel D. Wizard of Oz studies in HRI: A systematic review and new reporting guidelines. *Journal of Human-Robot Interaction*, 1(1):119–136, 2012. doi: 10.5898/JHRI.1.1.Riek.

Riek, Laurel D. Robotics technology in mental health care. In Luxton, David D., editor, *Artificial Intelligence in Behavioral and Mental Health Care*, pages 185–203. Elsevier, St. Louis, MO, 2016. doi: 10.1145/3127874.

Riek, Laurel D. Healthcare robotics. *Communications of the ACM*, 60(11):68–78, 2017. doi: 10.1145/3127874.

Riek, Laurel D., Paul, Philip C., and Robinson, Peter. When my robot smiles at me: Enabling human-robot rapport via real-time head gesture mimicry. *Journal on Multimodal User Interfaces*, 3(1–2):99–108, 2010, doi: 10.1007/s12193-009-0020-2.

Rizzolatti, Giacomo and Craighero, Layla. The mirror neuron-system. *Annual Review of Neuroscience*, 27(4):169–192, 2004. doi: 10.1146/annurev.neuro.27.070203.144230.

Robins, Ben, Dautenhahn, Kerstin, and Dickerson, Paul. From isolation to communication: A case study evaluation of robot assisted play for children with autism with a minimally expressive humanoid robot. In *2nd International Conferences on Advances in Computer-Human Interactions*, pages 205–211. Institute of Electrical and Electronics Engineers, Piscataway, NJ, 2009. ISBN 978-1-4244-3351-3. doi: 10.1109/ACHI.2009.32.

Robinson, Hayley, MacDonald, Bruce, and Broadbent, Elizabeth. The role of healthcare robots for older people at home: A review. *International Journal of Social Robotics*, 6(4):575–591, 2014. doi: 10.1007/s12369-014-0242-2.

Roesler, Eileen, Manzey, Dietrich, and Onnasch, Linda. A meta-analysis on the effectiveness of anthropomorphism in human-robot interaction. *Science Robotics*, 6(58):eabj5425, 2021. doi: 10.14279/depositonce-12447.

Roesler, Eileen, Naendrup-Poell, Lara, Manzey, Dietrich, and Onnasch, Linda. Why context matters: The influence of application domain on preferred degree of anthropomorphism and gender attribution in human–robot interaction. *International Journal of Social Robotics*, 14: 1155–1166, 2022. doi: 10.14279/depositonce-15458.

Rohlfing, Katharina, Brand, R. J., and Gogate, L. J. Multimodal motherese. In *Symposium at the X International Congress for Studies in Child Language IASCL 2005*, 2005. URL https://pub.uni-bielefeld.de/record/2618244.

Ros, Raquel, Lemaignan, Séverin, Sisbot, E. Akin, Alami, Rachid, Steinwender, Jasmin, Hamann, Katharina, and Warneken, Felix. Which one? Grounding the referent based on efficient human-robot interaction. In *19th International Symposium in Robot and Human Interactive Communication*, pages 570–575. Institute of Electrical and Electronics Engineers, Piscataway, NJ, 2010. ISBN 1944-9445. doi: 10.1109/ROMAN.2010.5598719.

Rossi, Silvia, Ferland, François, and Tapus, Adriana. User profiling and behavioral adaptation for HRI: A survey. *Pattern Recognition Letters*, 99:3–12, 2017. ISSN 0167-8655. doi: https://doi.org/10.1016/j.patrec.2017.06.002. URL www.sciencedirect.com/science/article/pii/S0167865517301976.

Rothe, Rasmus, Timofte, Radu, and Gool, Luc Van. Deep expectation of real and apparent age from a single image without facial landmarks. *International Journal of Computer Vision (IJCV)*, 126(2):144–157, 2016. doi: 10.1007/s11263-016-0940-3.

Rothenbücher, Dirk, Li, Jamy, Sirkin, David, Mok, Brian, and Ju, Wendy. Ghost driver: A field study investigating the interaction between pedestrians and driverless vehicles. In *25th IEEE International Symposium on Robot and Human Interactive Communication*, pages 795–802. Institute of Electrical and Electronics Engineers, Piscataway, NJ, 2016. ISBN 978-1-5090-3930-2. doi: 10.1109/ROMAN.2016.7745210.

Ruijten, Peter A. M., Terken, Jacques M. B., and Chandramouli, Sanjeev N. Enhancing trust in autonomous vehicles through intelligent user interfaces that mimic human behavior. *Multimodal Technologies and Interaction*, 2(4):62, 2018. doi: 10.3390/mti2040062.

Russell, James A. A circumplex model of affect. *Journal of Personality and Social Psychology*, 39(6):1161–1178, 1980. doi: 10.1037/h0077714.

Russell, James A. and Barrett, Lisa Feldman. Core affect, prototypical emotional episodes, and other things called emotion: Dissecting the elephant. *Journal of Personality and Social Psychology*, 76(5):805, 1999. doi: 10.1037//0022-3514.76.5.805.

Russell, James A., Lewicka, Maria, and Niit, Toomas. A cross-cultural study of a circumplex model of affect. *Journal of Personality and Social Psychology*, 57(5):848–856, 1989. doi: 10.1037/0022-3514.57.5.848.

Russell, Stuart and Norvig, Peter. *Artificial Intelligence: A Modern Approach*. Pearson, Essex, UK, 4th edition, 2022. ISBN 978-1292401133. URL www.worldcat.org/oclc/1242911311.

Rutherford, Mel D. and Towns, Ashley M. Scan path differences and similarities during emotion perception in those with and without autism spectrum disorders. *Journal of Autism and Developmental Disorders*, 38(7):1371–1381, 2008. doi: 10.1007/s10803-007-0525-7.

Rymarczyk, Krystyna, Żurawski, Łukasz, Jankowiak-Siuda, Kamila, and Szatkowska, Iwona. Neural correlates of facial mimicry: simultaneous measurements of EMG and BOLD responses during perception of dynamic compared to static facial expressions. *Frontiers in Psychology*, 9:52, 2018. doi: 10.3389/fpsyg.2018.00052.

Šabanović, Selma. Imagine all the robots: Developing a critical practice of cultural and disciplinary traversals in social robotics. PhD thesis, Doctoral Thesis Faculty of Rensselaer Polytechnic Institute, 2007. URL https://hdl.handle.net/20.500.13015/4057.

Šabanović, Selma. Emotion in robot cultures: Cultural models of affect in social robot design. In *Proceedings of the Conference on Design & Emotion (D&E2010)*, pages 4–11, 2010. doi: 10.5281/zenodo.2596814.

Šabanović, Selma and Chang, Wan-Ling. Socializing robots: Constructing robotic sociality in the design and use of the assistive robot PARO. *AI & Society*, 31(4):537–551, 2016. doi: 10.1007/s00146-015-0636-1.

Šabanović, Selma, Michalowski, Marek P., and Simmons, Reid. Robots in the wild: Observing human-robot social interaction outside the lab. In *9th IEEE International Workshop on Advanced Motion Control*, pages 596–601. Institute of Electrical and Electronics Engineers, Piscataway, NJ, 2006. ISBN 0-7803-9511-1. doi: 10.1109/AMC.2006.1631758.

Šabanović, Selma, Reeder, Sarah M., and Kechavarzi, Bobak. Designing robots in the wild: In situ prototype evaluation for a break management robot. *Journal of Human-Robot Interaction*, 3(1):70–88, 2014. ISSN 2163-0364. doi: 10.5898/JHRI.3.1.Sabanovic.

Šabanović, Selma, Chang, Wan-Ling, Bennett, Casey C., Piatt, Jennifer A., and Hakken, David. A robot of my own: Participatory design of socially assistive robots for independently living older adults diagnosed with depression. In *International Conference on Human Aspects of IT for the Aged Population*, pages 104–114. Springer, Cham Switzerland, 2015. ISBN 978-3-319-20891-6. doi: 10.1007/978-3-319-20892-3_11.

Sabel, Charles F. Studied trust: Building new forms of cooperation in a volatile economy. *Human Relations*, 46(9):1133–1170, 1993. doi: 10.1177/00187267930460090.

Sacks, Harvey, Schegloff, Emanuel A., and Jefferson, Gail. A simplest systematics for the organization of turn-taking for conversation. *Language*, 50(4):696–735, 1974. doi: 10.2307/412243.

Saerbeck, Martin and Bartneck, Christoph. Perception of affect elicited by robot motion. In *5th ACM/IEEE International Conference on Human-Robot Interaction*, pages 53–60. Association for Computing Machinery, New York, 2010. ISBN 978-1-4244-4893-7. doi: 10.1145/1734454.1734473.

Saerbeck, Martin, Schut, Tom, Bartneck, Christoph, and Janse, Maddy. Expressive robots in education—Varying the degree of social supportive behavior of a robotic tutor. In *28th ACM Conference on Human Factors in Computing Systems (CHI2010)*, pages 1613–1622. Association for Computing Machinery, New York, 2010. ISBN 978-1-60558-929-9. doi: 10.1145/1753326.1753567.

Sakamoto, Daisuke, Kanda, Takayuki, Ono, Tetsuo, Ishiguro, Hiroshi, and Hagita, Norihiro. Android as a telecommunication medium with a human-like presence. In *2nd ACM/IEEE International Conference on Human-Robot Interaction*, pages 193–200. Institute of Electrical and Electronics Engineers, Piscataway, NJ, 2007. ISBN 978-1-59593-617-2. doi: 10.1145/1228716.1228743.

Salem, Maha, Eyssel, Friederike, Rohlfing, Katharina, Kopp, Stefan, and Joublin, Frank. To err is human(-like): Effects of robot gesture on perceived anthropomorphism and likability.

International Journal of Social Robotics, 5(3):313–323, 2013. doi: 10.1007/s12369-013-0 196-9.

Salvini, P., Ciaravella, G., Yu, W., Ferri, G., Manzi, A., Mazzolai, B., Laschi, C., Oh, S. R., and Dario, P. How safe are service robots in urban environments? Bullying a robot. In *19th International Symposium in Robot and Human Interactive Communication*, pages 368–374. Institute of Electrical and Electronics Engineers, Piscataway, NJ, 2010. ISBN 978-1-4244-7991-7. doi: 10.1109/ROMAN.2010.5654677.

Sandoval, Eduardo Benítez, Brandstatter, Jürgen, Yalçin, Ütku, and Bartneck, Christoph. Robot likeability and reciprocity in human robot interaction: Using ultimatum game to determinate reciprocal likeable robot strategies. *International Journal of Social Robotics*, 13(4):851–862, 2021. doi: 10.1007/s12369-020-00658-5.

Sanghvi, Jyotirmay, Castellano, Ginevra, Leite, Iolanda, Pereira, André, McOwan, Peter W., and Paiva, Ana. Automatic analysis of affective postures and body motion to detect engagement with a game companion. In *6th ACM/IEEE International Conference on Human-Robot Interaction*, pages 305–311. Institute of Electrical and Electronics Engineers, Piscataway, NJ, 2011. ISBN 978-1-4503-0561-7. doi: 10.1145/1957656.1957781.

Sargent, Porter Edward. *The New Immoralities: Clearing the Way for a New Ethics*. Porter Sargent, Boston, MA, 2013. ISBN 978-1258541880. URL http://worldcat.org/oclc/379458 1.

Satake, Satoru, Kanda, Takayuki, Glas, Dylan F., Imai, Michita, Ishiguro, Hiroshi, and Hagita, Norihiro. How to approach humans? Strategies for social robots to initiate interaction. In *4th ACM/IEEE International Conference on Human-Robot Interaction*, pages 109–116. Association for Computing Machinery, New York, 2009. ISBN 978-1-60558-404-1. doi: 10.1145/1514095.1514117.

Sauppé, Allison and Mutlu, Bilge. The social impact of a robot co-worker in industrial settings. In *33rd Annual ACM Conference on Human Factors in Computing Systems*, pages 3613–3622. Association for Computing Machinery, New York, 2015. ISBN 978-1-4503-3145-6. doi: 10.1145/2702123.2702181.

Scassellati, Brian. Imitation and mechanisms of joint attention: A developmental structure for building social skills on a humanoid robot. In L., Nehaniv C., editor, *Computation for Metaphors, Analogy, and Agents*, volume 1562 of Lecture Notes in Computer Science, pages 176–195. Springer, Berlin, 1999. ISBN 978-3-540-65959-4. doi: 10.1007/3-540-488 34-0_11.

Scassellati, Brian. Investigating models of social development using a humanoid robot. In Webb, Barbara and Consi, Thomas, editors, *Biorobotics: Methods and Applications*, pages 145–168. MIT Press, Cambridge, MA, 2000. ISBN 9780262731416. URL http://worldcat .org/oclc/807529041.

Scassellati, Brian, Admoni, Henny, and Matarić, Maja. Robots for use in autism research. *Annual Review of Biomedical Engineering*, 14:275–294, 2012. doi: 10.1146/annurev-bioeng-071811-150036.

Schaefer, Kristin E., Chen, Jessie Y. C., Szalma, James L., and Hancock, Peter A. A meta-analysis of factors influencing the development of trust in automation: Implications for understanding autonomy in future systems. *Human Factors*, 58(3):377–400, 2016. doi: 10.1177/0018720816634228.

Scheepers, Daan, Spears, Russell, Doosje, Bertjan, and Manstead, Antony S. R. The social functions of ingroup bias: Creating, confirming, or changing social reality. *European Review of Social Psychology*, 17(1):359–396, 2006. doi: 10.1080/10463280601088773.

Scherer, Klaus R. Emotion as a multicomponent process: A model and some cross-cultural data. *Review of Personality & Social Psychology*, 5:37–63, 1984. URL https://doi.org/psyc info/1986-17269-001.

Schilbach, Leonhard, Wilms, Marcus, Eickhoff, Simon B., Romanzetti, Sandro, Tepest, Ralf, Bente, Gary, Shah, N. Jon, Fink, Gereon R., and Vogeley, Kai. Minds made for sharing: Initiating joint attention recruits reward-related neurocircuitry. *Journal of Cognitive Neuroscience*, 22(12):2702–2715, 2010. doi: 10.1162/jocn.2009.21401.

Schmiedel, Theresa, Zhong, Vivienne Jia, and Jäger, Janine. Value-sensitive design for AI technologies: Proposition of basic research principles based on social robotics research. In *Proceedings of the 4th Upper-Rhine Artificial Intelligence Symposium*, pages 74–79. Furtwangen University, Furtwangen im Schwarzwald, 2022. ISBN 978-3-00-073637-7. doi: http://doi.org/10.13140/RG.2.2.17162.77762.

Schnoebelen, Tyler and Kuperman, Victor. Using Amazon Mechanical Turk for linguistic research. *Psihologija*, 43(4):441–464, 2010. doi: 10.2298/PSI1004441S.

Schoen, Andrew, Sullivan, Dakota, Zhang, Ze Dong, Rakita, Daniel, and Mutlu, Bilge. Lively: Enabling multimodal, lifelike, and extensible real-time robot motion. In *Proceedings of the 2023 ACM/IEEE International Conference on Human-Robot Interaction*, pages 594–602. Association for Computing Machinery, New York, 2023. doi: 10.1145/3568162.3576982.

Schonenberg, Billy and Bartneck, Christoph. Mysterious machines. In *5th ACM/IEEE International Conference on Human-Robot Interaction*, pages 349–350. Association for Computing Machinery, New York, 2010. ISBN 978-1-4244-4893-7. doi: 10.1145/1734454.1734572.

Schouten, Alexander P., Portegies, Tijs C., Withuis, Iris, Willemsen, Lotte M., and Mazerant-Dubois, Komala. Robomorphism: Examining the effects of telepresence robots on between-student cooperation. *Computers in Human Behavior*, 126:106980, 2022. doi: 10.1016/j.chb.2021.106980.

Schreier, dir., Jake. *Robot and Frank*. Sony Pictures Home Entertainment, Culver City, CA, 2013. URL www.imdb.com/title/tt1990314/.

Seaborn, Katie, Barbareschi, Giulia, and Chandra, Shruti. Not only WEIRD but "uncanny"? A systematic review of diversity in human–robot interaction research. *International Journal of Social Robotics*, 15:1841–1870, 2023. doi: 10.1007/s12369-023-00968-4.

Searle, John. The Chinese room. In Wilson, Robert A. and Keil, Frank C., editors, *The MIT Encyclopedia of the Cognitive Sciences*. MIT Press, Cambridge, MA, 1999. URL https://rintintin.colorado.edu/~vancecd/phil201/Searle.pdf.

Searle, John R. Minds, brains and programs. *Behavioral and Brain Sciences*, 3(3):417–457, 1980. doi: 10.1017/S0140525X00005756.

Sebo, Sarah, Stoll, Brett, Scassellati, Brian, and Jung, Malte F. Robots in groups and teams: A literature review. *Proceedings of the ACM on Human-Computer Interaction*, 4(CSCW2): 1–36, 2020. doi: 10.1145/3415247.

Seeger, Anna-Maria and Heinzl, Armin. Human versus machine: Contingency factors of anthropomorphism as a trust-inducing design strategy for conversational agents. In *Information Systems and Neuroscience*, pages 129–139. Springer, Cham, Switzerland, 2018. doi: 10.1007/978-3-319-67431-5_15.

Seger, Charles R., Smith, Eliot R., Percy, Elise James, and Conrey, Frederica R. Reach out and reduce prejudice: The impact of interpersonal touch on intergroup liking. *Basic and Applied Social Psychology*, 36(1):51–58, 2014. doi: 10.1080/01973533.2013.856786.

Seibt, Johanna, Vestergaard, Christina, and Damholdt, Malene F. The complexity of human social interactions calls for mixed methods in HRI: Comment on "A Primer for Conducting Experiments in Human-robot Interaction," by G. Hoffman and X. Zhao. *ACM Transactions on Human-Robot Interaction (THRI)*, 10(1):1–4, 2021. doi: 10.1145/3439715.

Sequeira, Pedro, Alves-Oliveira, Patrícia, Ribeiro, Tiago, Di Tullio, Eugenio, Petisca, Sofia, Melo, Francisco S., Castellano, Ginevra, and Paiva, Ana. Discovering social interaction strategies for robots from restricted-perception Wizard-of-Oz studies. In *2016 11th ACM/IEEE International Conference on Human-Robot Interaction (HRI)*, pages 197–204. IEEE, Institute of Electrical and Electronics Engineers, Piscataway, NJ, 2016. doi: 10.1109/HRI.2016.7451752.

Shankar, Aparna, Hamer, Mark, McMunn, Anne, and Steptoe, Andrew. Social isolation and loneliness: Relationships with cognitive function during 4 years of follow-up in the English Longitudinal Study of Ageing. *Psychosomatic Medicine*, 75(2):161–170, 2013. doi: 10.1097/PSY.0b013e31827f09cd.

Sharkey, Amanda and Sharkey, Noel. Granny and the robots: Ethical issues in robot care for the elderly. *Ethics and Information Technology*, 14:27–40, 2012. doi: 10.1007/s10676-010 -9234-6.

Sharkey, Amanda J. C. Should we welcome robot teachers? *Ethics and Information Technology*, 18(4):283–297, 2016. doi: 10.1007/s10676-016-9387-z.

Sharma, Megha, Hildebrandt, Dale, Newman, Gem, Young, James E., and Eskicioglu, Rasit. Communicating affect via flight path: Exploring use of the Laban effort system for designing affective locomotion paths. In *8th ACM/IEEE International Conference on Human-Robot Interaction*, pages 293–300. Institute of Electrical and Electronics Engineers, Piscataway, NJ, 2013. ISBN 978-1-4673-3099-2. doi: 10.1109/HRI.2013.6483602.

Shaw-Garlock, Glenda. Looking forward to sociable robots. *International Journal of Social Robotics*, 1(3):249–260, 2009. ISSN 1875-4805. doi: 10.1007/s12369-009-0021-7.

Shi, Chao, Shiomi, Masahiro, Smith, Christian, Kanda, Takayuki, and Ishiguro, Hiroshi. A model of distributional handing interaction for a mobile robot. In Newman, Paul, Fox, Dieter, and Hsu, David, editors, *Robotics: Science and Systems*, pages 24–28. RSS Proceedings, 2013. URL http://roboticsproceedings.org/rss09/p55.pdf.

Shibata, Takanori. Therapeutic seal robot as biofeedback medical device: Qualitative and quantitative evaluations of robot therapy in dementia care. *Proceedings of the IEEE*, 100 (8):2527–2538, 2012. doi: 10.1109/JPROC.2012.2200559.

Shibata, Takanori, Wada, Kazuyoshi, Ikeda, Yousuke, and Šabanović, Selma. Cross-cultural studies on subjective evaluation of a seal robot. *Advanced Robotics*, 23(4):443–458, 2009. doi: 10.1163/156855309X408826.

Shiffrin, Richard M. and Schneider, Walter. Automatic and controlled processing revisited. *Psychological Review*, 91(2):269–276, 1984. doi: 10.1037/0033-295X.91.2.269.

Shiomi, Masahiro, Kanda, Takayuki, Ishiguro, Hiroshi, and Hagita, Norihiro. Interactive humanoid robots for a science museum. In *Proceedings of the 1st ACM SIGCHI/SIGART Conference on Human-Robot Interaction*, pages 305–312. Association for Computing Machinery, New York, 2006. ISBN 1-59593-294-1. doi: 10.1145/1121241.1121293.

Shiomi, Masahiro, Zanlungo, Francesco, Hayashi, Kotaro, and Kanda, Takayuki. Towards a socially acceptable collision avoidance for a mobile robot navigating among pedestrians using a pedestrian model. *International Journal of Social Robotics*, 6(3):443–455, 2014. doi: 10.1007/s12369-014-0238-y.

Shiwa, Toshiyuki, Kanda, Takayuki, Imai, Michita, Ishiguro, Hiroshi, and Hagita, Norihiro. How quickly should communication robots respond? In *2008 3rd ACM/IEEE International Conference on Human-Robot Interaction (HRI)*, pages 153–160. Institute of Electrical and Electronics Engineers, Piscataway, NJ, 2008. URL https://doi.org/10.1145/1349822.1349 843.

Shourmasti, Elaheh Shahmir, Colomo-Palacios, Ricardo, Holone, Harald, and Demi, Selina. User experience in social robots. *Sensors*, 21(15):5052, 2021. doi: 10.3390/s21155052.

Siciliano, Bruno and Khatib, Oussama. *Springer Handbook of Robotics*. Springer, Berlin, 2016. ISBN 9783319325507. URL www.worldcat.org/oclc/945745190.

Sidnell, Jack. *Conversation Analysis: An Introduction*, volume 45. John Wiley & Sons, New York, 2011. ISBN 978-1405159012. URL http://worldcat.org/oclc/973423100.

Sidner, Candace L., Lee, Christopher, Kidd, Cory D., Lesh, Neal, and Rich, Charles. Explorations in engagement for humans and robots. *Artificial Intelligence*, 166(1–2):140–164, 2005. doi: 10.1016/j.artint.2005.03.005.

Simon, Herbert Alexander. *The Sciences of the Artificial*. MIT Press, Cambridge, MA, 3rd edition, 1996. ISBN 0262691914. URL http://worldcat.org/oclc/552080160.

Singer, Peter W. *Wired for War: The Robotics Revolution and Conflict in the Twenty-First Century*. Penguin, New York, 2009. ISBN 9781594201981. URL http://worldcat.org/oclc/ 857636246.

Singh, Ashish and Young, James E. Animal-inspired human-robot interaction: A robotic tail for communicating state. In *7th ACM/IEEE International Conference on Human-Robot*

Interaction, pages 237–238. Institute of Electrical and Electronics Engineers, Piscataway, NJ, 2012. ISBN 978-1-4503-1063-5. doi: 10.1145/2157689.2157773.

Sirkin, David, Mok, Brian, Yang, Stephen, and Ju, Wendy. Mechanical ottoman: How robotic furniture offers and withdraws support. In *10th Annual ACM/IEEE International Conference on Human-Robot Interaction*, pages 11–18. Association for Computing Machinery, New York, 2015. ISBN 978-1-4503-2883-8. doi: 10.1145/2696454.2696461.

Sisbot, Emrah Akin, Marin-Urias, Luis F., Alami, Rachid, and Simeon, Thierry. A human aware mobile robot motion planner. *IEEE Transactions on Robotics*, 23(5):874–883, 2007. doi: 10.1109/TRO.2007.904911.

Siu, Ka-Chun, Suh, Irene H, Mukherjee, Mukul, Oleynikov, Dmitry, and Stergiou, Nick. The effect of music on robot-assisted laparoscopic surgical performance. *Surgical Innovation*, 17(4):306–311, 2010. doi: 10.1177/1553350610381087.

Sloman, Steven A. The empirical case for two systems of reasoning. *Psychological Bulletin*, 119(1):3–22, 1996. doi: 10.1037/0033-2909.119.1.3.

Smith, Aaron. US views of technology and the future: Science in the next 50 years. Pew Research Center, April 17, 2014. URL http://assets.pewresearch.org/wp-content/uploads/sites/14/2014/04/US-Views-of-Technology-and-the-Future.pdf.

Smith, Colin Tucker and De Houwer, Jan. The impact of persuasive messages on iat performance is moderated by source attractiveness and likeability. *Social Psychology*, 45(6):437, 2014. doi: 10.1027/1864-9335/a000208.

Smith, Eliot R. and DeCoster, Jamie. Dual-process models in social and cognitive psychology: Conceptual integration and links to underlying memory systems. *Personality and Social Psychology Review*, 4(2):108–131, 2000. doi: 10.1207/S15327957PSPR0402_01.

Solon, Olivia. Roomba creator responds to reports of "Poopocalypse": "We see this a lot." *The Guardian*, 2016. URL www.theguardian.com/technology/2016/aug/15/roomba-robot-vacuum-poopocalypse-facebook-post.

Sosnowski, Stefan, Bittermann, Ansgar, Kuhnlenz, Kolja, and Buss, Martin. Design and evaluation of emotion-display EDDIE. In *IEEE/RSJ International Conference on Intelligent Robots and Systems*, pages 3113–3118. Institute of Electrical and Electronics Engineers, Piscataway, NJ, 2006. ISBN 1-4244-0258-1. doi: 10.1109/IROS.2006.282330.

Sparrow, Robert. Robotic weapons and the future of war. In Tripodi, Paolo and Wolfendale, Jessica, editors, *New Wars and New Soldiers: Military Ethics in the Contemporary World*, pages 117–133. Ashgate, Surrey, UK, 2011. ISBN 978-1-4094-0105-6. URL http://worldcat.org/oclc/960210186.

Sparrow, Robert. Robots, rape, and representation. *International Journal of Social Robotics*, 9 (4):465–477, 2017. ISSN 1875-4805. doi: 10.1007/s12369-017-0413-z.

Sparrow, Robert and Howard, Mark. When human beings are like drunk robots: Driverless vehicles, ethics, and the future of transport. *Transportation Research Part C: Emerging Technologies*, 80:206–215, 2017. doi: 10.1016/j.trc.2017.04.014.

Sparrow, Robert and Sparrow, Linda. In the hands of machines? The future of aged care. *Minds and Machines*, 16(2):141–161, 2006. doi: 10.1007/s11023-006-9030-6.

Spatola, Nicolas and Wudarczyk, Olga A. Ascribing emotions to robots: Explicit and implicit attribution of emotions and perceived robot anthropomorphism. *Computers in Human Behavior*, 124:106934, 2021. doi: 10.1016/j.chb.2021.106934.

Spatola, Nicolas, Kühnlenz, Barbara, and Cheng, Gordon. Perception and evaluation in human–robot interaction: The human–robot interaction evaluation scale (HRIES)—A multicomponent approach of anthropomorphism. *International Journal of Social Robotics*, 13(7):1517–1539, 2021. doi: 10.1007/s12369-020-00667-4.

Spatola, Nicolas, Marchesi, Serena, and Wykowska, Agnieszka. Different models of anthropomorphism across cultures and ontological limits in current frameworks the integrative framework of anthropomorphism. *Frontiers in Robotics and AI*, 9:863319, 2022. doi: 10.3389/frobt.2022.863319.

Spexard, Thorsten, Li, Shuyin, Wrede, Britta, Fritsch, Jannik, Sagerer, Gerhard, Booij, Olaf, Zivkovic, Zoran, Terwijn, Bas, and Krose, Ben. BIRON, where are you? Enabling a robot to learn new places in a real home environment by integrating spoken dialog and visual localization. In *IEEE/RSJ International Conference on Intelligent Robots and Systems*, pages 934–940. Institute of Electrical and Electronics Engineers, Piscataway, NJ, 2006. ISBN 1-4244-0258-1. doi: 10.1109/IROS.2006.281770.

Stahl, Bernd Carsten and Coeckelbergh, Mark. Ethics of healthcare robotics: Towards responsible research and innovation. *Robotics and Autonomous Systems*, 86:152–161, 2016. doi: 10.1016/j.robot.2016.08.018.

Stapels, Julia G. and Eyssel, Friederike. Let's not be indifferent about robots! Neutral ratings on bipolar measures mask ambivalence in attitudes towards robots. *PloS One*, 16(1):e0244697, 2021. doi: 10.1371/journal.pone.0244697.

Stapels, Julia G. and Eyssel, Friederike. Robocalypse? Yes, please! The role of robot autonomy in the development of ambivalent attitudes towards robots. *International Journal of Social Robotics*, 14(3):683–697, 2022. doi: 10.1007/s12369-021-00817-2.

Stedeman, Alison, Sutherland, Dean, and Bartneck, Christoph. *Learning ROILA*. CreateSpace, Charleston, SC, 2011. ISBN 978-1466494978.

Steels, Luc. The artificial life roots of artificial intelligence. *Artificial Life*, 1(1/2):75–110, 1993. doi: 10.1162/artl.1993.1.1_2.75.

Steil, Jochen, Finas, Dominique, Beck, Susanne, Manzeschke, Arne, and Haux, Reinhold. Robotic systems in operating theaters: New forms of team–machine interaction in health care. *Methods of Information in Medicine*, 58(S 01):e14–e25, 2019. doi: 10.1055/s-0039-1 692465.

Stein, Nancy L. and Oatley, Keith. Basic emotions: Theory and measurement. *Cognition & Emotion*, 6(3–4):161–168, 1992. doi: 10.1080/02699939208411067.

Stel, Mariëlle, Van Baaren, Rick B., and Vonk, Roos. Effects of mimicking: Acting prosocially by being emotionally moved. *European Journal of Social Psychology*, 38(6):965–976, 2008. doi: 10.1002/ejsp.472.

Stoll, Marlene, Kerwer, Martin, Lieb, Klaus, and Chasiotis, Anita. Plain language summaries: A systematic review of theory, guidelines and empirical research. *PloS One*, 17(6):e0268789, 2022. doi: 10.1371/journal.pone.0268789.

Strack, Fritz, Martin, Leonard L., and Stepper, Sabine. Inhibiting and facilitating conditions of the human smile: A nonobtrusive test of the facial feedback hypothesis. *Journal of Personality and Social Psychology*, 54(5):768, 1988. doi: 10.1037/0022-3514.54.5.768.

Strömbergsson, Sofia, Hjalmarsson, Anna, Edlund, Jens, and House, David. Timing responses to questions in dialogue. In *Proceedings of Interspeech*, pages 2584–2588. International Speech Communication Association, 2013. URL www.isca-speech.org/archive/interspeec h_2013/strombergsson13_interspeech.html.

Sugiyama, Osamu, Kanda, Takayuki, Imai, Michita, Ishiguro, Hiroshi, and Hagita, Norihiro. Natural deictic communication with humanoid robots. In *IEEE/RSJ International Conference on Intelligent Robots and Systems*, pages 1441–1448. Institute of Electrical and Electronics Engineers, Piscataway, NJ, 2007. ISBN 978-1-4244-0911-2. doi: 10.1109/ IROS.2007.4399120.

Suguitan, Michael and Hoffman, Guy. Blossom: A handcrafted open-source robot. *Journal of Human-Robot Interaction*, 8(1), 2019. doi: 10.1145/3310356.

Sung, Ja-Young, Guo, Lan, Grinter, Rebecca E., and Christensen, Henrik I. "My Roomba is Rambo": Intimate home appliances. In *9th International Conference on Ubiquitous Computing*, pages 145–162. Springer-Verlag, Berlin, 2007. ISBN 978-3-540-74852-6. doi: 10.1007/978-3-540-74853-3_9.

Sung, JaYoung, Grinter, Rebecca E., and Christensen, Henrik I. "Pimp my Roomba": Designing for personalization. In *Proceedings of the SIGCHI Conference on Human Factors in Computing Systems*, pages 193–196. Association for Computing Machinery, New York, 2009. ISBN 978-1-60558-246-7. doi: 10.1145/1518701.1518732.

Suri, Siddharth and Watts, Duncan J. Cooperation and contagion in web-based, networked public goods experiments. *PloS One*, 6(3):e16836, 2011. doi: 10.1371/journal.pone.0016836.

Sweigart, Al. *Scratch Programming Playground: Learn to Program by Making Cool Games*. No Starch Press, San Francisco, CA, 2016. ISBN 9781718500211. URL https://worldcat.o rg/en/title/1125157436.

Szafir, Daniel, Mutlu, Bilge, and Fong, Terry. Communicating directionality in flying robots. In *The 10th Annual ACM/IEEE International Conference on Human-Robot Interaction*, pages 19–26. Association for Computing Machinery, New York, 2015. ISBN 978-1-4503-2883-8. doi: 10.1145/2696454.2696475.

Taichi, Tajika, Takahiro, Miyashita, Hiroshi, Ishiguro, and Norihiro, Hagita. Automatic categorization of haptic interactions—What are the typical haptic interactions between a human and a robot? In *6th IEEE-RAS International Conference on Humanoid Robots*, pages 490–496. Institute of Electrical and Electronics Engineers, Piscataway, NJ, 2006. ISBN 1-4244-0199-2. doi: 10.1109/ICHR.2006.321318.

Takayama, Leila, Dooley, Doug, and Ju, Wendy. Expressing thought: Improving robot readability with animation principles. In *Proceedings of the 6th International Conference on Human-Robot Interaction*, pages 69–76. Association for Computing Machinery, New York, 2011. ISBN 978-1-4673-4393-0. doi: 10.1145/1957656.1957674.

Takayama, Leila A. Throwing voices: Investigating the psychological effects of the spatial location of projected voices. PhD thesis, Stanford University, 2008. URL https://searchworks .stanford.edu/view/7860025.

Tan, Xiang Zhi, Vázquez, Marynel, Carter, Elizabeth J., Morales, Cecilia G., and Steinfeld, Aaron. Inducing bystander interventions during robot abuse with social mechanisms. In *Proceedings of the 13th ACM/IEEE International Conference on Human-Robot Interaction (HRI)*, pages 169–177. Association for Computing Machinery, New York, 2018. doi: 10.1 145/3171221.3171247.

Tanaka, Fumihide and Kimura, Takeshi. Care-receiving robot as a tool of teachers in child education. *Interaction Studies*, 11(2):263–268, 2010. doi: 10.1075/is.11.2.14tan.

Tanaka, Fumihide, Cicourel, Aaron, and Movellan, Javier R. Socialization between toddlers and robots at an early childhood education center. *Proceedings of the National Academy of Sciences*, 104(46):17954–17958, 2007. doi: 10.1073/pnas.0707769104.

Tapus, Adriana, Mataric, Maja J., and Scassellati, Brian. Socially assistive robotics [Grand Challenges of Robotics]. *IEEE Robotics & Automation Magazine*, 14(1):35–42, 2007. doi: 10.1109/MRA.2007.339605.

Tapus, Adriana, Peca, Andreea, Aly, Amir, Pop, Cristina, Jisa, Lavinia, Pintea, Sebastian, Rusu, Alina S., and David, Daniel O. Children with autism social engagement in interaction with Nao, an imitative robot: A series of single case experiments. *Interaction Studies*, 13(3): 315–347, 2012. doi: 10.1075/is.13.3.01tap.

Taylor, Ross, Kardas, Marcin, Cucurull, Guillem, Scialom, Thomas, Hartshorn, Anthony, Saravia, Elvis, Poulton, Andrew, Kerkez, Viktor, and Stojnic, Robert. Galactica: A large language model for science. arXiv, arXiv:2211.09085, 2022. doi: 10.48550/ARXIV.2211. 09085.

Temtsin, Sharon, Proudfoot, Diane, and Bartneck, C. A bona fide Turing test. In *Proceedings of the Human-Agent Interaction Conference*, pages 250–252. Association for Computing Machinery, New York, 2022. doi: 10.1145/3527188.3563918.

Thellman, Sam, de Graaf, Maartje, and Ziemke, Tom. Mental state attribution to robots: A systematic review of conceptions, methods, and findings. *ACM Transactions on Human-Robot Interaction (THRI)*, 11(4):1–51, 2022. doi: 10.1145/3526112.

Thill, Serge, Pop, Cristina A., Belpaeme, Tony, Ziemke, Tom, and Vanderborght, Bram. Robot-assisted therapy for autism spectrum disorders with (partially) autonomous control: Challenges and outlook. *Paladyn, Journal of Behavioral Robotics*, 3(4):209–217, 2012. doi: 10.2478/s13230-013-0107-7.

Thomas, Frank, Johnston, Ollie, and Frank, Thomas. *The Illusion of Life: Disney Animation*. Hyperion, New York, 1995. ISBN 978-0786860708. URL http://worldcat.org/oclc/974772 586.

Thrun, Sebastian, Burgard, Wolfram, and Fox, Dieter. *Probabilistic Robotics*. MIT Press, Cambridge, MA, 2005. ISBN 978-0-2622-0162-9. URL http://worldcat.org/oclc/7055 85641.

Togler, Jonas, Hemmert, Fabian, and Wettach, Reto. Living interfaces: The thrifty faucet. In *Proceedings of the 3rd International Conference on Tangible and Embedded Interaction*, pages 43–44. Association for Computing Machinery, New York, 2009. ISBN 978-1-60558-493-5. doi: 10.1145/1517664.1517680.

Trafton, J. Gregory, Cassimatis, Nicholas L., Bugajska, Magdalena D., Brock, Derek P., Mintz, Farilee E., and Schultz, Alan C. Enabling effective human-robot interaction using perspective-taking in robots. *IEEE Transactions on Systems, Man, and Cybernetics. Part A: Systems and Humans*, 35(4):460–470, 2005. doi: 10.1109/TSMCA.2005.850592.

Trappl, Robert, Petta, Paolo, and Payr, Sabine. *Emotions in Humans and Artifacts*. MIT Press, Cambridge, MA, 2003. ISBN 978-0262201421. URL https://mitpress.mit.edu/books/emotions-humans-and-artifacts.

Triebel, Rudolph, Arras, Kai, Alami, Rachid, Beyer, Lucas, Breuers, Stefan, Chatila, Raja, Chetouani, Mohamed, Cremers, Daniel, Evers, Vanessa, Fiore, Michelangelo, et al. Spencer: A socially aware service robot for passenger guidance and help in busy airports. In *Field and Service Robotics*, pages 607–622. Springer, Cham, Switzerland, 2016. ISBN 978-3-319-27700-4. doi: 10.1007/978-3-319-27702-8_40.

Troshani, Indrit, Rao Hill, Sally, Sherman, Claire, and Arthur, Damien. Do we trust in AI? Role of anthropomorphism and intelligence. *Journal of Computer Information Systems*, 61 (5):481–491, 2021. doi: 10.1080/08874417.2020.1788473.

Tunstall, Lewis, Von Werra, Leandro, and Wolf, Thomas. *Natural Language Processing with Transformers*. O'Reilly, Sebastopol, CA, 2022. ISBN 9781098136796. URL www.worldcat.org/title/1321899597.

Turing, Alan M. Computing machinery and intelligence. *Mind*, 59(236):433–460, 1950. doi: 10.1007/978-1-4020-6710-5_3.

Turkle, Sherry. *Reclaiming Conversation: The Power of Talk in a Digital Age*. Penguin, New York, 2016. ISBN 978-0143109792. URL http://worldcat.org/oclc/960703115.

Turkle, Sherry. *Alone Together: Why We Expect More from Technology and Less from Each Other*. Basic Books, New York, 2017. ISBN 9780465031467. URL www.basicbooks.com/titles/sherry-turkle/alone-together/9780465093663/.

Urquiza-Haas, Esmeralda G. and Kotrschal, Kurt. The mind behind anthropomorphic thinking: attribution of mental states to other species. *Animal Behaviour*, 109:167–176, 2015. doi: 10.1016/j.anbehav.2015.08.011.

Vaes, Jeroen, Paladino, Maria Paola, Castelli, Luigi, Leyens, Jacques-Philippe, and Giovanazzi, Anna. On the behavioral consequences of infrahumanization: The implicit role of uniquely human emotions in intergroup relations. *Journal of Personality and Social Psychology*, 85 (6):1016–1034, 2003. doi: 10.1037/0022-3514.85.6.1016.

Vaillan, George E. *Triumphs of Experience: The Men of the Harvard Grant Study*. Belknap Press, Cambridge, MA, 2015. ISBN 978-0674503816. URL http://worldcat.org/oclc/9109 69527.

van Breemen, Albert, Yan, Xue, and Meerbeek, Bernt. iCat: An animated user-interface robot with personality. In *Proceedings of the 4th International Joint Conference on Autonomous Agents and Multiagent Systems*, pages 143–144. Association for Computing Machinery, New York, 2005. ISBN 1-59593-093-0. doi: 10.1145/1082473.1082823.

Van de Schoot, Rens, Winter, Sonja D, Ryan, Oisín, Zondervan-Zwijnenburg, Mariëlle, and Depaoli, Sarah. A systematic review of Bayesian articles in psychology: The last 25 years. *Psychological Methods*, 22(2):217, 2017. doi: 10.1037/met0000100.

van den Oord, Aaron, Dieleman, Sander, Zen, Heiga, Simonyan, Karen, Vinyals, Oriol, Graves, Alex, Kalchbrenner, Nal, Senior, Andrew, and Kavukcuoglu, Koray. Wavenet: A generative model for raw audio. arXiv, arXiv:1609.03499, 2016. URL http://arxiv.org/abs/1609.03499.

Van Erp, Jan B. F. and Toet, Alexander. How to touch humans: Guidelines for social agents and robots that can touch. In *Humaine Association Conference on Affective Computing and Intelligent Interaction*, pages 780–785. Institute of Electrical and Electronics Engineers, Piscataway, NJ, 2013. ISBN 978-0-7695-5048-0. doi: 10.1109/ACII.2013.145.

van Harreveld, Frenk, Nohlen, Hannah U., and Schneider, Iris K. The ABC of ambivalence: Affective, behavioral, and cognitive consequences of attitudinal conflict. In *Advances in Experimental Social Psychology*, volume 52, pages 285–324. Elsevier, St. Louis, MO, 2015. doi: 10.1016/bs.aesp.2015.01.002.

Van Wynsberghe, Aimee. *Healthcare Robots: Ethics, Design and Implementation*. Routledge, Milton Park, Abingdon, Oxfordshire, UK, 2016. ISBN 1032098600. URL www.worldcat.org/title/1246143567.

Vandevelde, Cesar, Wyffels, Francis, Ciocci, Maria-Cristina, Vanderborght, Bram, and Saldien, Jelle. Design and evaluation of a DIY construction system for educational robot kits. *International Journal of Technology and Design Education*, 26:521–540, 2016. doi: 10.1007/s10798-015-9324-1.

VanLehn, Kurt. The relative effectiveness of human tutoring, intelligent tutoring systems, and other tutoring systems. *Educational Psychologist*, 46(4):197–221, 2011. doi: 10.1080/00461520.2011.611369.

Venture, Gentiane, Kadone, Hideki, Zhang, Tianxiang, Grèzes, Julie, Berthoz, Alain, and Hicheur, Halim. Recognizing emotions conveyed by human gait. *International Journal of Social Robotics*, 6(4):621–632, 2014. doi: 10.1007/s12369-014-0243-1.

Vertesi, Janet. *Seeing Like a Rover: How Robots, Teams, and Images Craft Knowledge of Mars*. University of Chicago Press, Chicago, 2015. ISBN 978-0226155968. URL www.worldcat.org/oclc/904790036.

Veruggio, Gianmarco, Operto, Fiorella, and Bekey, George. Roboethics: Social and ethical implications. In Siciliano, Bruno and Khatib, Oussama, editors, *Springer Handbook of Robotics*, pages 2135–2160. Springer, New York, 2016. ISBN 978-3-319-32550-7. doi: 10.1007/978-3-319-32552-1.

Vincent, James. A drunk man was arrested for knocking over Silicon Valley's crime-fighting robot. *The Verge*, April 2017. URL www.theverge.com/2017/4/26/15432280/security-robot-knocked-over-drunk-man-knightscope-k5-mountain-view.

Vincenti, Walter G. *What Engineers Know and How They Know It: Analytical Studies from Aeronautical History*. Johns Hopkins Studies in the History of Technology. Johns Hopkins University Press, Baltimore, MD, 1990. ISBN 0801839742. URL http://worldcat.org/oclc/877307767.

Vollmer, Anna-Lisa, Read, Robin, Trippas, Dries, and Belpaeme, Tony. Children conform, adults resist: A robot group induced peer pressure on normative social conformity. *Science Robotics*, 3(21):eaat7111, 2018. doi: 10.1126/scirobotics.aat7111.

Vredenburg, Karel, Mao, Ji-Ye, Smith, Paul W., and Carey, Tom. A survey of user-centered design practice. In *Proceedings of the SIGCHI Conference on Human Factors in Computing Systems*, pages 471–478. Association for Computing Machinery, New York, 2002. ISBN 1-58113-453-3. doi: 10.1145/503376.503460.

Wada, Kazuyoshi and Shibata, Takanori. Living with seal robots—Its sociopsychological and physiological influences on the elderly at a care house. *IEEE Transactions on Robotics*, 23(5):972–980, 2007. doi: 10.1109/TRO.2007.906261.

Walczyk, Jeffrey J., Roper, Karen S., Seemann, Eric, and Humphrey, Angela M. Cognitive mechanisms underlying lying to questions: Response time as a cue to deception. *Applied Cognitive Psychology*, 17(7):755–774, 2003. doi: 10.1002/acp.914.

Walden, Justin, Jung, Eun Hwa, Sundar, S. Shyam, and Johnson, Ariel Celeste. Mental models of robots among senior citizens: An interview study of interaction expectations and design implications. *Interaction Studies*, 16(1):68–88, 2015. doi: 10.1075/is.16.1.04wal.

Walters, Michael L., Dautenhahn, Kerstin, Te Boekhorst, René, Koay, Kheng Lee, Kaouri, Christina, Woods, Sarah, Nehaniv, Chrystopher, Lee, David, and Werry, Iain. The influence of subjects' personality traits on personal spatial zones in a human-robot interaction experiment. In *IEEE International Workshop on Robot and Human Interactive Communication*, pages 347–352. Association for Computing Machinery, New York, 2005. ISBN 0-7803-9274-4. URL https://doi.org/10.1109/ROMAN.2005.1513803.

Walters, Michael L., Syrdal, Dag Sverre, Koay, Kheng Lee, Dautenhahn, Kerstin, and Te Boekhorst, René. Human approach distances to a mechanical-looking robot with different robot voice styles. In *RO-MAN 2008—The 17th IEEE International Symposium on Robot and Human Interactive Communication*, pages 707–712. Institute of Electrical and Electronics Engineers, Piscataway, NJ, 2008. doi: 10.1109/ROMAN.2008.4600750.

Walters, Michael L., Dautenhahn, Kerstin, Te Boekhorst, René, Koay, Kheng Lee, Syrdal, Dag Sverre, and Nehaniv, Chrystopher L. An empirical framework for human-robot proxemics. *Proceedings of New Frontiers in Human-Robot Interaction*, 2009. URL http://hdl.handle.net/2299/9670.

Wang, Lin, Rau, Pei-Luen Patrick, Evers, Vanessa, Robinson, Benjamin Krisper, and Hinds, Pamela. When in Rome: The role of culture & context in adherence to robot recommendations. In *5th ACM/IEEE International Conference on Human-Robot Interaction*, pages 359–366, Piscataway, NJ, USA, 2010. IEEE. ISBN 978-1-4244-4893-7. doi: 10.1109/HRI.2010.5453165.

Warner, Rebecca M., Malloy, Daniel, Schneider, Kathy, Knoth, Russell, and Wilder, Bruce. Rhythmic organization of social interaction and observer ratings of positive affect and involvement. *Journal of Nonverbal Behavior*, 11(2):57–74, 1987. doi: 10.1007/BF00990958.

Watanabe, Miki, Ogawa, Kohei, and Ishiguro, Hiroshi. Can androids be salespeople in the real world? In *Proceedings of the 33rd Annual ACM Conference Extended Abstracts on Human Factors in Computing Systems*, pages 781–788. Association for Computing Machinery, New York, 2015. ISBN 978-1-4503-3146-3. doi: 10.1145/2702613.2702967.

Wayland, Michael. GM ups spending on EVs and autonomous vehicles by 30% to $35 billion by 2025 on higher profits. CNBC News, 2021. URL www.cnbc.com/2021/06/16/gm-ups-spending-on-evs-and-autonomous-vehicles-to-35-billion-by-2025.html.

Waymo. Waymo safety report. Report, Waymo, 2020. URL https://storage.googleapis.com/sdc-prod/v1/safety-report/2020-09-waymo-safety-report.pdf.

Waytz, Adam, Cacioppo, John, and Epley, Nicholas. Who sees human? The stability and importance of individual differences in anthropomorphism. *Perspectives on Psychological Science*, 5(3):219–232, 2010. doi: 10.1177/1745691610369336.

Waytz, Adam, Heafner, Joy, and Epley, Nicholas. The mind in the machine: Anthropomorphism increases trust in an autonomous vehicle. *Journal of Experimental Social Psychology*, 52:113–117, 2014. doi: 10.1016/j.jesp.2014.01.005.

Whitby, Blay. Sometimes it's hard to be a robot: A call for action on the ethics of abusing artificial agents. *Interacting with Computers*, 20(3):326–333, 2008. doi: 10.1016/j.intcom.2008.02.002.

Whiten, Andrew, Goodall, Jane, McGrew, William C., Nishida, Toshisada, Reynolds, Vernon, Sugiyama, Yukimaru, Tutin, Caroline E. G., Wrangham, Richard W., and Boesch, Christophe. Cultures in chimpanzees. *Nature*, 399(6737):682–685, 1999. doi: 10.1038/21415.

Wiese, Eva, Weis, Patrick P., Bigman, Yochanan, Kapsaskis, Kyra, and Gray, Kurt. It's a match: Task assignment in human–robot collaboration depends on mind perception. *International Journal of Social Robotics*, 14(1):141–148, 2022. doi: 10.1007/s12369-021-00771-z.

Willemse, Christian J. A. M., Huisman, Gijs, Jung, Merel M., van Erp, Jan B. F., and Heylen, Dirk K. J. Observing touch from video: The influence of social cues on pleasantness perceptions. In *International Conference on Human Haptic Sensing and Touch Enabled Computer Applications*, pages 196–205. Springer, Cham, Switzerland, 2016. ISBN 978-3-319-42323-4. doi: 10.1007/978-3-319-42324-1_20.

Williams, Kipling D. Ostracism. *Annual Review of Psychology*, 58(1):425–452, 2007. doi: 10.1146/annurev.psych.58.110405.085641.

Williams, Lawrence E. and Bargh, John A. Keeping one's distance: The influence of spatial distance cues on affect and evaluation. *Psychological Science*, 19(3):302–308, 2008. doi: 10.1111/j.1467-9280.2008.02084.x.

Williams, Tom, Thames, Daria, Novakoff, Julia, and Scheutz, Matthias. Thank you for sharing that interesting fact: Effects of capability and context on indirect speech act use in task-based human-robot dialogue. In *Proceedings of the ACM/IEEE International Conference on Human-Robot Interaction*, pages 298–306. Association for Computing Machinery, New York, 2018. ISBN 978-1-4503-4953-6. doi: 10.1145/3171221.3171246.

Wills, Paul, Baxter, Paul, Kennedy, James, Senft, Emmanuel, and Belpaeme, Tony. Socially contingent humanoid robot head behaviour results in increased charity donations. In *The 11th ACM/IEEE International Conference on Human-Robot Interaction*, pages 533–534. Institute of Electrical and Electronics Engineers, Piscataway, NJ, 2016. ISBN 978-1-4673-8370-7. doi: 10.1109/HRI.2016.7451842.

Wilson, Daniel H. *How to Survive a Robot Uprising: Tips on Defending Yourself against the Coming Rebellion*. Bloomsbury, London, New York, 2005. ISBN 9781582345925. URL http://worldcat.org/oclc/1029483559.

Winkle, Katie, Caleb-Solly, Praminda, Turton, Ailie, and Bremner, Paul. Social robots for engagement in rehabilitative therapies: Design implications from a study with therapists. In *Proceedings of the ACM/IEEE International Conference on Human-Robot Interaction*, pages 289–297. Association for Computing Machinery, New York, 2018. ISBN 978-1-4503-4953-6. doi: 10.1145/3171221.3171273.

Winkle, Katie, Lagerstedt, Erik, Torre, Ilaria, and Offenwanger, Anna. 15 years of (Who) man robot interaction: Reviewing the H in human-robot interaction. *ACM Transactions on Human-Robot Interaction*, 12(3):1–28, 2023a. doi: 10.1145/3571718.

Winkle, Katie, McMillan, Donald, Arnelid, Maria, Harrison, Katherine, Balaam, Madeline, Johnson, Ericka, and Leite, Iolanda. Feminist human-robot interaction: Disentangling power, principles and practice for better, more ethical hri. In *Proceedings of the 2023 ACM/IEEE International Conference on Human-Robot Interaction*, pages 72–82. Association for Computing Machinery, New York, 2023b. doi: 10.1145/3568162.3576973.

Wistort, Ryan and Breazeal, Cynthia. Tofu: A socially expressive robot character for child interaction. In *8th International Conference on Interaction Design and Children*, pages 292–293. Association for Computing Machinery, New York, 2009. ISBN 978-1-60558-395-2. doi: 10.1145/1551788.1551862.

Wojciechowska, Anna, Frey, Jeremy, Sass, Sarit, Shafir, Roy, and Cauchard, Jessica R. Collocated human-drone interaction: Methodology and approach strategy. In *2019 14th ACM/IEEE International Conference on Human-Robot Interaction (HRI)*, pages 172–181. Institute of Electrical and Electronics Engineers, Piscataway, NJ, 2019. doi: 10.1109/HRI.2019.8673127.

Wojciszke, Bogdan. Morality and competence in person-and self-perception. *European Review of Social Psychology*, 16(1):155–188, 2005. doi: 10.1080/10463280500229619.

Wolfe, Jeremy M., Kluender, Keith R., Levi, Dennis M., Bartoshuk, Linda M., Herz, Rachel S., Klatzky, Roberta L., Lederman, Susan J., and Merfeld, Daniel M. *Sensation & Perception*. Sinauer, Sunderland, MA, 2006. ISBN 9780197551967. URL www.worldcat.org/title/128 7073270.

Wolfert, Pieter, Robinson, Nicole, and Belpaeme, Tony. A review of evaluation practices of gesture generation in embodied conversational agents. *IEEE Transactions on Human-Machine Systems*, 52(3):379–389, 2022. doi: 10.1109/THMS.2022.3149173.

Wrede, Britta, Fritsch, Jannik, and Rohlfing, Katharina. How can prosody help to learn actions? In *Proceedings of the 4th International Conference on Development and Learning, 2005*, pages 163–163. Institute of Electrical and Electronics Engineers, Piscataway, NJ, 2005. doi: 10.1109/DEVLRN.2005.1490969.

Wullenkord, Ricarda. Messung und Veränderung von Einstellungen gegenüber Robotern-Untersuchung des Einflusses von imaginiertem Kontakt auf implizite und explizite Maße.

PhD thesis, University of Bielefeld, 2017. URL https://pub.uni-bielefeld.de/publication/29 13679.

Wullenkord, Ricarda and Eyssel, Friederike. Societal and ethical issues in HRI. *Current Robotics Reports*, 1(3):85–96, 2020. doi: 10.1007/s43154-020-00010-9.

Wullenkord, Ricarda, Fraune, Marlena R., Eyssel, Friederike, and Šabanović, Selma. Getting in touch: How imagined, actual, and physical contact affect evaluations of robots. In *25th IEEE International Symposium on Robot and Human Interactive Communication*, pages 980–985. Institute of Electrical and Electronics Engineers, Piscataway, NJ, 2016. ISBN 978 1 5090-3930 2. doi: 10.1109/ROMAN.2016.7745228.

Wykowska, Agnieszka. Robots as mirrors of the human mind. *Current Directions in Psychological Science*, 30(1):34–40, 2021. doi: 10.1177/0963721420978609.

Xu, Junchao, Broekens, Joost, Hindriks, Koen, and Neerincx, Mark A. Robot mood is contagious: Effects of robot body language in the imitation game. In *International Conference on Autonomous Agents and Multi-Agent Systems*, pages 973–980. International Foundation for Autonomous Agents and Multiagent Systems, Richland, SC, 2014. ISBN 978-1-4503-2738-1. URL https://dl.acm.org/citation.cfm?id=2617401.

Yamaji, Yuto, Miyake, Taisuke, Yoshiike, Yuta, De Silva, P. Ravindra S., and Okada, Michio. STB: Human-dependent sociable trash box. In *5th ACM/IEEE International Conference on Human-Robot Interaction*, pages 197–198. Institute of Electrical and Electronics Engineers, Piscataway, NJ, 2010. ISBN 978-1-4244-4892-0. doi: 10.1109/HRI.2010.5453196.

Yamaoka, Fumitaka, Kanda, Takayuki, Ishiguro, Hiroshi, and Hagita, Norihiro. "Lifelike" behavior of communication robots based on developmental psychology findings. In *5th IEEE-RAS International Conference on Humanoid Robots*, pages 406–411. Institute of Electrical and Electronics Engineers, Piscataway, NJ, 2005. ISBN 0-7803-9320-1. doi: 10.1109/ICHR.2005.1573601.

Yamaoka, Fumitaka, Kanda, Takayuki, Ishiguro, Hiroshi, and Hagita, Norihiro. A model of proximity control for information-presenting robots. *IEEE Transactions on Robotics*, 26 (1):187–195, 2010. doi: 10.1109/TRO.2009.2035747.

Yamashita, Yuki, Ishihara, Hisashi, Ikeda, Takashi, and Asada, Minoru. Path analysis for the halo effect of touch sensations of robots on their personality impressions. In *International Conference on Social Robotics*, pages 502–512. Springer, Cham, Switzerland, 2016. doi: 10.1007/978-3-319-47437-3_49.

Yeh, Alexander, Ratsamee, Photchara, Kiyokawa, Kiyoshi, Uranishi, Yuki, Mashita, Tomohiro, Takemura, Haruo, Fjeld, Morten, and Obaid, Mohammad. Exploring proxemics for human-drone interaction. In *Proceedings of the 5th International Conference on Human-Agent Interaction*, pages 81–88. Association for Computing Machinery, New York, 2017. doi: 10.1145/3125739.3125773.

Yogeswaran, Nivasan, Dang, Wenting, Navaraj, William Taube, Shakthivel, Dhayalan, Khan, Saleem, Polat, Emre Ozan, Gupta, Shoubhik, Heidari, Hadi, Kaboli, Mohsen, Lorenzelli, Leandro, et al. New materials and advances in making electronic skin for interactive robots. *Advanced Robotics*, 29(21):1359–1373, 2015. doi: 10.1080/01691864.2015.1095653.

Yohanan, Steve and MacLean, Karon E. The role of affective touch in human-robot interaction: Human intent and expectations in touching the haptic creature. *International Journal of Social Robotics*, 4(2):163–180, 2012. doi: 10.1007/s12369-011-0126-7.

Yoon, Youngwoo, Wolfert, Pieter, Kucherenko, Taras, Viegas, Carla, Nikolov, Teodor, Tsakov, Mihail, and Henter, Gustav Eje. The GENEA challenge 2022: A large evaluation of data-driven co-speech gesture generation. In Tumuluri, Raj, Sebe, Nicu, Pingali, Gopal, Jayagopi, Dinesh Babu, Dhall, Abhinav, Singh, Richa, Anthony, Lisa, and Salah, Albert Ali, editors, *Proceedings of the 2022 International Conference on Multimodal Interaction*, pages 736–747. Association for Computing Machinery, New York, 2022. doi: 10.1145/3536221.3558058.

Young, James E., Sung, JaYoung, Voida, Amy, Sharlin, Ehud, Igarashi, Takeo, Christensen, Henrik I., and Grinter, Rebecca E. Evaluating human-robot interaction. *International Journal of Social Robotics*, 3(1):53–67, 2011. doi: 10.1007/s12369-010-0081-8.

Yu, Chen and Smith, Linda B. Joint attention without gaze following: Human infants and their parents coordinate visual attention to objects through eye-hand coordination. *PloS One*, 8 (11):e79659, 2013. doi: 10.1371/journal.pone.0079659.

Zaga, Cristina. The design of robothings: Non-anthropomorphic and non-verbal robots to promote children's collaboration through play. PhD thesis, Univesity of Twente, 2021. URL https://doi.org/10.1109/RO-MAN46459.2019.8956427.

Zajonc, Robert B. Attitudinal effects of mere exposure. *Journal of Personality and Social Psychology*, 9(2p2):1–27, 1968. doi: 10.1037/h0025848.

Zaveri, Mihir. NYPD robot dog's run is cut short after fierce backlash. *New York Times*, 2021. URL www.nytimes.com/2021/04/28/nyregion/nypd-robot-dog-backlash.html.

Zen, Heiga, Tokuda, Keiichi, and Black, Alan W. Statistical parametric speech synthesis. *Speech Communication*, 51(11):1039–1064, 2009. doi: 10.1016/j.specom.2009.04.004.

Zeng, Zhihong, Pantic, Maja, Roisman, Glenn I., and Huang, Thomas S. A survey of affect recognition methods: Audio, visual, and spontaneous expressions. *IEEE Transactions on Pattern Analysis and Machine Intelligence*, 31(1):39–58, 2009. doi: 10.1109/TPAMI.2008.52.

Zhang, Yu, Park, Daniel S., Han, Wei, Qin, James, Gulati, Anmol, Shor, Joel, Jansen, Aren, Xu, Yuanzhong, Huang, Yanping, Wang, Shibo, et al. Bigssl: Exploring the frontier of large-scale semi-supervised learning for automatic speech recognition. *IEEE Journal of Selected Topics in Signal Processing*, 16(6):1519–1532, 2022. doi: 10.1109/JSTSP.2022.3182537.

Zhou, Chen, Miao, Ming-Cheng, Chen, Xin-Ran, Hu, Yi-Fei, Chang, Qi, Yan, Ming-Yuan, and Kuai, Shu-Guang. Human-behaviour-based social locomotion model improves the humanization of social robots. *Nature Machine Intelligence*, 4:1040–1052, 2022. doi: 10.1038/s42256-022-00542-z.

Złotowski, Jakub, Yogeeswaran, Kumar, and Bartneck, Christoph. Can we control it? Autonomous robots are perceived as threatening. *International Journal of Human-Computer Studies*, 100:48–54, 2017. doi: 10.1016/j.ijhcs.2016.12.008.

Złotowski, Jakub, Sumioka, Hidenobu, Eyssel, Friederike, Nishio, Shuichi, Bartneck, Christoph, and Ishiguro, Hiroshi. Model of dual anthropomorphism: The relationship between the media equation effect and implicit anthropomorphism. *International Journal of Social Robotics*, 10(5):701–714, 2018. doi: 10.1007/s12369-018-0476-5.

Index

Printed in the United States
by Baker & Taylor Publisher Services